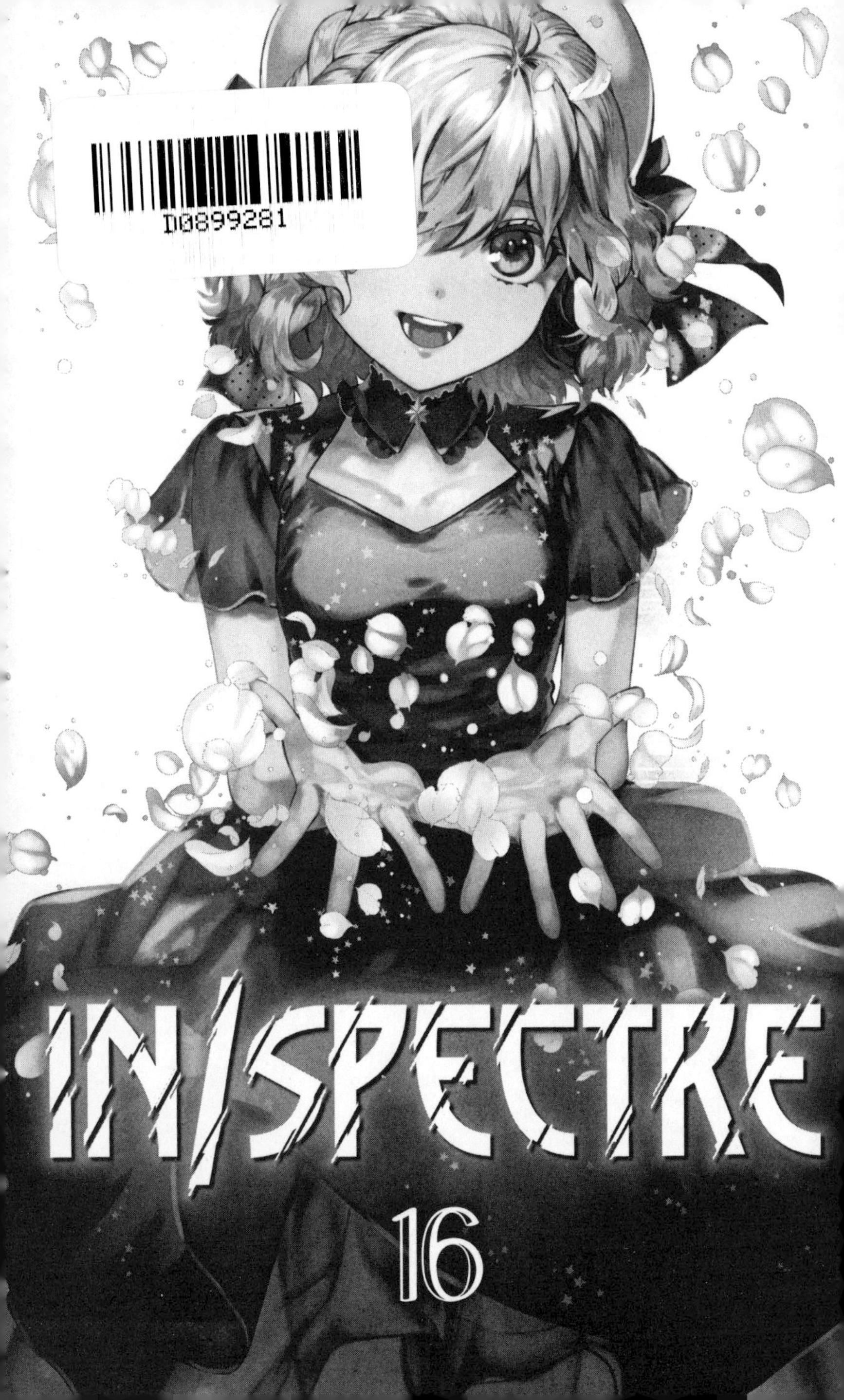
IN/SPECTRE
16

CONTENTS

CHAPTER 45: "THE RETALIATION AND DEFEAT OF KOTOKO IWANAGA PART 7"

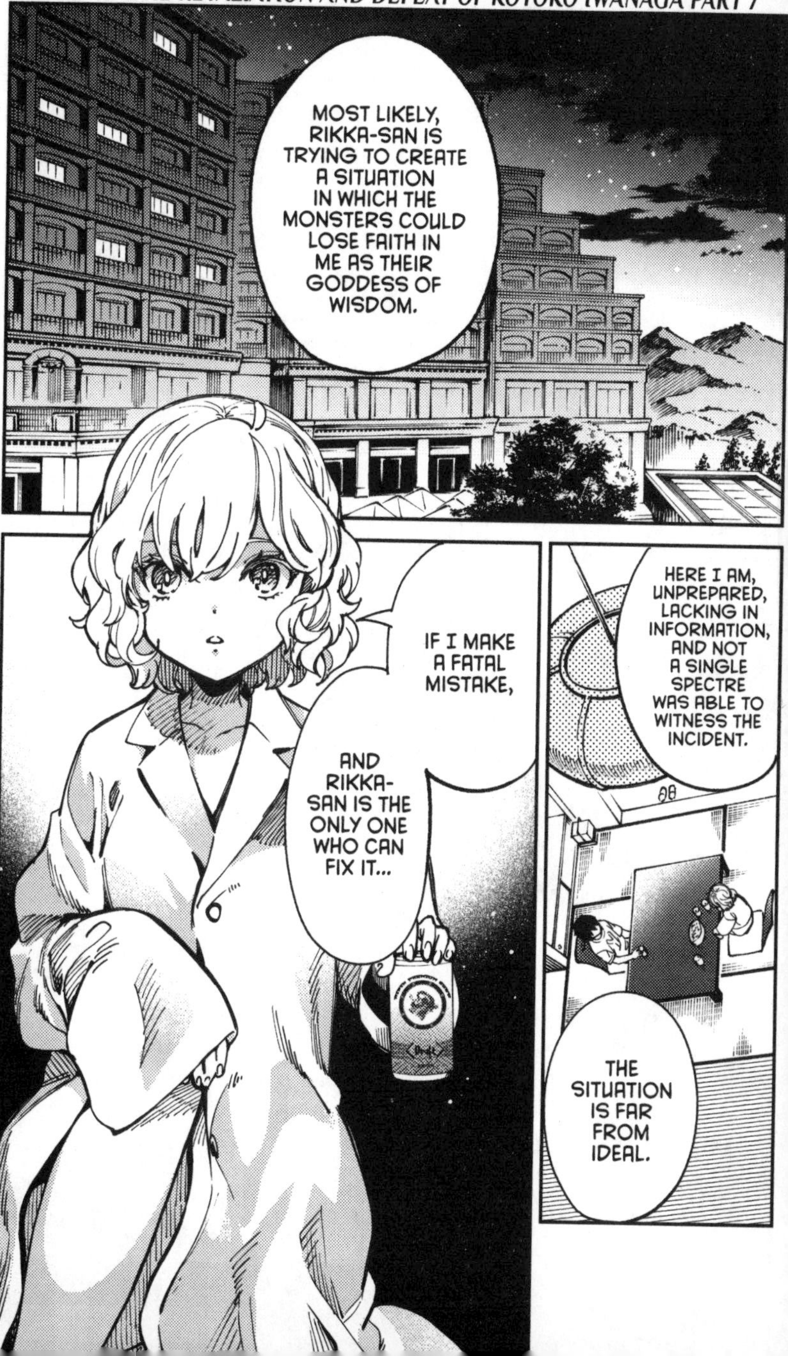
MOST LIKELY, RIKKA-SAN IS TRYING TO CREATE A SITUATION IN WHICH THE MONSTERS COULD LOSE FAITH IN ME AS THEIR GODDESS OF WISDOM.
HERE I AM, UNPREPARED, LACKING IN INFORMATION, AND NOT A SINGLE SPECTRE WAS ABLE TO WITNESS THE INCIDENT.
THE SITUATION IS FAR FROM IDEAL.
IF I MAKE A FATAL MISTAKE,
AND RIKKA-SAN IS THE ONLY ONE WHO CAN FIX IT...

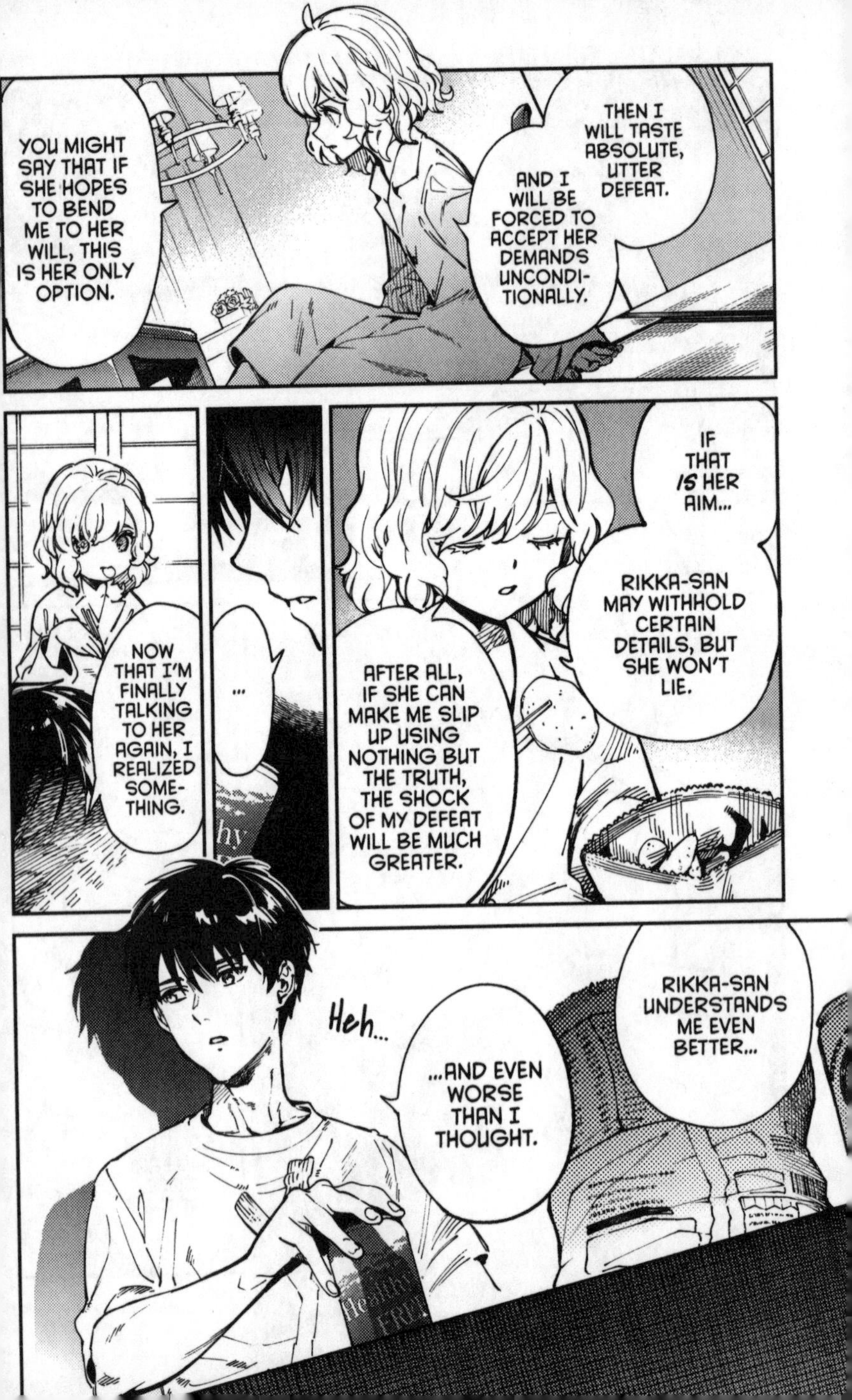
THEN I WILL TASTE ABSOLUTE, UTTER DEFEAT.
AND I WILL BE FORCED TO ACCEPT HER DEMANDS UNCONDITIONALLY.
YOU MIGHT SAY THAT IF SHE HOPES TO BEND ME TO HER WILL, THIS IS HER ONLY OPTION.
IF THAT *IS* HER AIM...
RIKKA-SAN MAY WITHHOLD CERTAIN DETAILS, BUT SHE WON'T LIE.
AFTER ALL, IF SHE CAN MAKE ME SLIP UP USING NOTHING BUT THE TRUTH, THE SHOCK OF MY DEFEAT WILL BE MUCH GREATER.
...
NOW THAT I'M FINALLY TALKING TO HER AGAIN, I REALIZED SOME-THING.
RIKKA-SAN UNDERSTANDS ME EVEN BETTER...
Heh...
...AND EVEN WORSE THAN I THOUGHT.

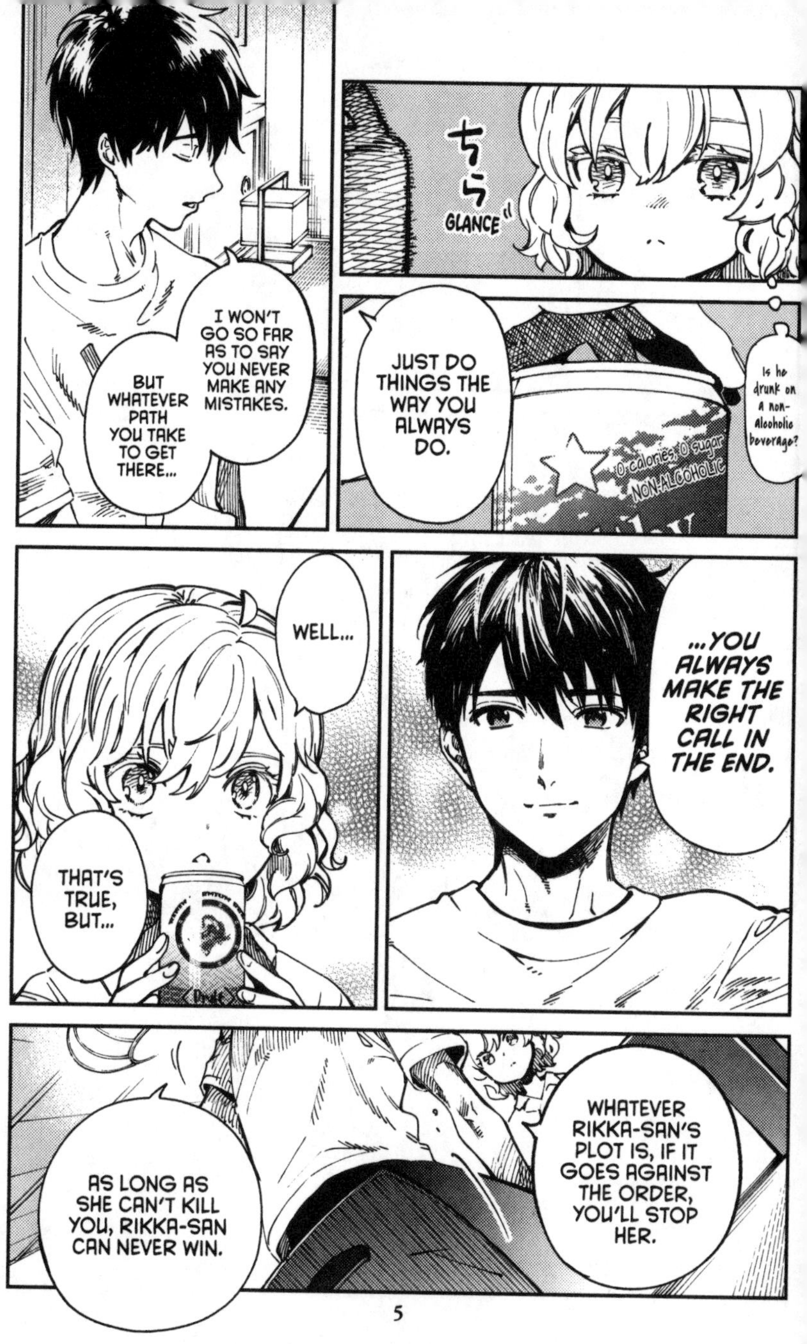

ちら
GLANCE
Is he drunk on a non-alcoholic beverage?
JUST DO THINGS THE WAY YOU ALWAYS DO.
0 calories, 0 sugar
NON-ALCOHOLIC
I WON'T GO SO FAR AS TO SAY YOU NEVER MAKE ANY MISTAKES.
BUT WHATEVER PATH YOU TAKE TO GET THERE...
...YOU ALWAYS MAKE THE RIGHT CALL IN THE END.
WELL...
THAT'S TRUE, BUT...
WHATEVER RIKKA-SAN'S PLOT IS, IF IT GOES AGAINST THE ORDER, YOU'LL STOP HER.
AS LONG AS SHE CAN'T KILL YOU, RIKKA-SAN CAN NEVER WIN.

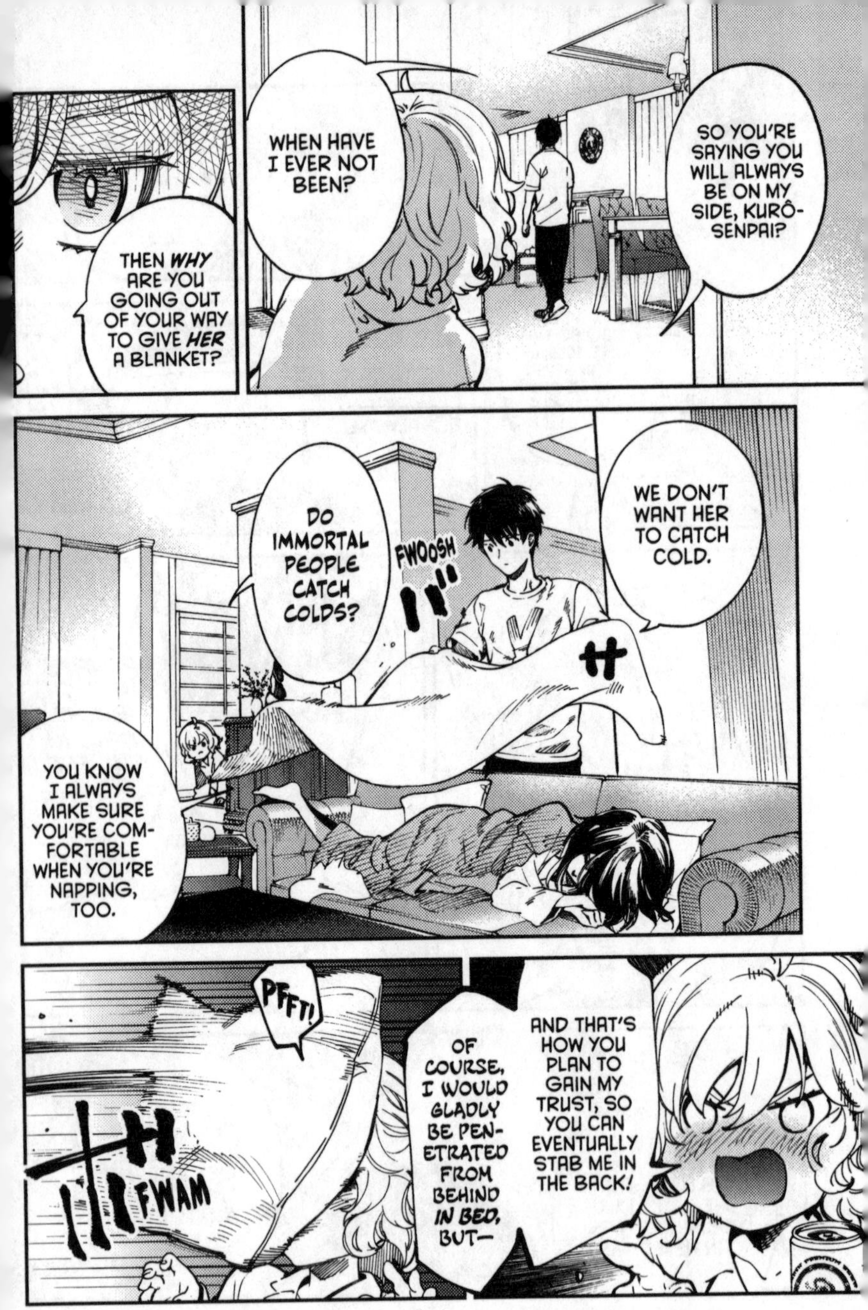
SO YOU'RE SAYING YOU WILL ALWAYS BE ON MY SIDE, KURÔ-SENPAI?
WHEN HAVE I EVER NOT BEEN?
THEN *WHY* ARE YOU GOING OUT OF YOUR WAY TO GIVE *HER* A BLANKET?
WE DON'T WANT HER TO CATCH COLD.
DO IMMORTAL PEOPLE CATCH COLDS?
FWOOSH
YOU KNOW I ALWAYS MAKE SURE YOU'RE COM-FORTABLE WHEN YOU'RE NAPPING, TOO.
AND THAT'S HOW YOU PLAN TO GAIN MY TRUST, SO YOU CAN EVENTUALLY STAB ME IN THE BACK!
OF COURSE, I WOULD GLADLY BE PEN-ETRATED FROM BEHIND *IN BED,* BUT—
PFFT!
FWAM

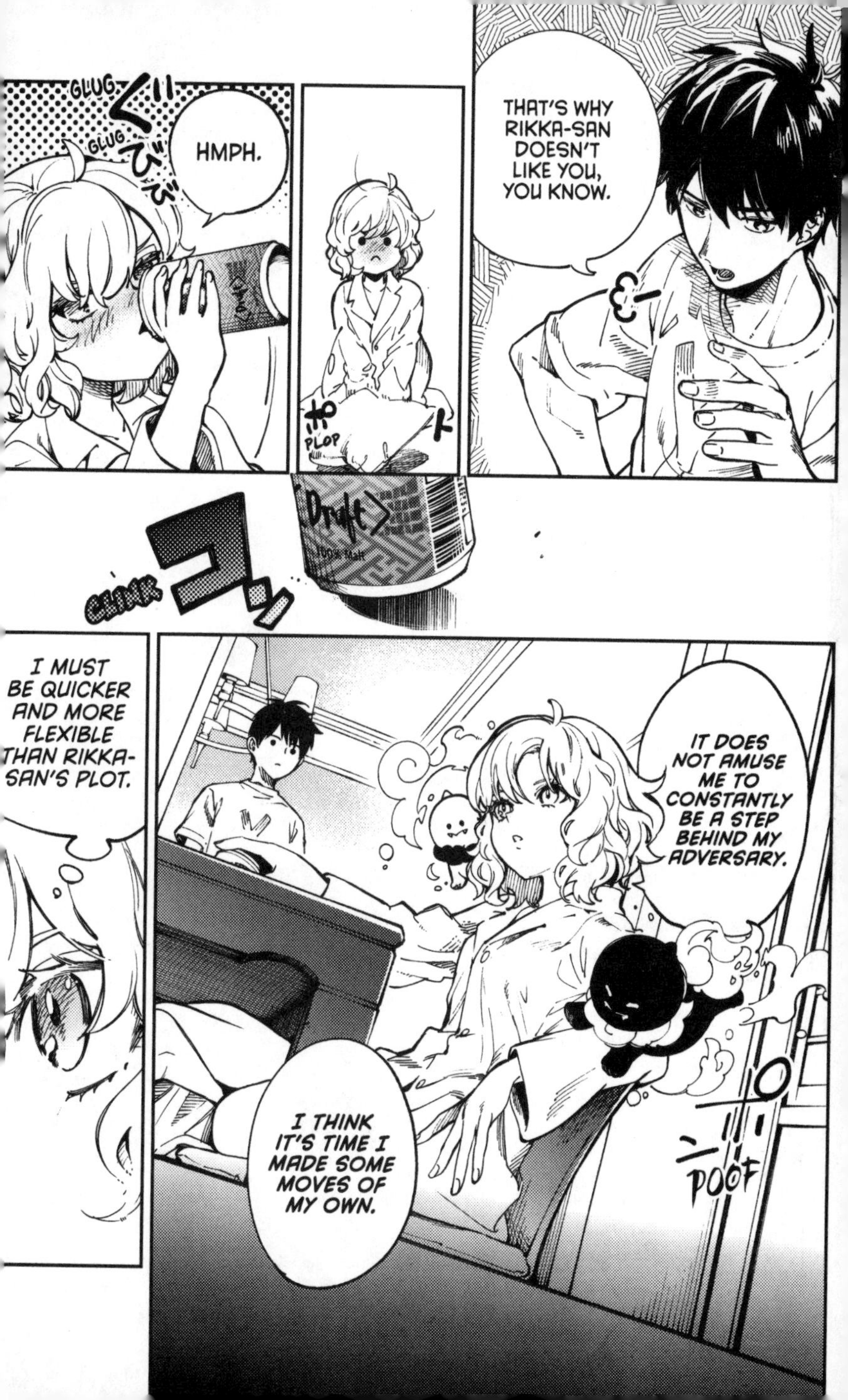
THAT'S WHY RIKKA-SAN DOESN'T LIKE YOU, YOU KNOW.
PLOP
GLUG
GLUG
HMPH.
CLINK
Drift
IT DOES NOT AMUSE ME TO CONSTANTLY BE A STEP BEHIND MY ADVERSARY.
I THINK IT'S TIME I MADE SOME MOVES OF MY OWN.
POOF
I MUST BE QUICKER AND MORE FLEXIBLE THAN RIKKA-SAN'S PLOT.

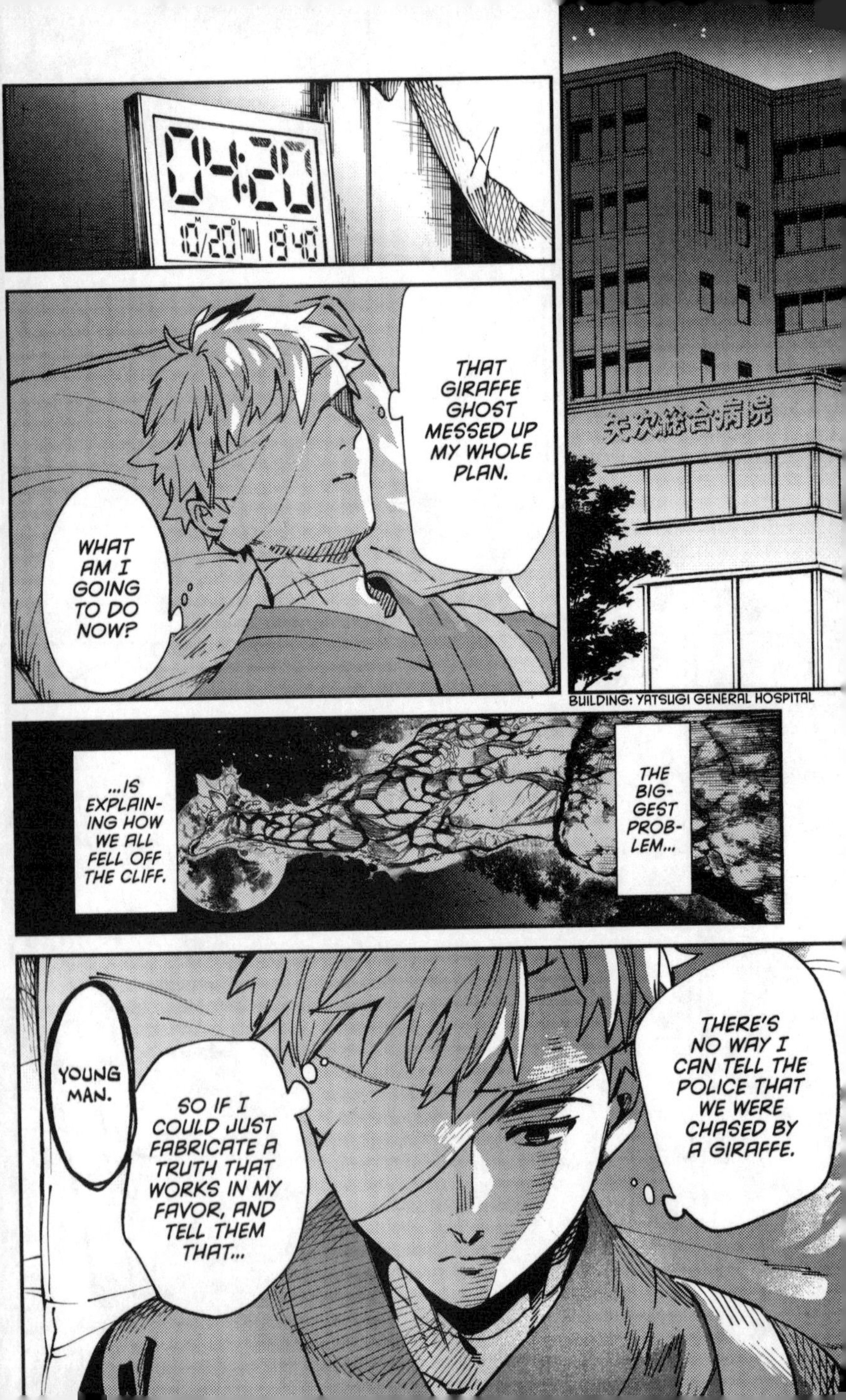
BUILDING: YATSUGI GENERAL HOSPITAL
THAT GIRAFFE GHOST MESSED UP MY WHOLE PLAN.
WHAT AM I GOING TO DO NOW?
THE BIG-GEST PROB-LEM...
...IS EXPLAIN-ING HOW WE ALL FELL OFF THE CLIFF.
THERE'S NO WAY I CAN TELL THE POLICE THAT WE WERE CHASED BY A GIRAFFE.
SO IF I COULD JUST FABRICATE A TRUTH THAT WORKS IN MY FAVOR, AND TELL THEM THAT...
YOUNG MAN.

YOU APPEAR TO BE HAVING TROUBLE SLEEPING.

WHOOOO!

I UNDERSTAND YOU HAVE AMNESIA? NO WONDER YOU'RE SO RESTLESS.

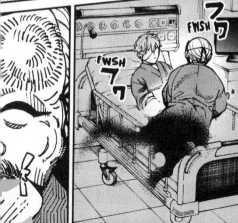

FWSH

FWSH

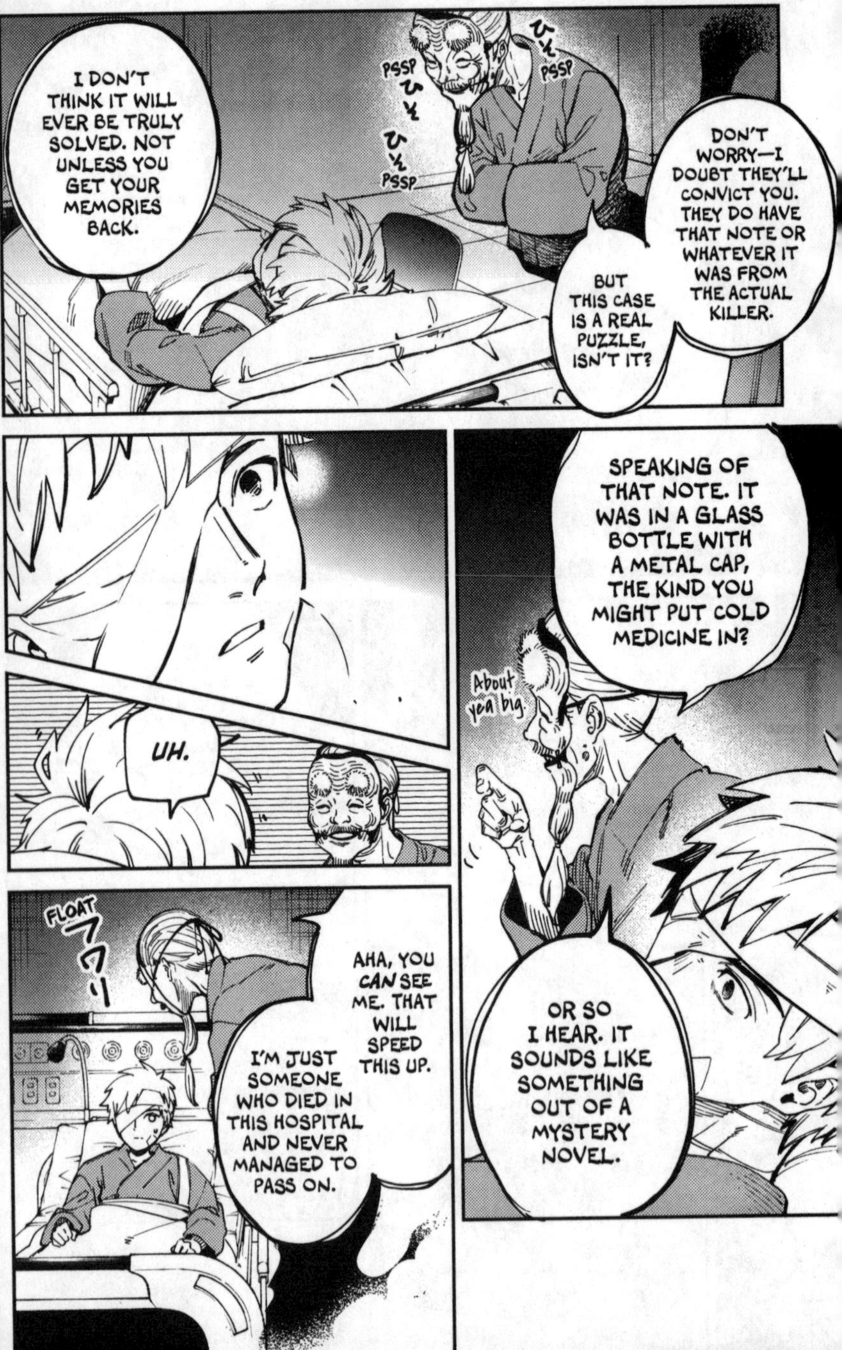
PSSP
ひそ
PSSP
ひそ
PSSP
ひそ
DON'T WORRY—I DOUBT THEY'LL CONVICT YOU. THEY DO HAVE THAT NOTE OR WHATEVER IT WAS FROM THE ACTUAL KILLER.
BUT THIS CASE IS A REAL PUZZLE, ISN'T IT?
I DON'T THINK IT WILL EVER BE TRULY SOLVED. NOT UNLESS YOU GET YOUR MEMORIES BACK.
SPEAKING OF THAT NOTE. IT WAS IN A GLASS BOTTLE WITH A METAL CAP, THE KIND YOU MIGHT PUT COLD MEDICINE IN?
About yea big.
OR SO I HEAR. IT SOUNDS LIKE SOMETHING OUT OF A MYSTERY NOVEL.
UH.
FLOAT
AHA, YOU CAN SEE ME. THAT WILL SPEED THIS UP.
I'M JUST SOMEONE WHO DIED IN THIS HOSPITAL AND NEVER MANAGED TO PASS ON.

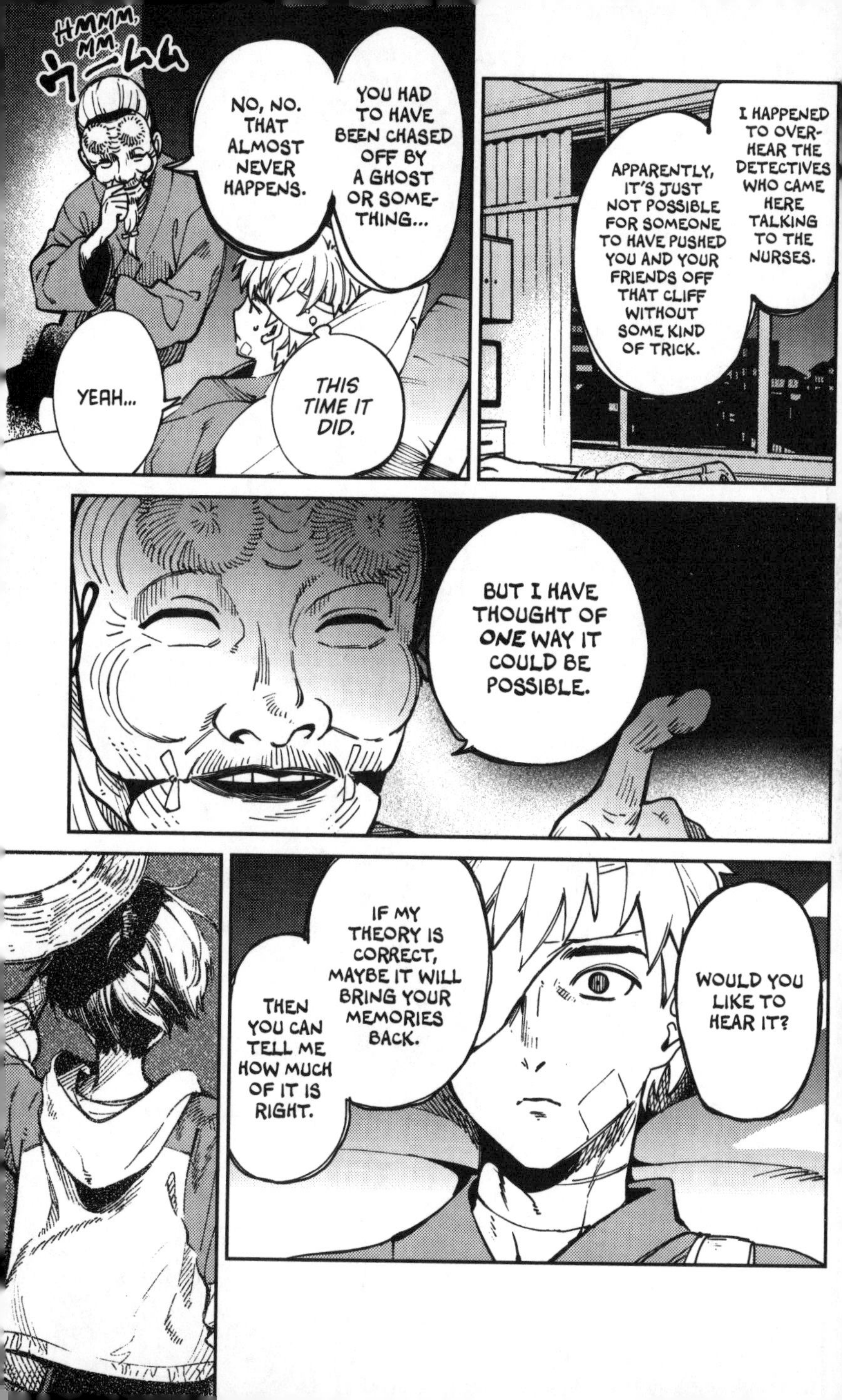
I HAPPENED TO OVER-HEAR THE DETECTIVES WHO CAME HERE TALKING TO THE NURSES.
APPARENTLY, IT'S JUST NOT POSSIBLE FOR SOMEONE TO HAVE PUSHED YOU AND YOUR FRIENDS OFF THAT CLIFF WITHOUT SOME KIND OF TRICK.
YOU HAD TO HAVE BEEN CHASED OFF BY A GHOST OR SOME-THING...
NO, NO. THAT ALMOST NEVER HAPPENS.
HMMM, MM.
ウームム
THIS TIME IT DID.
YEAH...
BUT I HAVE THOUGHT OF ONE WAY IT COULD BE POSSIBLE.
WOULD YOU LIKE TO HEAR IT?
IF MY THEORY IS CORRECT, MAYBE IT WILL BRING YOUR MEMORIES BACK.
THEN YOU CAN TELL ME HOW MUCH OF IT IS RIGHT.

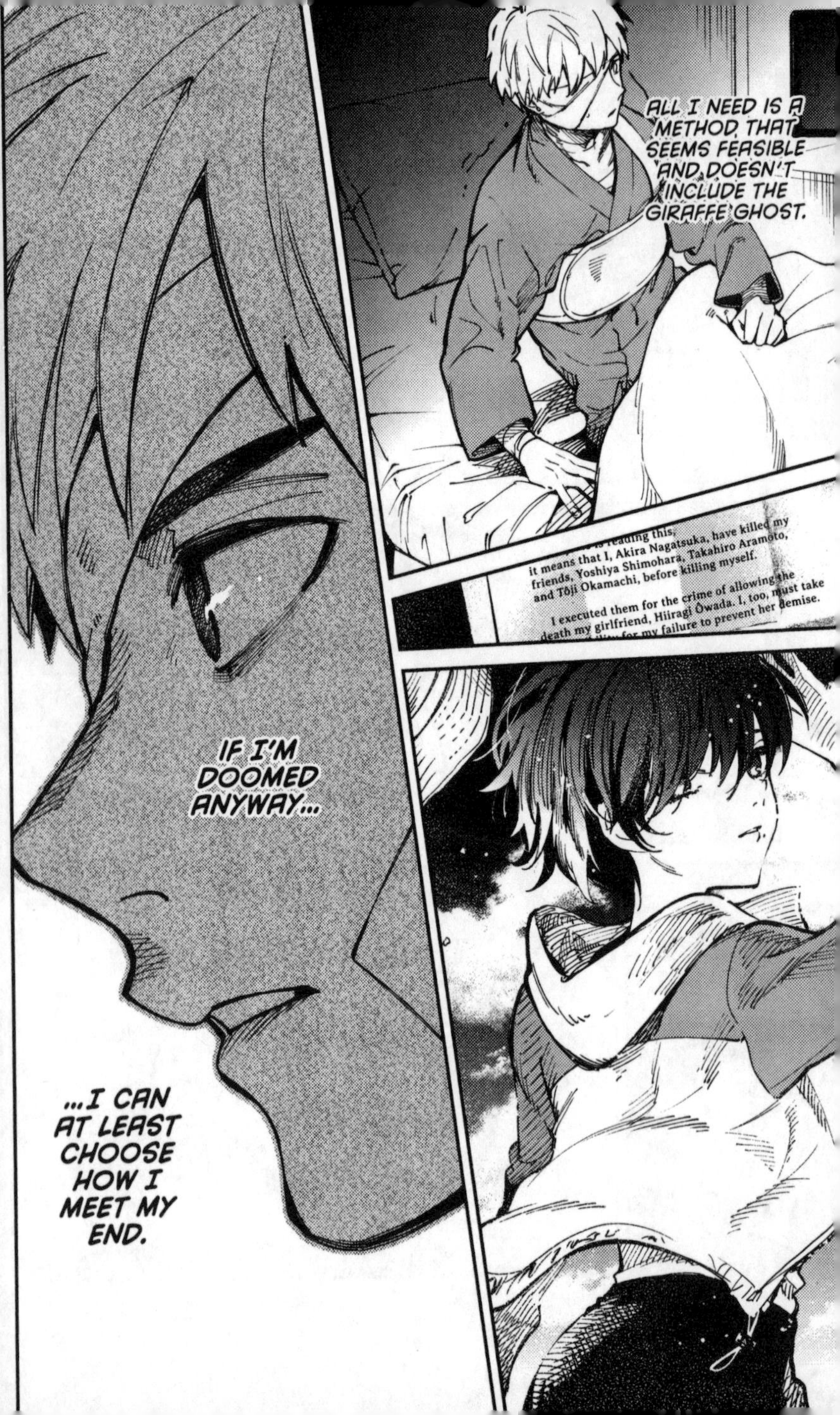
ALL I NEED IS A METHOD THAT SEEMS FEASIBLE AND DOESN'T INCLUDE THE GIRAFFE GHOST.
is reading this,
it means that I, Akira Nagatsuka, have killed my
friends, Yoshiya Shimohara, Takahiro Aramoto,
and Tōji Okamachi, before killing myself.
I executed them for the crime of allowing the
death my girlfriend, Hiiragi Ōwada. I, too, must take
for my failure to prevent her demise.
IF I'M DOOMED ANYWAY...
...I CAN AT LEAST CHOOSE HOW I MEET MY END.

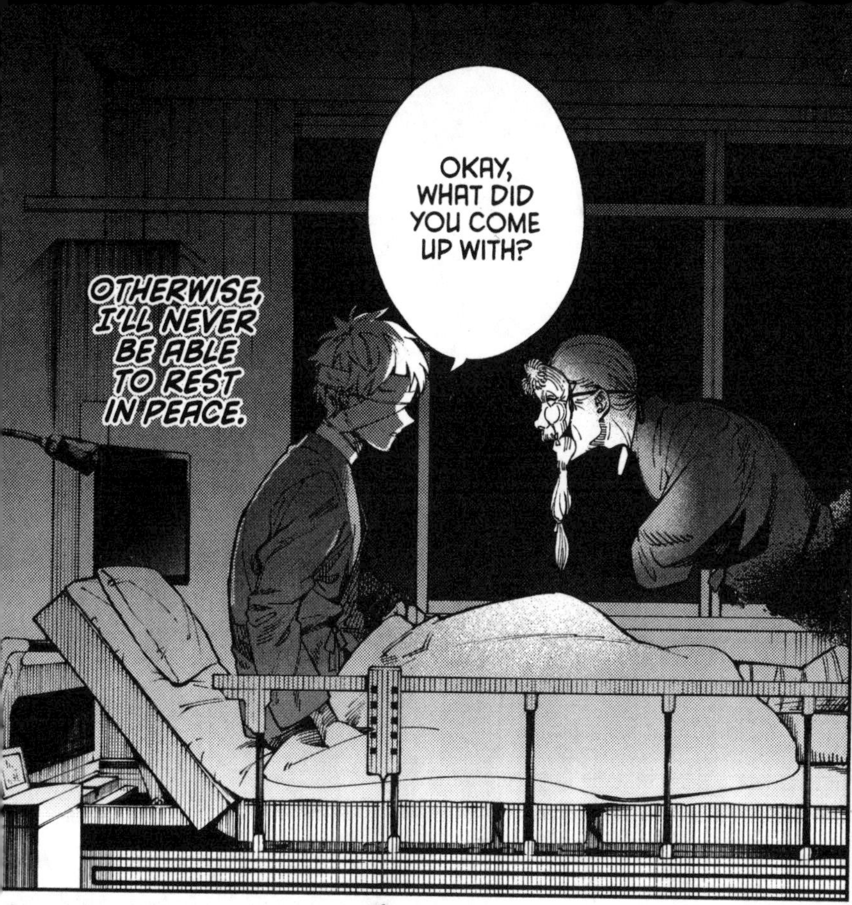
OKAY, WHAT DID YOU COME UP WITH?
OTHERWISE, I'LL NEVER BE ABLE TO REST IN PEACE.

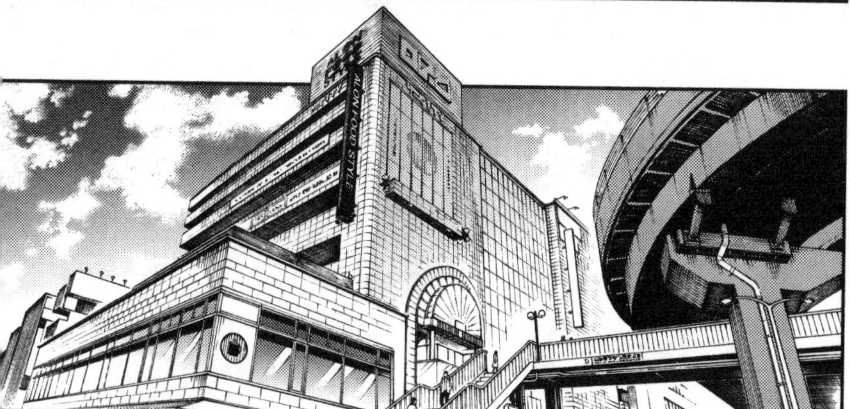
ALON FOOD STYLE

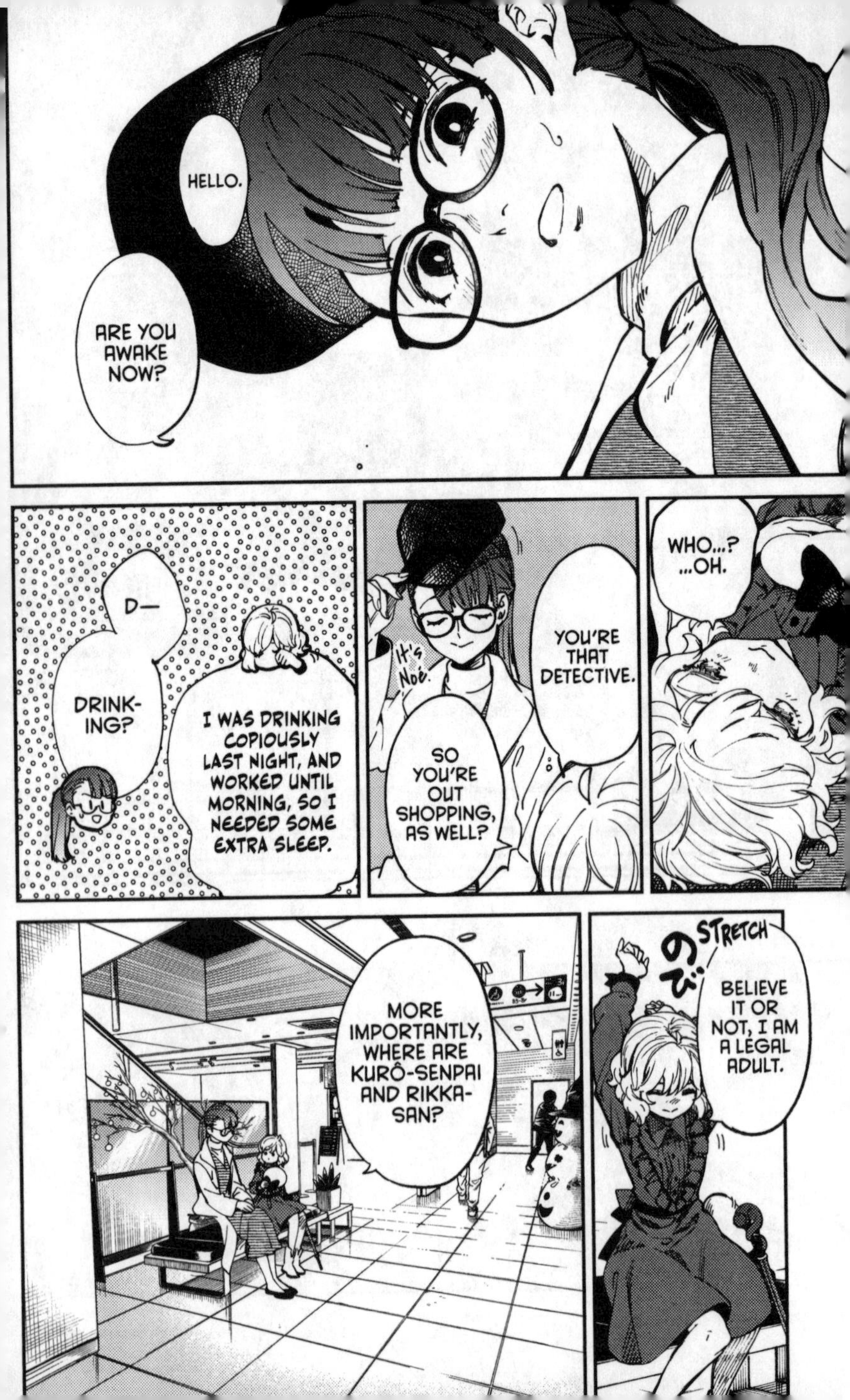
HELLO.
ARE YOU AWAKE NOW?
WHO...? ...OH.
YOU'RE THAT DETECTIVE.
It's Noé.
SO YOU'RE OUT SHOPPING, AS WELL?
I WAS DRINKING COPIOUSLY LAST NIGHT, AND WORKED UNTIL MORNING, SO I NEEDED SOME EXTRA SLEEP.
D—
DRINK-ING?
のび
STRETCH
BELIEVE IT OR NOT, I AM A LEGAL ADULT.
MORE IMPORTANTLY, WHERE ARE KURÔ-SENPAI AND RIKKA-SAN?

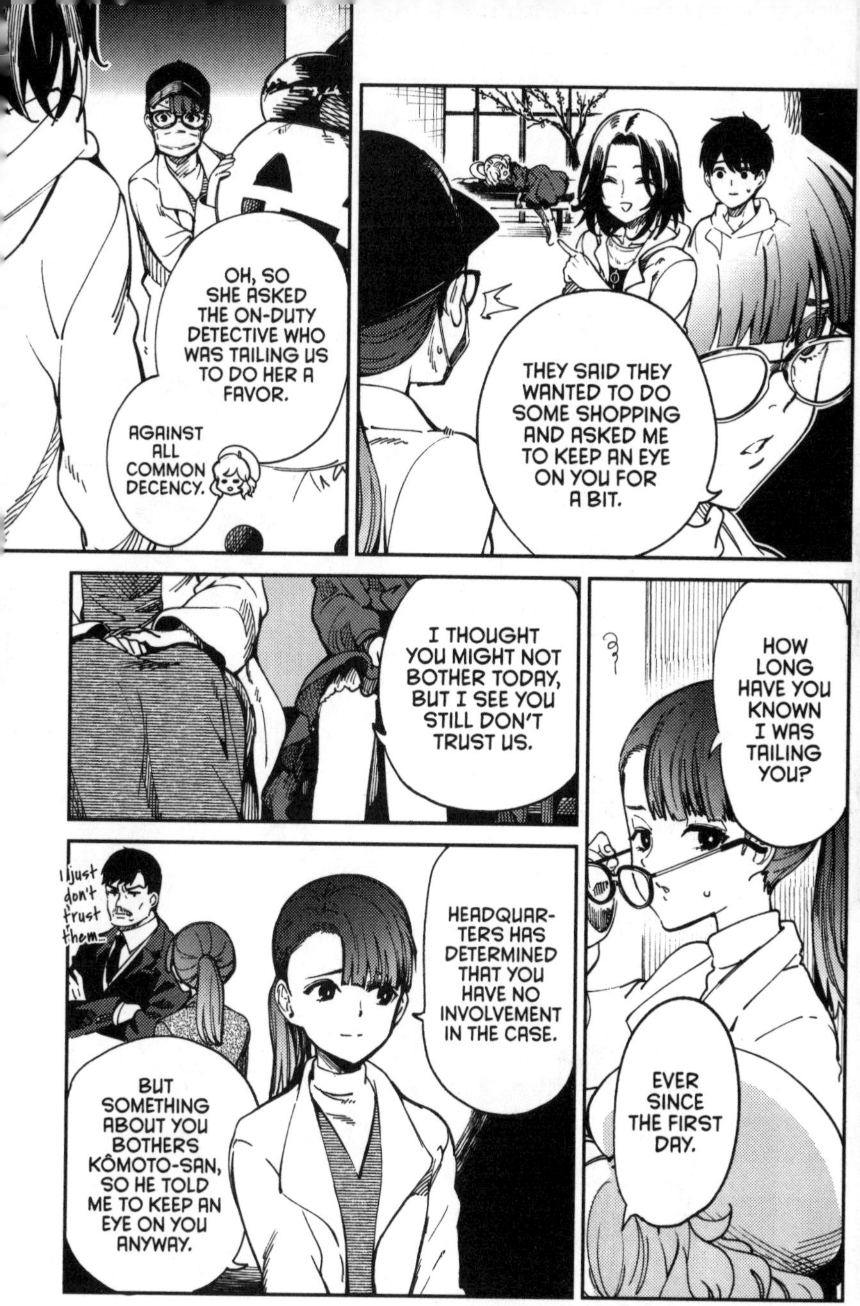
THEY SAID THEY WANTED TO DO SOME SHOPPING AND ASKED ME TO KEEP AN EYE ON YOU FOR A BIT.
OH, SO SHE ASKED THE ON-DUTY DETECTIVE WHO WAS TAILING US TO DO HER A FAVOR.
AGAINST ALL COMMON DECENCY.
HOW LONG HAVE YOU KNOWN I WAS TAILING YOU?
EVER SINCE THE FIRST DAY.
I THOUGHT YOU MIGHT NOT BOTHER TODAY, BUT I SEE YOU STILL DON'T TRUST US.
HEADQUARTERS HAS DETERMINED THAT YOU HAVE NO INVOLVEMENT IN THE CASE.
I just don't trust them...
BUT SOMETHING ABOUT YOU BOTHERS KÔMOTO-SAN, SO HE TOLD ME TO KEEP AN EYE ON YOU ANYWAY.

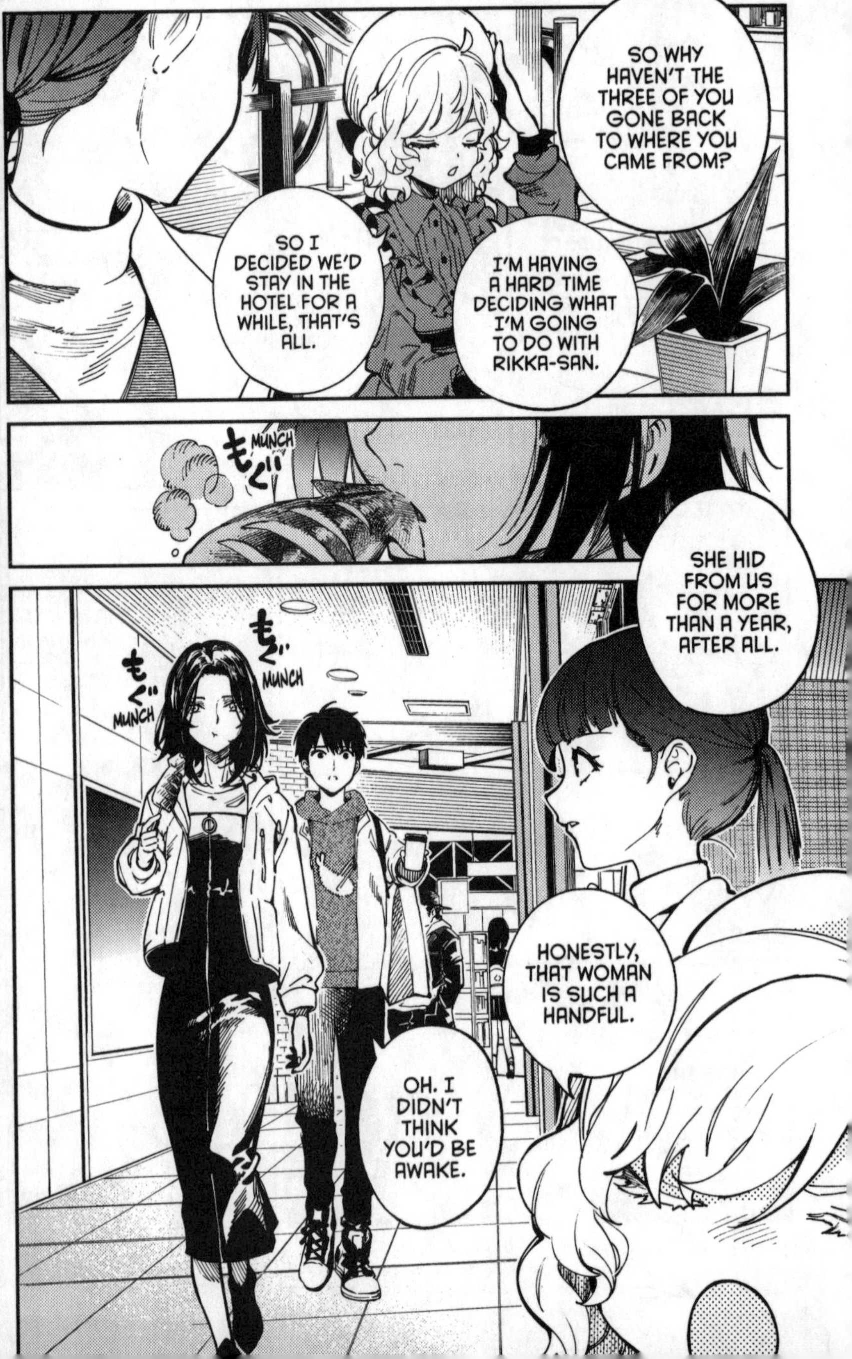
SO WHY HAVEN'T THE THREE OF YOU GONE BACK TO WHERE YOU CAME FROM?
I'M HAVING A HARD TIME DECIDING WHAT I'M GOING TO DO WITH RIKKA-SAN.
SO I DECIDED WE'D STAY IN THE HOTEL FOR A WHILE, THAT'S ALL.
もぐ MUNCH
SHE HID FROM US FOR MORE THAN A YEAR, AFTER ALL.
HONESTLY, THAT WOMAN IS SUCH A HANDFUL.
もぐ MUNCH
もぐ MUNCH
OH. I DIDN'T THINK YOU'D BE AWAKE.

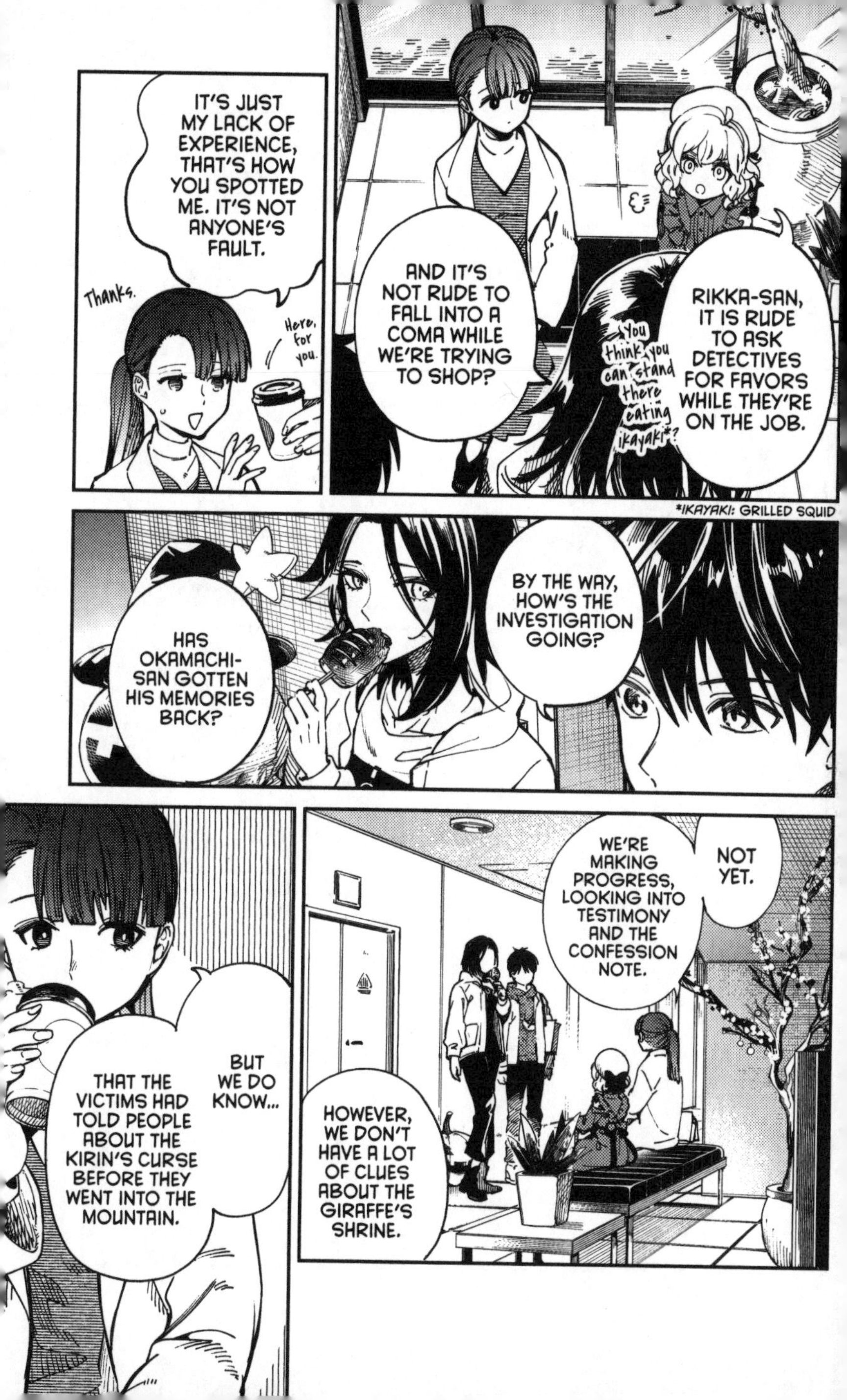
RIKKA-SAN, IT IS RUDE TO ASK DETECTIVES FOR FAVORS WHILE THEY'RE ON THE JOB.
You think you can stand there eating ikayaki*?
AND IT'S NOT RUDE TO FALL INTO A COMA WHILE WE'RE TRYING TO SHOP?
IT'S JUST MY LACK OF EXPERIENCE, THAT'S HOW YOU SPOTTED ME. IT'S NOT ANYONE'S FAULT.
Here, for you.
Thanks.
BY THE WAY, HOW'S THE INVESTIGATION GOING?
HAS OKAMACHI-SAN GOTTEN HIS MEMORIES BACK?
NOT YET.
WE'RE MAKING PROGRESS, LOOKING INTO TESTIMONY AND THE CONFESSION NOTE.
HOWEVER, WE DON'T HAVE A LOT OF CLUES ABOUT THE GIRAFFE'S SHRINE.
BUT WE DO KNOW...
THAT THE VICTIMS HAD TOLD PEOPLE ABOUT THE KIRIN'S CURSE BEFORE THEY WENT INTO THE MOUNTAIN.

*IKAYAKI: GRILLED SQUID

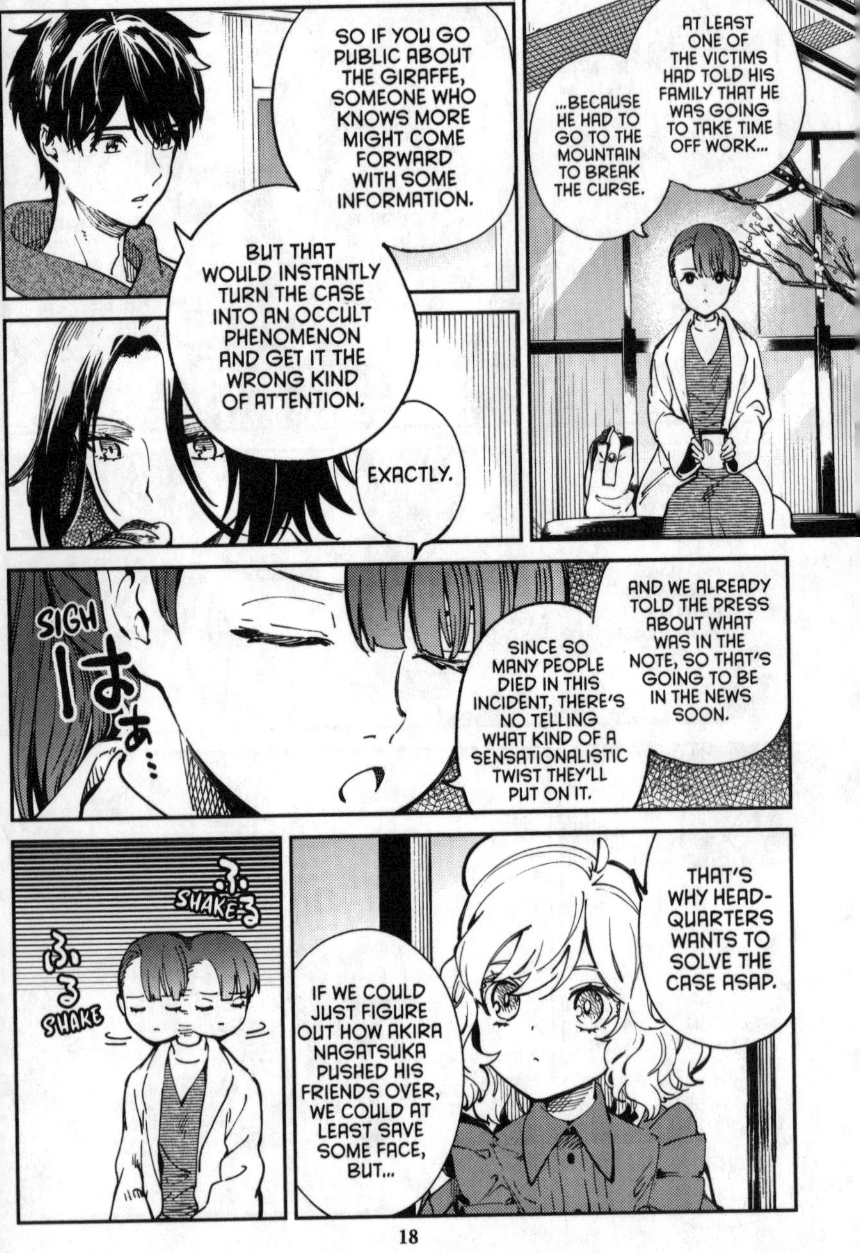
AT LEAST ONE OF THE VICTIMS HAD TOLD HIS FAMILY THAT HE WAS GOING TO TAKE TIME OFF WORK...
...BECAUSE HE HAD TO GO TO THE MOUNTAIN TO BREAK THE CURSE.
SO IF YOU GO PUBLIC ABOUT THE GIRAFFE, SOMEONE WHO KNOWS MORE MIGHT COME FORWARD WITH SOME INFORMATION.
BUT THAT WOULD INSTANTLY TURN THE CASE INTO AN OCCULT PHENOMENON AND GET IT THE WRONG KIND OF ATTENTION.
EXACTLY.
AND WE ALREADY TOLD THE PRESS ABOUT WHAT WAS IN THE NOTE, SO THAT'S GOING TO BE IN THE NEWS SOON.
SINCE SO MANY PEOPLE DIED IN THIS INCIDENT, THERE'S NO TELLING WHAT KIND OF A SENSATIONALISTIC TWIST THEY'LL PUT ON IT.
はぁ…
SIGH
THAT'S WHY HEAD-QUARTERS WANTS TO SOLVE THE CASE ASAP.
IF WE COULD JUST FIGURE OUT HOW AKIRA NAGATSUKA PUSHED HIS FRIENDS OVER, WE COULD AT LEAST SAVE SOME FACE, BUT...
ふる
SHAKE
ふる
SHAKE

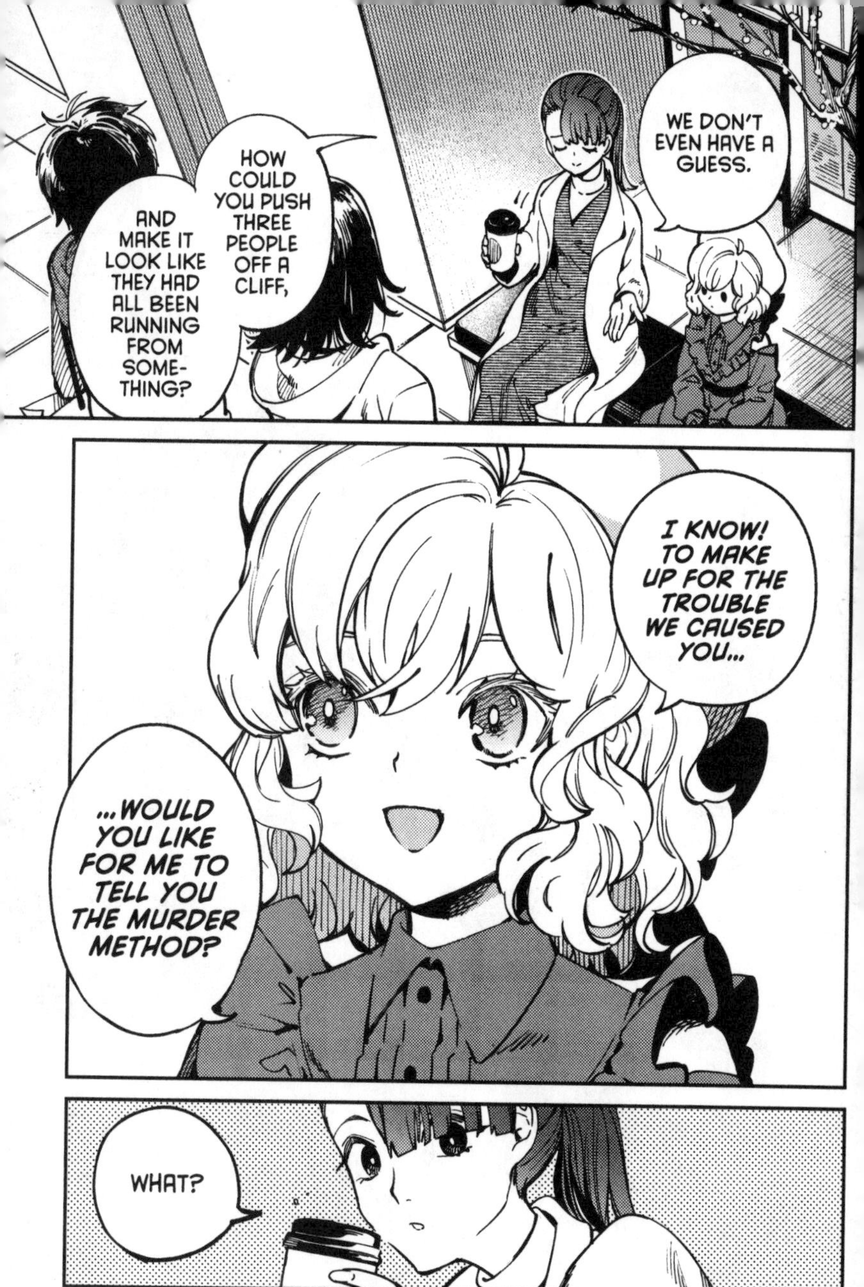
WE DON'T EVEN HAVE A GUESS.
HOW COULD YOU PUSH THREE PEOPLE OFF A CLIFF,
AND MAKE IT LOOK LIKE THEY HAD ALL BEEN RUNNING FROM SOME-THING?
I KNOW! TO MAKE UP FOR THE TROUBLE WE CAUSED YOU...
...WOULD YOU LIKE FOR ME TO TELL YOU THE MURDER METHOD?
WHAT?

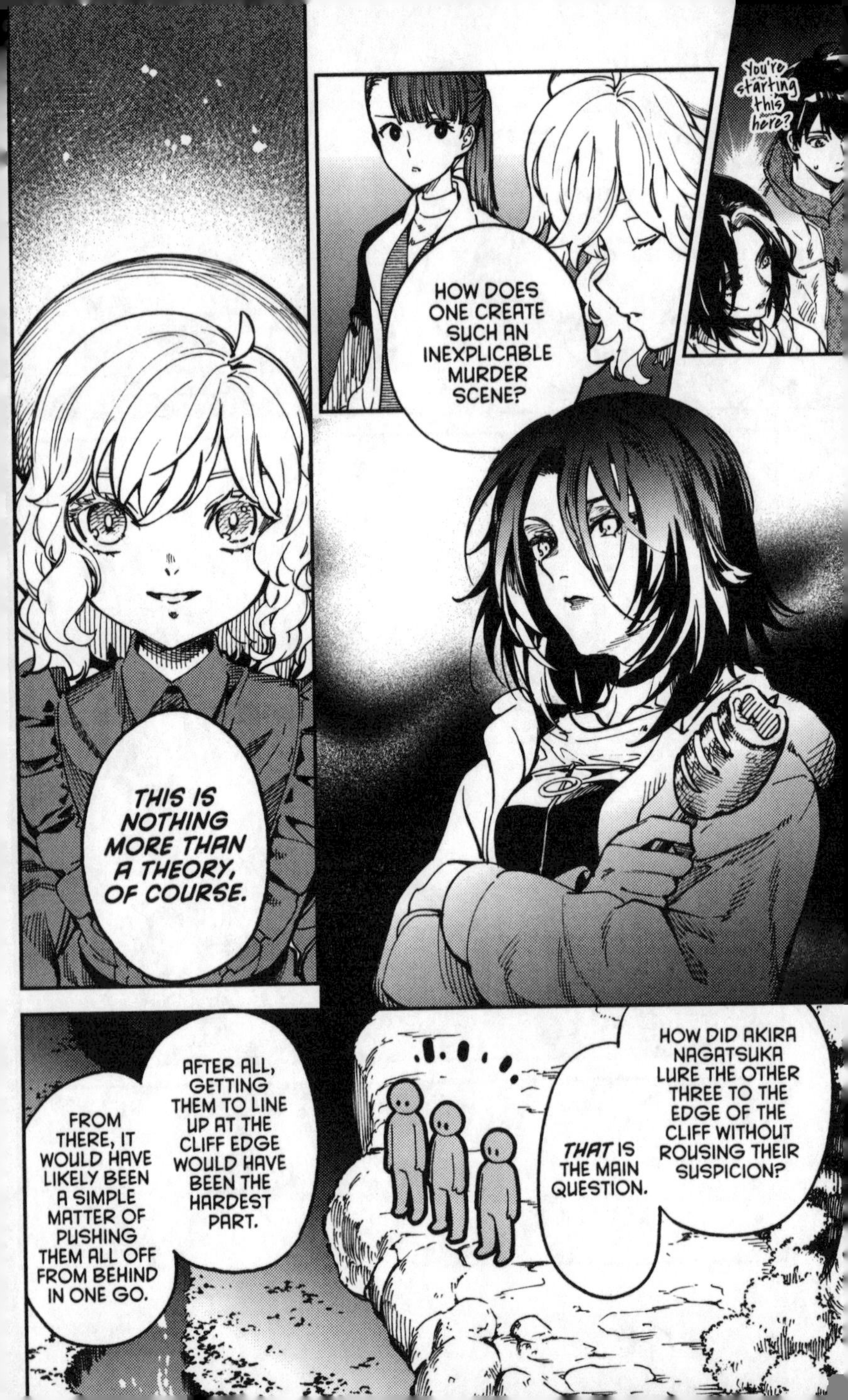
You're starting this here?
HOW DOES ONE CREATE SUCH AN INEXPLICABLE MURDER SCENE?
THIS IS NOTHING MORE THAN A THEORY, OF COURSE.
HOW DID AKIRA NAGATSUKA LURE THE OTHER THREE TO THE EDGE OF THE CLIFF WITHOUT ROUSING THEIR SUSPICION?
THAT IS THE MAIN QUESTION.
AFTER ALL, GETTING THEM TO LINE UP AT THE CLIFF EDGE WOULD HAVE BEEN THE HARDEST PART.
FROM THERE, IT WOULD HAVE LIKELY BEEN A SIMPLE MATTER OF PUSHING THEM ALL OFF FROM BEHIND IN ONE GO.

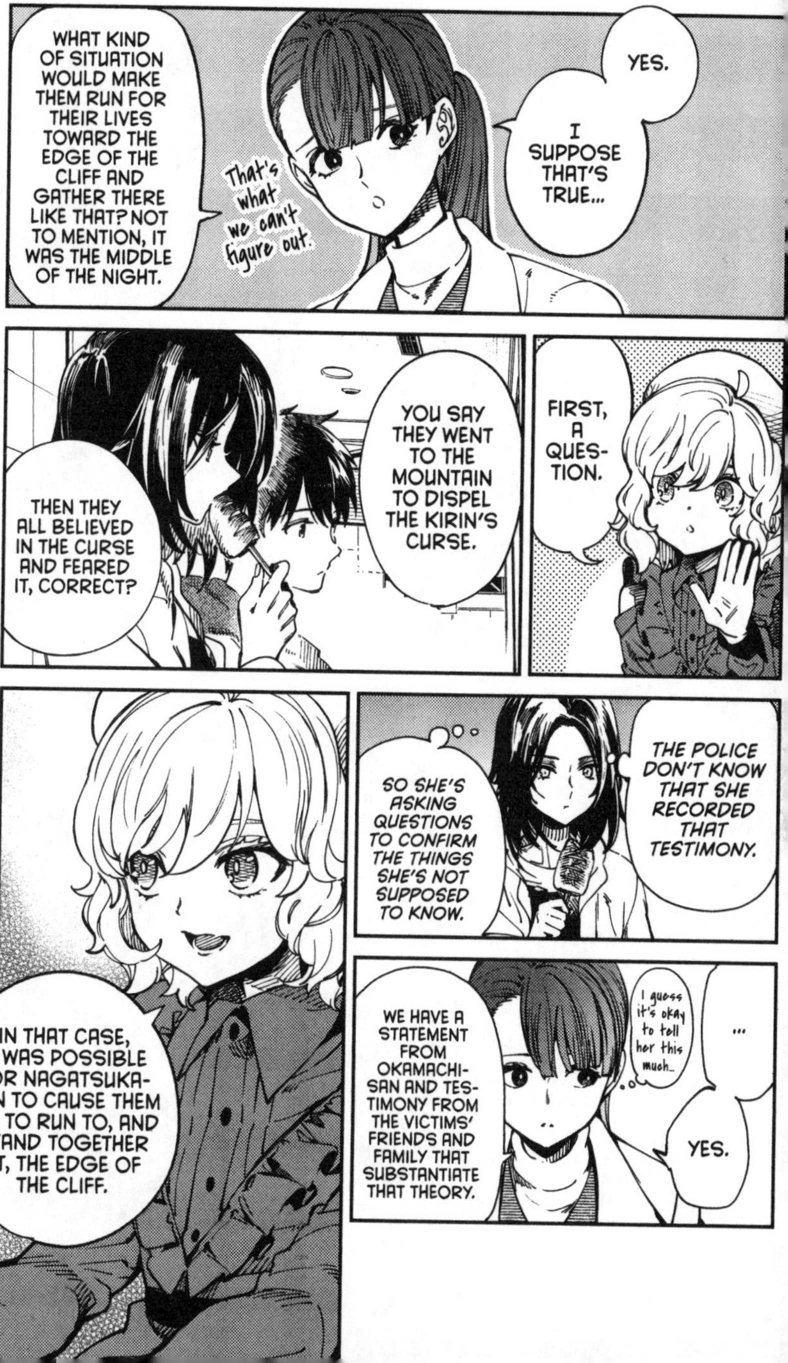
YES.
I SUPPOSE THAT'S TRUE...
That's what we can't figure out.
WHAT KIND OF SITUATION WOULD MAKE THEM RUN FOR THEIR LIVES TOWARD THE EDGE OF THE CLIFF AND GATHER THERE LIKE THAT? NOT TO MENTION, IT WAS THE MIDDLE OF THE NIGHT.
FIRST, A QUES-TION.
YOU SAY THEY WENT TO THE MOUNTAIN TO DISPEL THE KIRIN'S CURSE.
THEN THEY ALL BELIEVED IN THE CURSE AND FEARED IT, CORRECT?
THE POLICE DON'T KNOW THAT SHE RECORDED THAT TESTIMONY.
SO SHE'S ASKING QUESTIONS TO CONFIRM THE THINGS SHE'S NOT SUPPOSED TO KNOW.
...
I guess it's okay to tell her this much...
WE HAVE A STATEMENT FROM OKAMACHI-SAN AND TES-TIMONY FROM THE VICTIMS' FRIENDS AND FAMILY THAT SUBSTANTIATE THAT THEORY.
YES.
IN THAT CASE, IT WAS POSSIBLE FOR NAGATSUKA-SAN TO CAUSE THEM ALL TO RUN TO, AND STAND TOGETHER AT, THE EDGE OF THE CLIFF.

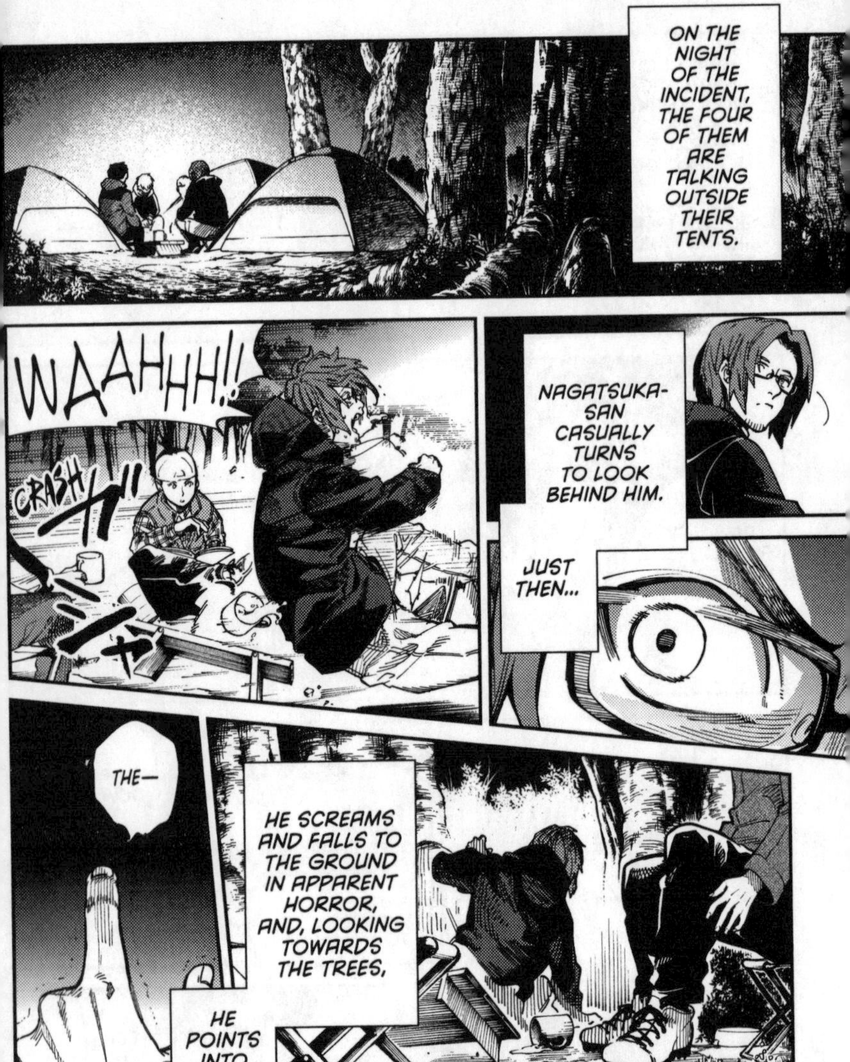
ON THE NIGHT OF THE INCIDENT, THE FOUR OF THEM ARE TALKING OUTSIDE THEIR TENTS.
NAGATSUKA-SAN CASUALLY TURNS TO LOOK BEHIND HIM.
JUST THEN...
WAAHHH!!
CRASH
HE SCREAMS AND FALLS TO THE GROUND IN APPARENT HORROR, AND, LOOKING TOWARDS THE TREES,
HE POINTS INTO THE DARKNESS.
THE—

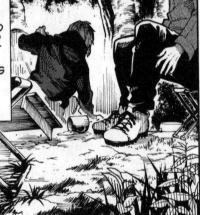

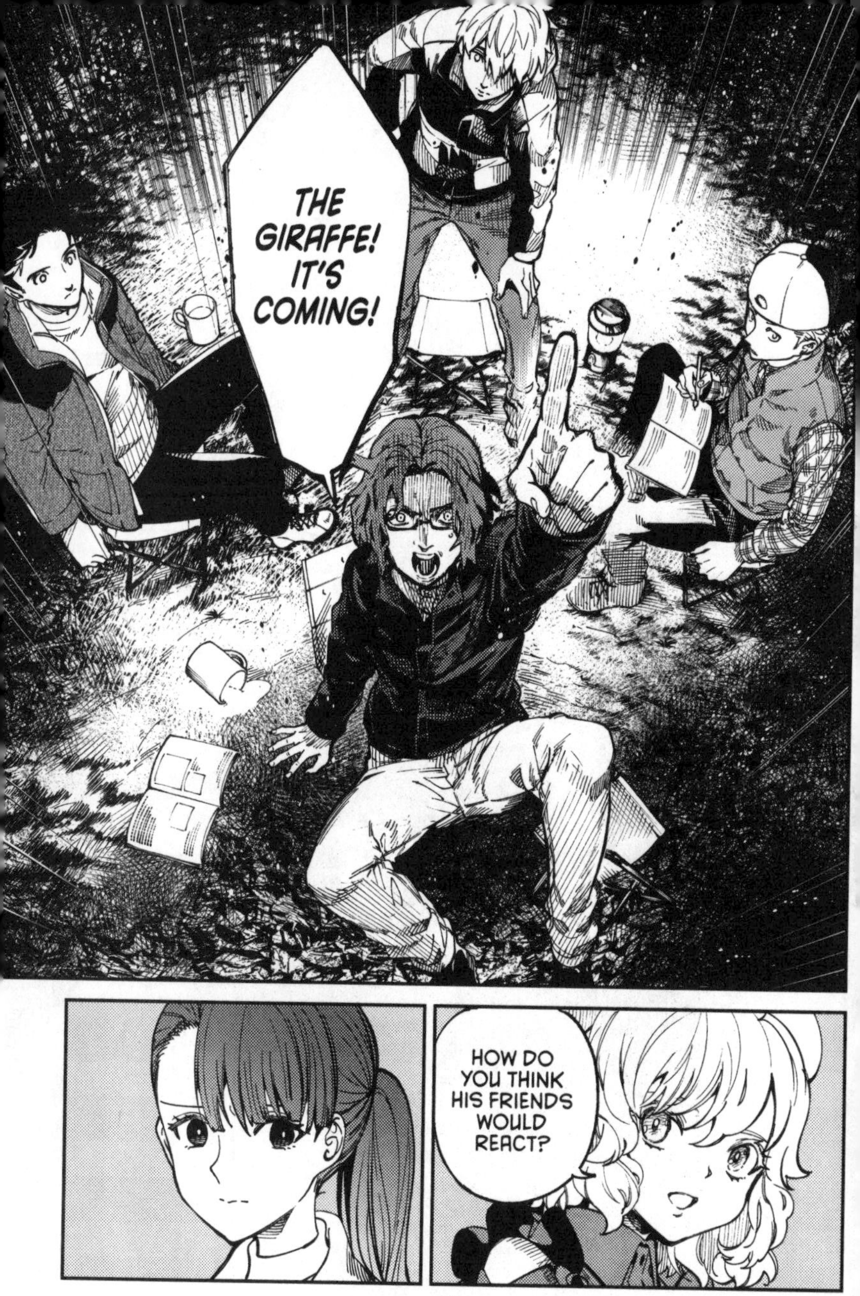
THE GIRAFFE! IT'S COMING!
HOW DO YOU THINK HIS FRIENDS WOULD REACT?

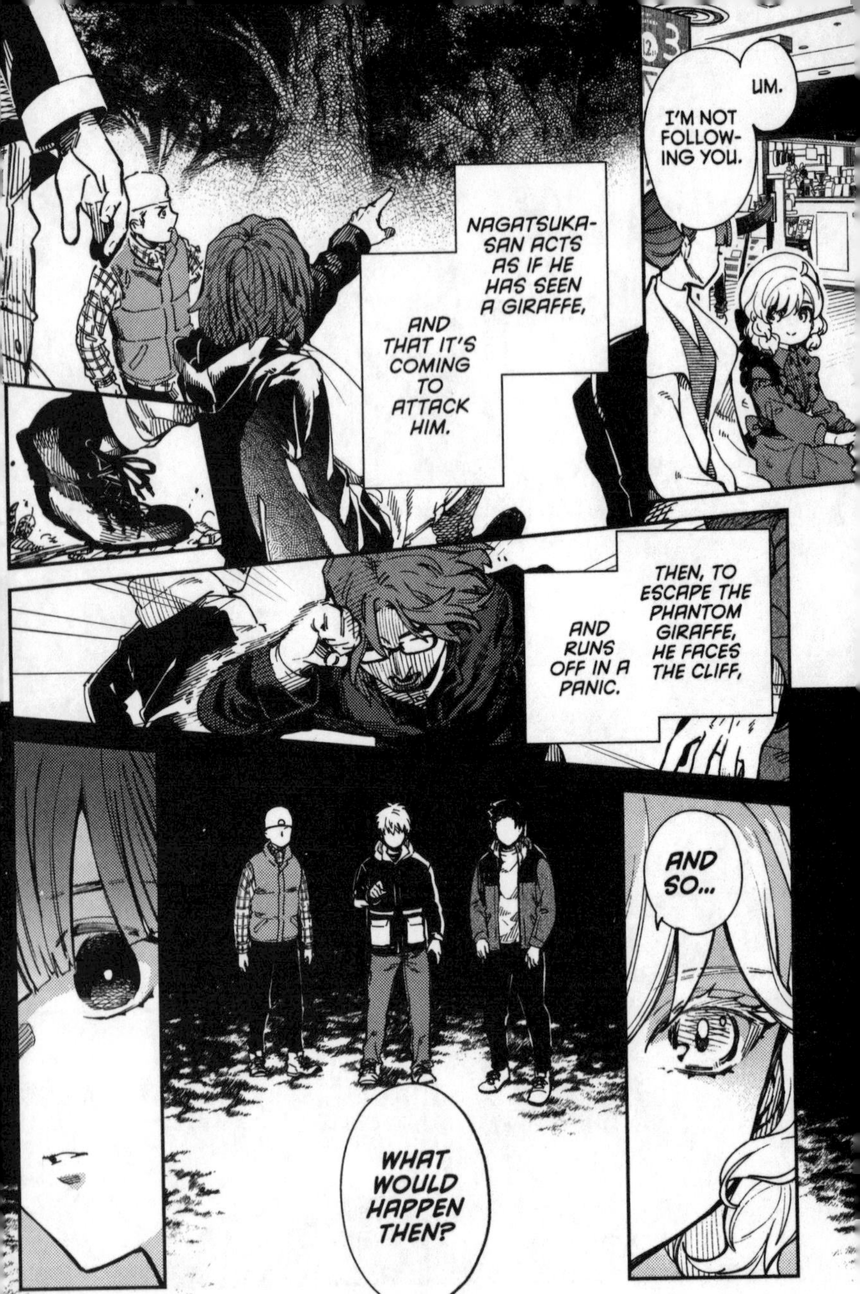
UM.
I'M NOT FOLLOWING YOU.
NAGATSUKA-SAN ACTS AS IF HE HAS SEEN A GIRAFFE,
AND THAT IT'S COMING TO ATTACK HIM.
THEN, TO ESCAPE THE PHANTOM GIRAFFE, HE FACES THE CLIFF,
AND RUNS OFF IN A PANIC.
AND SO...
WHAT WOULD HAPPEN THEN?

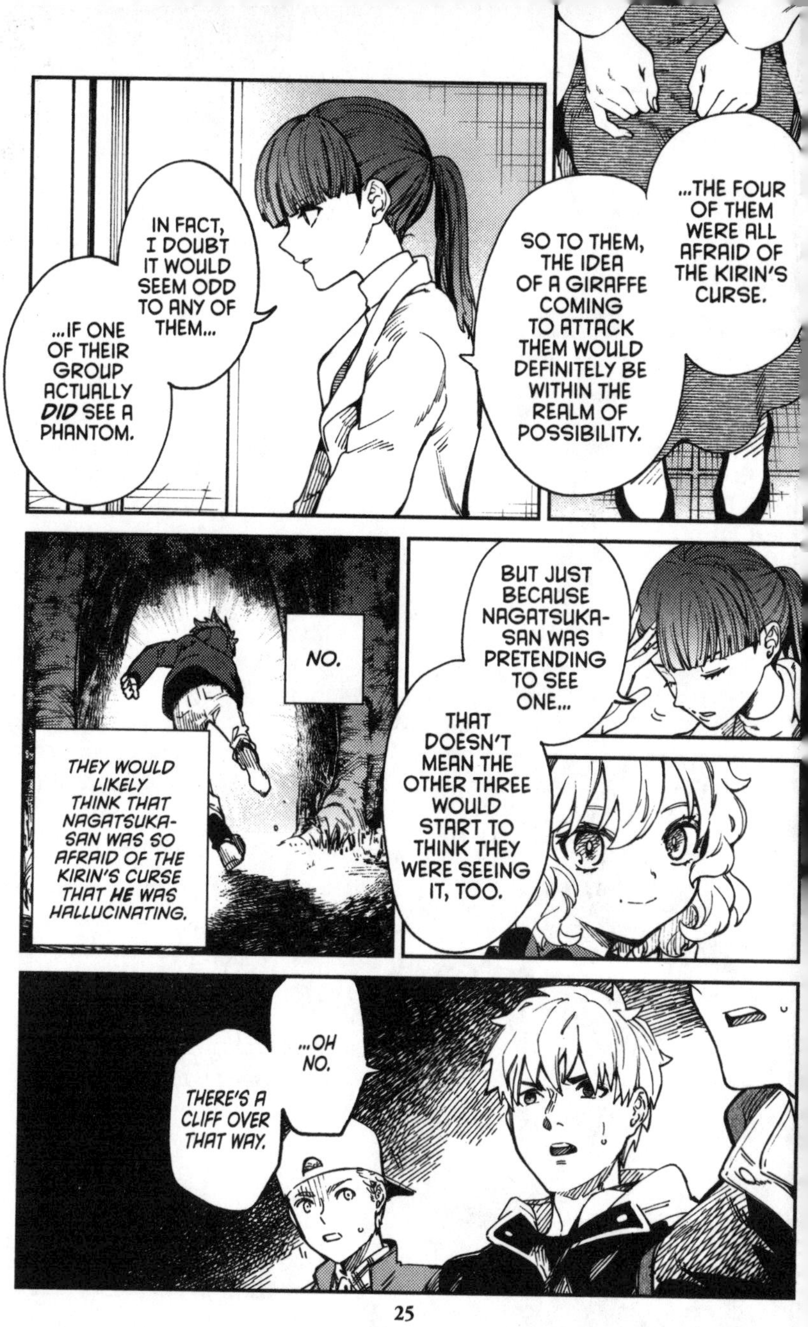
...THE FOUR OF THEM WERE ALL AFRAID OF THE KIRIN'S CURSE.
SO TO THEM, THE IDEA OF A GIRAFFE COMING TO ATTACK THEM WOULD DEFINITELY BE WITHIN THE REALM OF POSSIBILITY.
IN FACT, I DOUBT IT WOULD SEEM ODD TO ANY OF THEM...
...IF ONE OF THEIR GROUP ACTUALLY ***DID*** SEE A PHANTOM.
BUT JUST BECAUSE NAGATSUKA-SAN WAS PRETENDING TO SEE ONE...
THAT DOESN'T MEAN THE OTHER THREE WOULD START TO THINK THEY WERE SEEING IT, TOO.
NO.
*THEY WOULD LIKELY THINK THAT NAGATSUKA-SAN WAS SO AFRAID OF THE KIRIN'S CURSE THAT **HE** WAS HALLUCINATING.*
...OH NO.
THERE'S A CLIFF OVER THAT WAY.

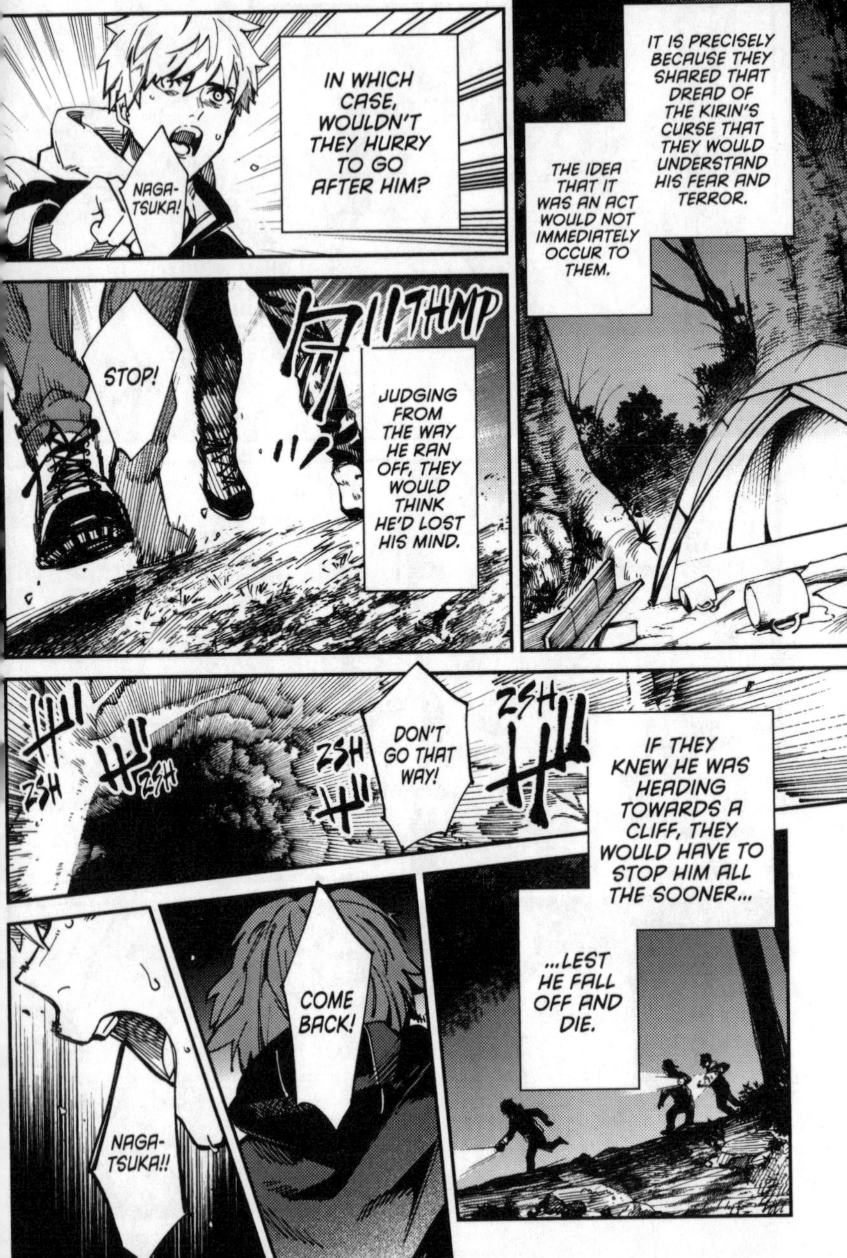

IT IS PRECISELY BECAUSE THEY SHARED THAT DREAD OF THE KIRIN'S CURSE THAT THEY WOULD UNDERSTAND HIS FEAR AND TERROR.
THE IDEA THAT IT WAS AN ACT WOULD NOT IMMEDIATELY OCCUR TO THEM.
IN WHICH CASE, WOULDN'T THEY HURRY TO GO AFTER HIM?
NAGA-TSUKA!
JUDGING FROM THE WAY HE RAN OFF, THEY WOULD THINK HE'D LOST HIS MIND.
THMP
STOP!
IF THEY KNEW HE WAS HEADING TOWARDS A CLIFF, THEY WOULD HAVE TO STOP HIM ALL THE SOONER...
ZSH
DON'T GO THAT WAY!
ZSH
ZSH
ZSH
...LEST HE FALL OFF AND DIE.
COME BACK!
NAGA-TSUKA!!

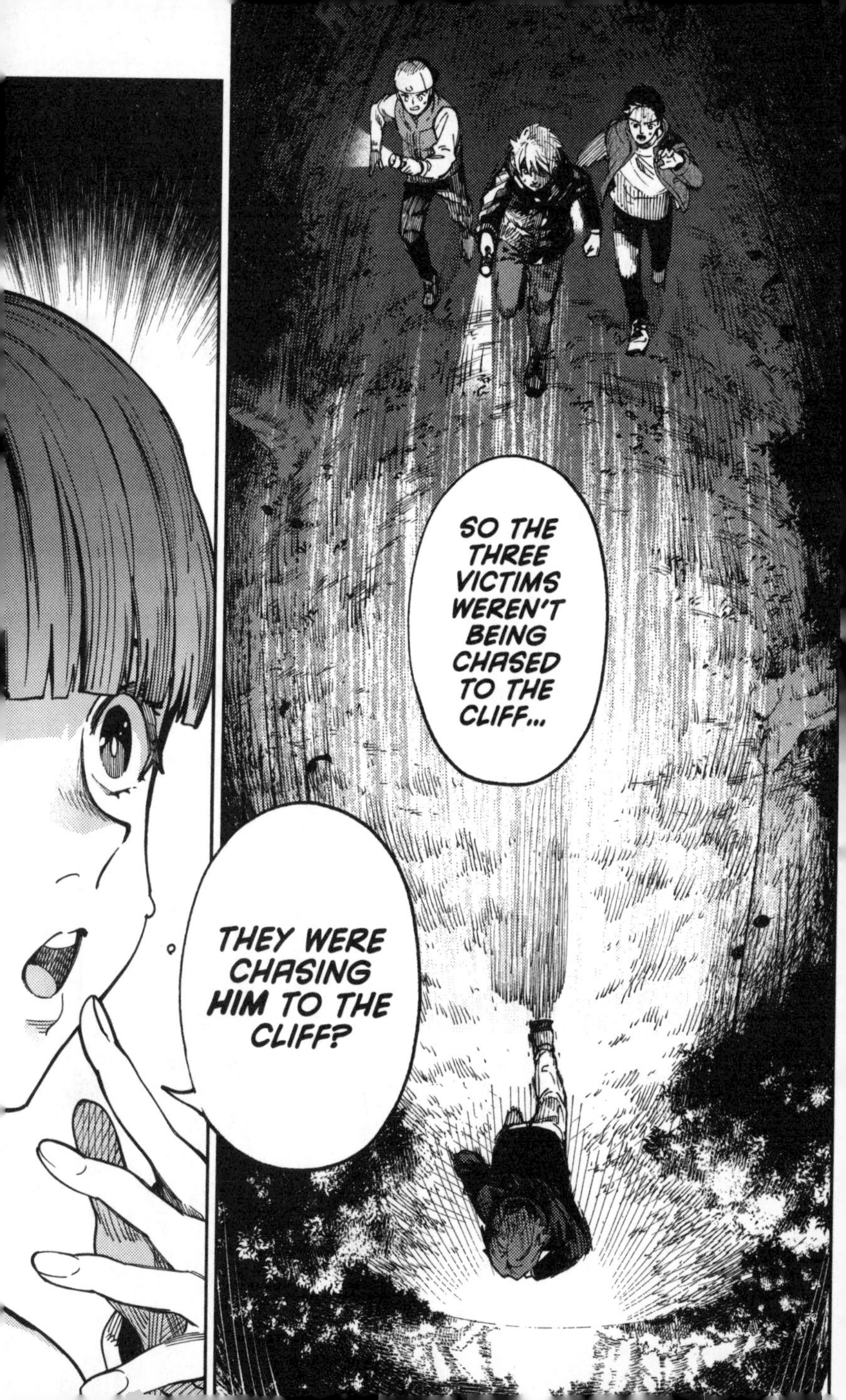
SO THE THREE VICTIMS WEREN'T BEING CHASED TO THE CLIFF...
THEY WERE CHASING HIM TO THE CLIFF?

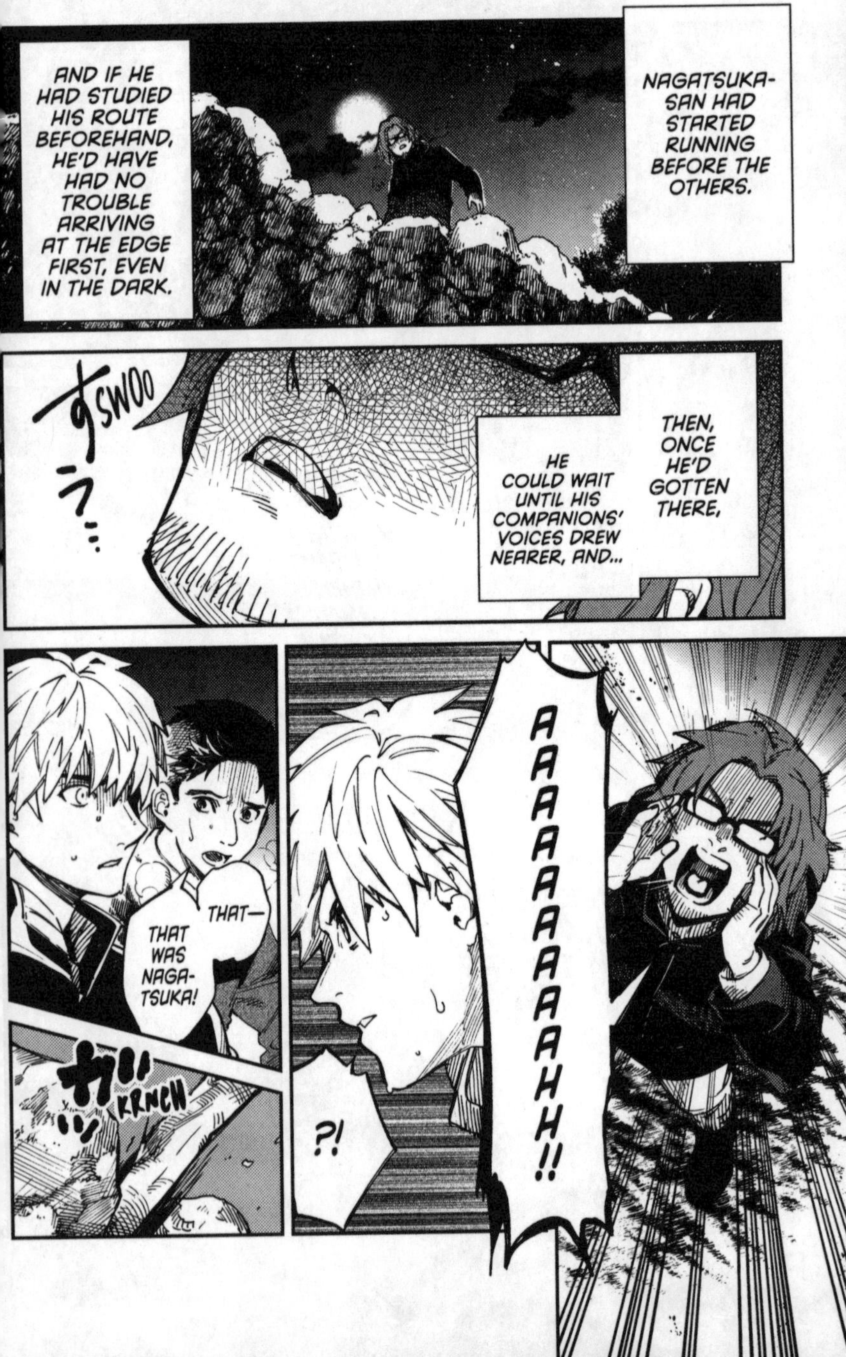
NAGATSUKA-SAN HAD STARTED RUNNING BEFORE THE OTHERS.
AND IF HE HAD STUDIED HIS ROUTE BEFOREHAND, HE'D HAVE HAD NO TROUBLE ARRIVING AT THE EDGE FIRST, EVEN IN THE DARK.
THEN, ONCE HE'D GOTTEN THERE,
HE COULD WAIT UNTIL HIS COMPANIONS' VOICES DREW NEARER, AND...
SWOO
AAAAAAAAAHH!!
?!
THAT—
THAT WAS NAGA-TSUKA!
KRNCH

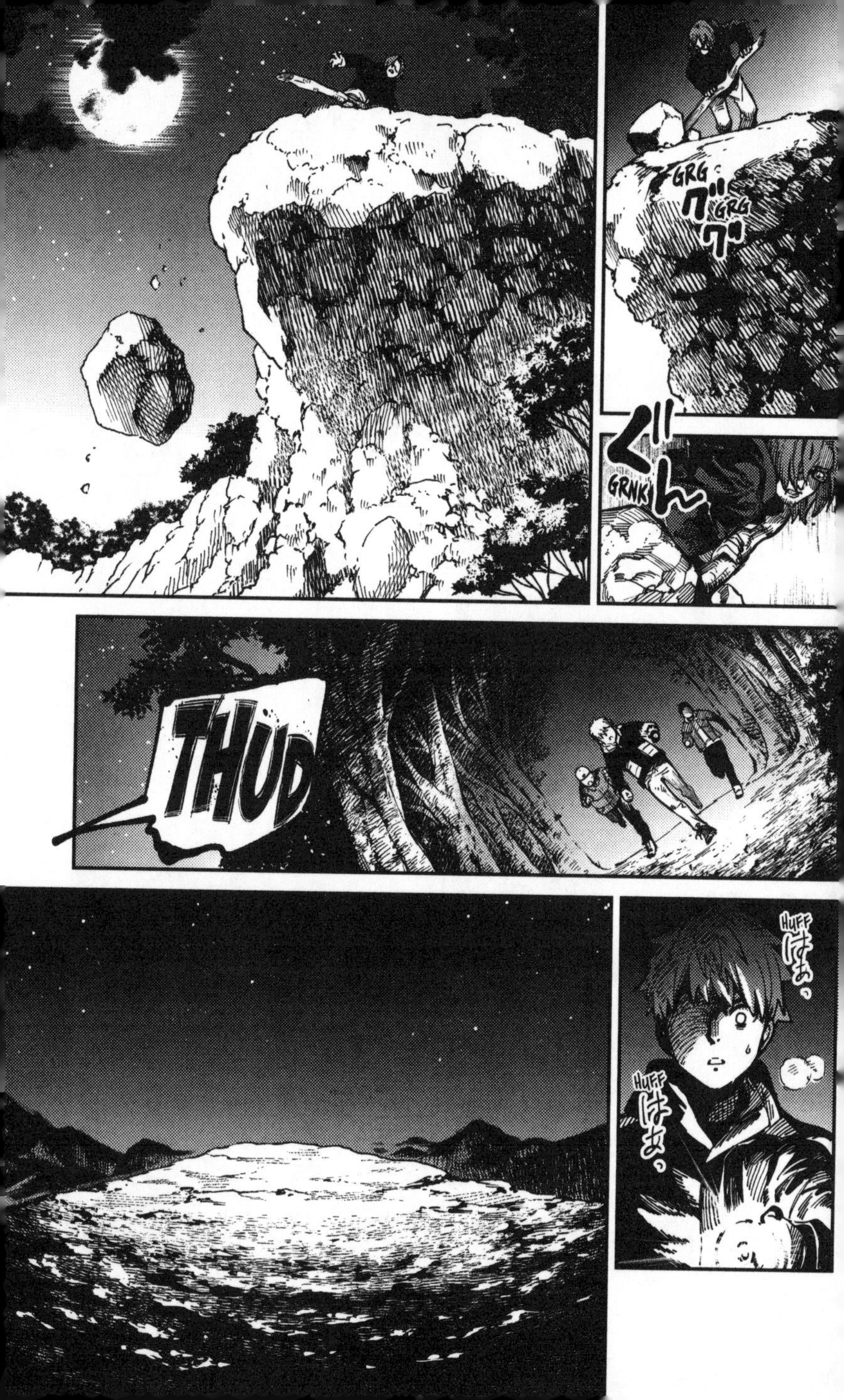
GRG ガ GRG ガ
GRNK ぐん
THUD
HUFF はあっ
HUFF はあっ

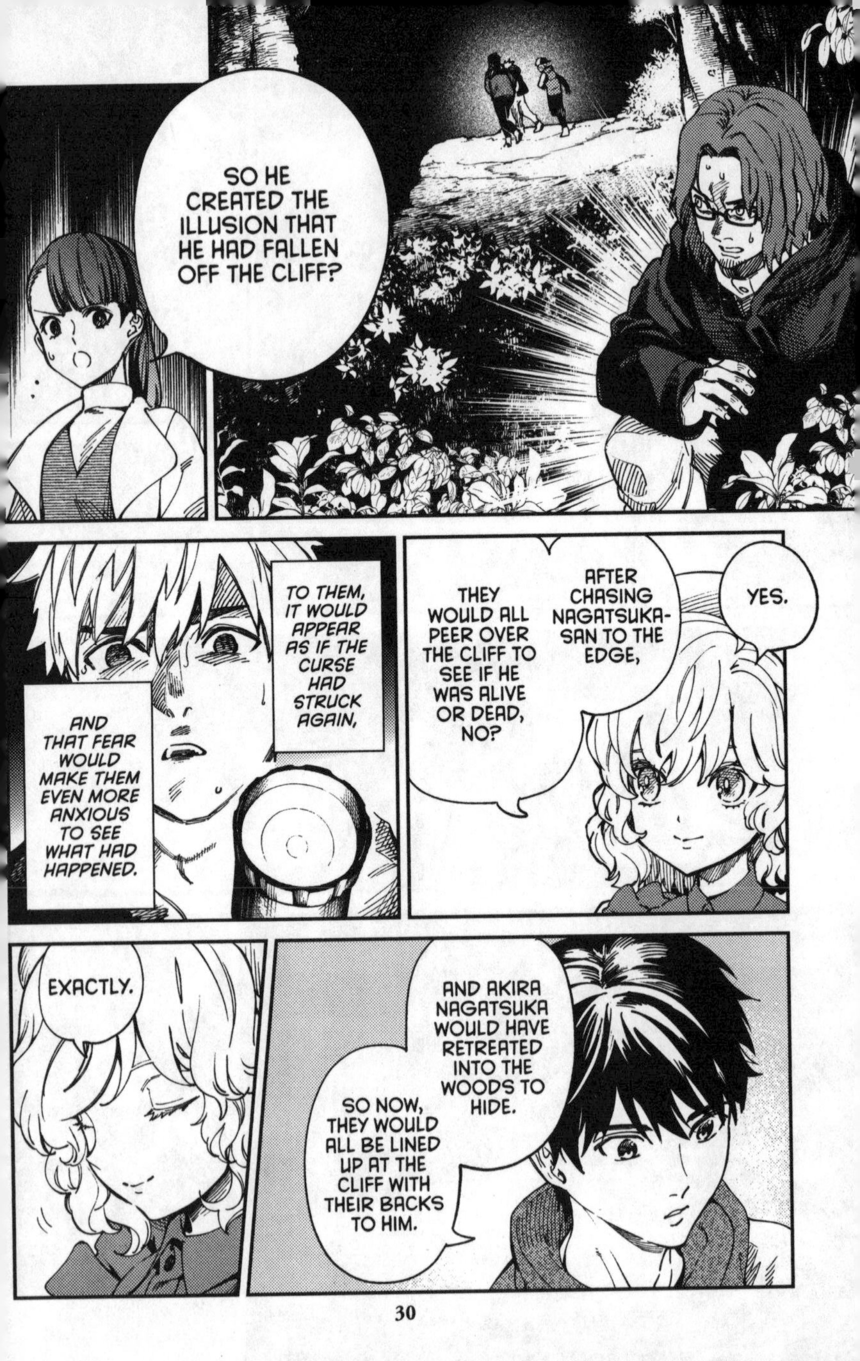
SO HE CREATED THE ILLUSION THAT HE HAD FALLEN OFF THE CLIFF?
YES.
AFTER CHASING NAGATSUKA-SAN TO THE EDGE,
THEY WOULD ALL PEER OVER THE CLIFF TO SEE IF HE WAS ALIVE OR DEAD, NO?
TO THEM, IT WOULD APPEAR AS IF THE CURSE HAD STRUCK AGAIN,
AND THAT FEAR WOULD MAKE THEM EVEN MORE ANXIOUS TO SEE WHAT HAD HAPPENED.
AND AKIRA NAGATSUKA WOULD HAVE RETREATED INTO THE WOODS TO HIDE.
SO NOW, THEY WOULD ALL BE LINED UP AT THE CLIFF WITH THEIR BACKS TO HIM.
EXACTLY.

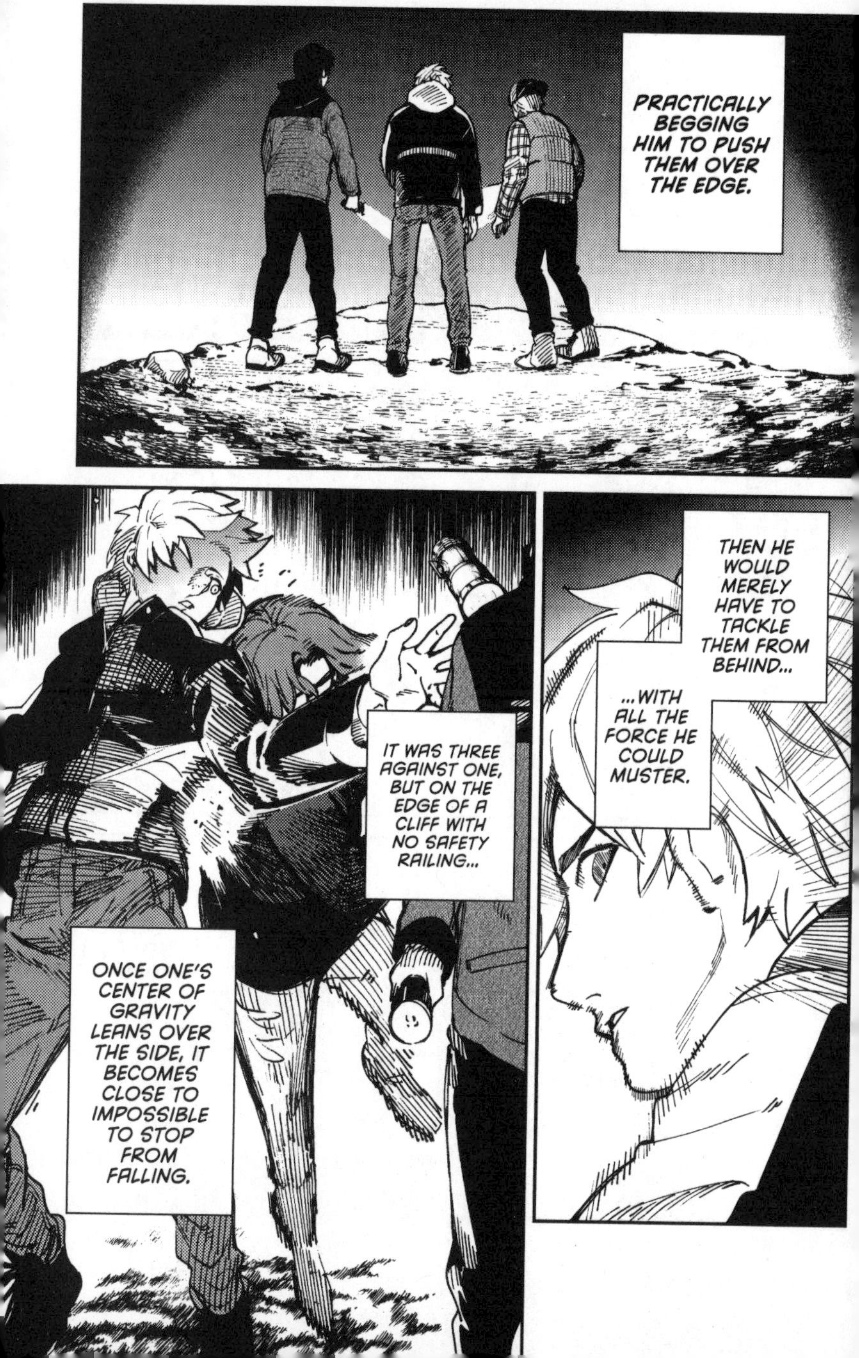
PRACTICALLY BEGGING HIM TO PUSH THEM OVER THE EDGE.
THEN HE WOULD MERELY HAVE TO TACKLE THEM FROM BEHIND...
...WITH ALL THE FORCE HE COULD MUSTER.
IT WAS THREE AGAINST ONE, BUT ON THE EDGE OF A CLIFF WITH NO SAFETY RAILING...
ONCE ONE'S CENTER OF GRAVITY LEANS OVER THE SIDE, IT BECOMES CLOSE TO IMPOSSIBLE TO STOP FROM FALLING.

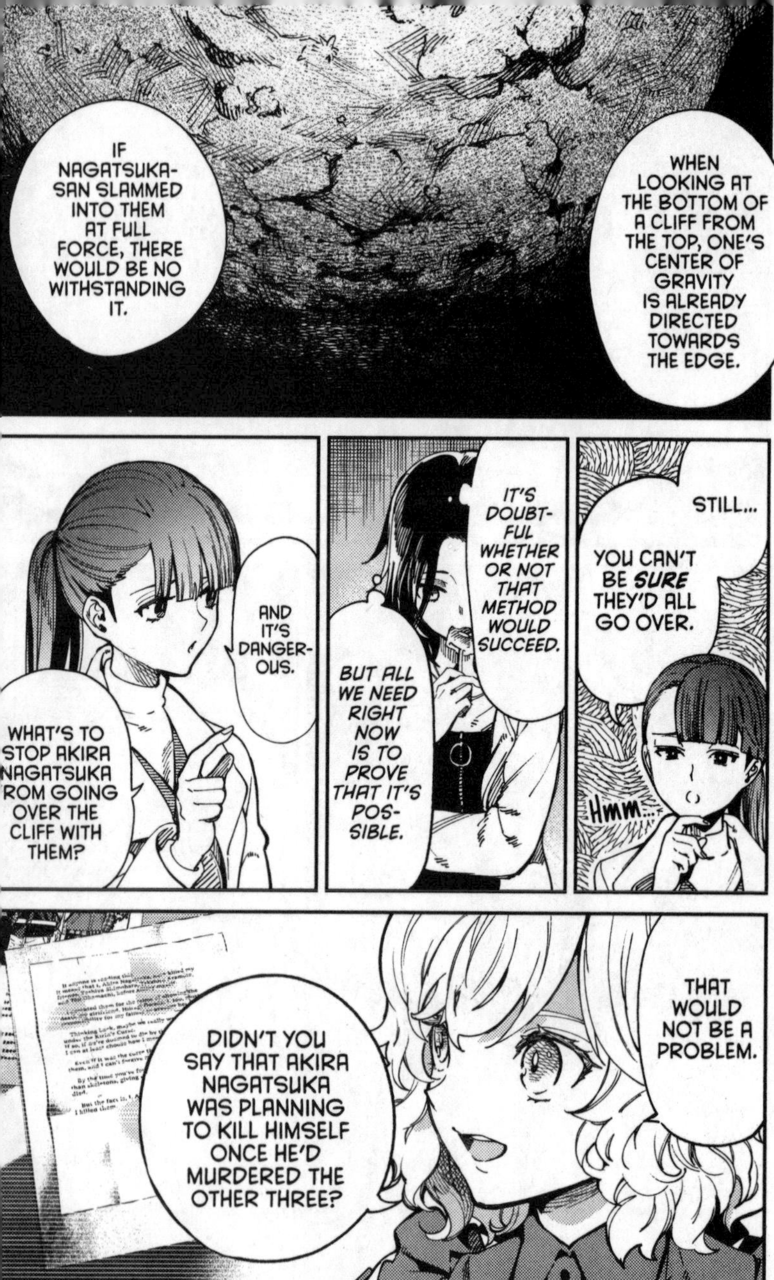
WHEN LOOKING AT THE BOTTOM OF A CLIFF FROM THE TOP, ONE'S CENTER OF GRAVITY IS ALREADY DIRECTED TOWARDS THE EDGE.
IF NAGATSUKA-SAN SLAMMED INTO THEM AT FULL FORCE, THERE WOULD BE NO WITHSTANDING IT.
STILL...
YOU CAN'T BE *SURE* THEY'D ALL GO OVER.
Hmm...
IT'S DOUBTFUL WHETHER OR NOT THAT METHOD WOULD SUCCEED.
BUT ALL WE NEED RIGHT NOW IS TO PROVE THAT IT'S POSSIBLE.
AND IT'S DANGEROUS.
WHAT'S TO STOP AKIRA NAGATSUKA ROM GOING OVER THE CLIFF WITH THEM?
THAT WOULD NOT BE A PROBLEM.
DIDN'T YOU SAY THAT AKIRA NAGATSUKA WAS PLANNING TO KILL HIMSELF ONCE HE'D MURDERED THE OTHER THREE?

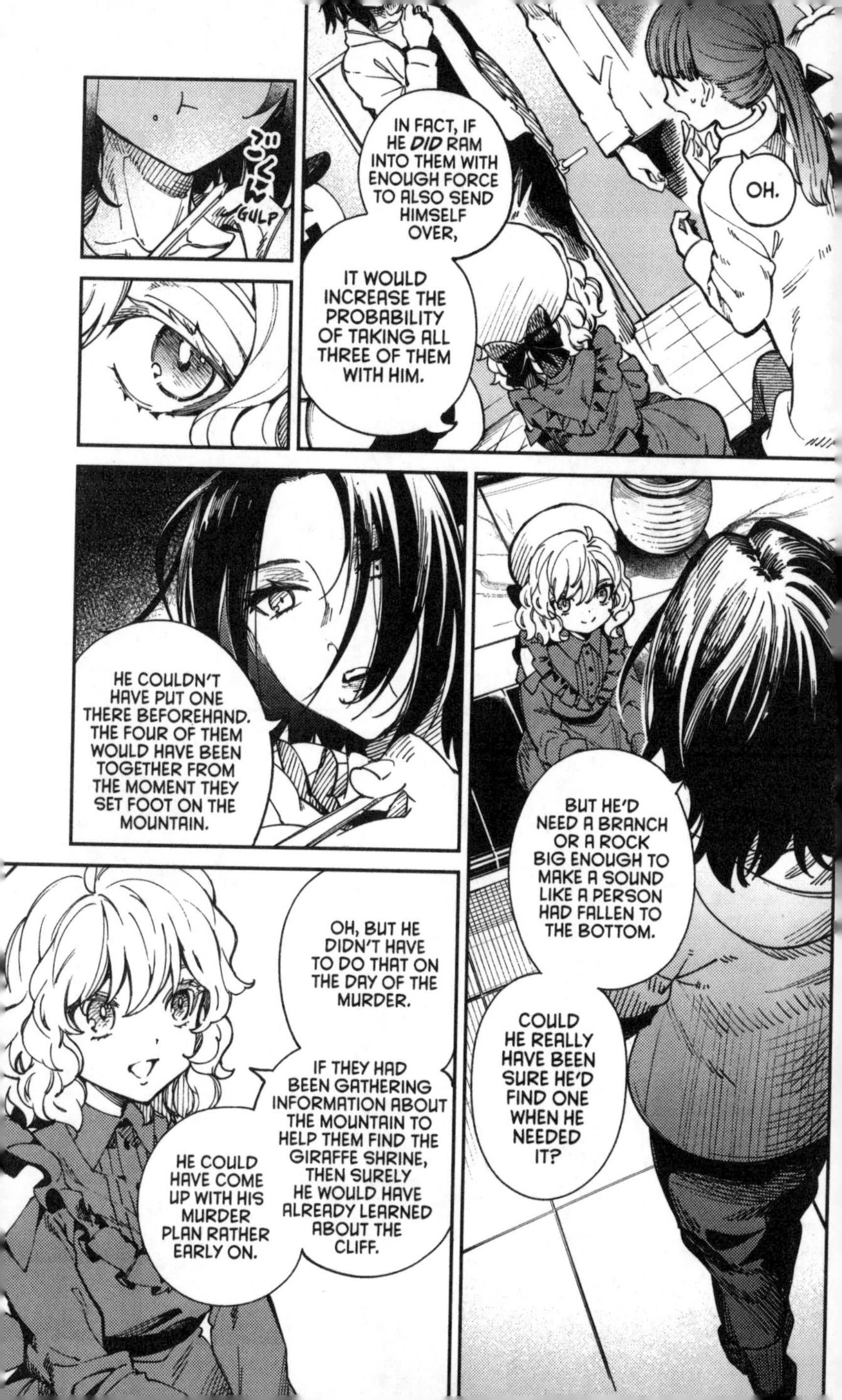
IN FACT, IF HE *DID* RAM INTO THEM WITH ENOUGH FORCE TO ALSO SEND HIMSELF OVER,
IT WOULD INCREASE THE PROBABILITY OF TAKING ALL THREE OF THEM WITH HIM.
OH.
ごくん GULP
BUT HE'D NEED A BRANCH OR A ROCK BIG ENOUGH TO MAKE A SOUND LIKE A PERSON HAD FALLEN TO THE BOTTOM.
COULD HE REALLY HAVE BEEN SURE HE'D FIND ONE WHEN HE NEEDED IT?
HE COULDN'T HAVE PUT ONE THERE BEFOREHAND. THE FOUR OF THEM WOULD HAVE BEEN TOGETHER FROM THE MOMENT THEY SET FOOT ON THE MOUNTAIN.
OH, BUT HE DIDN'T HAVE TO DO THAT ON THE DAY OF THE MURDER.
IF THEY HAD BEEN GATHERING INFORMATION ABOUT THE MOUNTAIN TO HELP THEM FIND THE GIRAFFE SHRINE, THEN SURELY HE WOULD HAVE ALREADY LEARNED ABOUT THE CLIFF.
HE COULD HAVE COME UP WITH HIS MURDER PLAN RATHER EARLY ON.

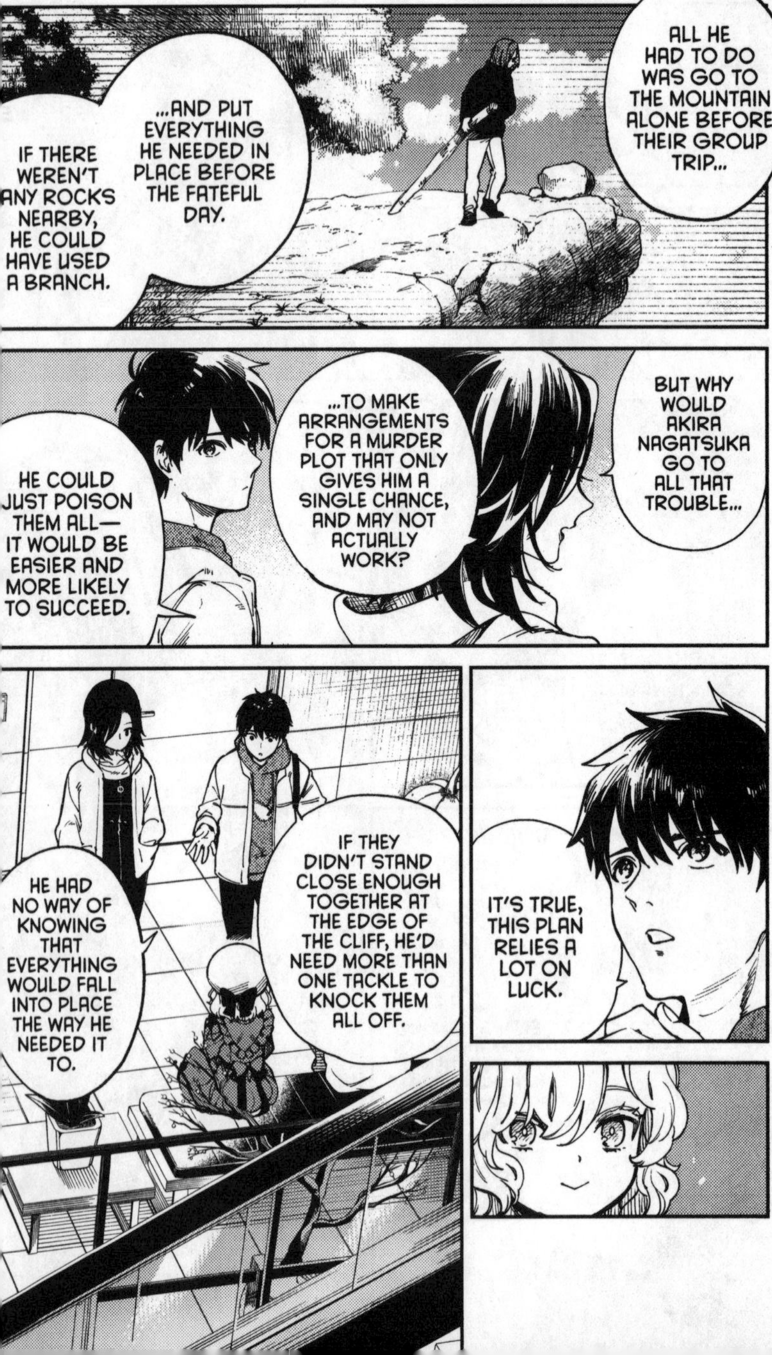
ALL HE HAD TO DO WAS GO TO THE MOUNTAIN ALONE BEFORE THEIR GROUP TRIP...
...AND PUT EVERYTHING HE NEEDED IN PLACE BEFORE THE FATEFUL DAY.
IF THERE WEREN'T ANY ROCKS NEARBY, HE COULD HAVE USED A BRANCH.
BUT WHY WOULD AKIRA NAGATSUKA GO TO ALL THAT TROUBLE...
...TO MAKE ARRANGEMENTS FOR A MURDER PLOT THAT ONLY GIVES HIM A SINGLE CHANCE, AND MAY NOT ACTUALLY WORK?
HE COULD JUST POISON THEM ALL—IT WOULD BE EASIER AND MORE LIKELY TO SUCCEED.
IT'S TRUE, THIS PLAN RELIES A LOT ON LUCK.
IF THEY DIDN'T STAND CLOSE ENOUGH TOGETHER AT THE EDGE OF THE CLIFF, HE'D NEED MORE THAN ONE TACKLE TO KNOCK THEM ALL OFF.
HE HAD NO WAY OF KNOWING THAT EVERYTHING WOULD FALL INTO PLACE THE WAY HE NEEDED IT TO.

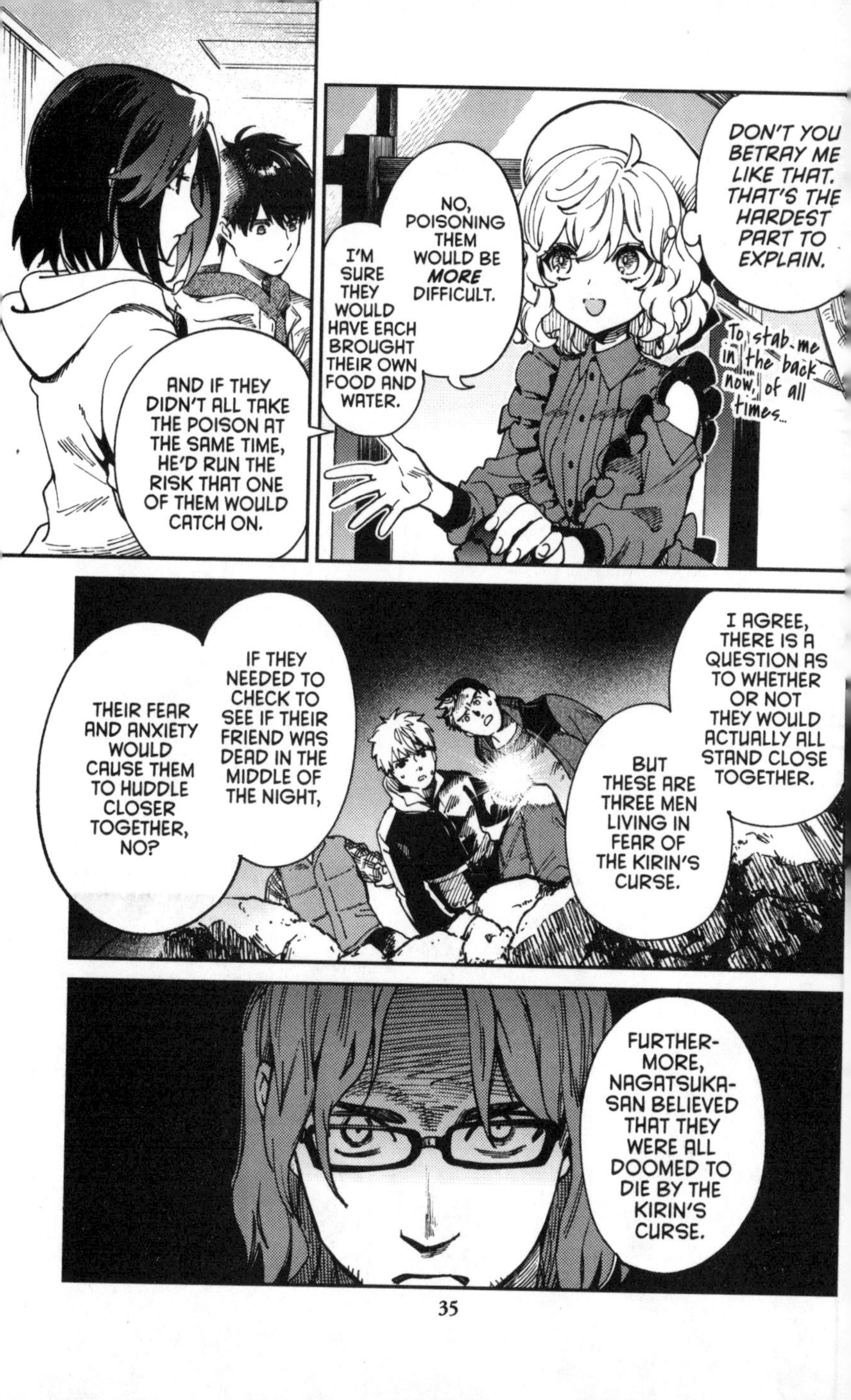
DON'T YOU BETRAY ME LIKE THAT. THAT'S THE HARDEST PART TO EXPLAIN.
To stab me in the back now, of all times...
NO, POISONING THEM WOULD BE *MORE* DIFFICULT.
I'M SURE THEY WOULD HAVE EACH BROUGHT THEIR OWN FOOD AND WATER.
AND IF THEY DIDN'T ALL TAKE THE POISON AT THE SAME TIME, HE'D RUN THE RISK THAT ONE OF THEM WOULD CATCH ON.
I AGREE, THERE IS A QUESTION AS TO WHETHER OR NOT THEY WOULD ACTUALLY ALL STAND CLOSE TOGETHER.
BUT THESE ARE THREE MEN LIVING IN FEAR OF THE KIRIN'S CURSE.
IF THEY NEEDED TO CHECK TO SEE IF THEIR FRIEND WAS DEAD IN THE MIDDLE OF THE NIGHT,
THEIR FEAR AND ANXIETY WOULD CAUSE THEM TO HUDDLE CLOSER TOGETHER, NO?
FURTHER-MORE, NAGATSUKA-SAN BELIEVED THAT THEY WERE ALL DOOMED TO DIE BY THE KIRIN'S CURSE.

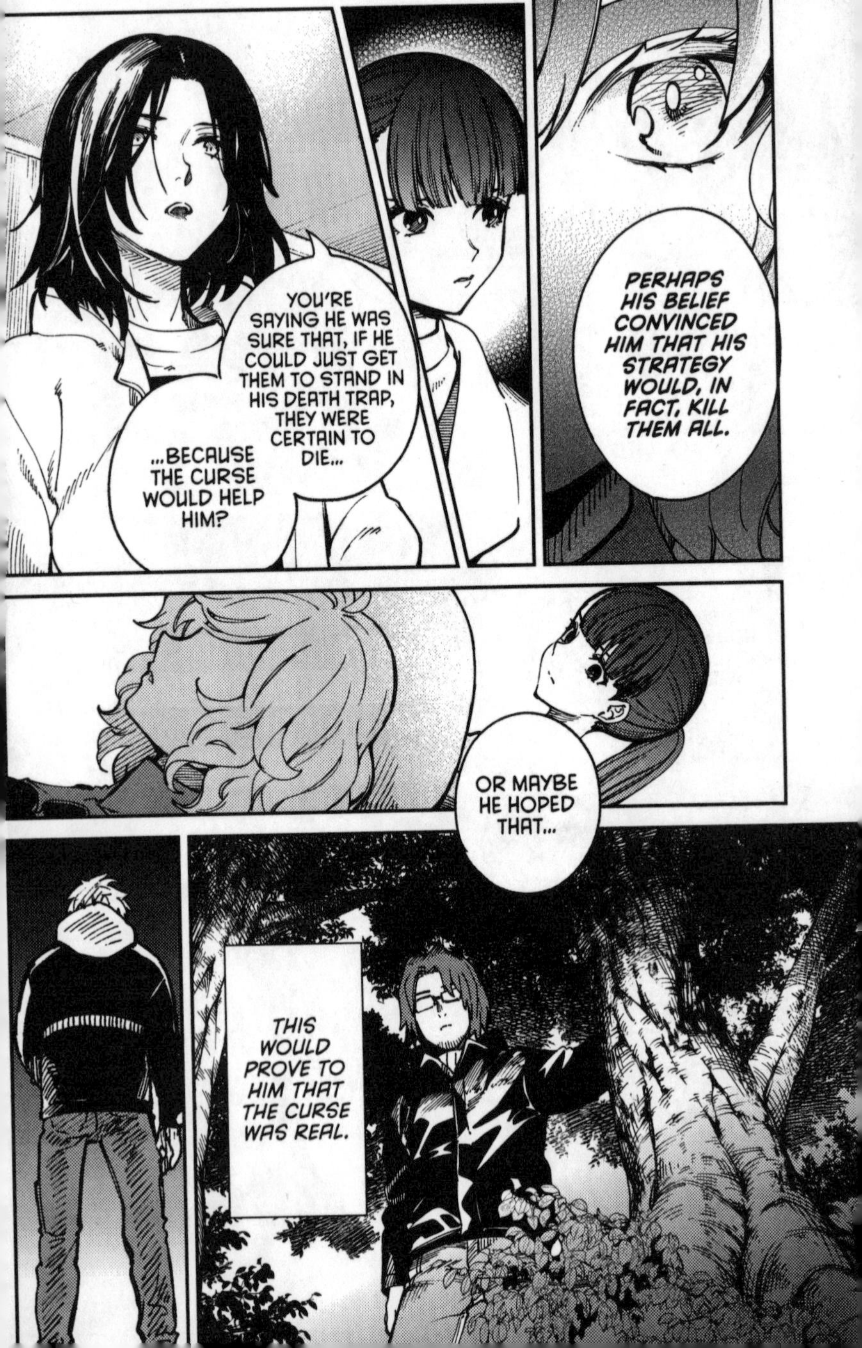
PERHAPS HIS BELIEF CONVINCED HIM THAT HIS STRATEGY WOULD, IN FACT, KILL THEM ALL.
YOU'RE SAYING HE WAS SURE THAT, IF HE COULD JUST GET THEM TO STAND IN HIS DEATH TRAP, THEY WERE CERTAIN TO DIE...
...BECAUSE THE CURSE WOULD HELP HIM?
OR MAYBE HE HOPED THAT...
THIS WOULD PROVE TO HIM THAT THE CURSE WAS REAL.

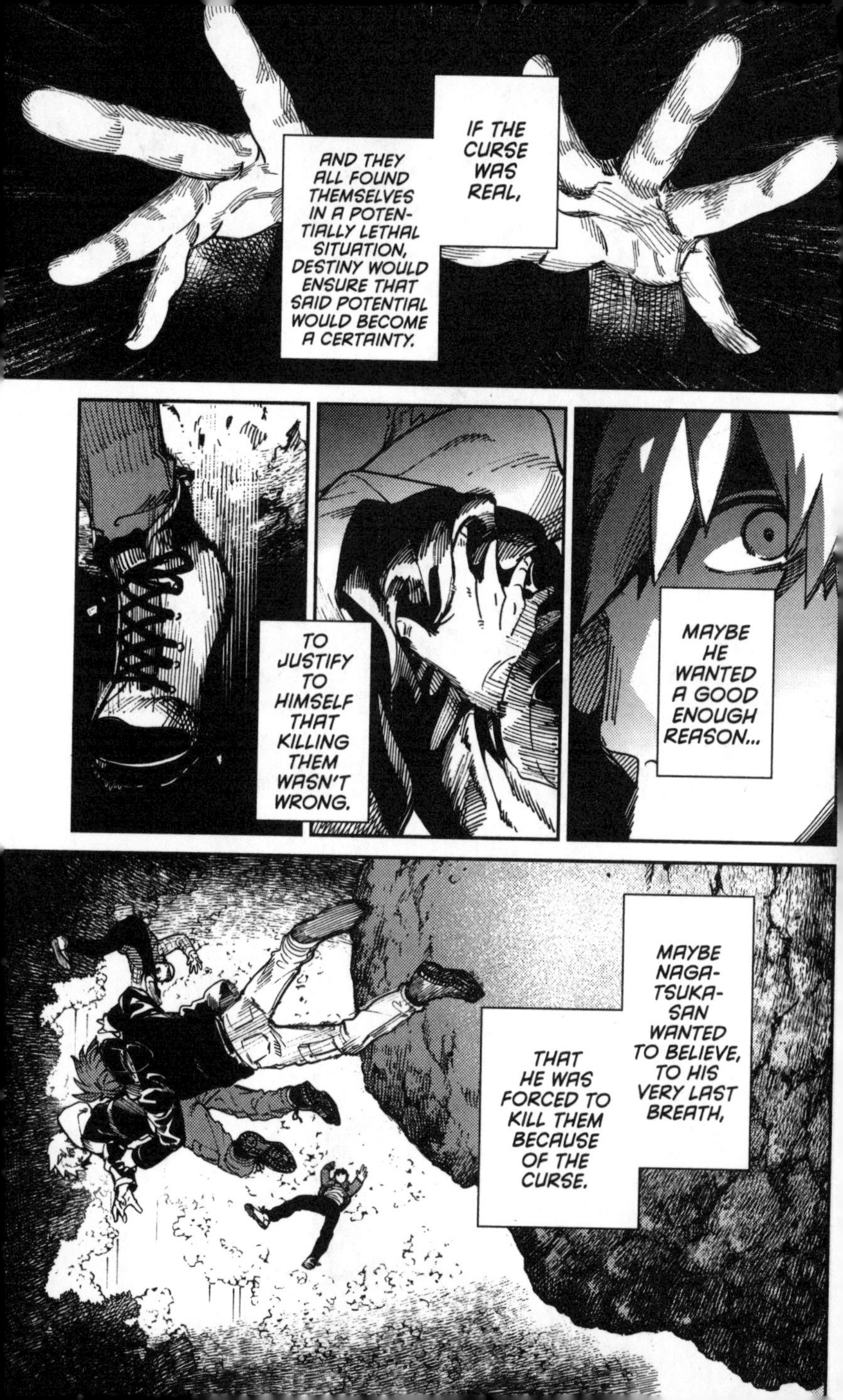
IF THE CURSE WAS REAL,
AND THEY ALL FOUND THEMSELVES IN A POTENTIALLY LETHAL SITUATION, DESTINY WOULD ENSURE THAT SAID POTENTIAL WOULD BECOME A CERTAINTY.
MAYBE HE WANTED A GOOD ENOUGH REASON...
TO JUSTIFY TO HIMSELF THAT KILLING THEM WASN'T WRONG.
MAYBE NAGATSUKA-SAN WANTED TO BELIEVE, TO HIS VERY LAST BREATH,
THAT HE WAS FORCED TO KILL THEM BECAUSE OF THE CURSE.

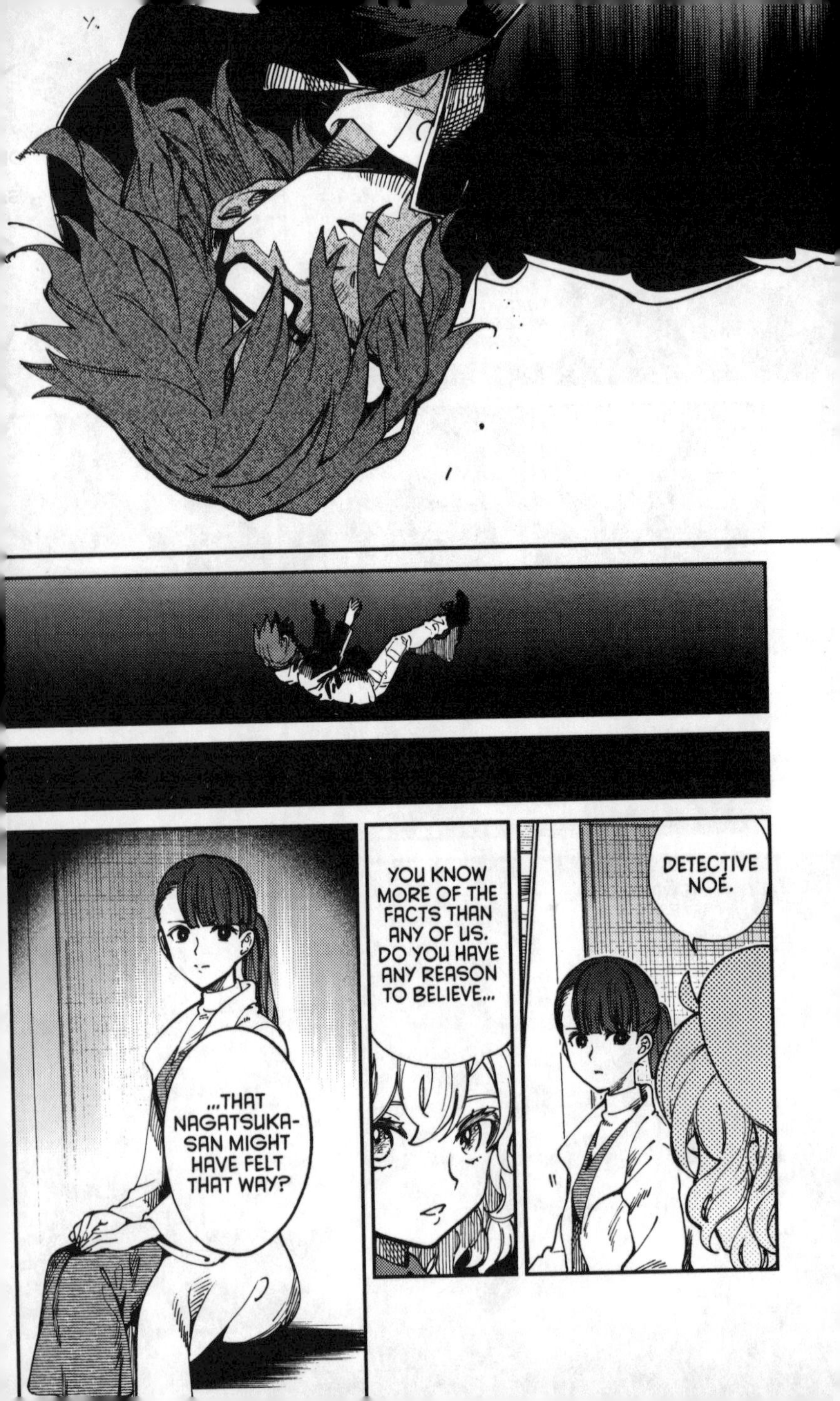
DETECTIVE NOÉ.
YOU KNOW MORE OF THE FACTS THAN ANY OF US. DO YOU HAVE ANY REASON TO BELIEVE...
...THAT NAGATSUKA-SAN MIGHT HAVE FELT THAT WAY?

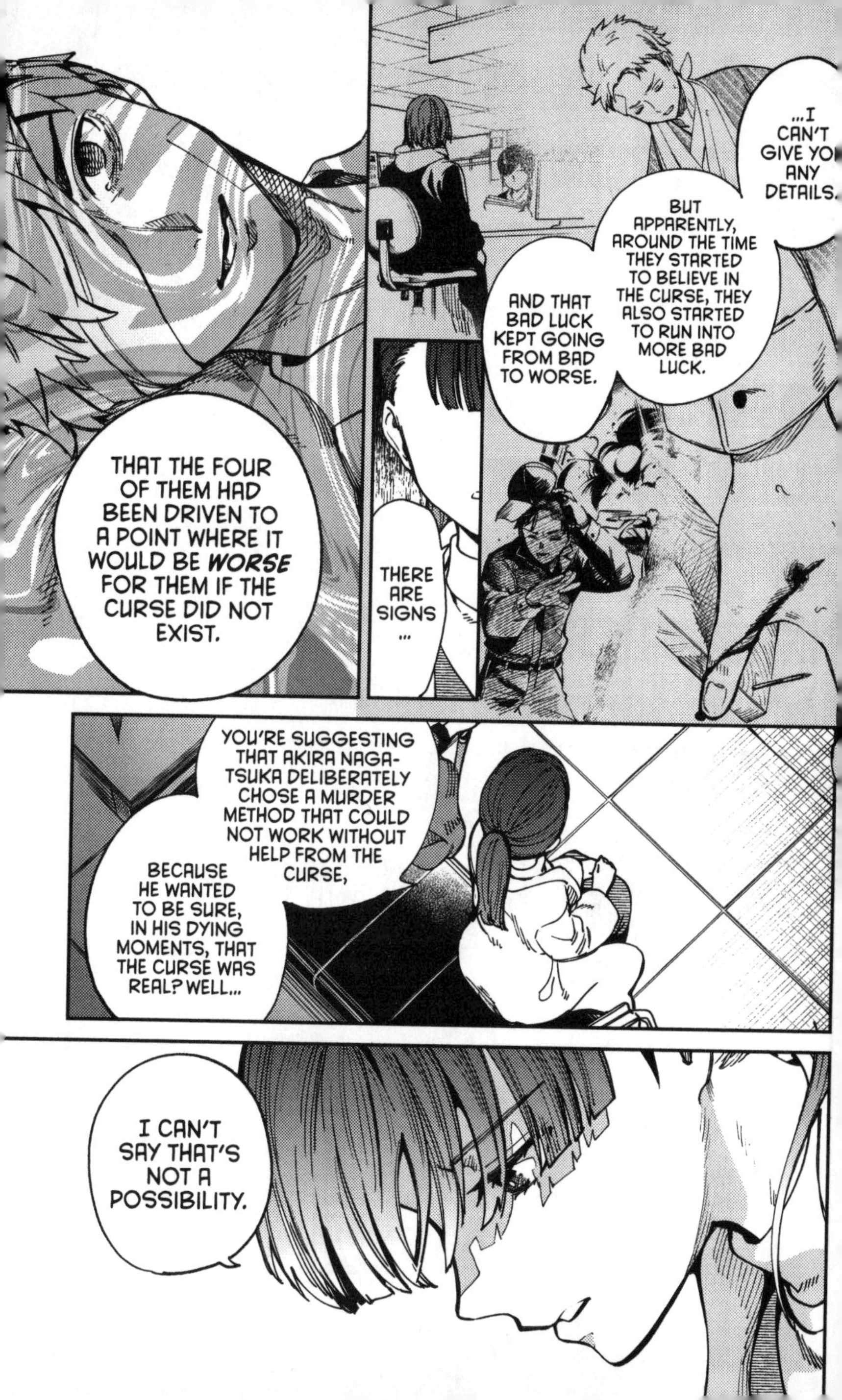

...I CAN'T GIVE YO ANY DETAILS.
BUT APPARENTLY, AROUND THE TIME THEY STARTED TO BELIEVE IN THE CURSE, THEY ALSO STARTED TO RUN INTO MORE BAD LUCK.
AND THAT BAD LUCK KEPT GOING FROM BAD TO WORSE.
THERE ARE SIGNS...
THAT THE FOUR OF THEM HAD BEEN DRIVEN TO A POINT WHERE IT WOULD BE *WORSE* FOR THEM IF THE CURSE DID NOT EXIST.
YOU'RE SUGGESTING THAT AKIRA NAGA-TSUKA DELIBERATELY CHOSE A MURDER METHOD THAT COULD NOT WORK WITHOUT HELP FROM THE CURSE,
BECAUSE HE WANTED TO BE SURE, IN HIS DYING MOMENTS, THAT THE CURSE WAS REAL? WELL...
I CAN'T SAY THAT'S NOT A POSSIBILITY.

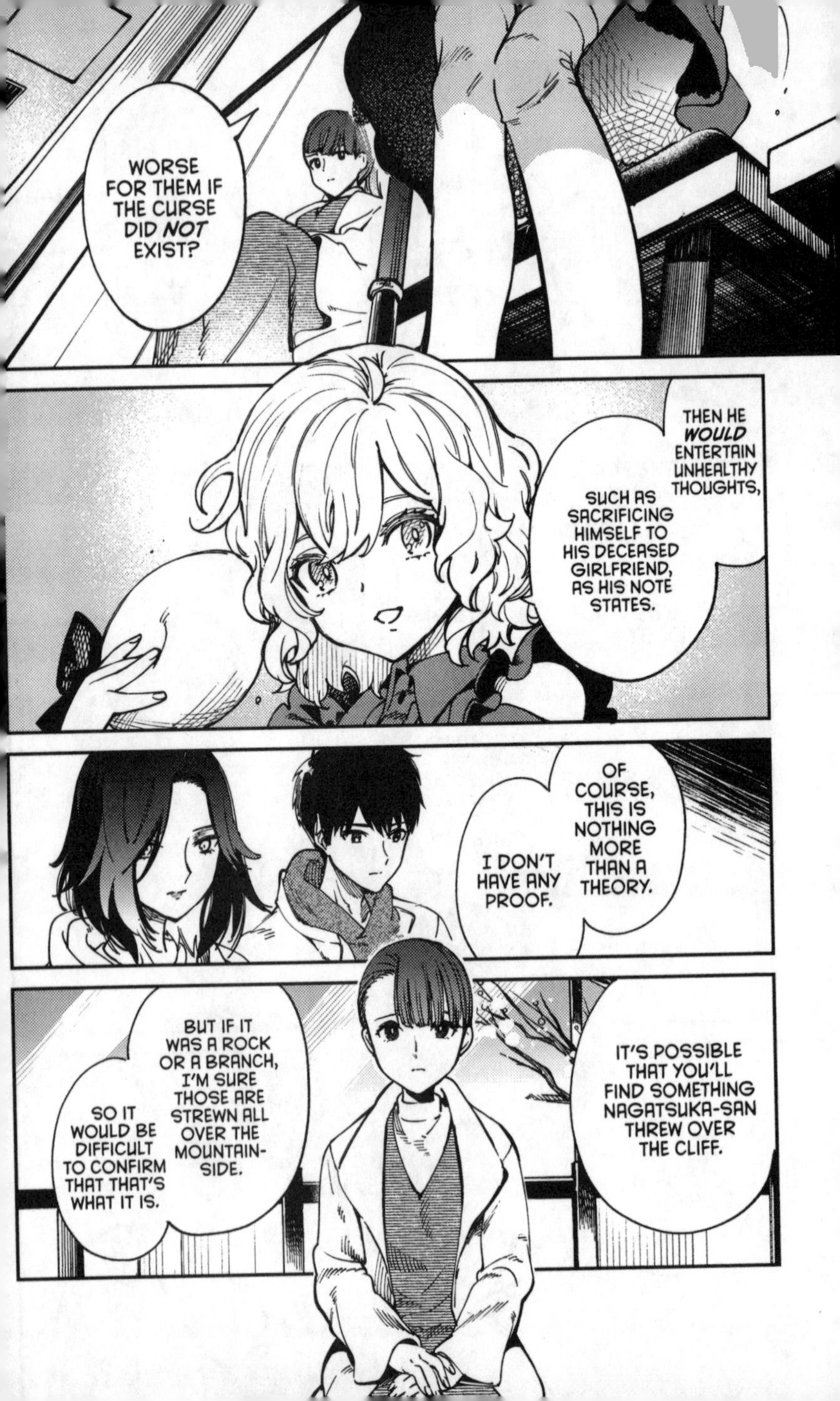
WORSE FOR THEM IF THE CURSE DID *NOT* EXIST?
THEN HE ***WOULD*** ENTERTAIN UNHEALTHY THOUGHTS,
SUCH AS SACRIFICING HIMSELF TO HIS DECEASED GIRLFRIEND, AS HIS NOTE STATES.
OF COURSE, THIS IS NOTHING MORE THAN A THEORY.
I DON'T HAVE ANY PROOF.
IT'S POSSIBLE THAT YOU'LL FIND SOMETHING NAGATSUKA-SAN THREW OVER THE CLIFF.
BUT IF IT WAS A ROCK OR A BRANCH, I'M SURE THOSE ARE STREWN ALL OVER THE MOUNTAIN-SIDE.
SO IT WOULD BE DIFFICULT TO CONFIRM THAT THAT'S WHAT IT IS.

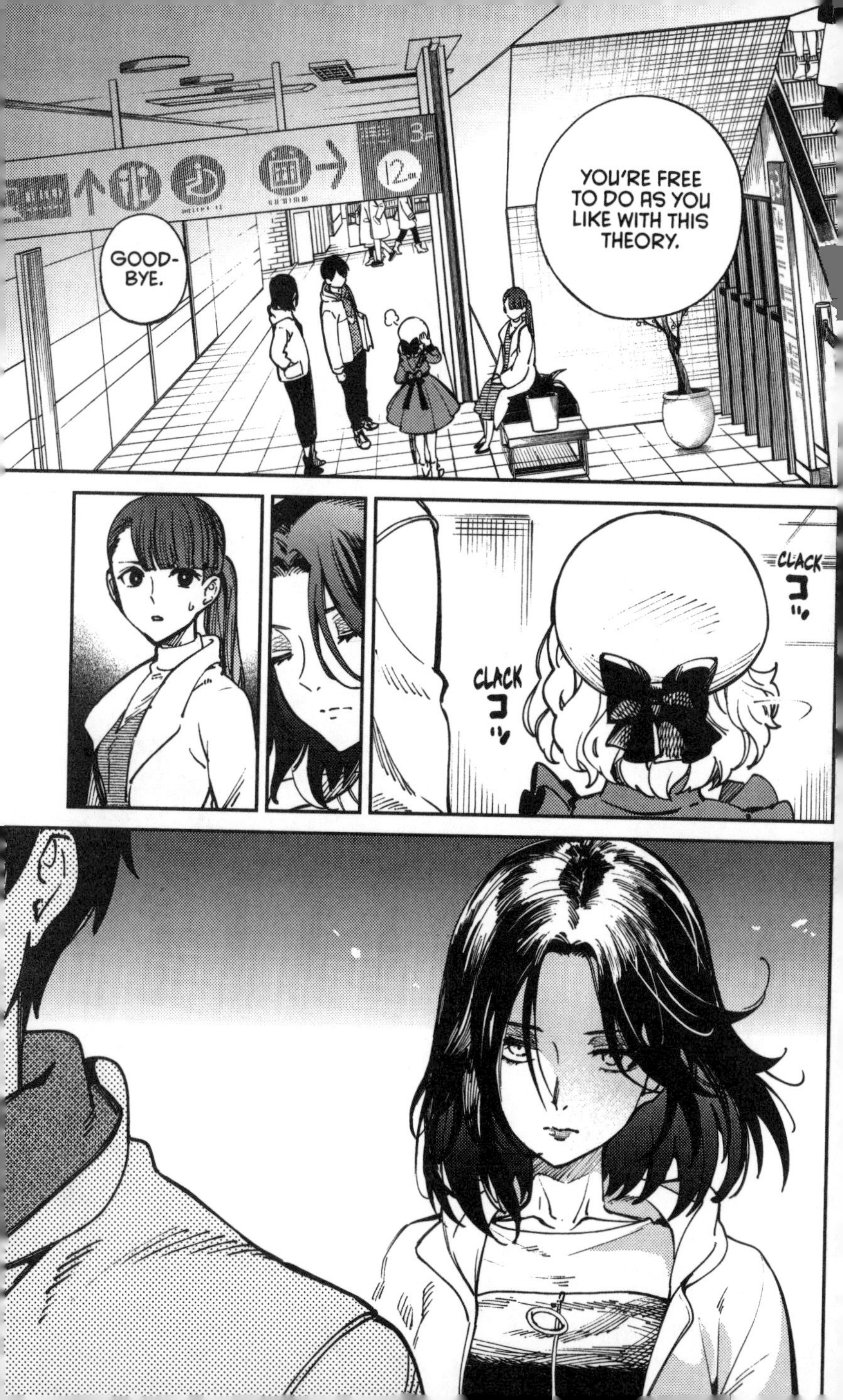
YOU'RE FREE TO DO AS YOU LIKE WITH THIS THEORY.
GOOD-BYE.
CLACK
コッ
CLACK
コッ

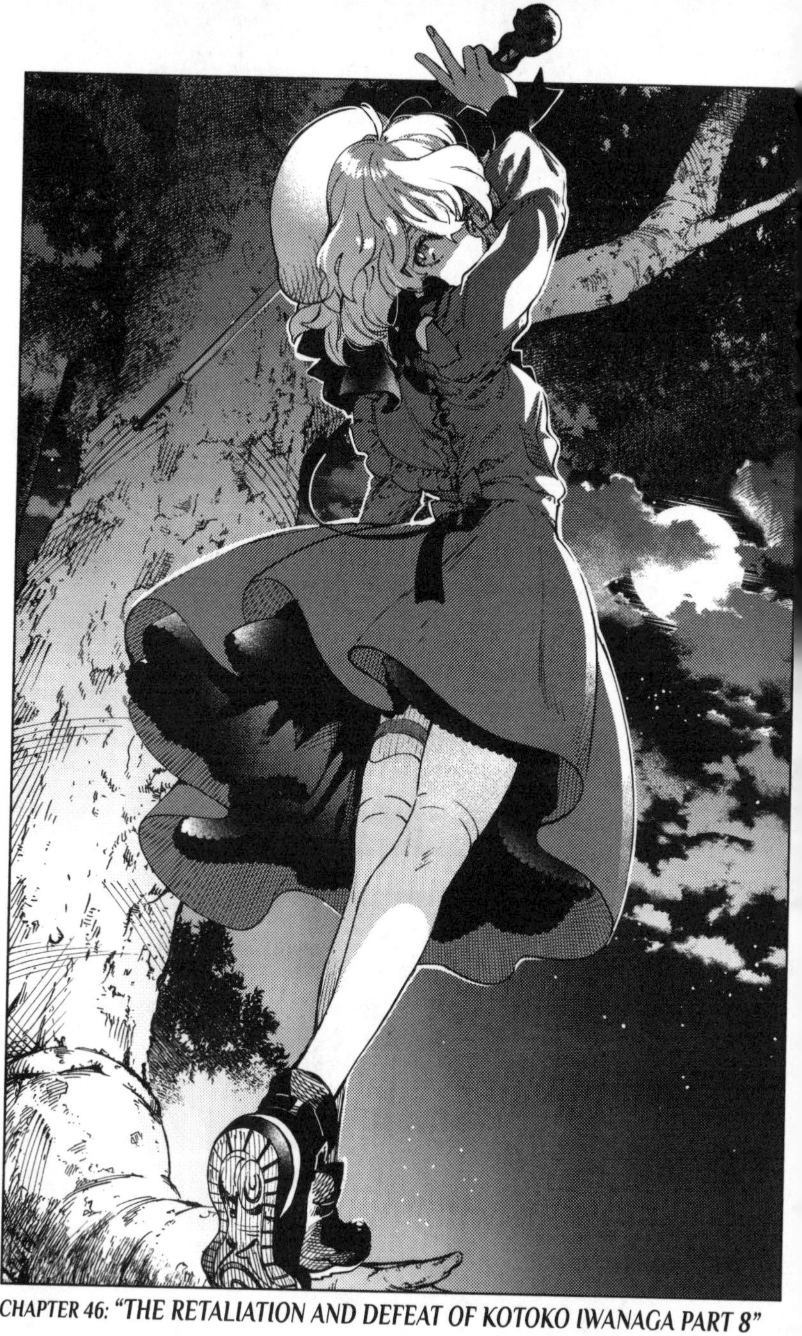

CHAPTER 46: "THE RETALIATION AND DEFEAT OF KOTOKO IWANAGA PART 8"

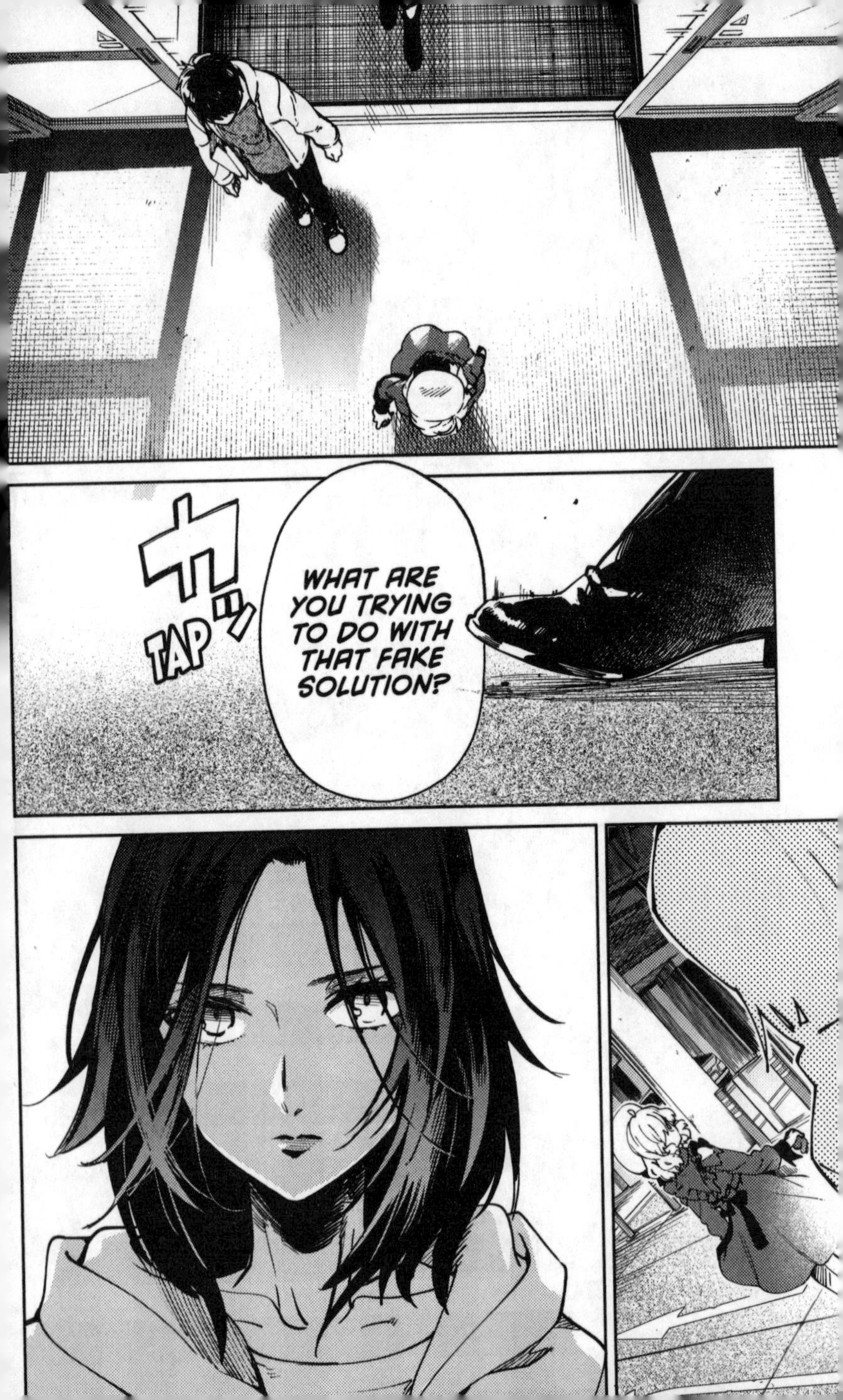
WHAT ARE YOU TRYING TO DO WITH THAT FAKE SOLUTION?
TAP

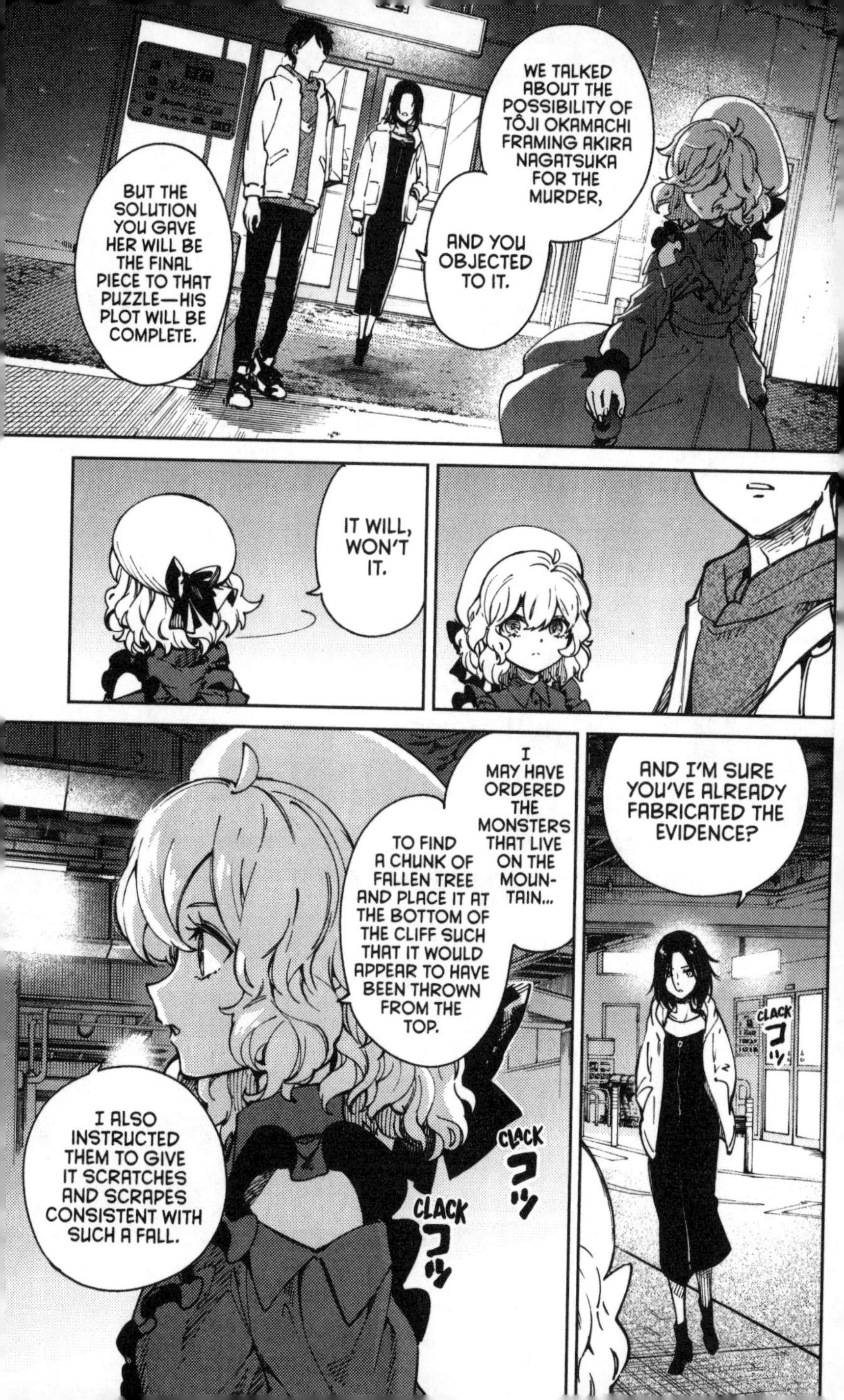
WE TALKED ABOUT THE POSSIBILITY OF TÔJI OKAMACHI FRAMING AKIRA NAGATSUKA FOR THE MURDER,
AND YOU OBJECTED TO IT.
BUT THE SOLUTION YOU GAVE HER WILL BE THE FINAL PIECE TO THAT PUZZLE—HIS PLOT WILL BE COMPLETE.
IT WILL, WON'T IT.
AND I'M SURE YOU'VE ALREADY FABRICATED THE EVIDENCE?
CLACK
コッ
I MAY HAVE ORDERED THE MONSTERS THAT LIVE ON THE MOUN-TAIN...
TO FIND A CHUNK OF FALLEN TREE AND PLACE IT AT THE BOTTOM OF THE CLIFF SUCH THAT IT WOULD APPEAR TO HAVE BEEN THROWN FROM THE TOP.
I ALSO INSTRUCTED THEM TO GIVE IT SCRATCHES AND SCRAPES CONSISTENT WITH SUCH A FALL.
CLACK
コッ
CLACK
コッ

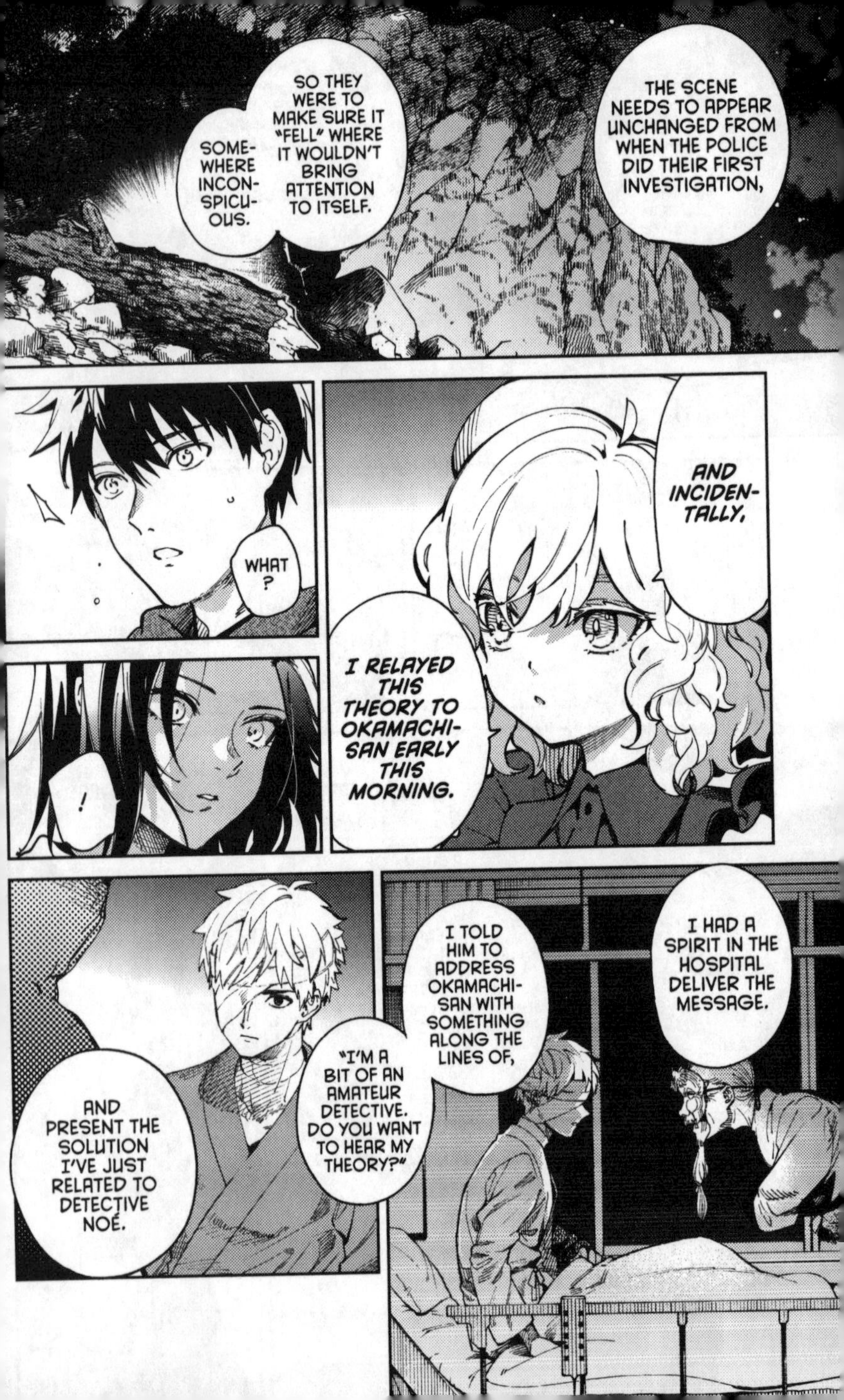
THE SCENE NEEDS TO APPEAR UNCHANGED FROM WHEN THE POLICE DID THEIR FIRST INVESTIGATION,
SO THEY WERE TO MAKE SURE IT "FELL" WHERE IT WOULDN'T BRING ATTENTION TO ITSELF.
SOME-WHERE INCON-SPICU-OUS.
AND INCIDEN-TALLY,
I RELAYED THIS THEORY TO OKAMACHI-SAN EARLY THIS MORNING.
WHAT?
!
I HAD A SPIRIT IN THE HOSPITAL DELIVER THE MESSAGE.
I TOLD HIM TO ADDRESS OKAMACHI-SAN WITH SOMETHING ALONG THE LINES OF,
"I'M A BIT OF AN AMATEUR DETECTIVE. DO YOU WANT TO HEAR MY THEORY?"
AND PRESENT THE SOLUTION I'VE JUST RELATED TO DETECTIVE NOÉ.

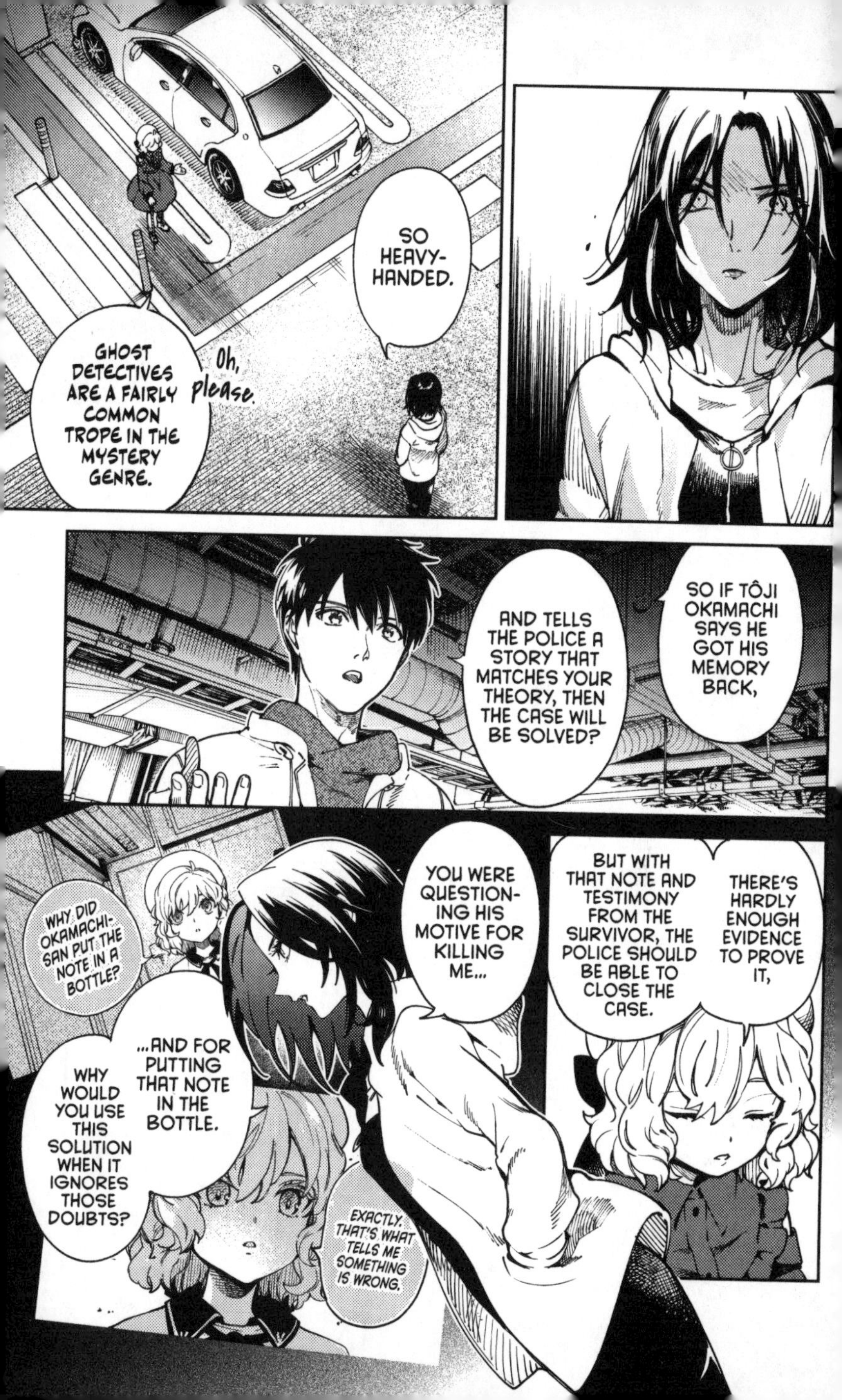

SO HEAVY-HANDED.
Oh, please.
GHOST DETECTIVES ARE A FAIRLY COMMON TROPE IN THE MYSTERY GENRE.
SO IF TÔJI OKAMACHI SAYS HE GOT HIS MEMORY BACK,
AND TELLS THE POLICE A STORY THAT MATCHES YOUR THEORY, THEN THE CASE WILL BE SOLVED?
THERE'S HARDLY ENOUGH EVIDENCE TO PROVE IT,
BUT WITH THAT NOTE AND TESTIMONY FROM THE SURVIVOR, THE POLICE SHOULD BE ABLE TO CLOSE THE CASE.
YOU WERE QUESTIONING HIS MOTIVE FOR KILLING ME...
WHY DID OKAMACHI-SAN PUT THE NOTE IN A BOTTLE?
...AND FOR PUTTING THAT NOTE IN THE BOTTLE.
WHY WOULD YOU USE THIS SOLUTION WHEN IT IGNORES THOSE DOUBTS?
EXACTLY. THAT'S WHAT TELLS ME SOMETHING IS WRONG.

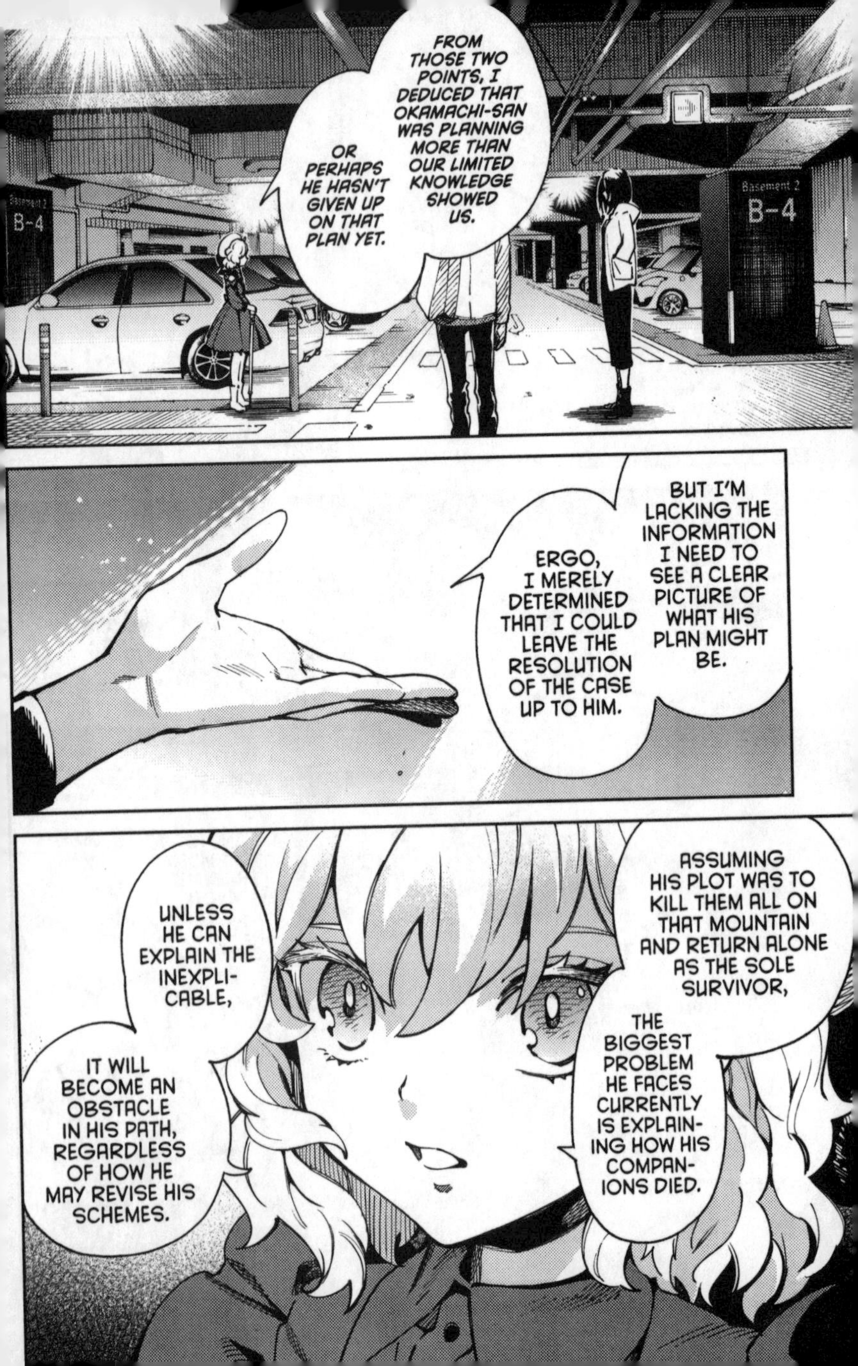

FROM THOSE TWO POINTS, I DEDUCED THAT OKAMACHI-SAN WAS PLANNING MORE THAN OUR LIMITED KNOWLEDGE SHOWED US.
OR PERHAPS HE HASN'T GIVEN UP ON THAT PLAN YET.
BUT I'M LACKING THE INFORMATION I NEED TO SEE A CLEAR PICTURE OF WHAT HIS PLAN MIGHT BE.
ERGO, I MERELY DETERMINED THAT I COULD LEAVE THE RESOLUTION OF THE CASE UP TO HIM.
ASSUMING HIS PLOT WAS TO KILL THEM ALL ON THAT MOUNTAIN AND RETURN ALONE AS THE SOLE SURVIVOR,
THE BIGGEST PROBLEM HE FACES CURRENTLY IS EXPLAINING HOW HIS COMPANIONS DIED.
UNLESS HE CAN EXPLAIN THE INEXPLICABLE,
IT WILL BECOME AN OBSTACLE IN HIS PATH, REGARDLESS OF HOW HE MAY REVISE HIS SCHEMES.

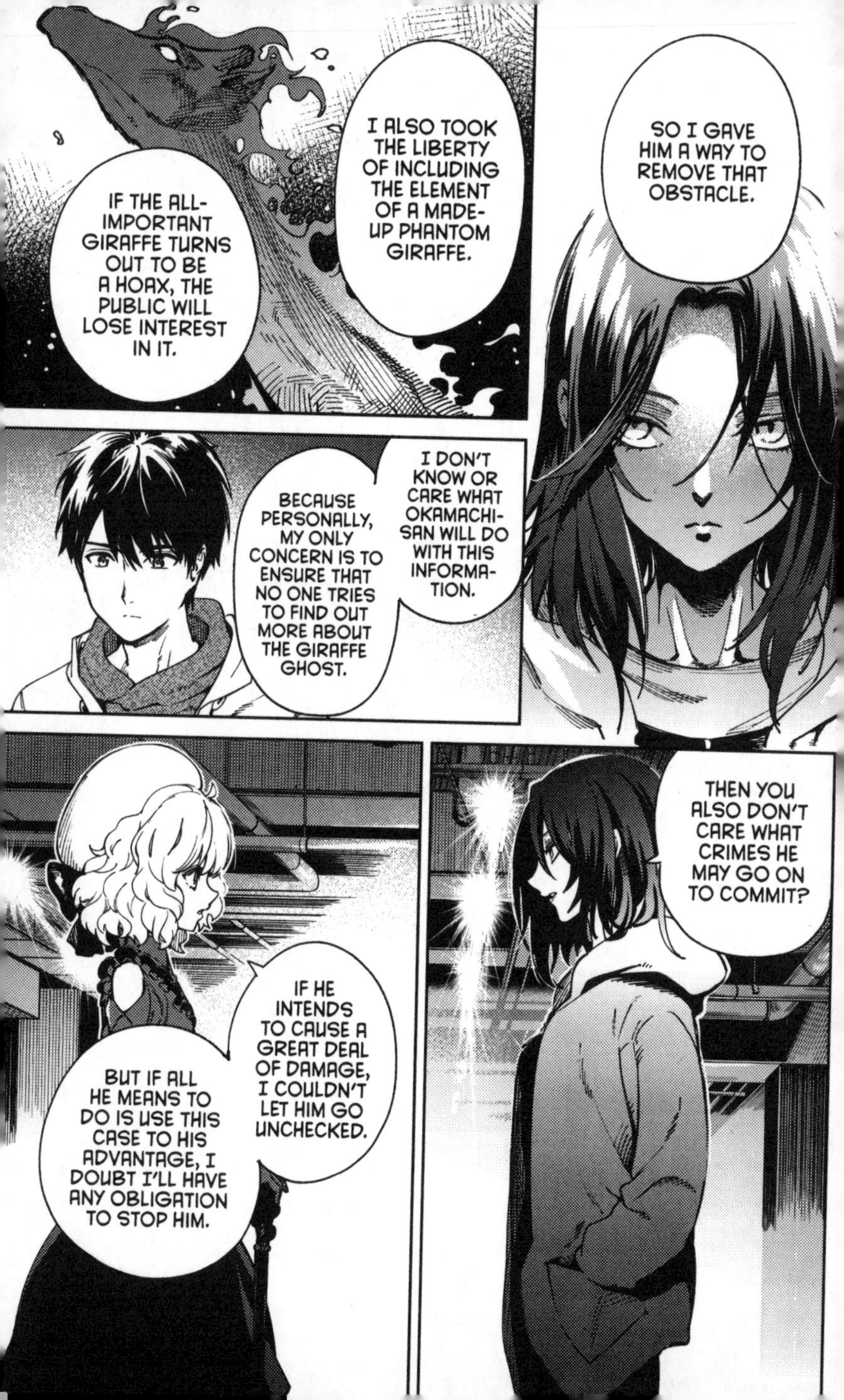
SO I GAVE HIM A WAY TO REMOVE THAT OBSTACLE.
I ALSO TOOK THE LIBERTY OF INCLUDING THE ELEMENT OF A MADE-UP PHANTOM GIRAFFE.
IF THE ALL-IMPORTANT GIRAFFE TURNS OUT TO BE A HOAX, THE PUBLIC WILL LOSE INTEREST IN IT.
I DON'T KNOW OR CARE WHAT OKAMACHI-SAN WILL DO WITH THIS INFORMATION.
BECAUSE PERSONALLY, MY ONLY CONCERN IS TO ENSURE THAT NO ONE TRIES TO FIND OUT MORE ABOUT THE GIRAFFE GHOST.
THEN YOU ALSO DON'T CARE WHAT CRIMES HE MAY GO ON TO COMMIT?
IF HE INTENDS TO CAUSE A GREAT DEAL OF DAMAGE, I COULDN'T LET HIM GO UNCHECKED.
BUT IF ALL HE MEANS TO DO IS USE THIS CASE TO HIS ADVANTAGE, I DOUBT I'LL HAVE ANY OBLIGATION TO STOP HIM.

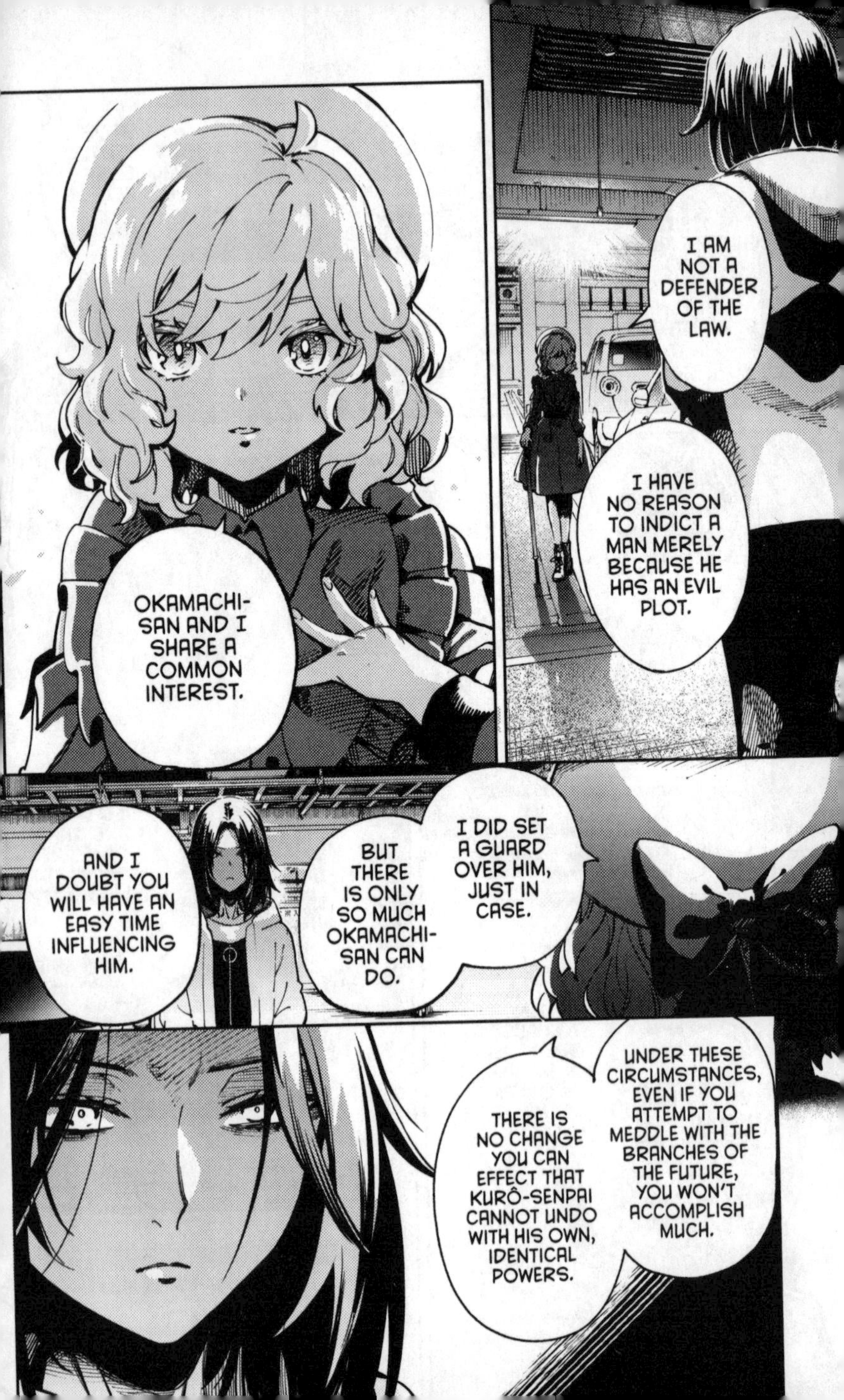
I AM NOT A DEFENDER OF THE LAW.
I HAVE NO REASON TO INDICT A MAN MERELY BECAUSE HE HAS AN EVIL PLOT.
OKAMACHI-SAN AND I SHARE A COMMON INTEREST.
I DID SET A GUARD OVER HIM, JUST IN CASE.
BUT THERE IS ONLY SO MUCH OKAMACHI-SAN CAN DO.
AND I DOUBT YOU WILL HAVE AN EASY TIME INFLUENCING HIM.
UNDER THESE CIRCUMSTANCES, EVEN IF YOU ATTEMPT TO MEDDLE WITH THE BRANCHES OF THE FUTURE, YOU WON'T ACCOMPLISH MUCH.
THERE IS NO CHANGE YOU CAN EFFECT THAT KURÔ-SENPAI CANNOT UNDO WITH HIS OWN, IDENTICAL POWERS.

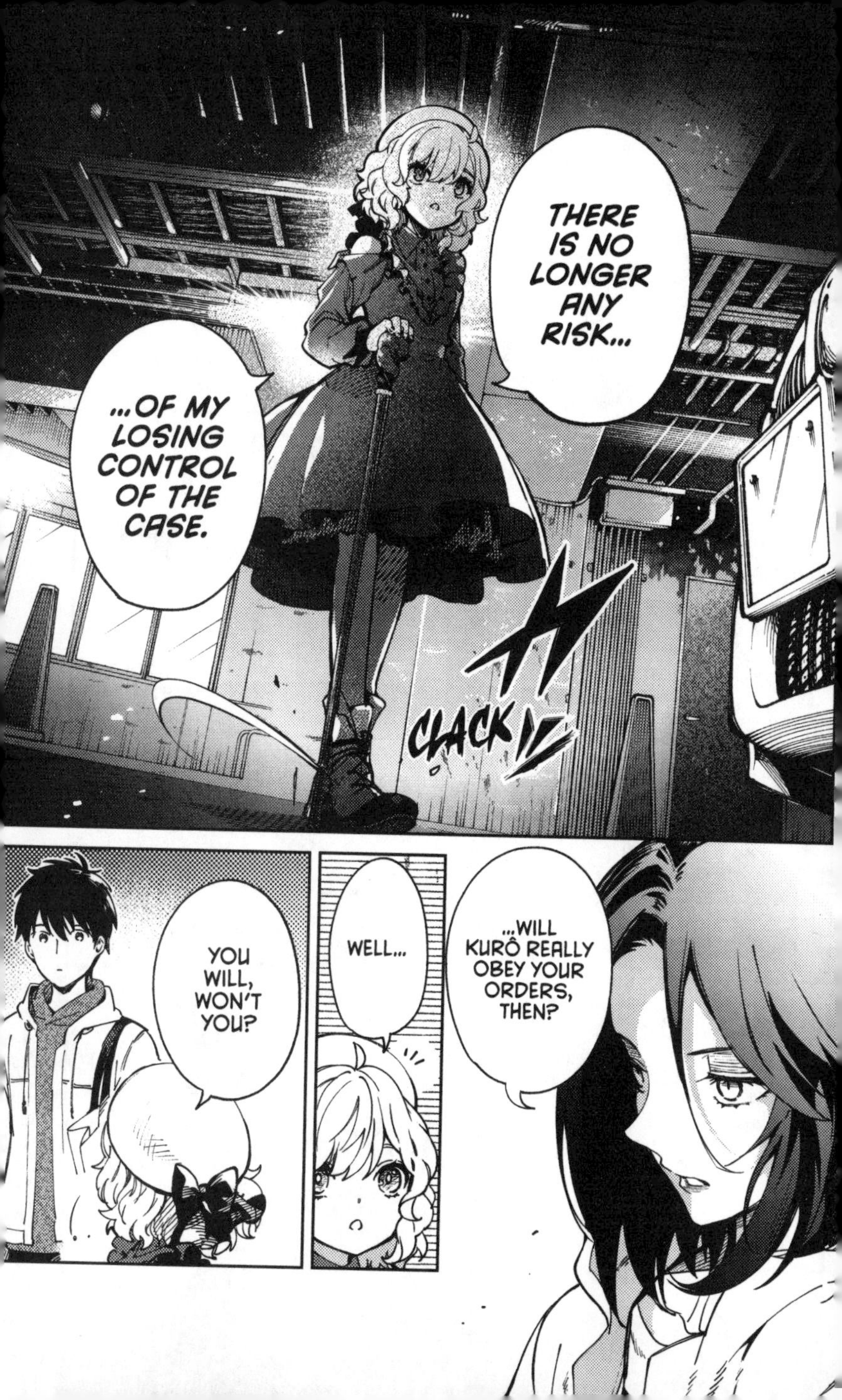
THERE IS NO LONGER ANY RISK...
...OF MY LOSING CONTROL OF THE CASE.
CLACK
...WILL KURÔ REALLY OBEY YOUR ORDERS, THEN?
WELL...
YOU WILL, WON'T YOU?

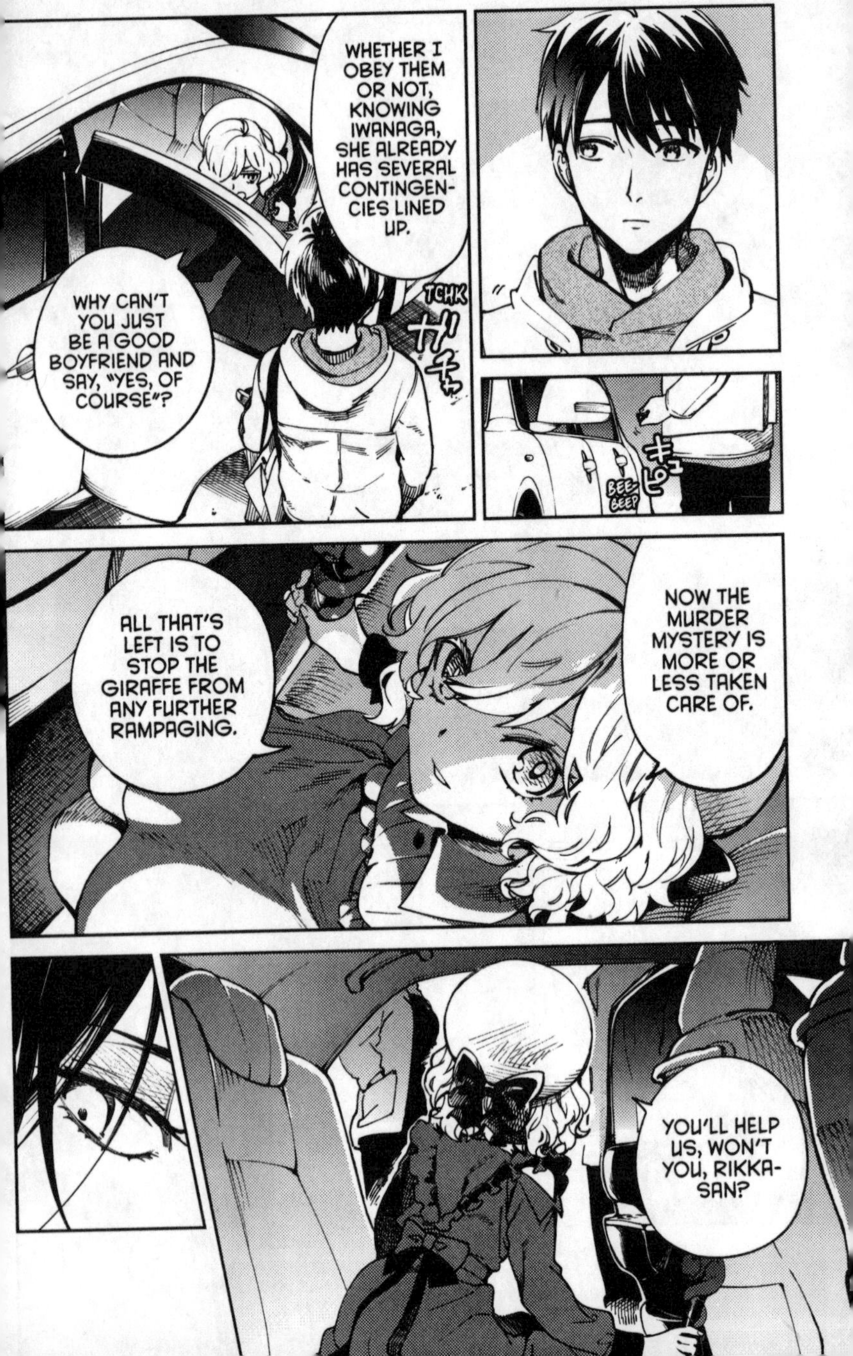
キュピ
BEE-BEEP
WHETHER I OBEY THEM OR NOT, KNOWING IWANAGA, SHE ALREADY HAS SEVERAL CONTINGEN-CIES LINED UP.
TCHK
ガチャ
WHY CAN'T YOU JUST BE A GOOD BOYFRIEND AND SAY, "YES, OF COURSE"?
NOW THE MURDER MYSTERY IS MORE OR LESS TAKEN CARE OF.
ALL THAT'S LEFT IS TO STOP THE GIRAFFE FROM ANY FURTHER RAMPAGING.
YOU'LL HELP US, WON'T YOU, RIKKA-SAN?

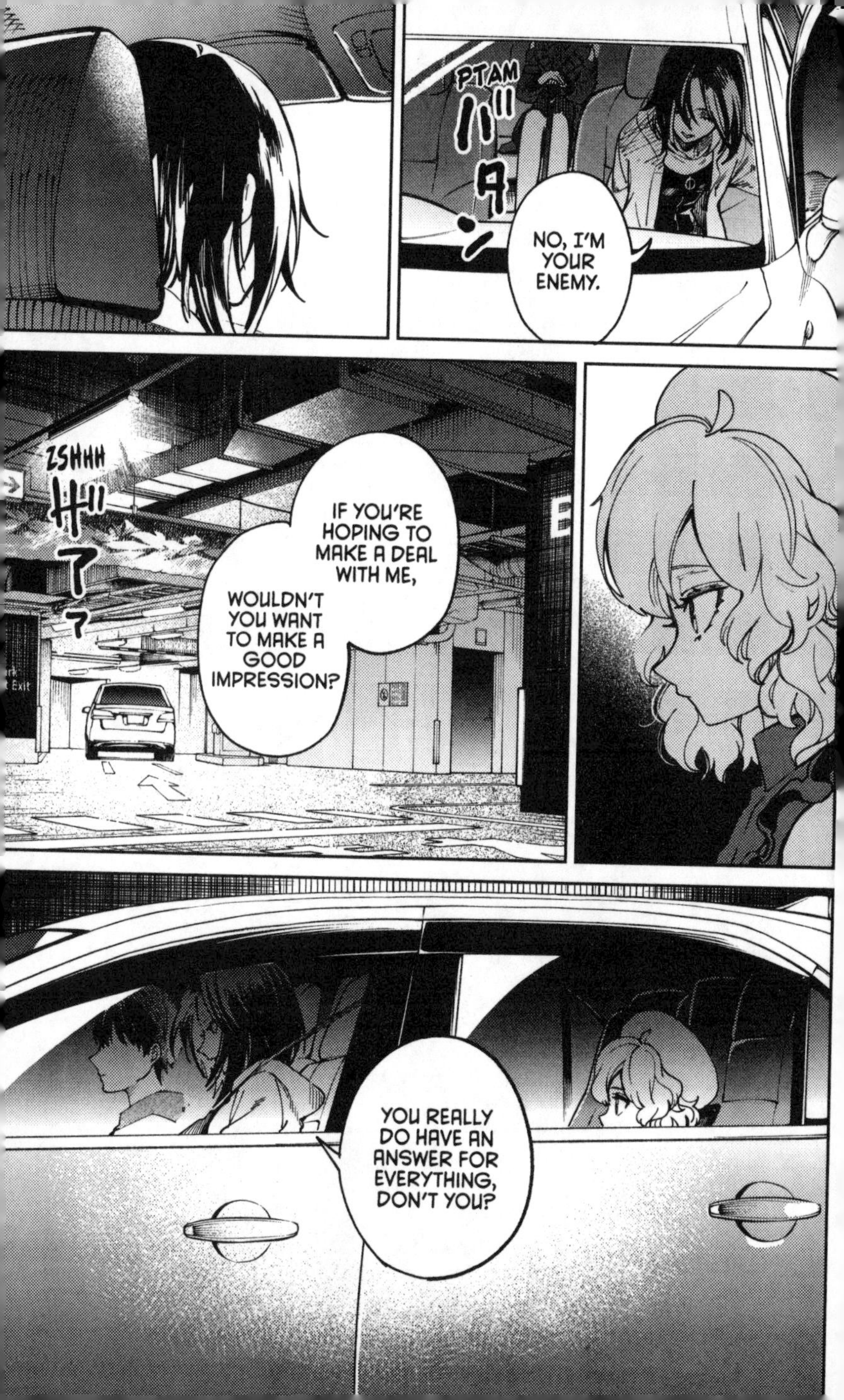
PTAM
バタン
NO, I'M YOUR ENEMY.
ZSHHH
ザァァ
IF YOU'RE HOPING TO MAKE A DEAL WITH ME,
WOULDN'T YOU WANT TO MAKE A GOOD IMPRESSION?
YOU REALLY DO HAVE AN ANSWER FOR EVERYTHING, DON'T YOU?

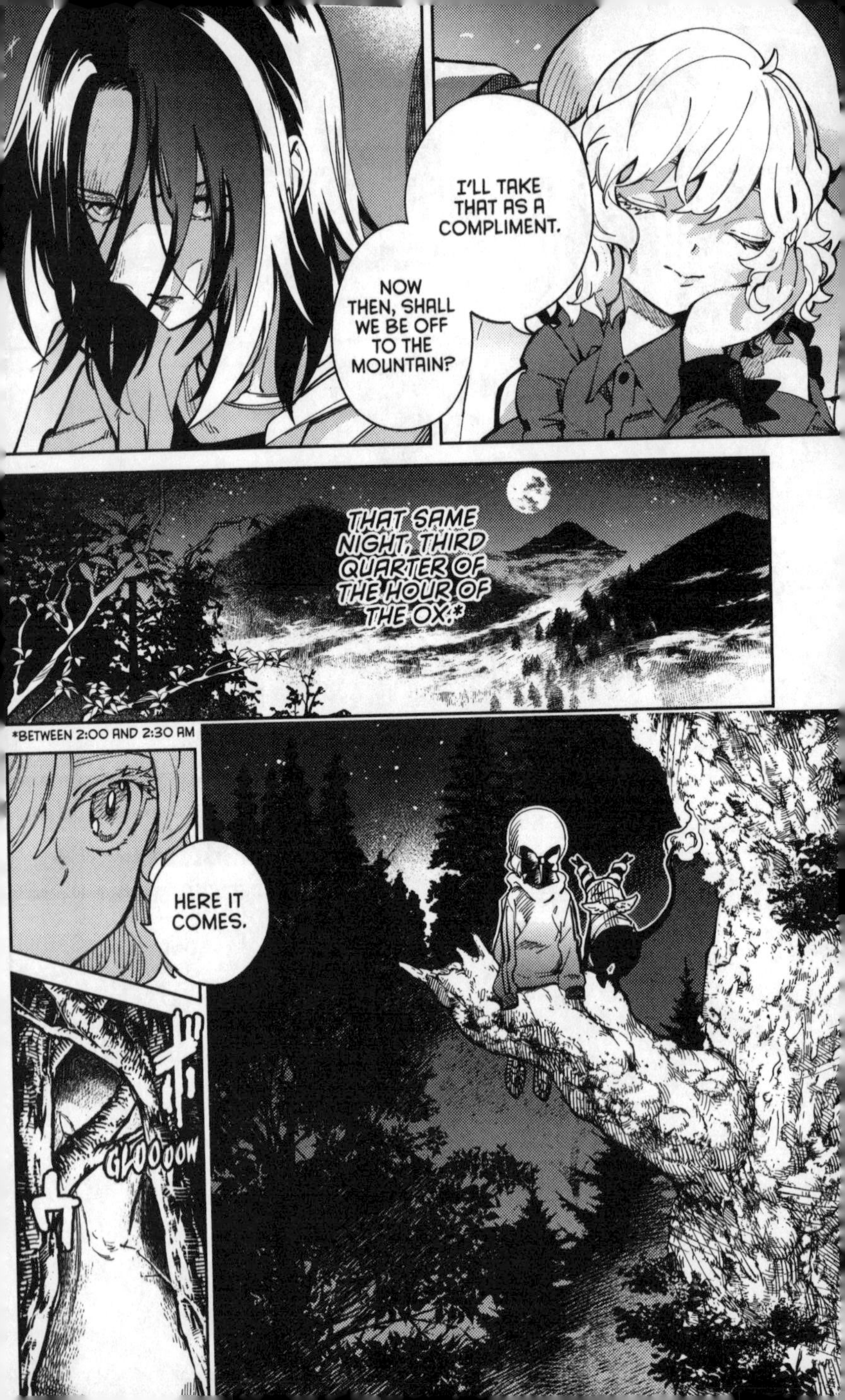
I'LL TAKE THAT AS A COMPLIMENT.
NOW THEN, SHALL WE BE OFF TO THE MOUNTAIN?
THAT SAME NIGHT, THIRD QUARTER OF THE HOUR OF THE OX.*
*BETWEEN 2:00 AND 2:30 AM
HERE IT COMES.
GLOOOOW

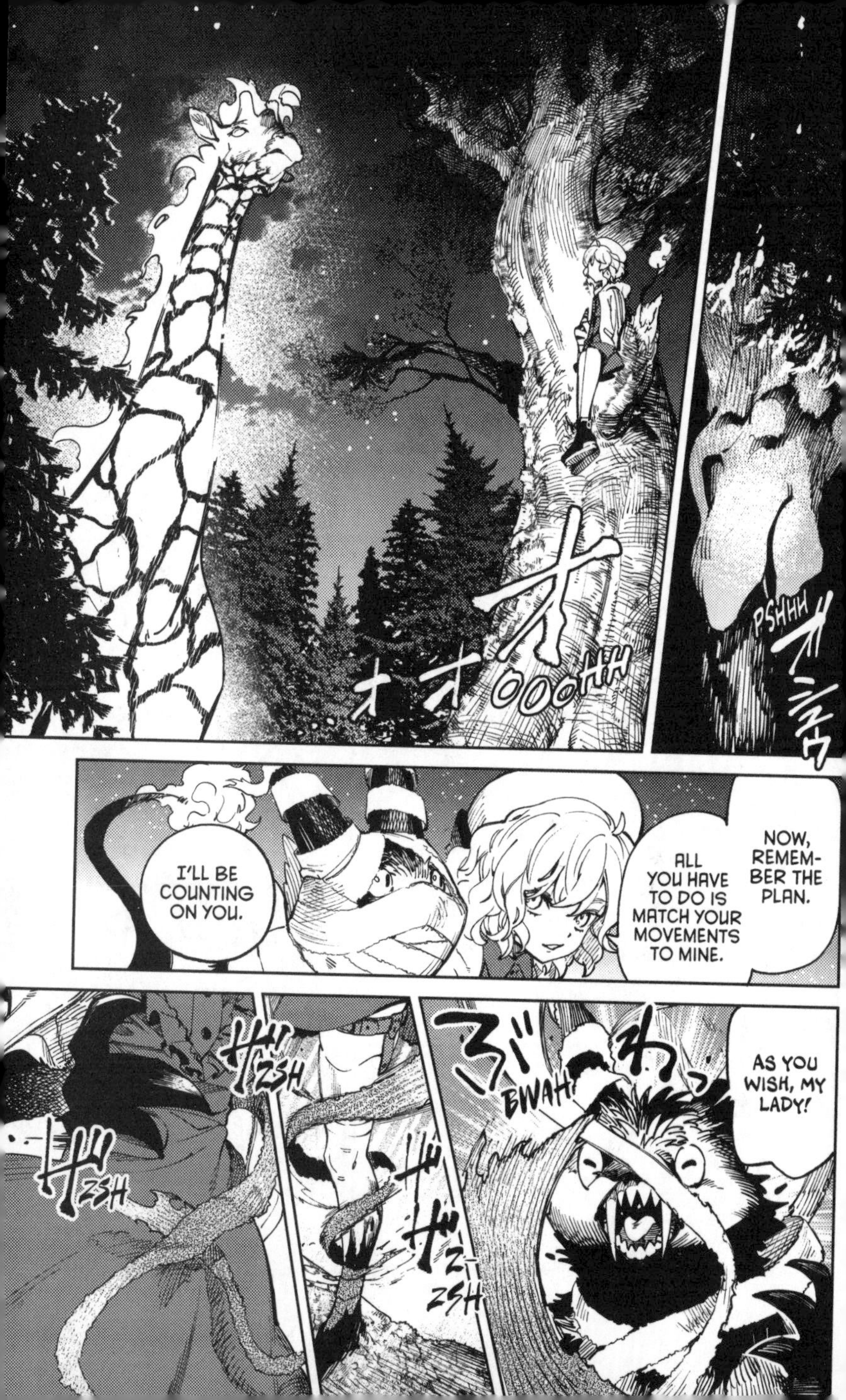
PSHHH
OOOHHH
NOW, REMEMBER THE PLAN.
ALL YOU HAVE TO DO IS MATCH YOUR MOVEMENTS TO MINE.
I'LL BE COUNTING ON YOU.
AS YOU WISH, MY LADY!
BWAH
ZSH
Z-ZSH
ZSH

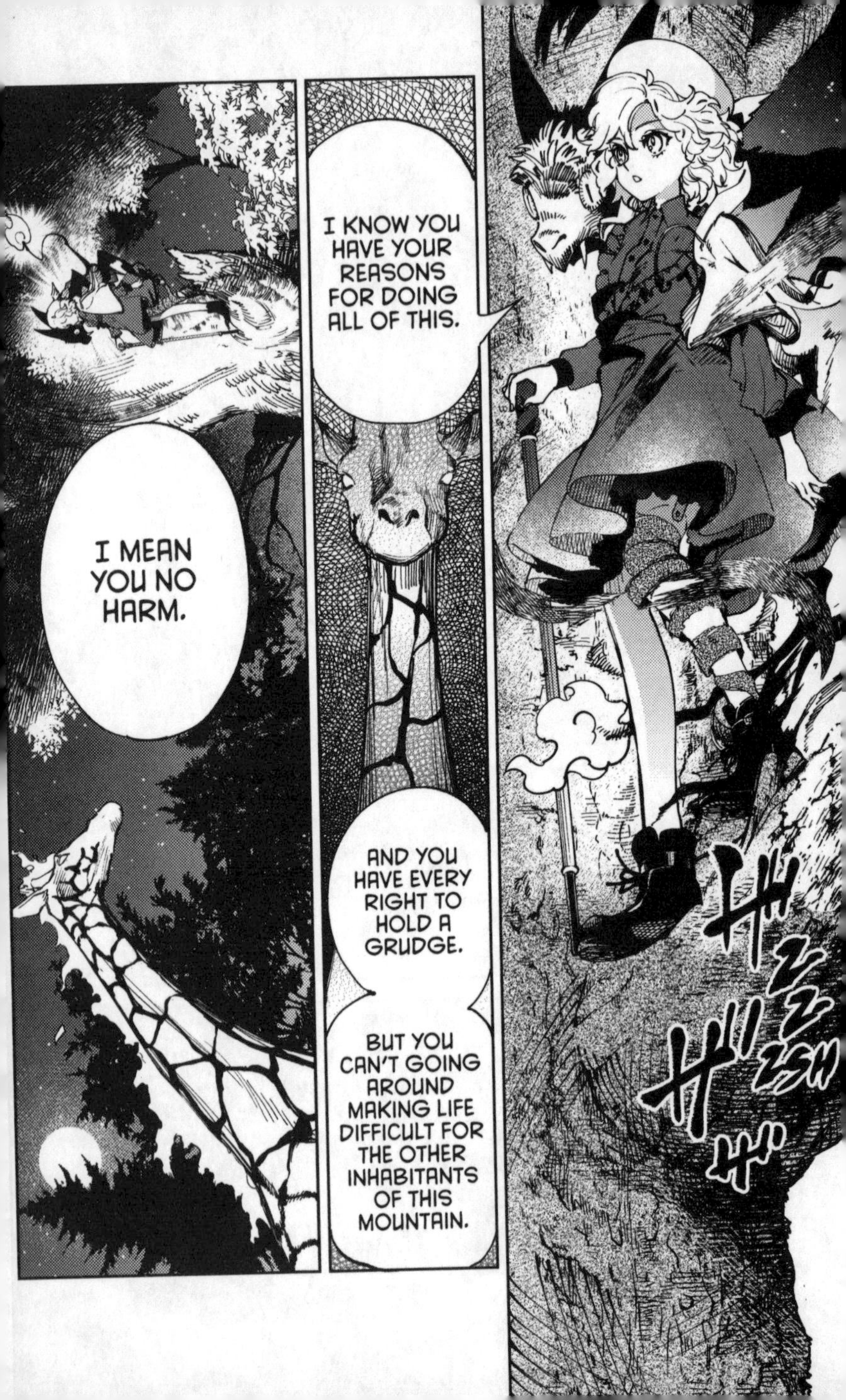
ZZZSH
I KNOW YOU HAVE YOUR REASONS FOR DOING ALL OF THIS.
AND YOU HAVE EVERY RIGHT TO HOLD A GRUDGE.
BUT YOU CAN'T GOING AROUND MAKING LIFE DIFFICULT FOR THE OTHER INHABITANTS OF THIS MOUNTAIN.
I MEAN YOU NO HARM.

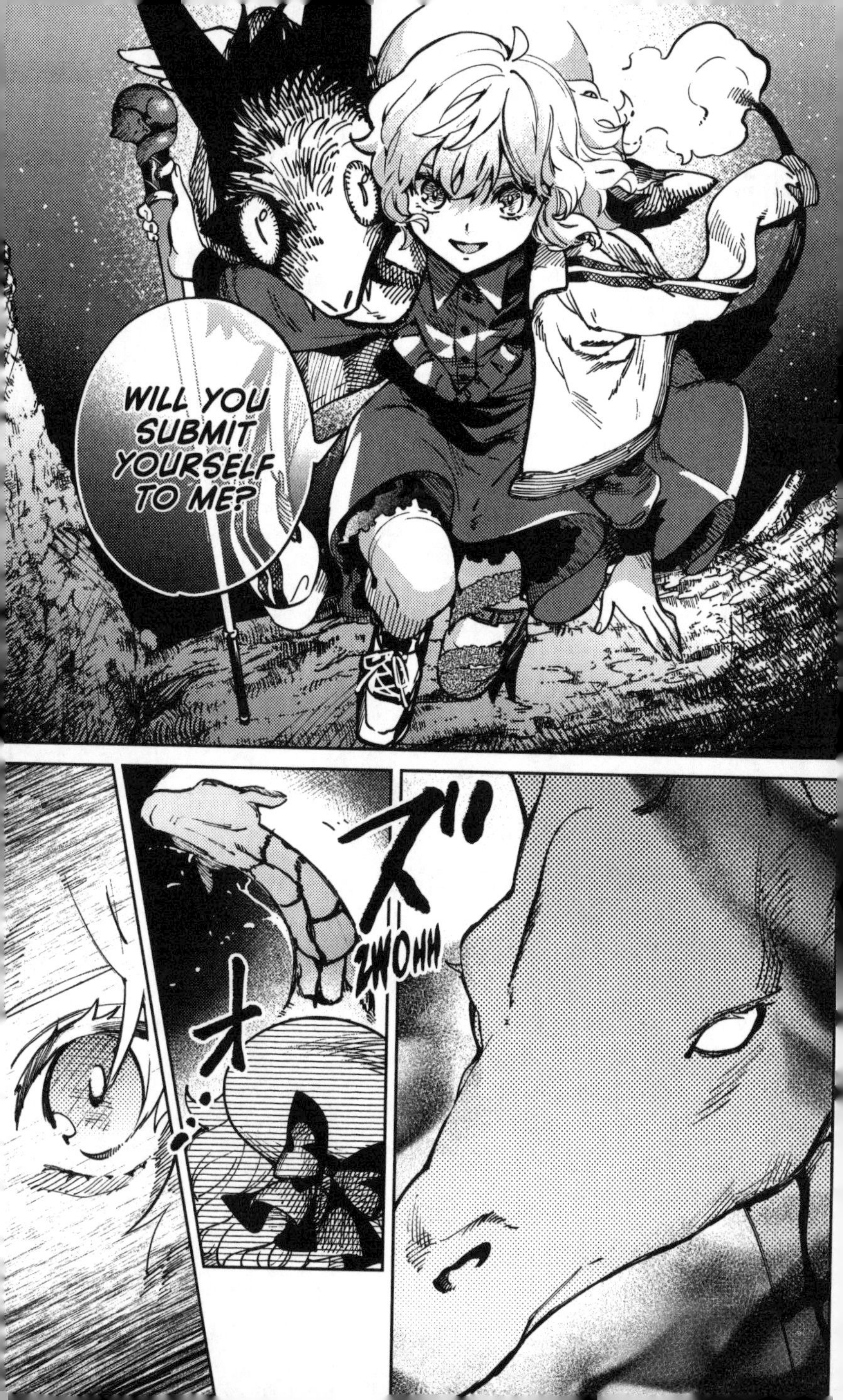
WILL YOU SUBMIT YOURSELF TO ME?
ズ
ZWOHH
オ

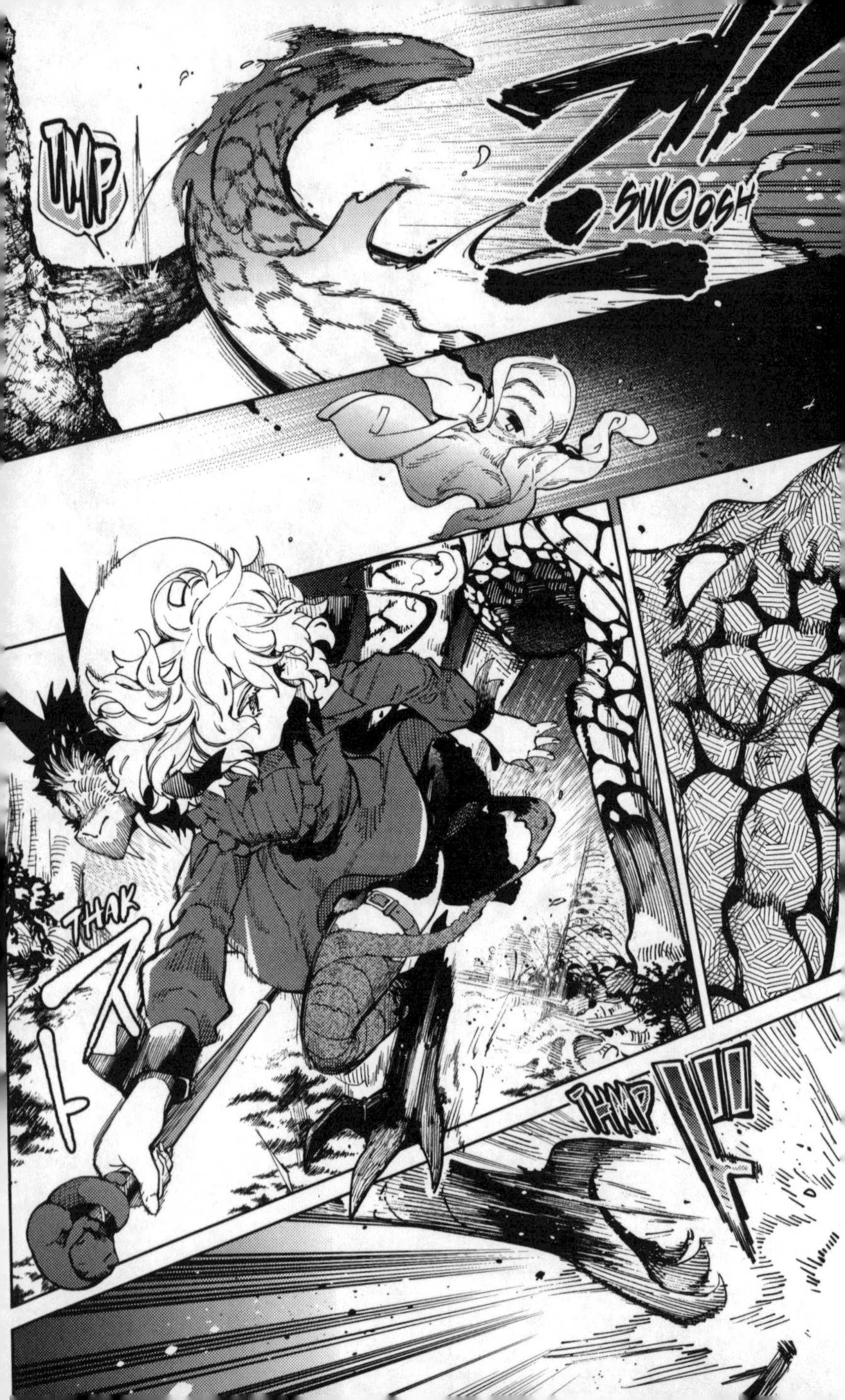
SWOOSH
TMP
THAK
THMP

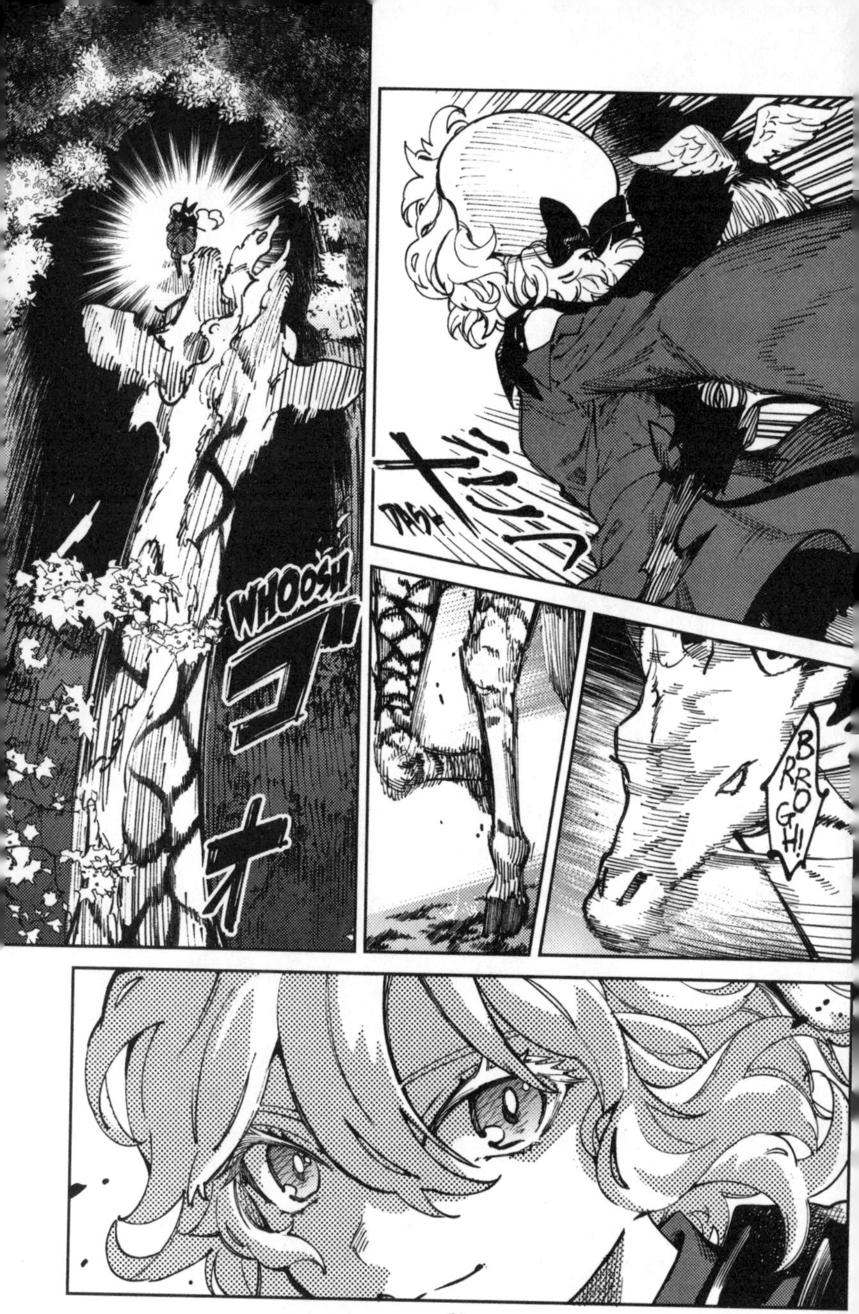
DASH
BRROGH!
WHOOSH

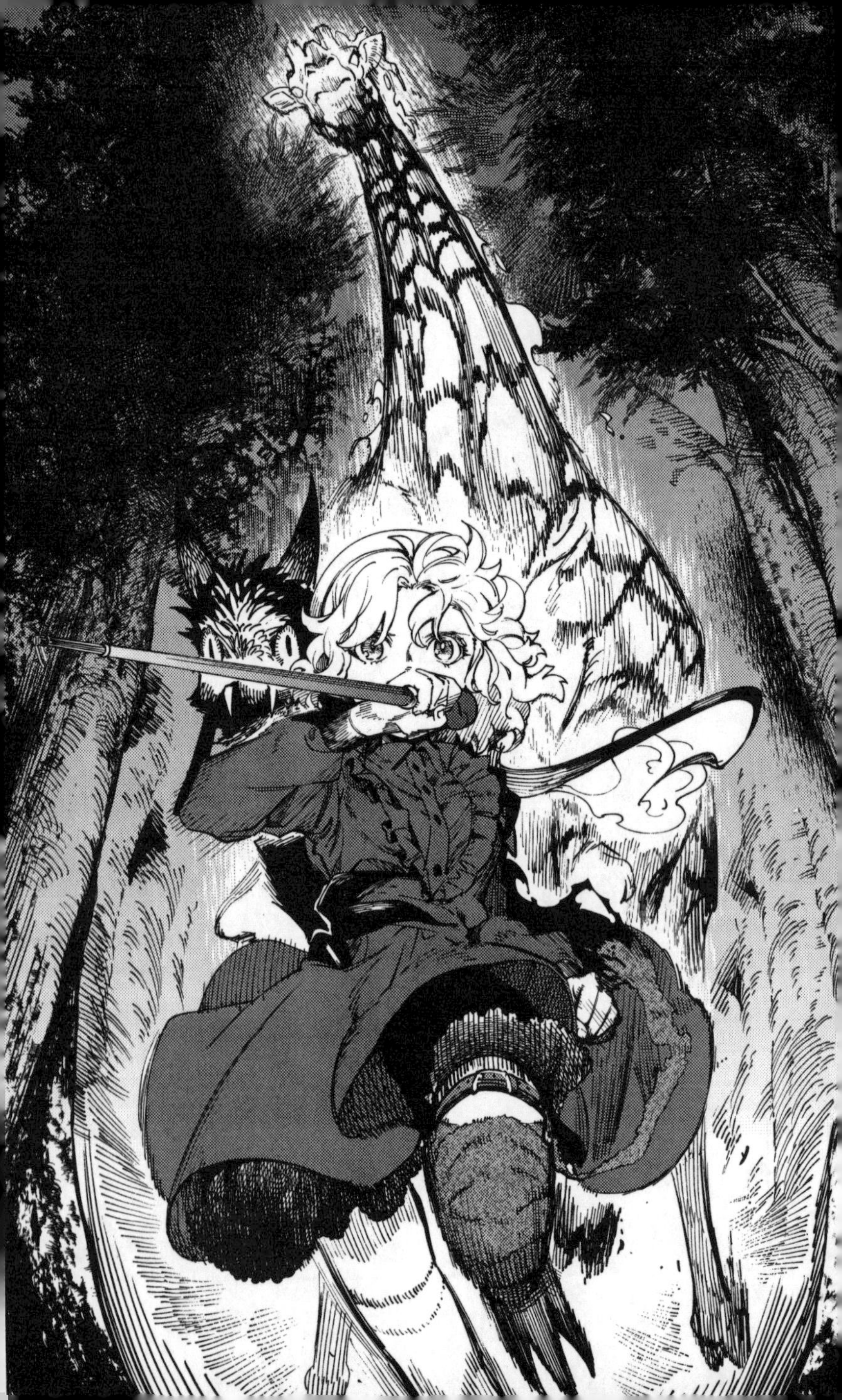

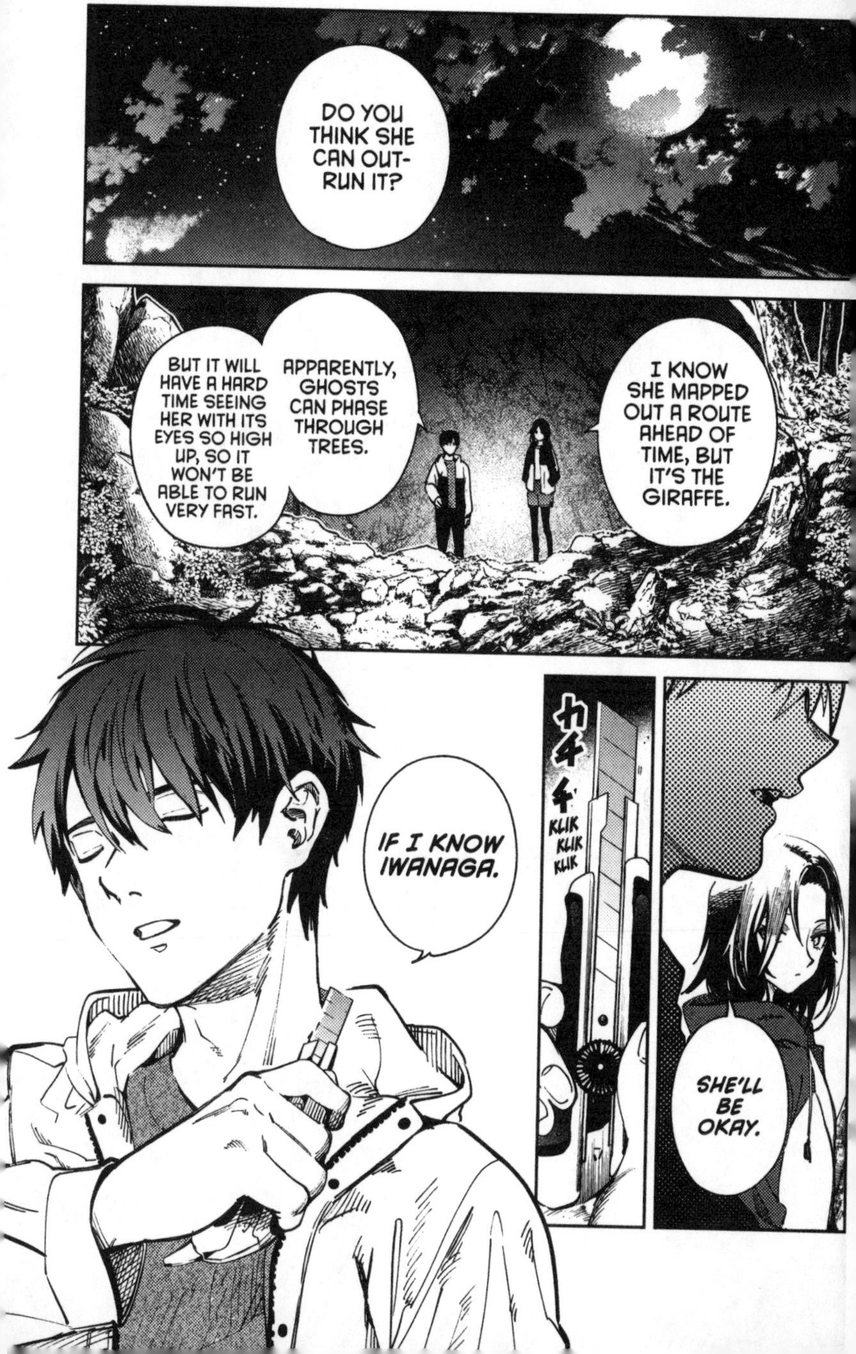
DO YOU THINK SHE CAN OUT-RUN IT?
I KNOW SHE MAPPED OUT A ROUTE AHEAD OF TIME, BUT IT'S THE GIRAFFE.
APPARENTLY, GHOSTS CAN PHASE THROUGH TREES.
BUT IT WILL HAVE A HARD TIME SEEING HER WITH ITS EYES SO HIGH UP, SO IT WON'T BE ABLE TO RUN VERY FAST.
SHE'LL BE OKAY.
KLIK KLIK KLIK
IF I KNOW IWANAGA.

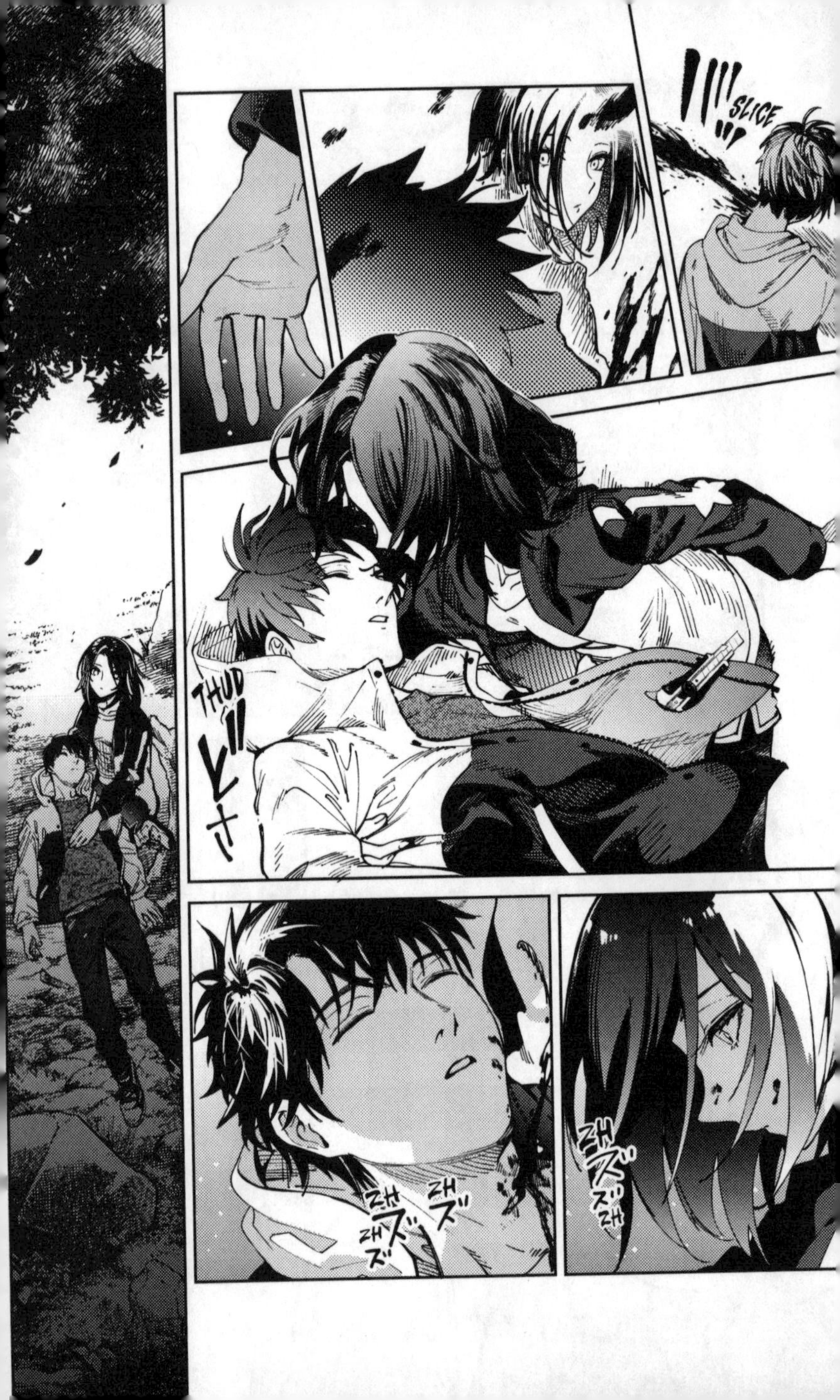
SLICE
THUD
ZH ZH
ZH ZH
ZH ZH

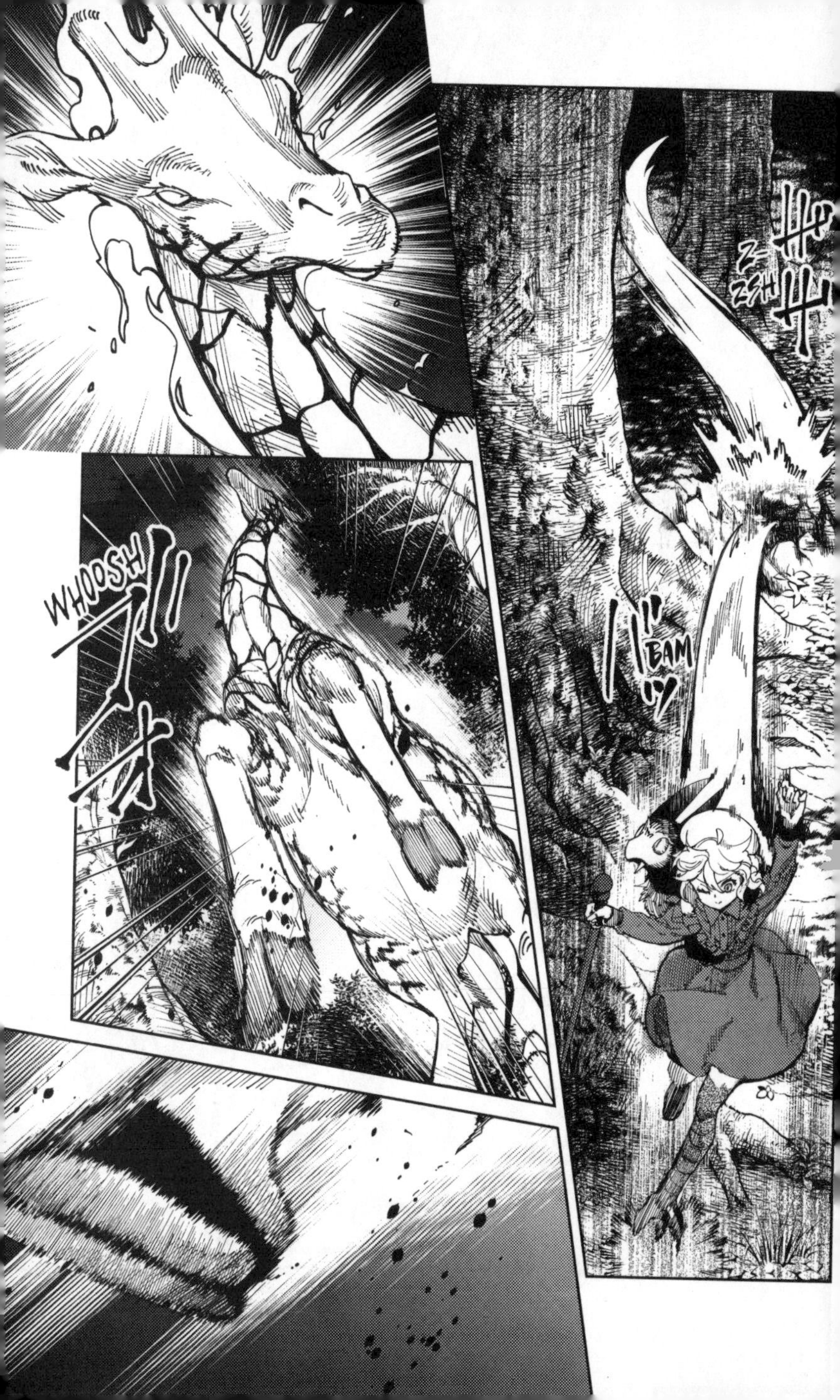
Z-ZSHH
BAM
WHOOSH

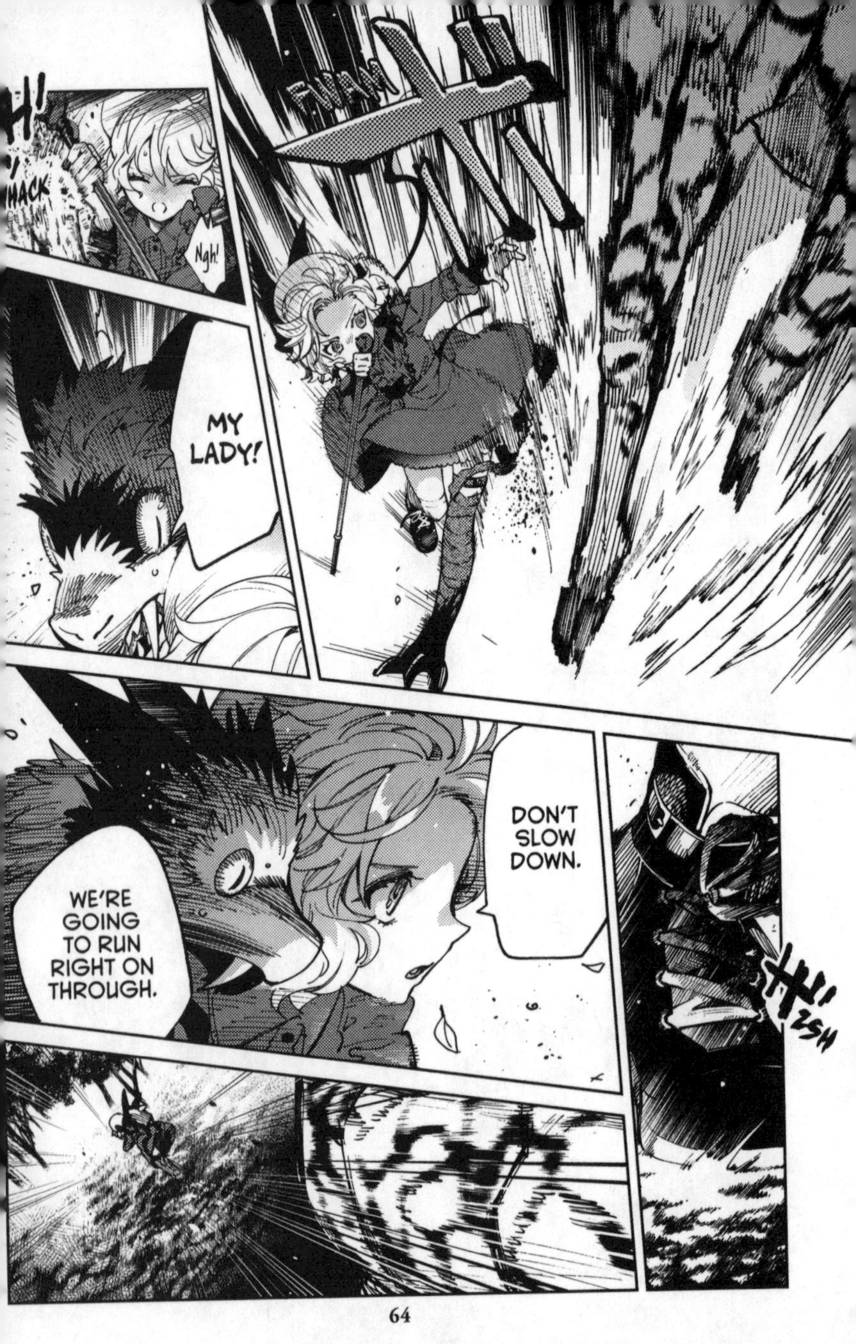
Ngh!
MY LADY!
DON'T SLOW DOWN.
WE'RE GOING TO RUN RIGHT ON THROUGH.

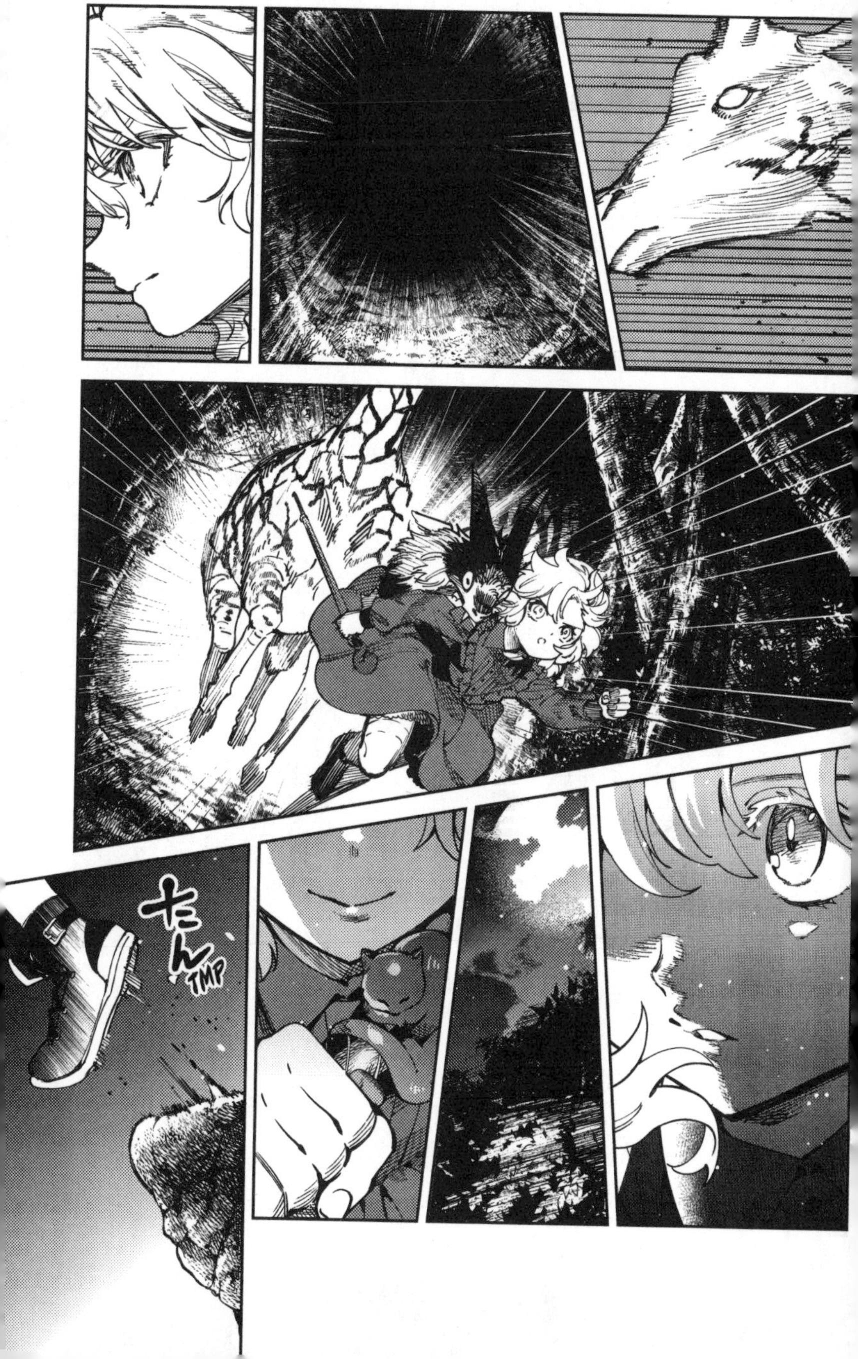
たん
TMP

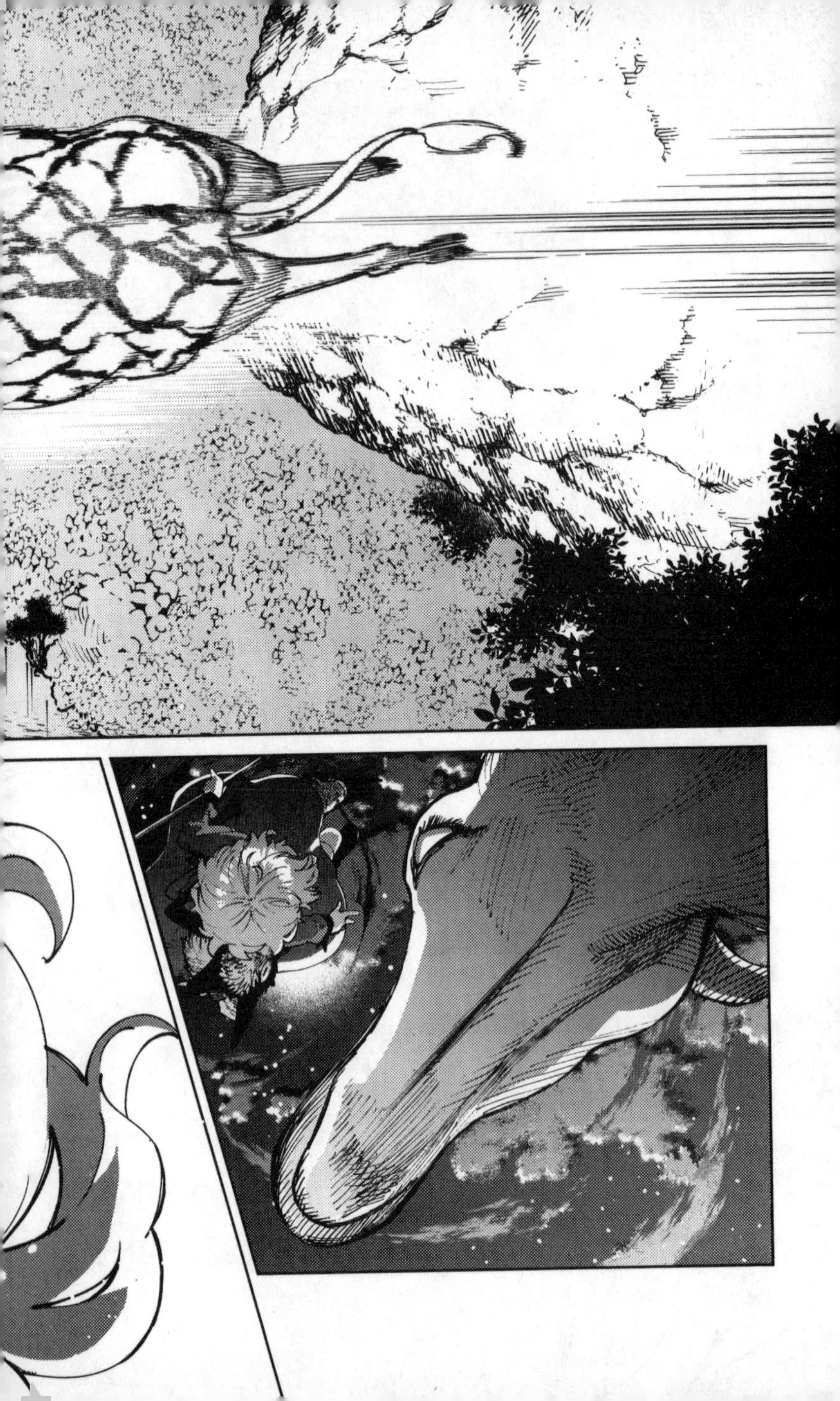

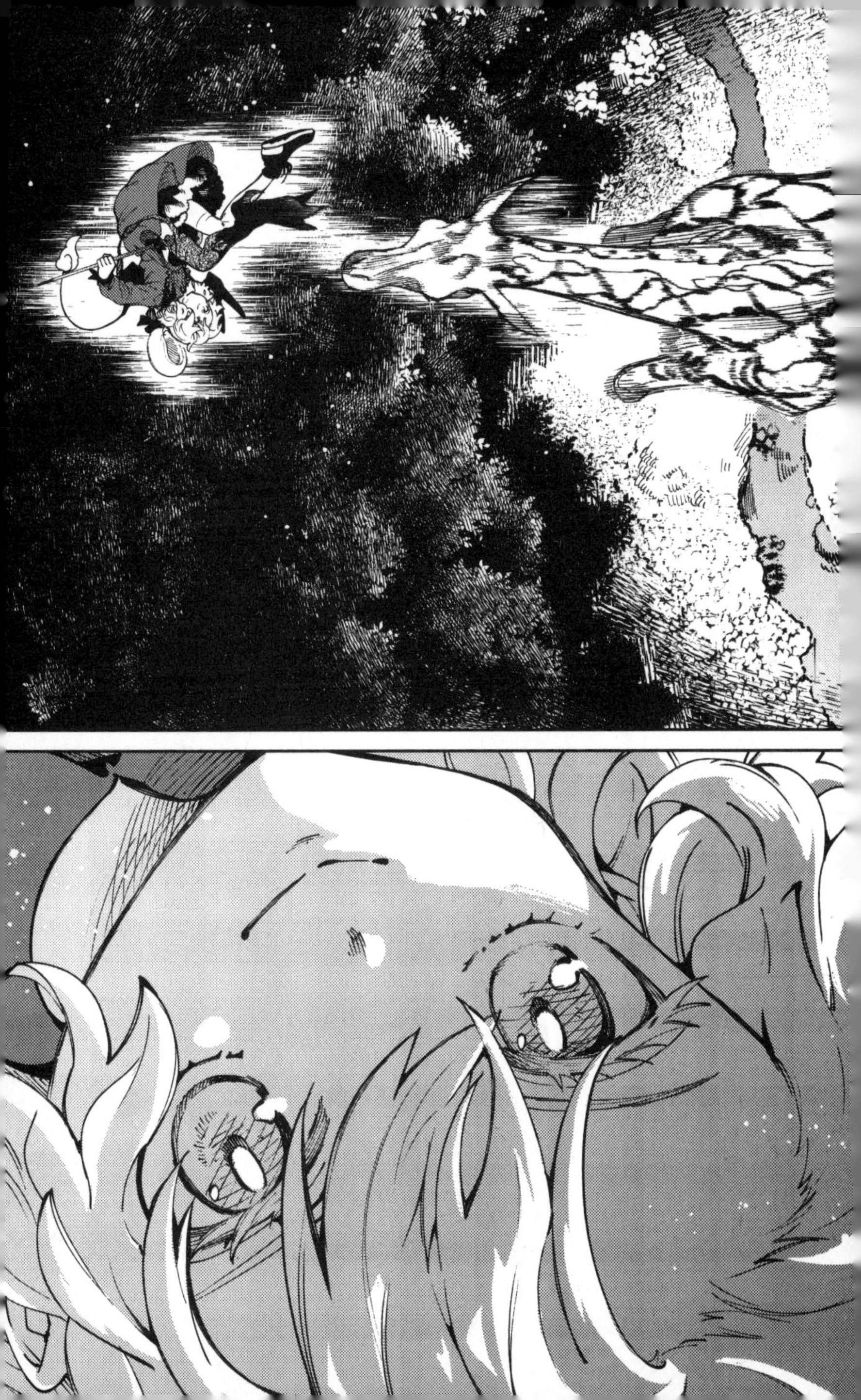

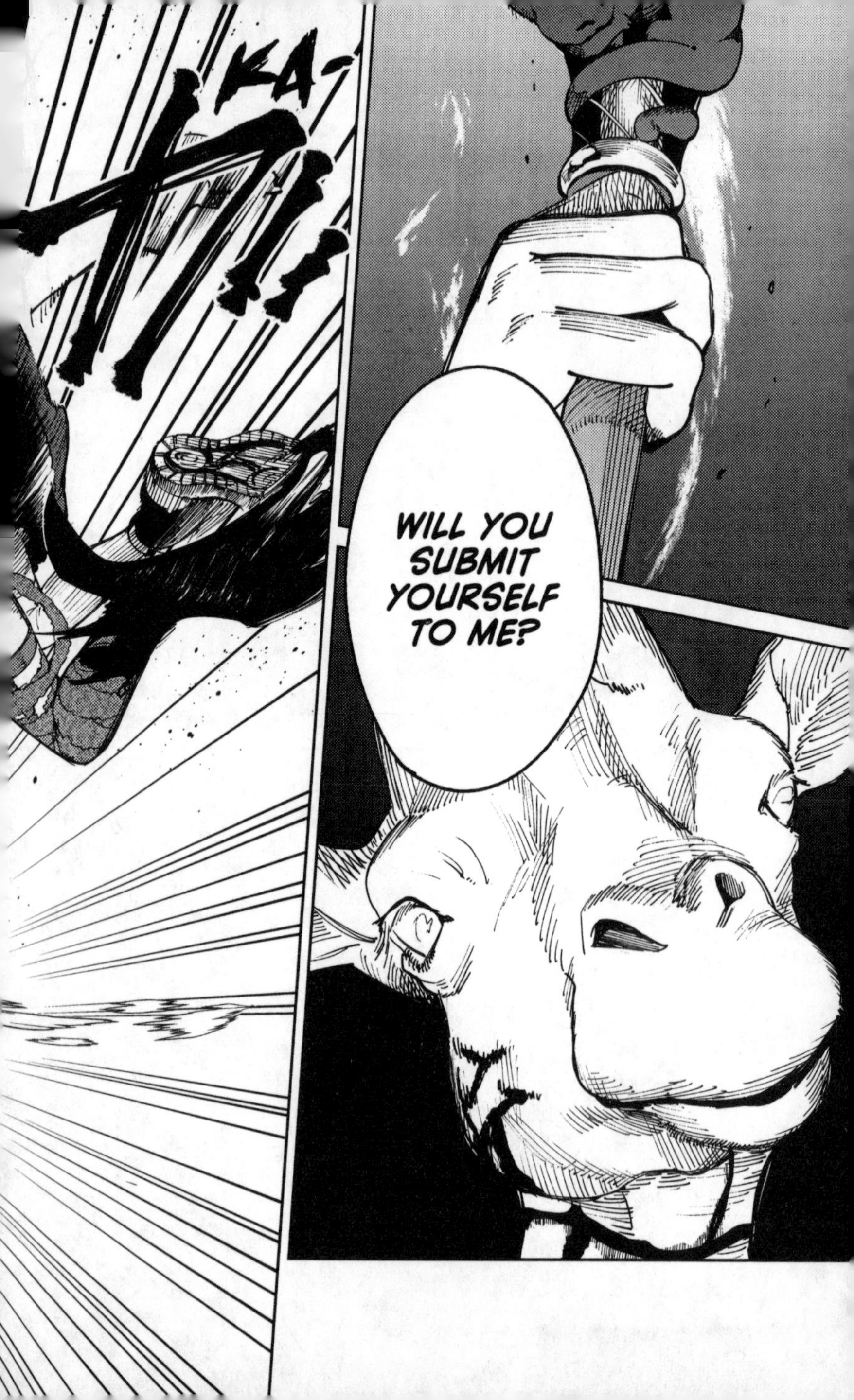
WILL YOU SUBMIT YOURSELF TO ME?
KA-

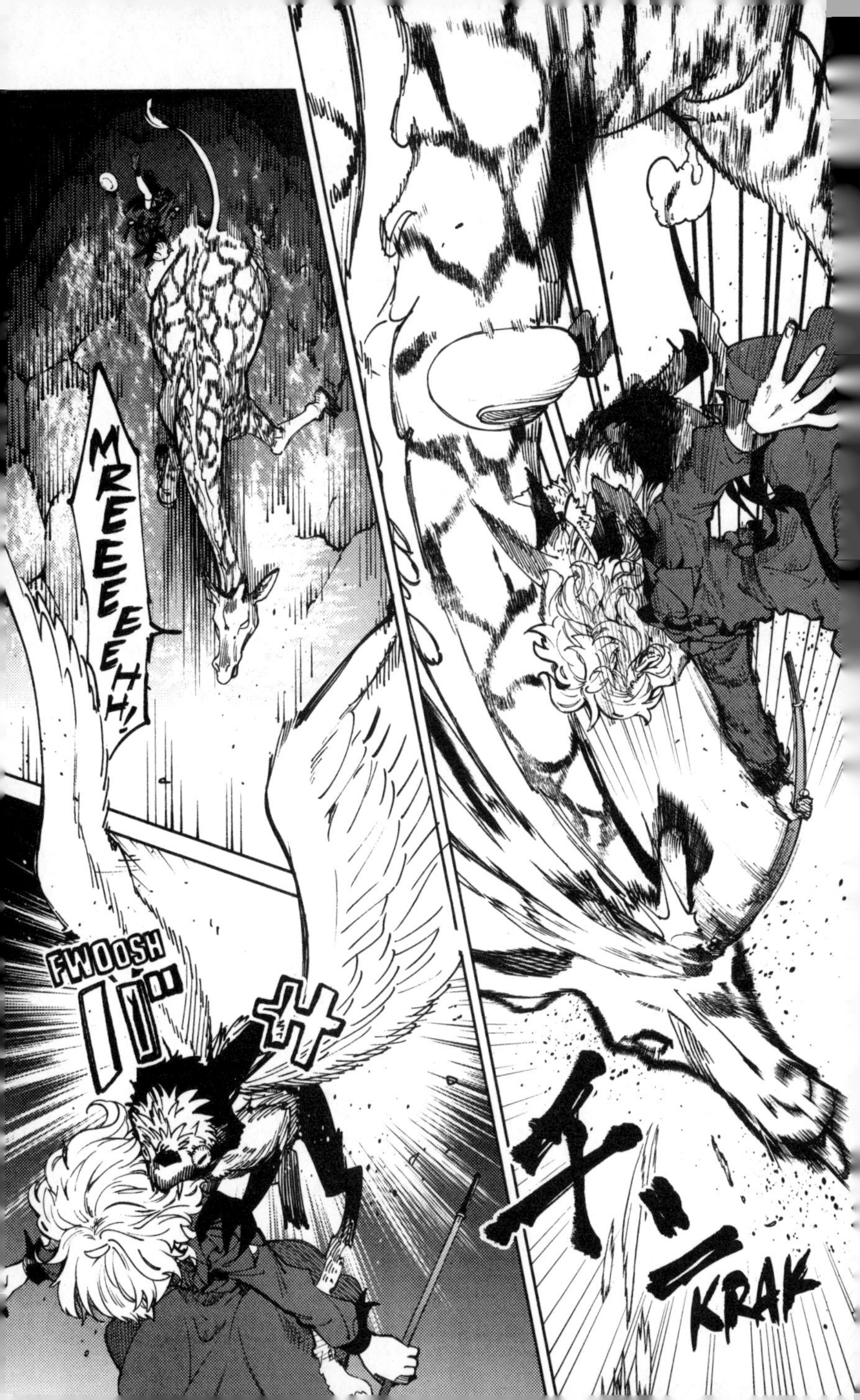
KRAK
MREEEEEEHH!
FWOOSH

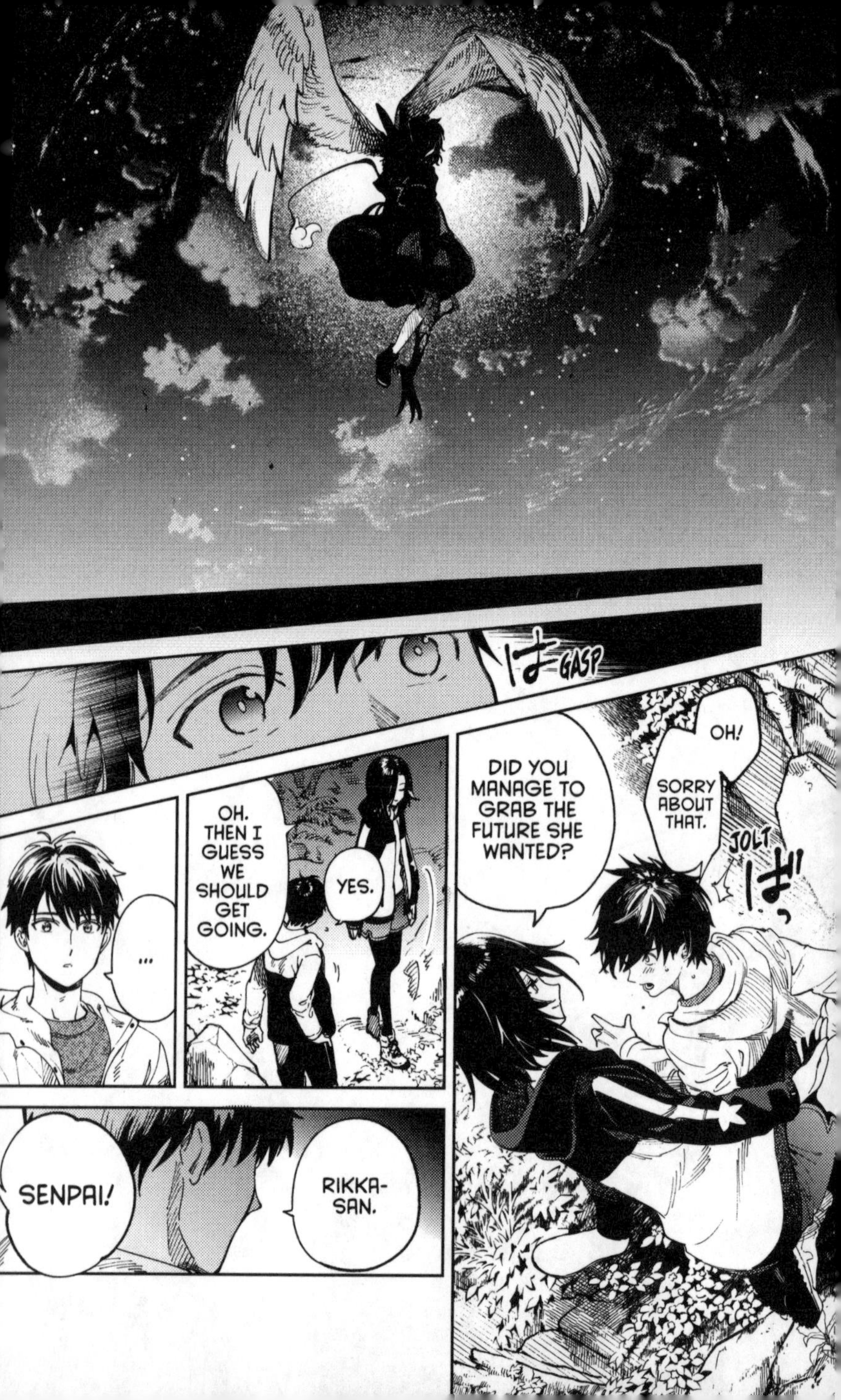
は
GASP
OH!
SORRY ABOUT THAT.
JOLT
ぱっ
DID YOU MANAGE TO GRAB THE FUTURE SHE WANTED?
OH. THEN I GUESS WE SHOULD GET GOING.
YES.
...
RIKKA-SAN.
SENPAI!

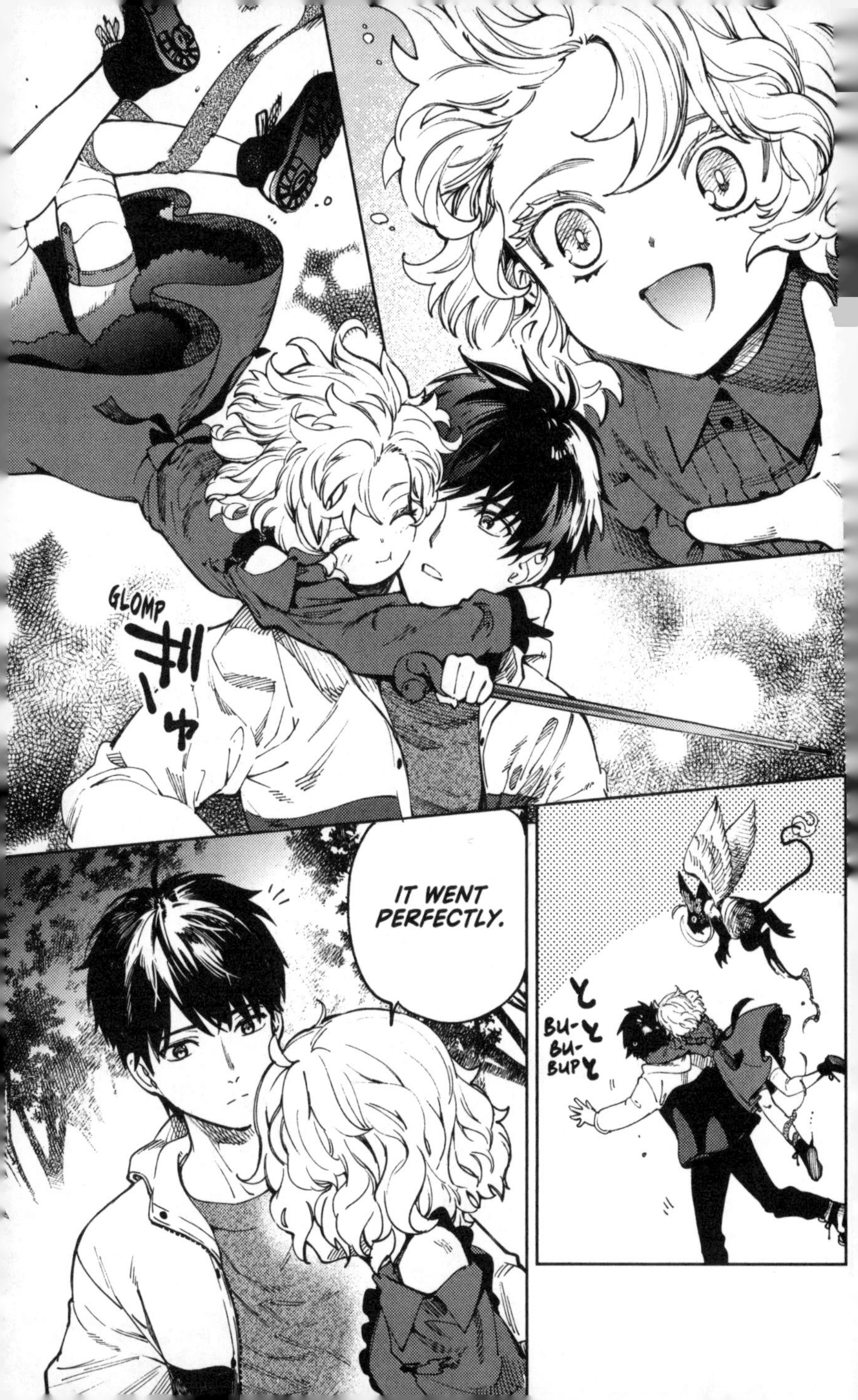
GLOMP
ギューッ
BU-BU-BUP
IT WENT PERFECTLY.

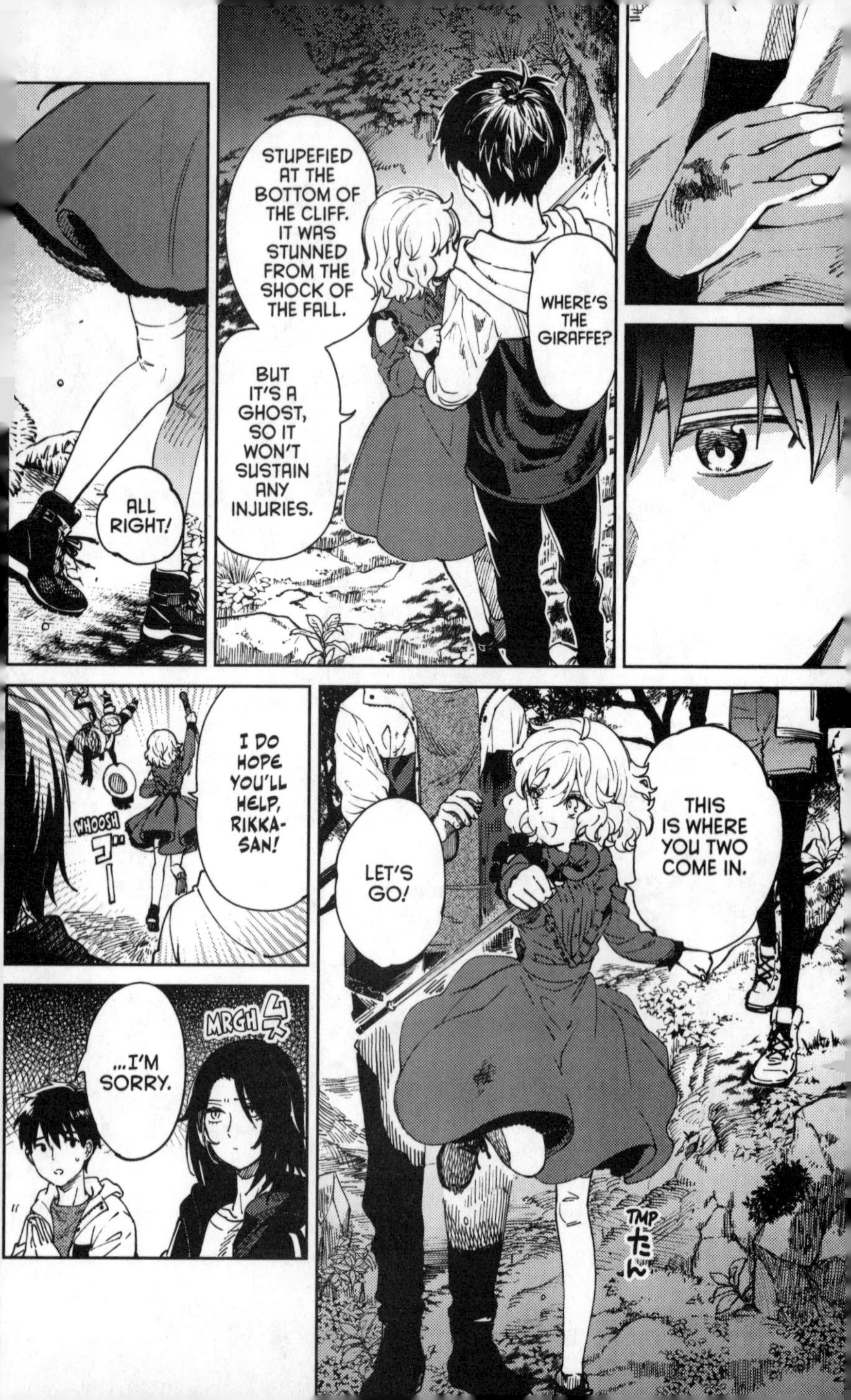
WHERE'S THE GIRAFFE?
STUPEFIED AT THE BOTTOM OF THE CLIFF. IT WAS STUNNED FROM THE SHOCK OF THE FALL.
BUT IT'S A GHOST, SO IT WON'T SUSTAIN ANY INJURIES.
ALL RIGHT!
THIS IS WHERE YOU TWO COME IN.
LET'S GO!
TMP
たん
I DO HOPE YOU'LL HELP, RIKKA-SAN!
WHOOSH
ゴー
MRGH
ムス
...I'M SORRY.

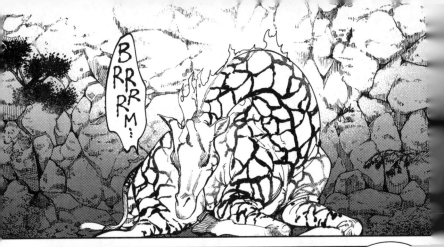

BRRRRM...
I UNDERSTAND. I'LL TELL THE MOUNTAIN SPECTRES TO RETURN YOUR BONES TO THEIR MOTHER EARTH.
AND I WILL ENSURE THAT EVERY BIT OF THE SHRINE IS DISMANTLED.
IF THAT IS WHAT WILL BRING YOU PEACE, THEN THE MONSTERS AROUND HERE WILL BE SURE TO HELP.
I WON'T TELL YOU TO FORGET ABOUT YOUR GRUDGE AGAINST HUMANS.
BUT IF HUMANS KEEP DYING MYSTERIOUS DEATHS, THEN THEY'LL START SWARMING THE MOUNTAIN AND MAKING THINGS DIFFICULT HERE.

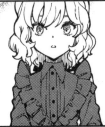

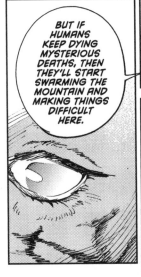

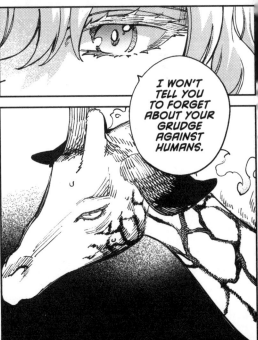

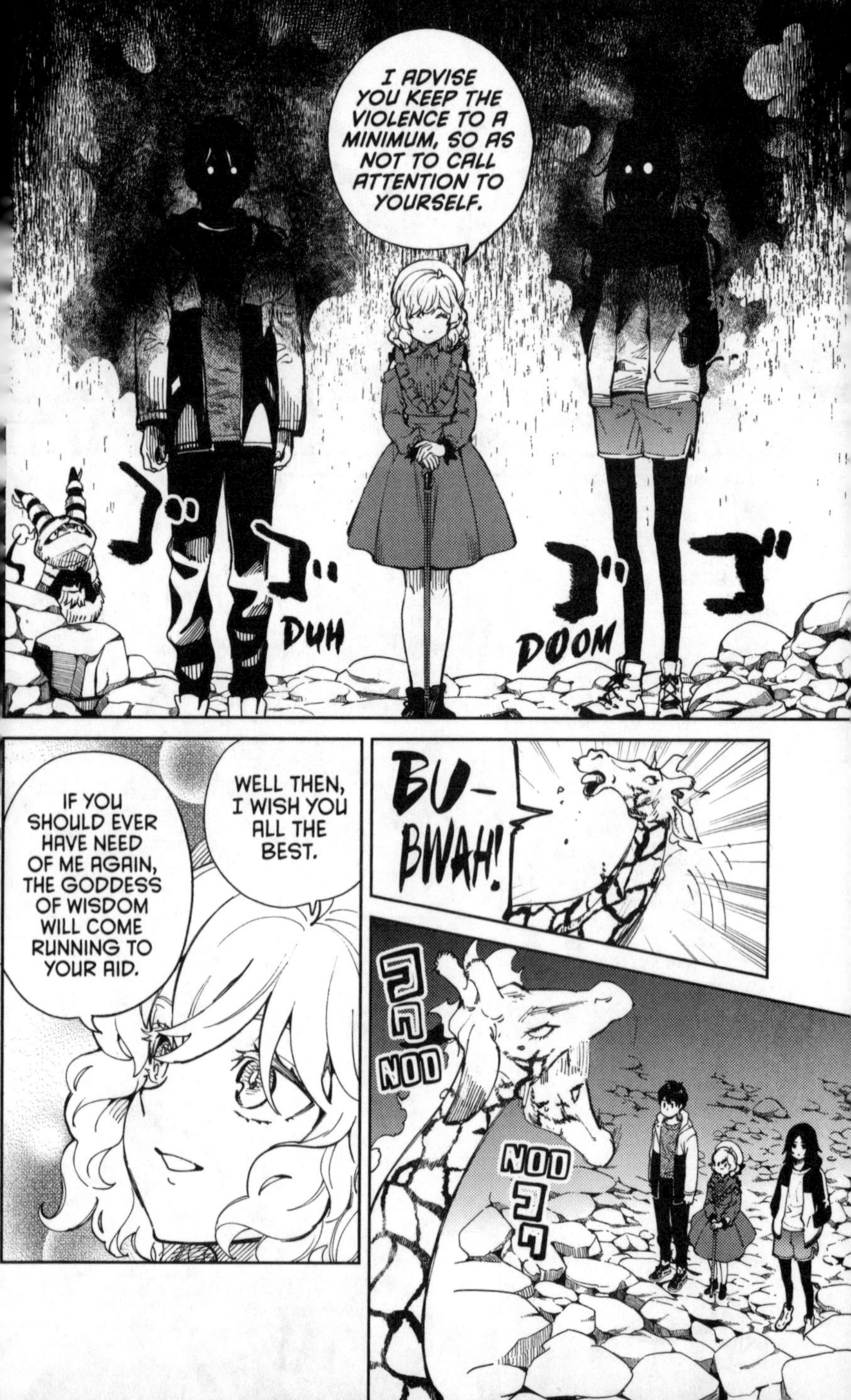

I ADVISE YOU KEEP THE VIOLENCE TO A MINIMUM, SO AS NOT TO CALL ATTENTION TO YOURSELF.
ゴゴ
DOOM
ゴゴ
DUH
BU-BWAH!
コク
NOD
NOD
コク
WELL THEN, I WISH YOU ALL THE BEST.
IF YOU SHOULD EVER HAVE NEED OF ME AGAIN, THE GODDESS OF WISDOM WILL COME RUNNING TO YOUR AID.

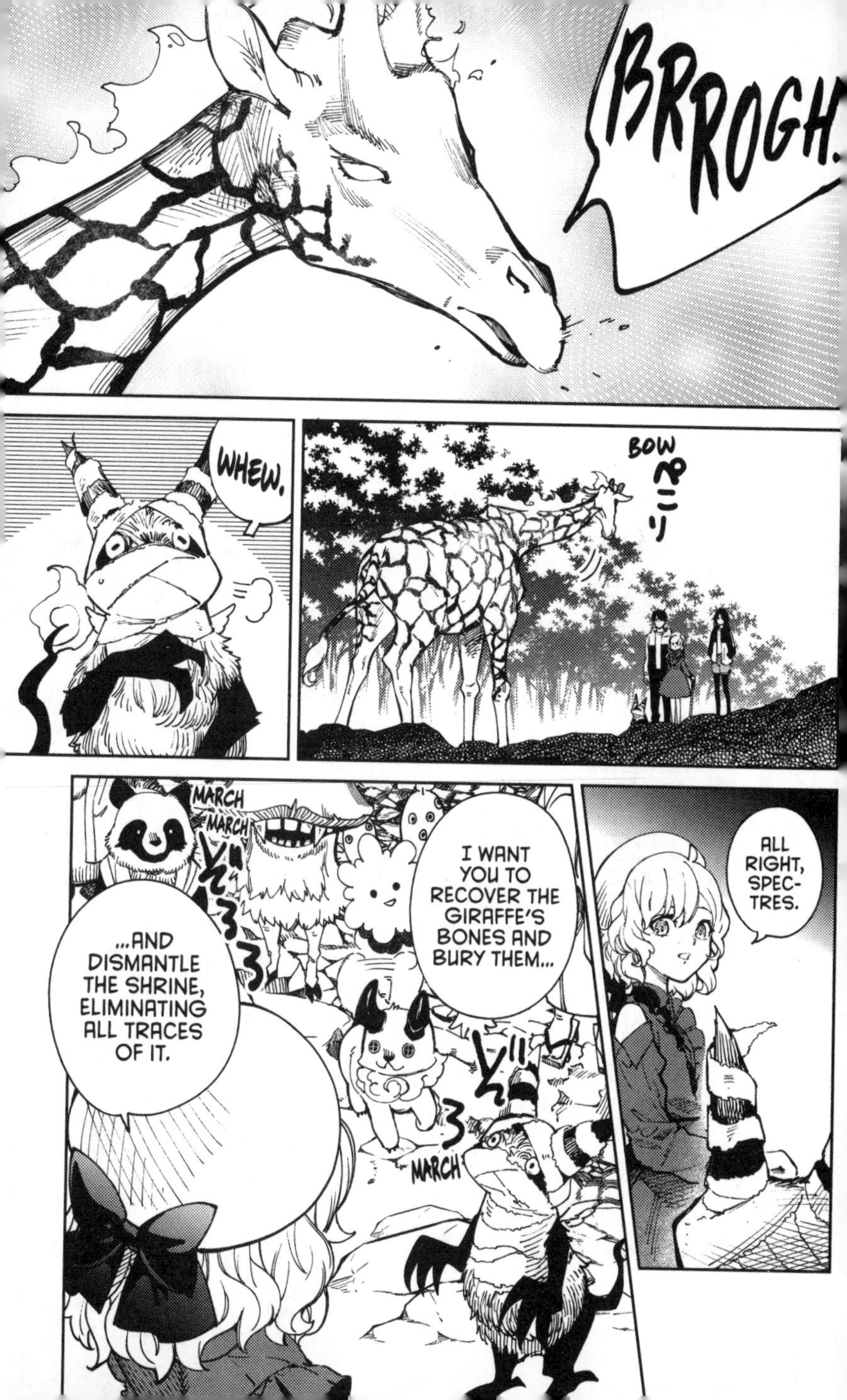
BRROGH.
BOW
ぺこり
WHEW.
ALL RIGHT, SPEC-TRES.
I WANT YOU TO RECOVER THE GIRAFFE'S BONES AND BURY THEM...
...AND DISMANTLE THE SHRINE, ELIMINATING ALL TRACES OF IT.
MARCH
MARCH
MARCH

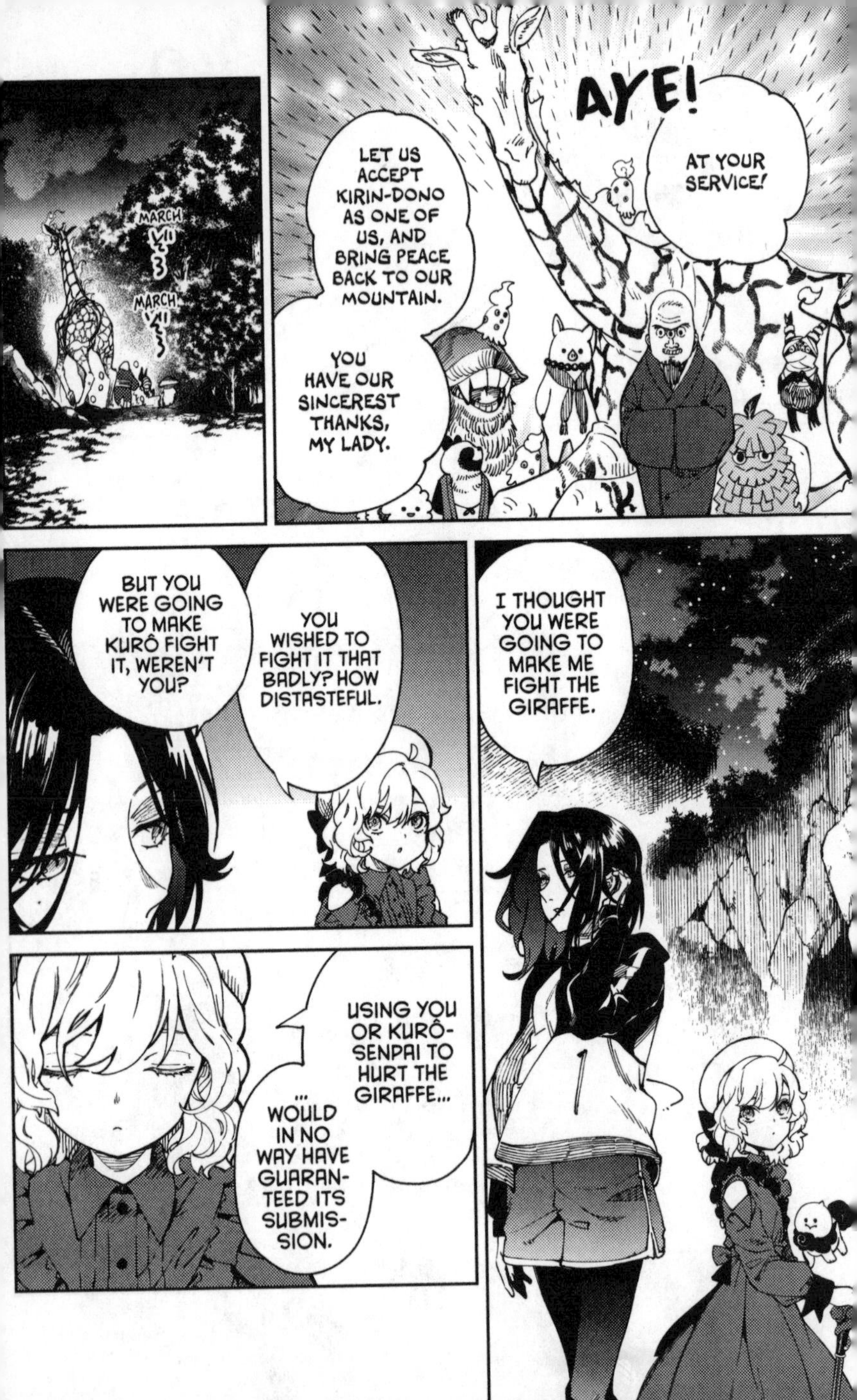
AYE!
AT YOUR SERVICE!
LET US ACCEPT KIRIN-DONO AS ONE OF US, AND BRING PEACE BACK TO OUR MOUNTAIN.
YOU HAVE OUR SINCEREST THANKS, MY LADY.
MARCH
MARCH
I THOUGHT YOU WERE GOING TO MAKE ME FIGHT THE GIRAFFE.
YOU WISHED TO FIGHT IT THAT BADLY? HOW DISTASTEFUL.
BUT YOU WERE GOING TO MAKE KURÔ FIGHT IT, WEREN'T YOU?
USING YOU OR KURÔ-SENPAI TO HURT THE GIRAFFE...
...WOULD IN NO WAY HAVE GUARANTEED ITS SUBMISSION.

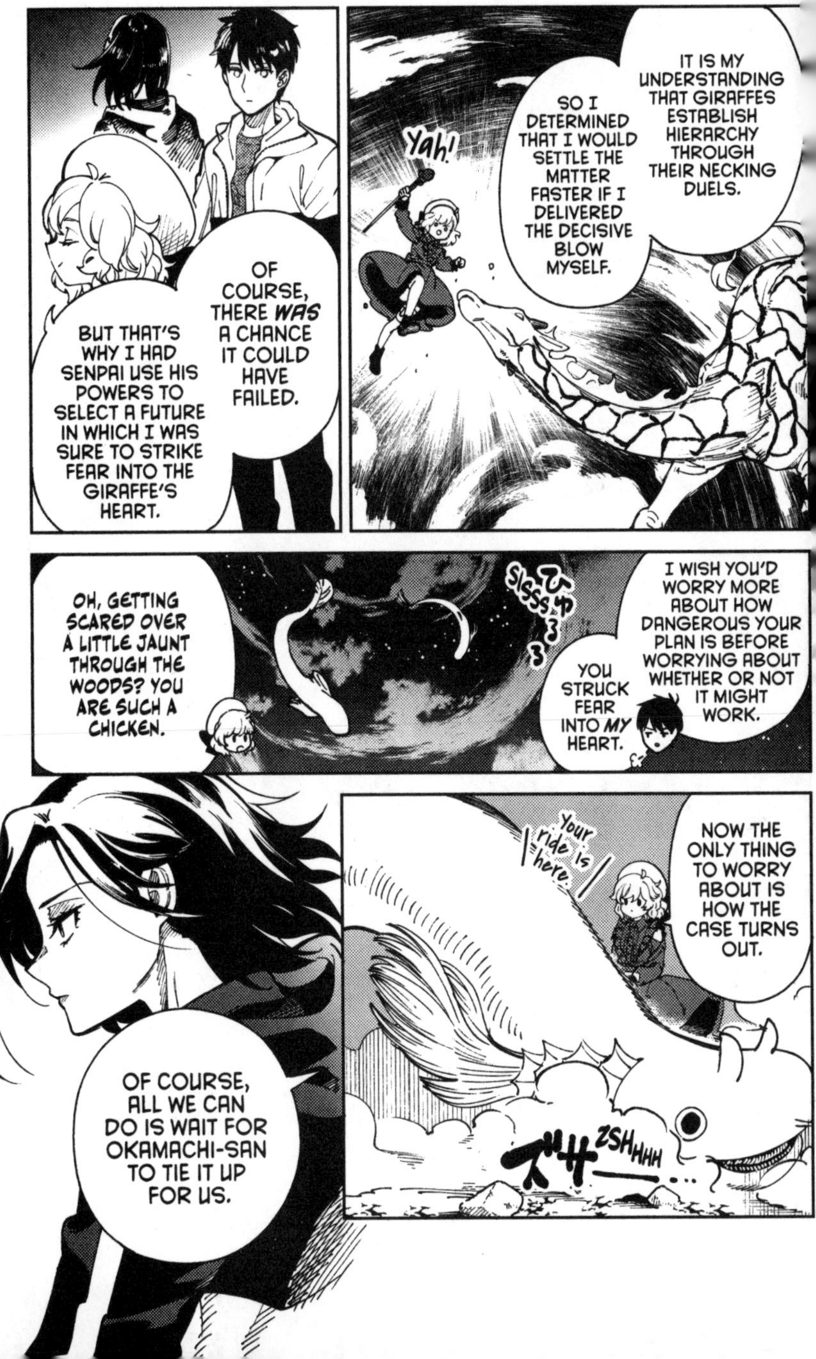
IT IS MY UNDERSTANDING THAT GIRAFFES ESTABLISH HIERARCHY THROUGH THEIR NECKING DUELS.
SO I DETERMINED THAT I WOULD SETTLE THE MATTER FASTER IF I DELIVERED THE DECISIVE BLOW MYSELF.
Yah!
OF COURSE, THERE *WAS* A CHANCE IT COULD HAVE FAILED.
BUT THAT'S WHY I HAD SENPAI USE HIS POWERS TO SELECT A FUTURE IN WHICH I WAS SURE TO STRIKE FEAR INTO THE GIRAFFE'S HEART.
I WISH YOU'D WORRY MORE ABOUT HOW DANGEROUS YOUR PLAN IS BEFORE WORRYING ABOUT WHETHER OR NOT IT MIGHT WORK.
YOU STRUCK FEAR INTO *MY* HEART.
SISSSS
OH, GETTING SCARED OVER A LITTLE JAUNT THROUGH THE WOODS? YOU ARE SUCH A CHICKEN.
NOW THE ONLY THING TO WORRY ABOUT IS HOW THE CASE TURNS OUT.
Your ride is here.
ZSHHHHH...
OF COURSE, ALL WE CAN DO IS WAIT FOR OKAMACHI-SAN TO TIE IT UP FOR US.

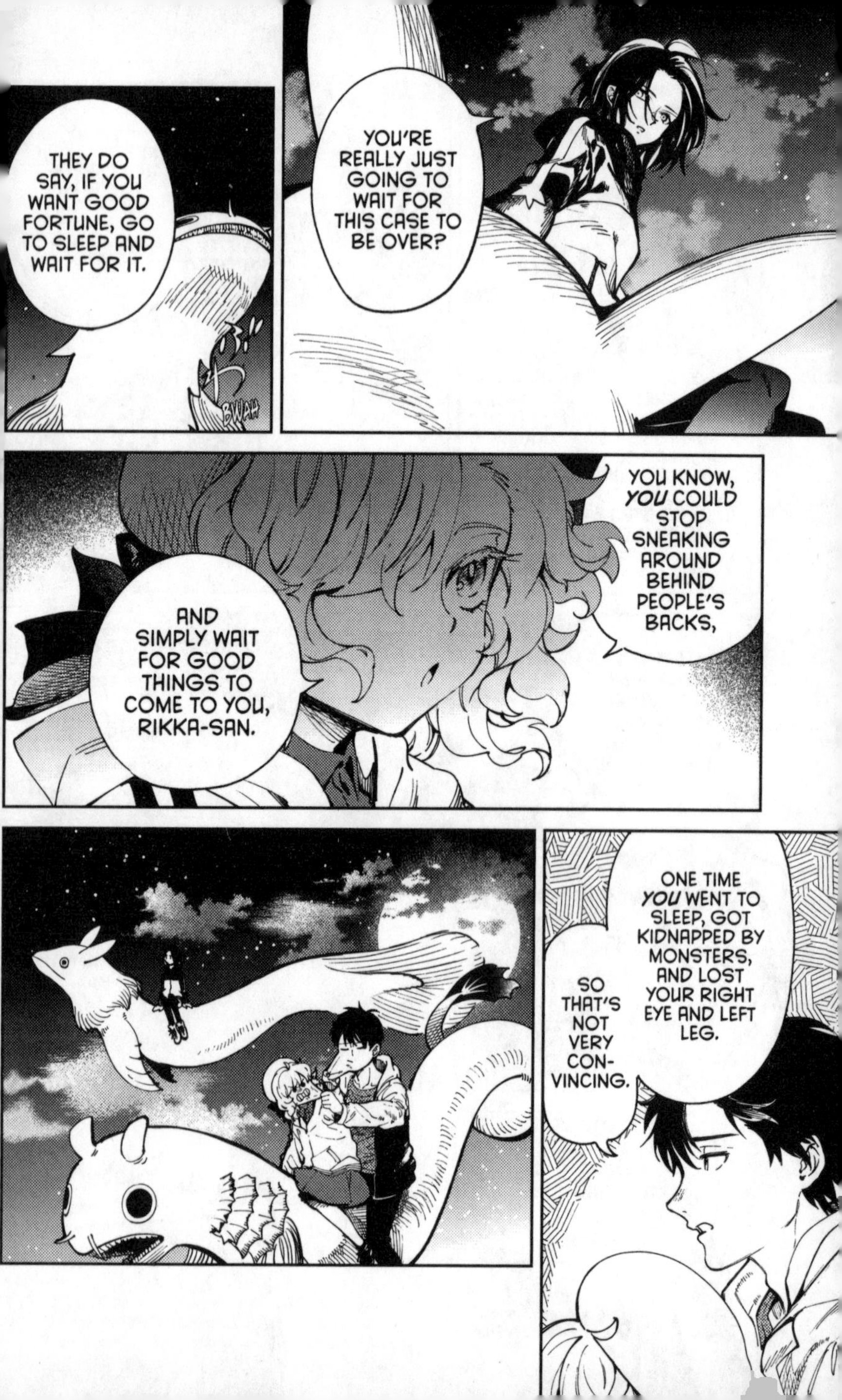
YOU'RE REALLY JUST GOING TO WAIT FOR THIS CASE TO BE OVER?
THEY DO SAY, IF YOU WANT GOOD FORTUNE, GO TO SLEEP AND WAIT FOR IT.
BWAH
YOU KNOW, *YOU* COULD STOP SNEAKING AROUND BEHIND PEOPLE'S BACKS,
AND SIMPLY WAIT FOR GOOD THINGS TO COME TO YOU, RIKKA-SAN.
ONE TIME *YOU* WENT TO SLEEP, GOT KIDNAPPED BY MONSTERS, AND LOST YOUR RIGHT EYE AND LEFT LEG.
SO THAT'S NOT VERY CON-VINCING.

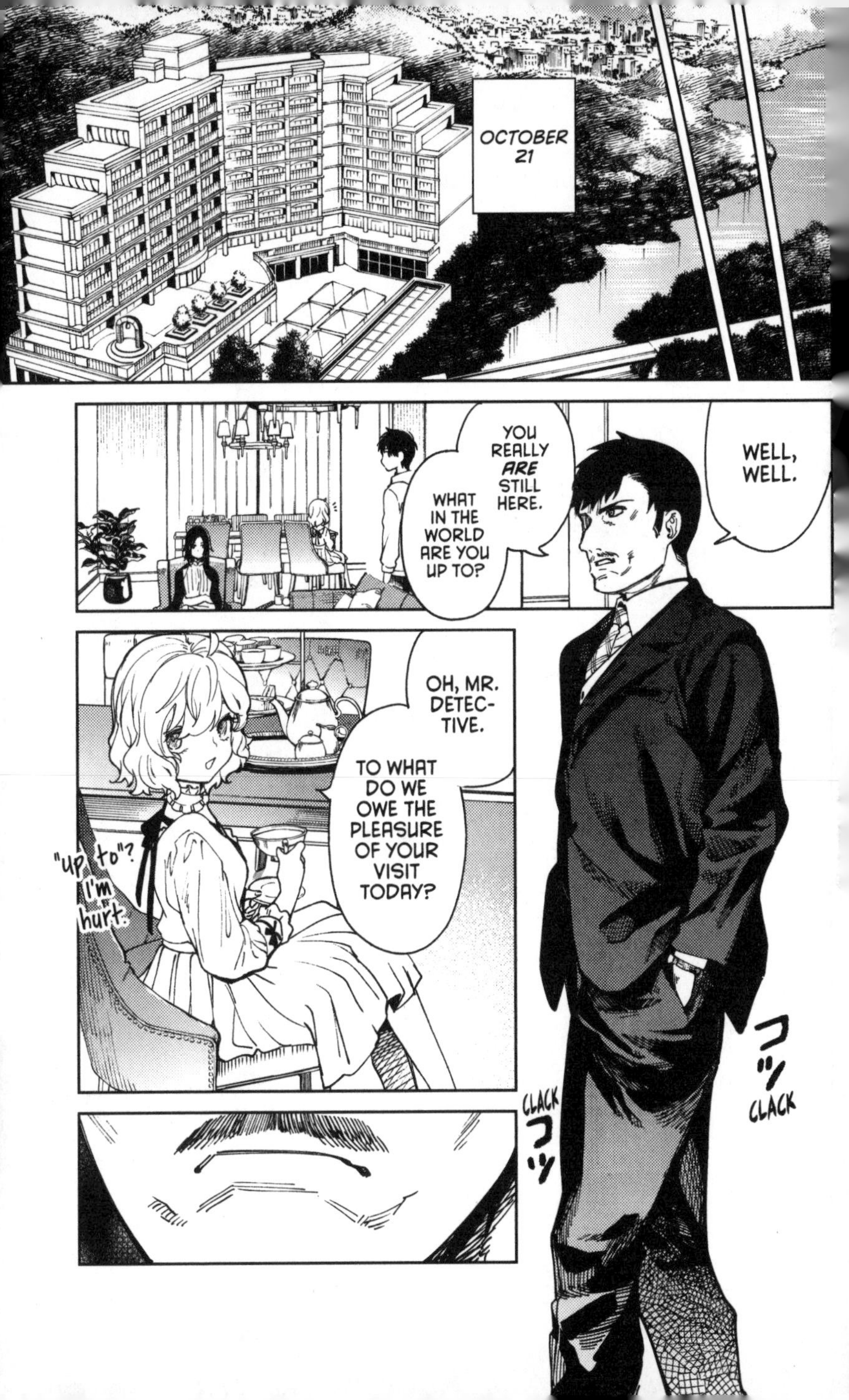
OCTOBER 21
WELL, WELL.
YOU REALLY *ARE* STILL HERE.
WHAT IN THE WORLD ARE YOU UP TO?
OH, MR. DETECTIVE.
TO WHAT DO WE OWE THE PLEASURE OF YOUR VISIT TODAY?
"up to"? I'm hurt.
CLACK
CLACK

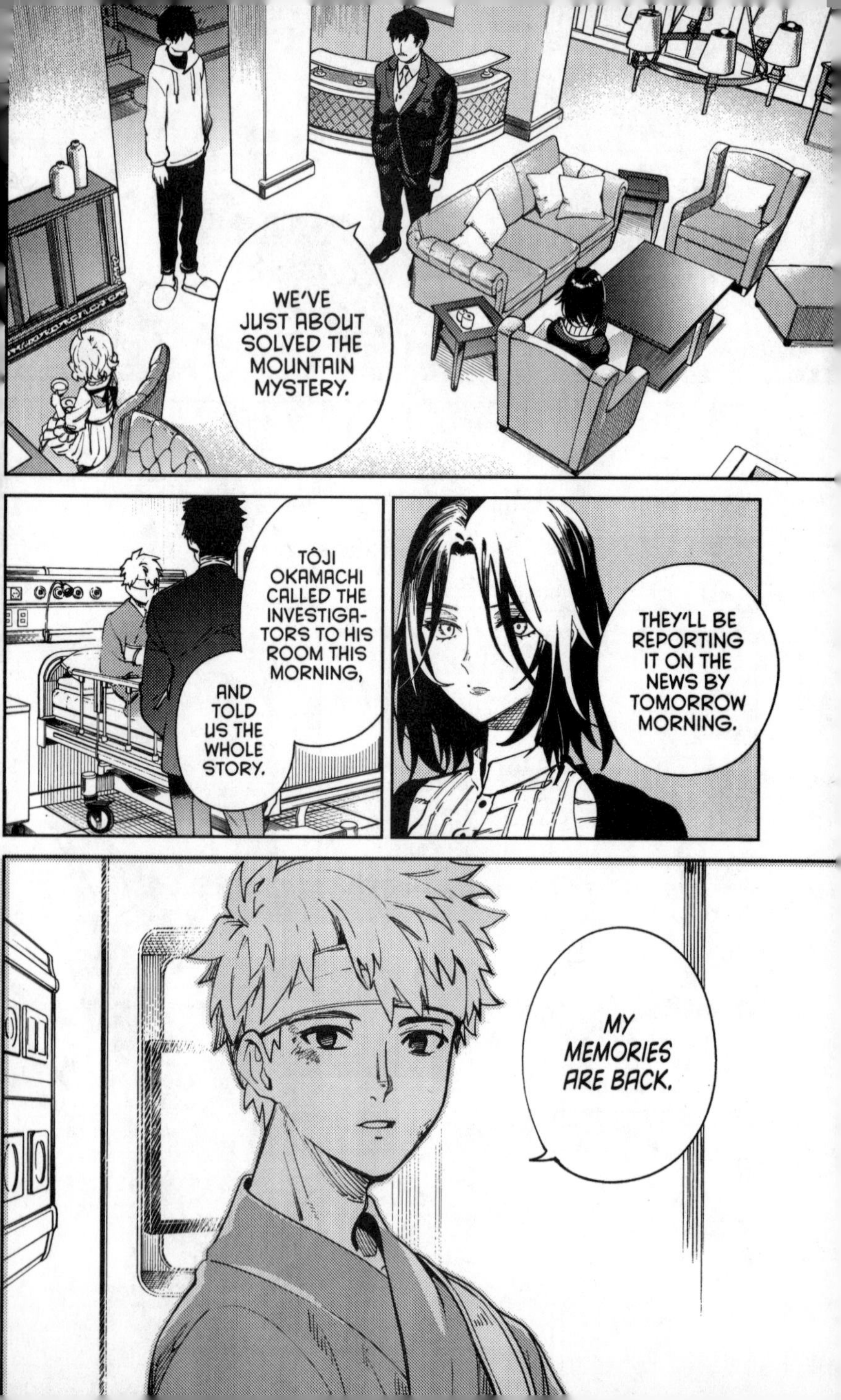
WE'VE JUST ABOUT SOLVED THE MOUNTAIN MYSTERY.
THEY'LL BE REPORTING IT ON THE NEWS BY TOMORROW MORNING.
TÔJI OKAMACHI CALLED THE INVESTIGA-TORS TO HIS ROOM THIS MORNING,
AND TOLD US THE WHOLE STORY.
MY MEMORIES ARE BACK.

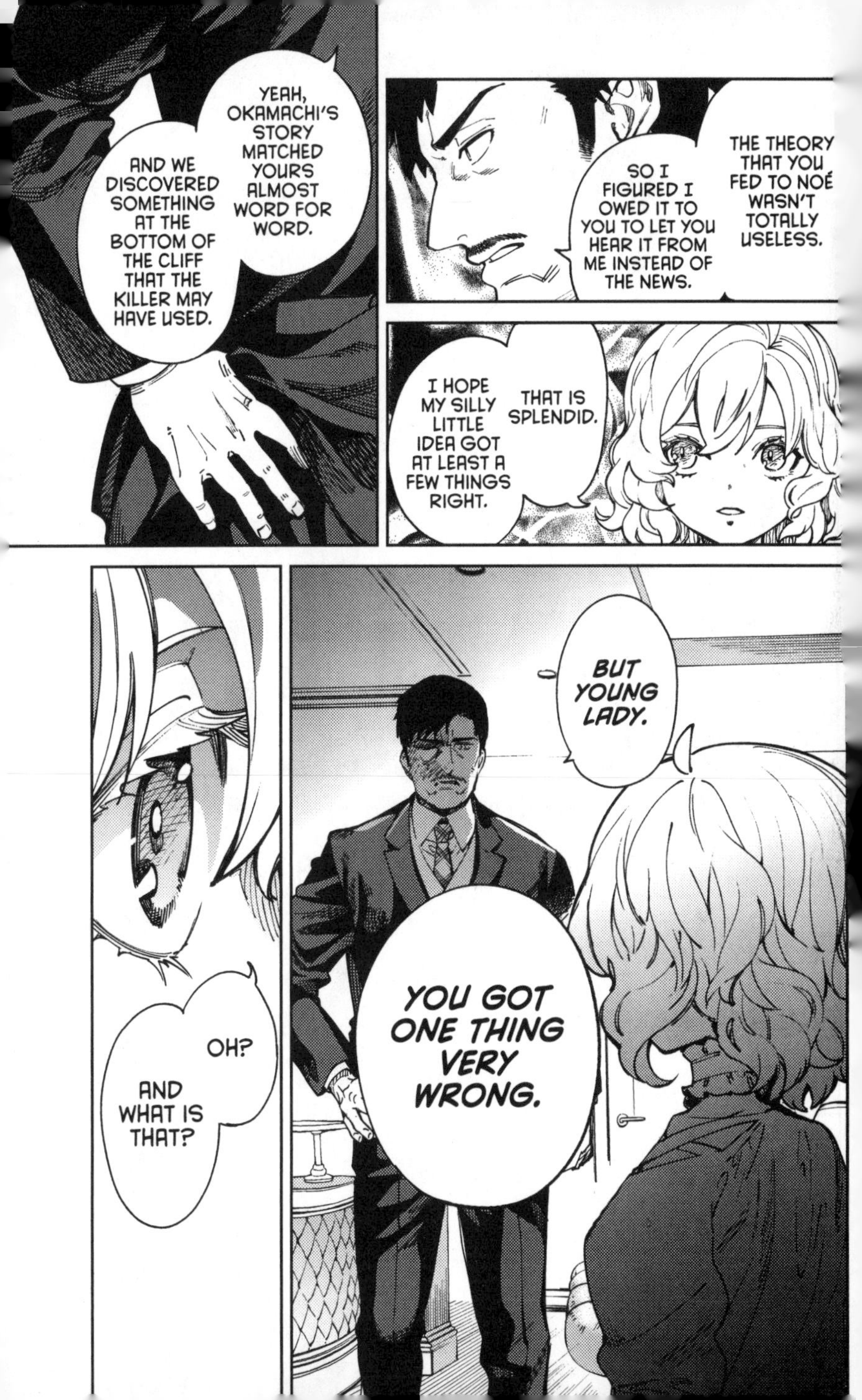
THE THEORY THAT YOU FED TO NOÉ WASN'T TOTALLY USELESS.
SO I FIGURED I OWED IT TO YOU TO LET YOU HEAR IT FROM ME INSTEAD OF THE NEWS.
THAT IS SPLENDID.
I HOPE MY SILLY LITTLE IDEA GOT AT LEAST A FEW THINGS RIGHT.
YEAH, OKAMACHI'S STORY MATCHED YOURS ALMOST WORD FOR WORD.
AND WE DISCOVERED SOMETHING AT THE BOTTOM OF THE CLIFF THAT THE KILLER MAY HAVE USED.
BUT YOUNG LADY.
YOU GOT ONE THING VERY WRONG.
OH?
AND WHAT IS THAT?

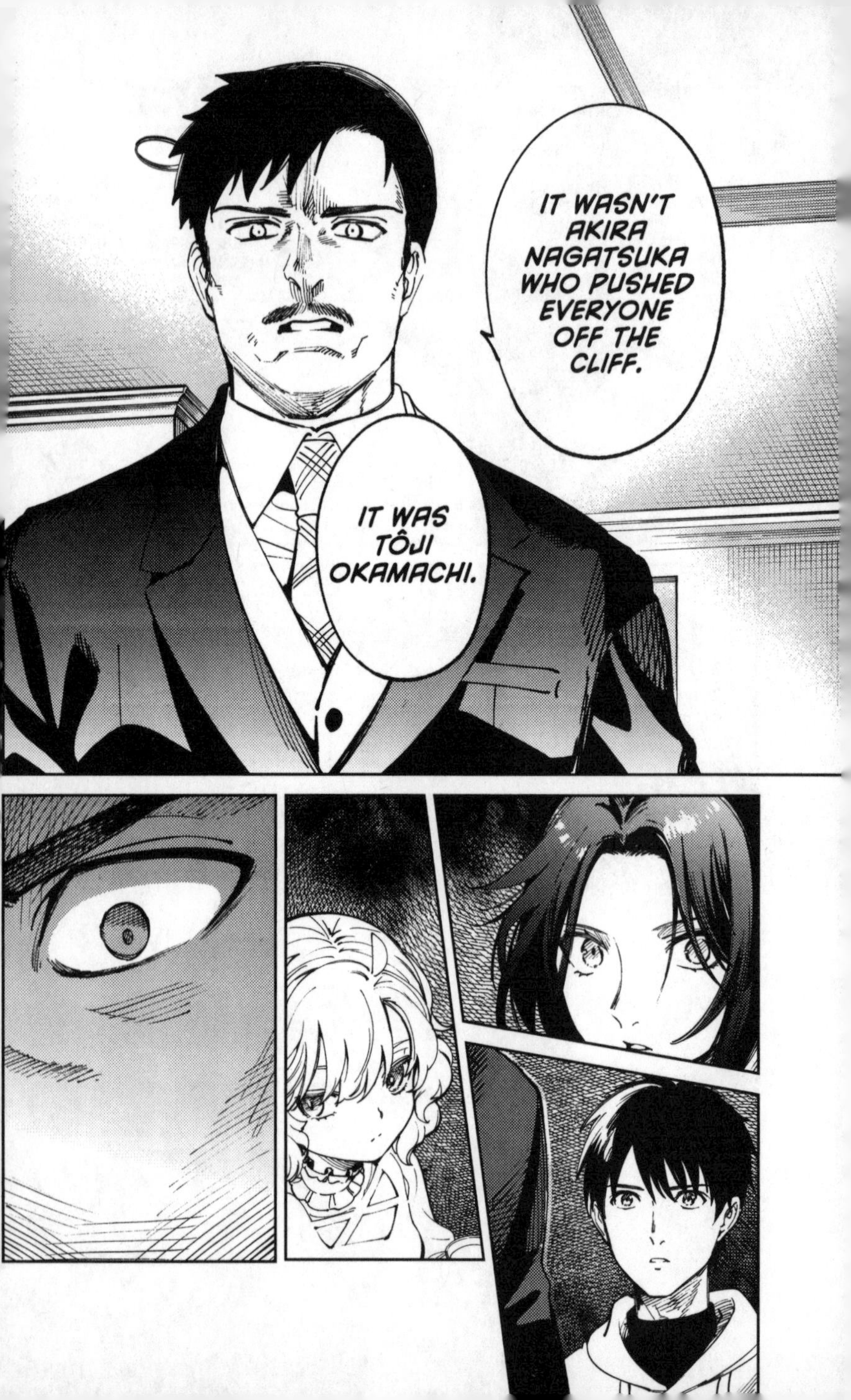
IT WASN'T AKIRA NAGATSUKA WHO PUSHED EVERYONE OFF THE CLIFF.
IT WAS TÔJI OKAMACHI.

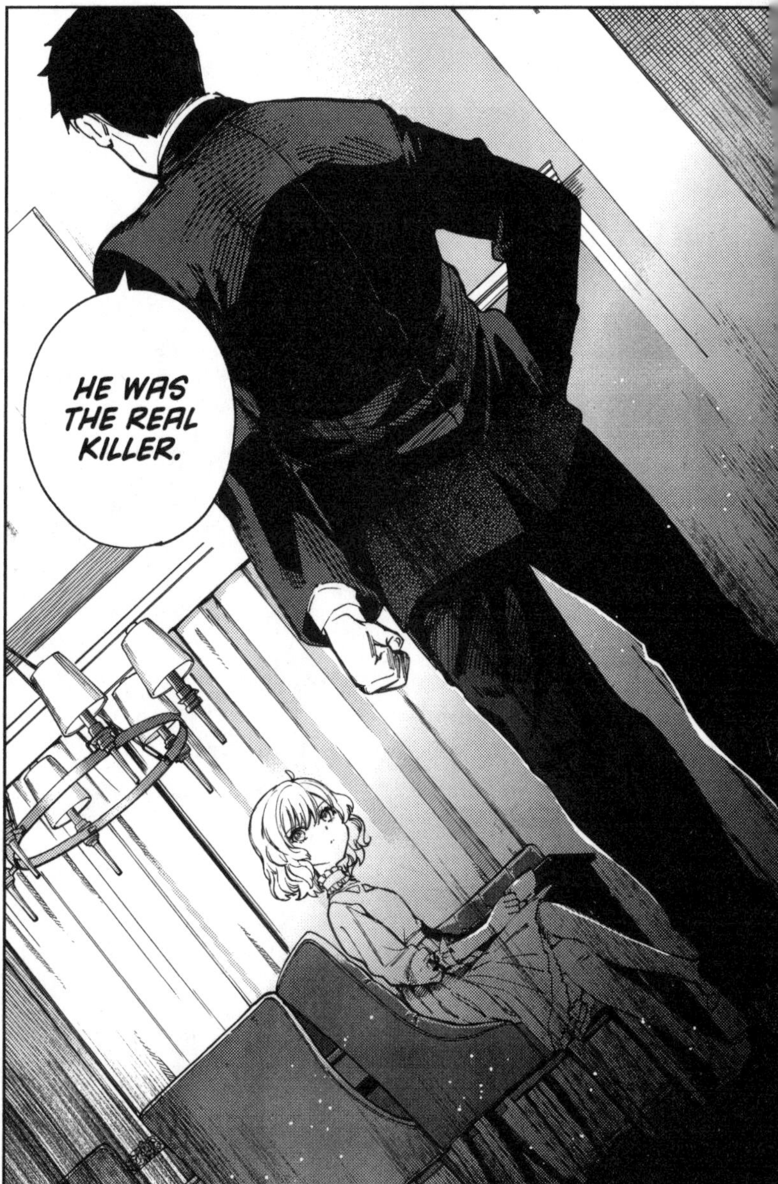
HE WAS THE REAL KILLER.

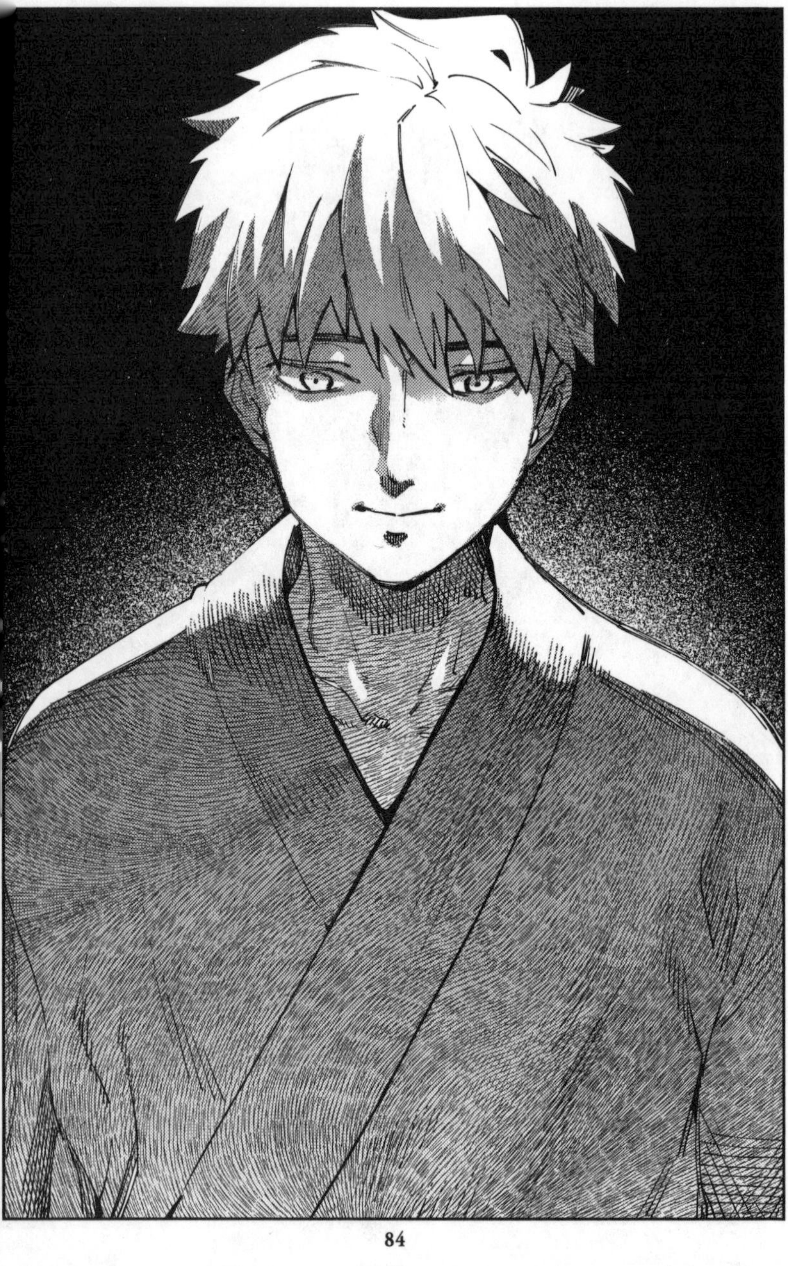

IN/SPECTRE

Rikka-san is supposed to be even taller than Kurō, who is supposed to be tall.

CHAPTER 47: "THE RETALIATION AND DEFEAT OF KOTOKO IWANAGA PART 9"

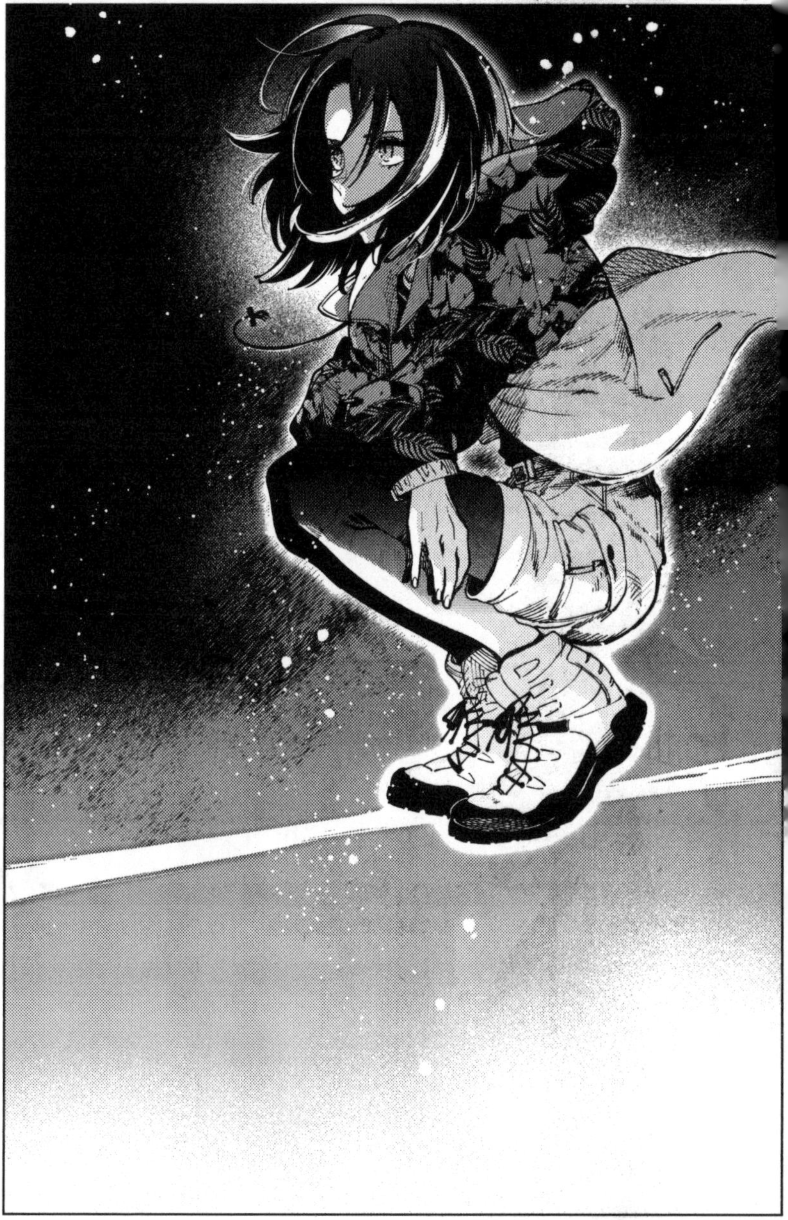

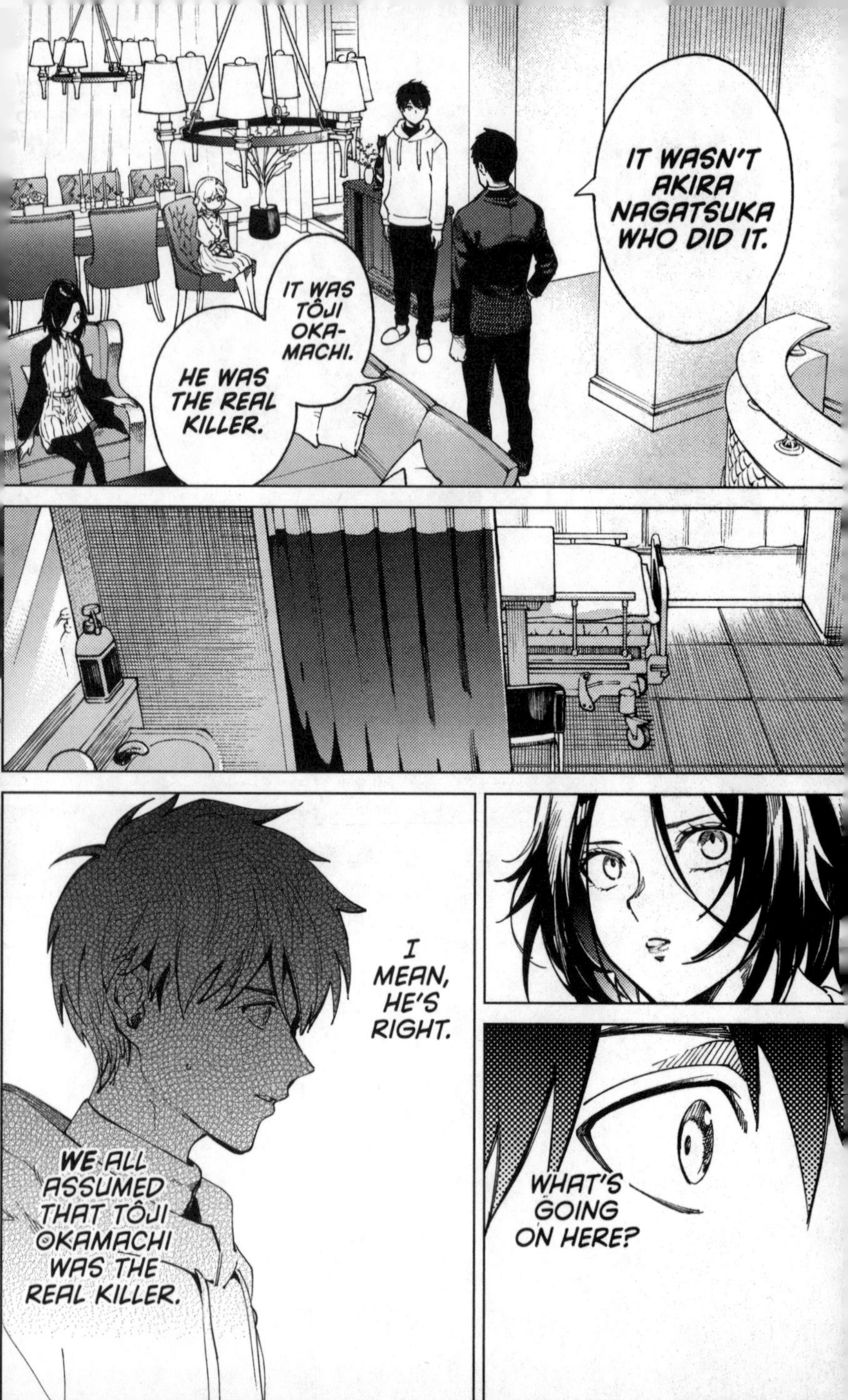
IT WASN'T AKIRA NAGATSUKA WHO DID IT.
IT WAS TÔJI OKA-MACHI.
HE WAS THE REAL KILLER.
WHAT'S GOING ON HERE?
I MEAN, HE'S RIGHT.
WE ALL ASSUMED THAT TÔJI OKAMACHI WAS THE REAL KILLER.

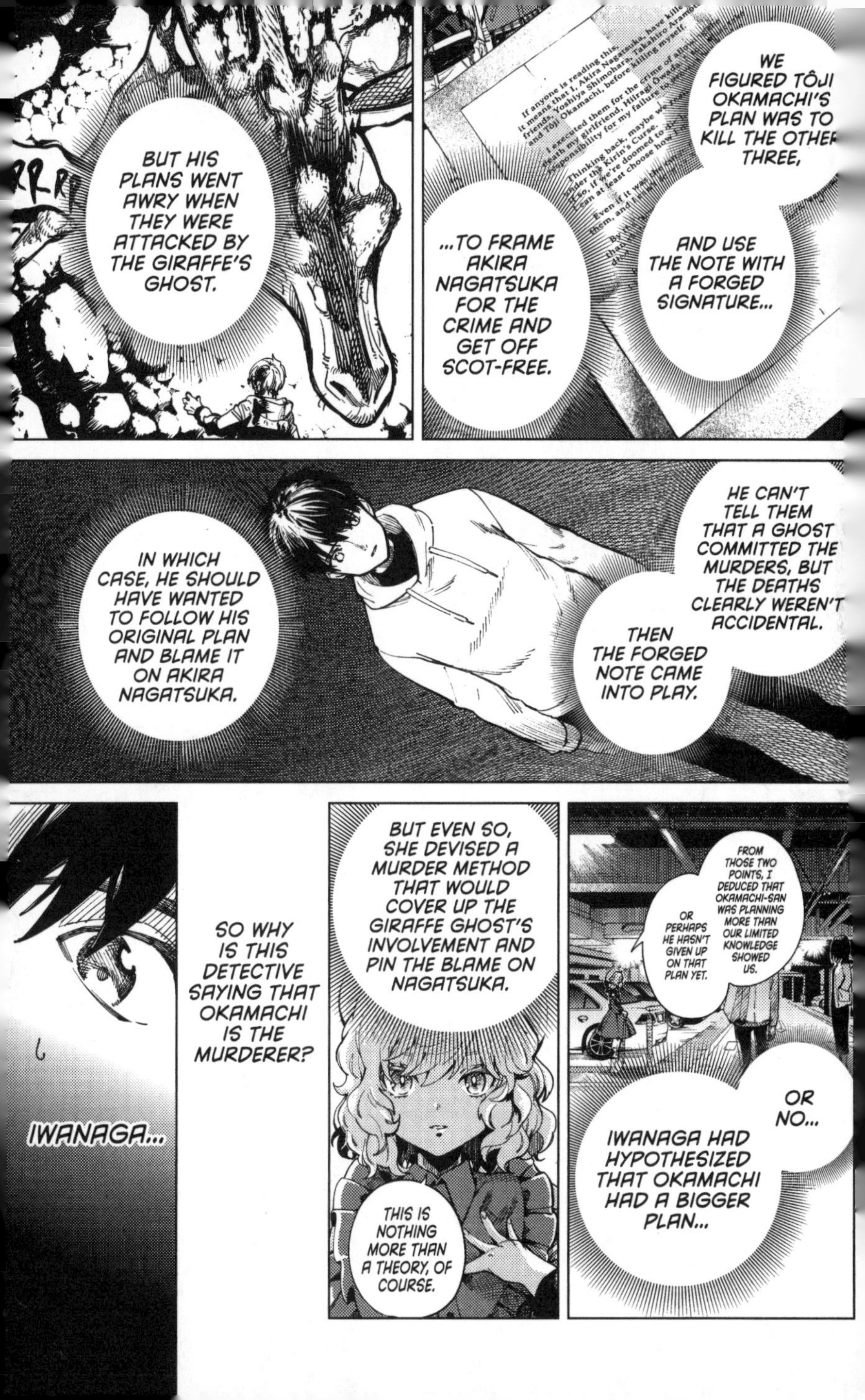
WE FIGURED TÔJI OKAMACHI'S PLAN WAS TO KILL THE OTHER THREE,
AND USE THE NOTE WITH A FORGED SIGNATURE...
...TO FRAME AKIRA NAGATSUKA FOR THE CRIME AND GET OFF SCOT-FREE.
BUT HIS PLANS WENT AWRY WHEN THEY WERE ATTACKED BY THE GIRAFFE'S GHOST.
HE CAN'T TELL THEM THAT A GHOST COMMITTED THE MURDERS, BUT THE DEATHS CLEARLY WEREN'T ACCIDENTAL.
THEN THE FORGED NOTE CAME INTO PLAY.
IN WHICH CASE, HE SHOULD HAVE WANTED TO FOLLOW HIS ORIGINAL PLAN AND BLAME IT ON AKIRA NAGATSUKA.
FROM THOSE TWO POINTS, I DEDUCED THAT OKAMACHI-SAN WAS PLANNING MORE THAN OUR LIMITED KNOWLEDGE SHOWED US.
OR PERHAPS HE HASN'T GIVEN UP ON THAT PLAN YET.
OR NO...
IWANAGA HAD HYPOTHESIZED THAT OKAMACHI HAD A BIGGER PLAN...
BUT EVEN SO, SHE DEVISED A MURDER METHOD THAT WOULD COVER UP THE GIRAFFE GHOST'S INVOLVEMENT AND PIN THE BLAME ON NAGATSUKA.
THIS IS NOTHING MORE THAN A THEORY, OF COURSE.
SO WHY IS THIS DETECTIVE SAYING THAT OKAMACHI IS THE MURDERER?
IWANAGA...

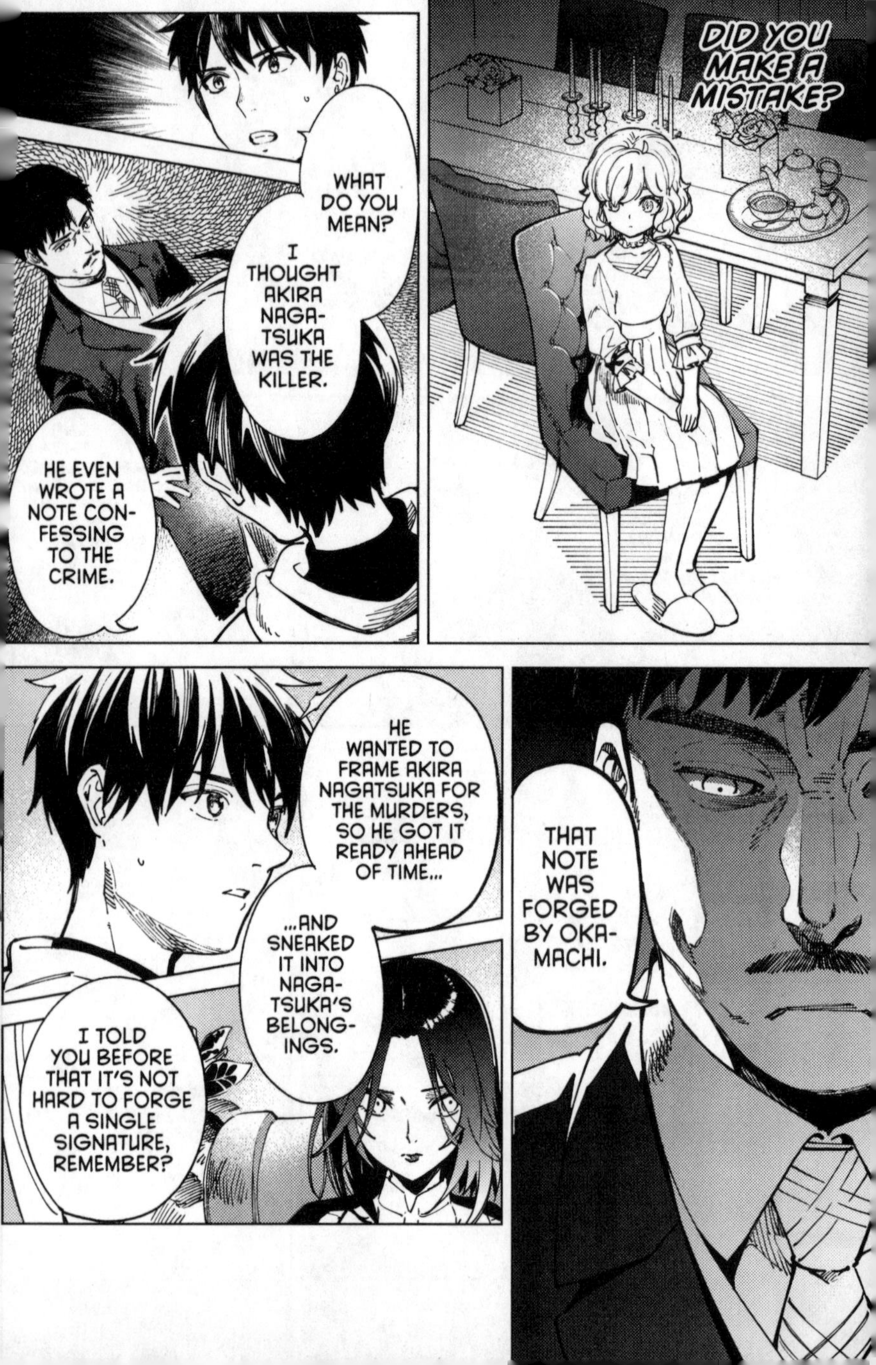
DID YOU MAKE A MISTAKE?
WHAT DO YOU MEAN?
I THOUGHT AKIRA NAGATSUKA WAS THE KILLER.
HE EVEN WROTE A NOTE CONFESSING TO THE CRIME.
THAT NOTE WAS FORGED BY OKAMACHI.
HE WANTED TO FRAME AKIRA NAGATSUKA FOR THE MURDERS, SO HE GOT IT READY AHEAD OF TIME...
...AND SNEAKED IT INTO NAGATSUKA'S BELONGINGS.
I TOLD YOU BEFORE THAT IT'S NOT HARD TO FORGE A SINGLE SIGNATURE, REMEMBER?

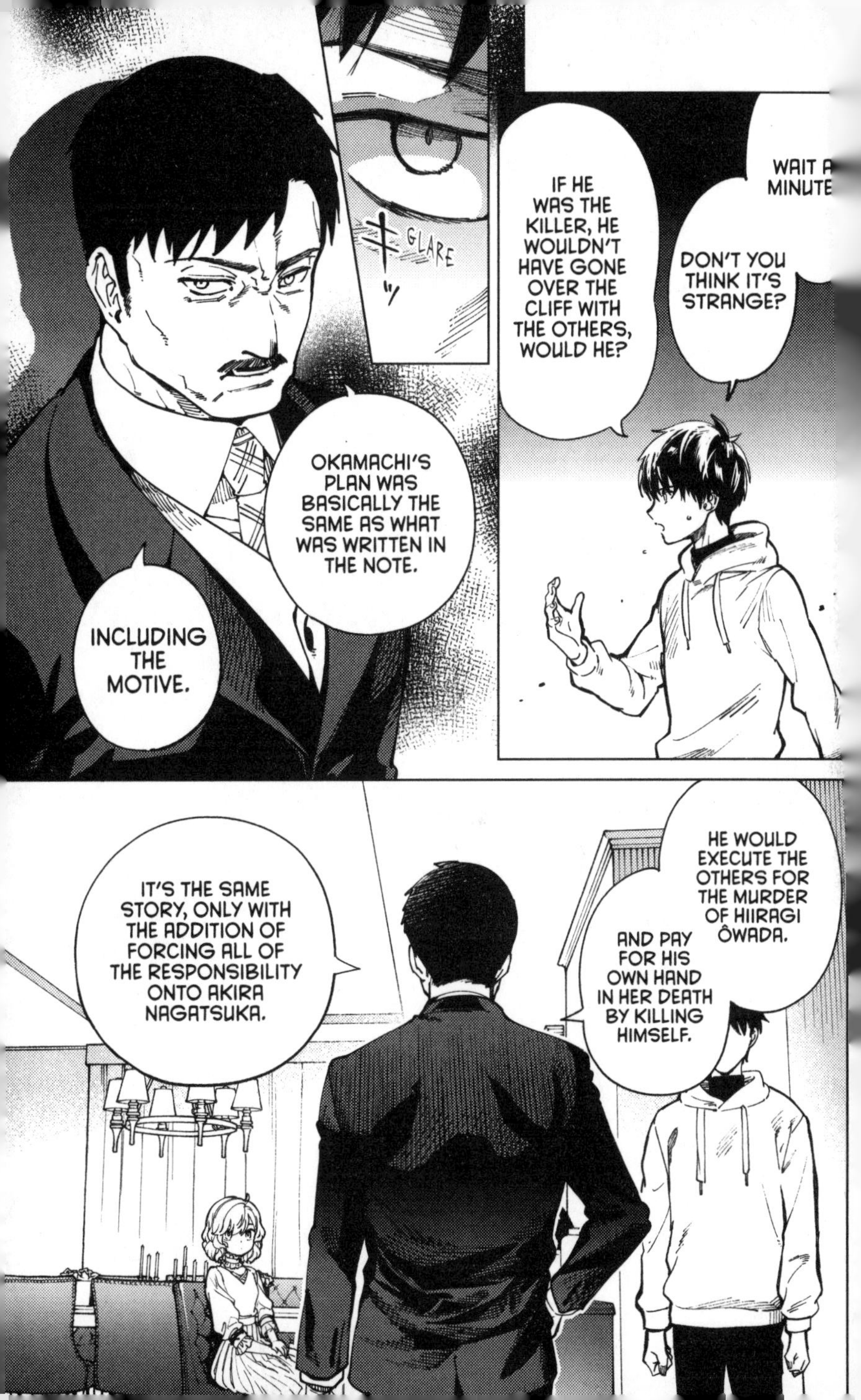
WAIT A MINUTE
DON'T YOU THINK IT'S STRANGE?
IF HE WAS THE KILLER, HE WOULDN'T HAVE GONE OVER THE CLIFF WITH THE OTHERS, WOULD HE?
GLARE
OKAMACHI'S PLAN WAS BASICALLY THE SAME AS WHAT WAS WRITTEN IN THE NOTE.
INCLUDING THE MOTIVE.
HE WOULD EXECUTE THE OTHERS FOR THE MURDER OF HIIRAGI ÔWADA.
AND PAY FOR HIS OWN HAND IN HER DEATH BY KILLING HIMSELF.
IT'S THE SAME STORY, ONLY WITH THE ADDITION OF FORCING ALL OF THE RESPONSIBILITY ONTO AKIRA NAGATSUKA.

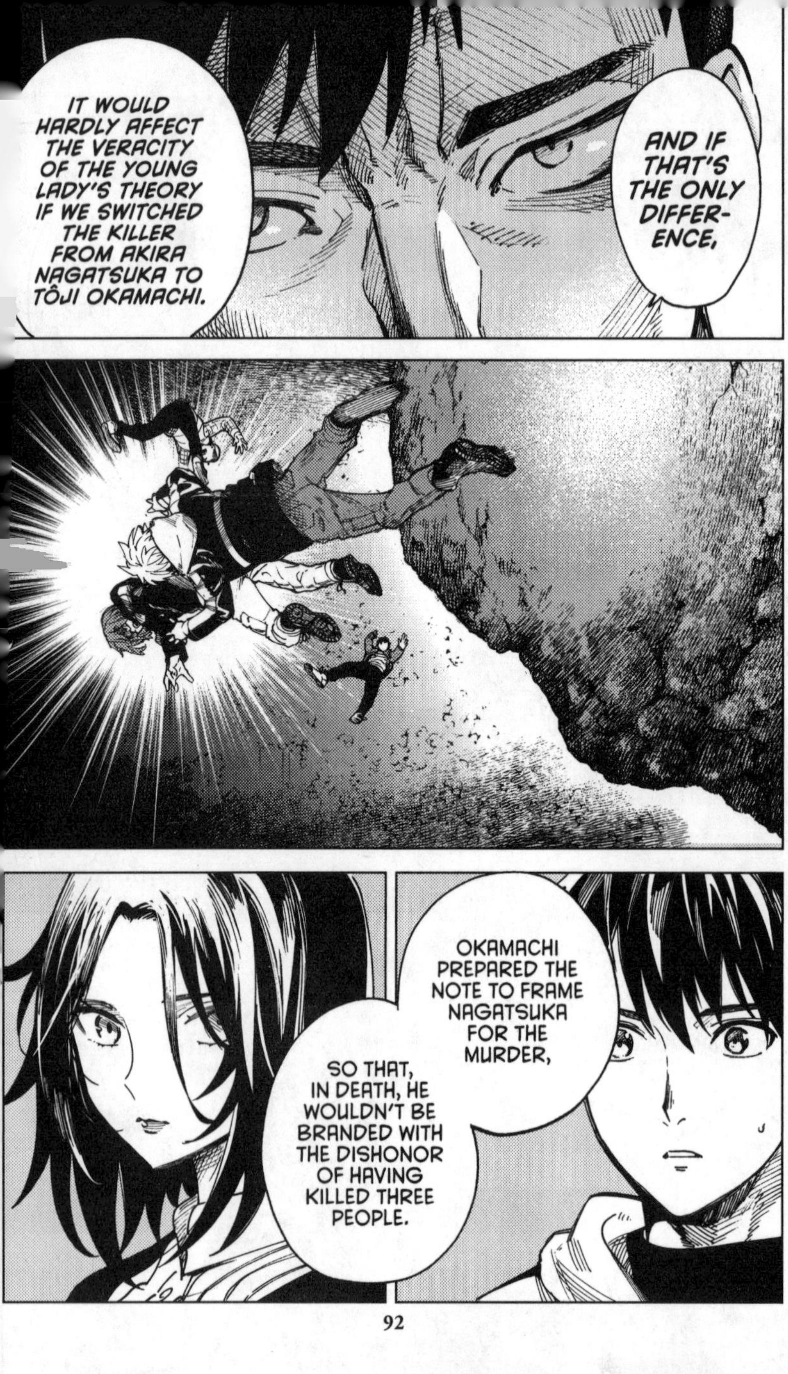
AND IF THAT'S THE ONLY DIFFER-ENCE,
IT WOULD HARDLY AFFECT THE VERACITY OF THE YOUNG LADY'S THEORY IF WE SWITCHED THE KILLER FROM AKIRA NAGATSUKA TO TÔJI OKAMACHI.
OKAMACHI PREPARED THE NOTE TO FRAME NAGATSUKA FOR THE MURDER,
SO THAT, IN DEATH, HE WOULDN'T BE BRANDED WITH THE DISHONOR OF HAVING KILLED THREE PEOPLE.

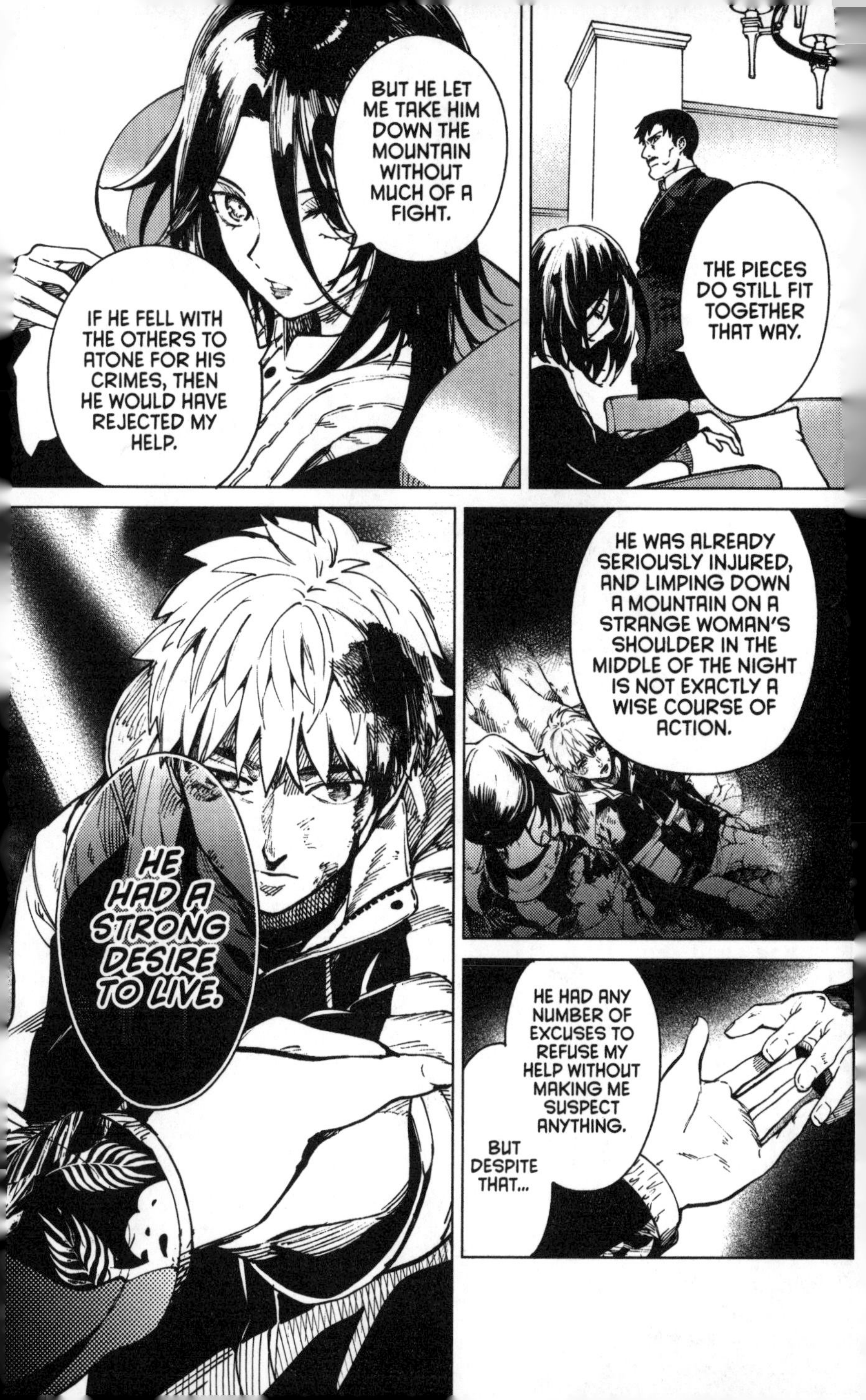
THE PIECES DO STILL FIT TOGETHER THAT WAY.
BUT HE LET ME TAKE HIM DOWN THE MOUNTAIN WITHOUT MUCH OF A FIGHT.
IF HE FELL WITH THE OTHERS TO ATONE FOR HIS CRIMES, THEN HE WOULD HAVE REJECTED MY HELP.
HE WAS ALREADY SERIOUSLY INJURED, AND LIMPING DOWN A MOUNTAIN ON A STRANGE WOMAN'S SHOULDER IN THE MIDDLE OF THE NIGHT IS NOT EXACTLY A WISE COURSE OF ACTION.
HE HAD ANY NUMBER OF EXCUSES TO REFUSE MY HELP WITHOUT MAKING ME SUSPECT ANYTHING.
BUT DESPITE THAT...
HE HAD A STRONG DESIRE TO LIVE.

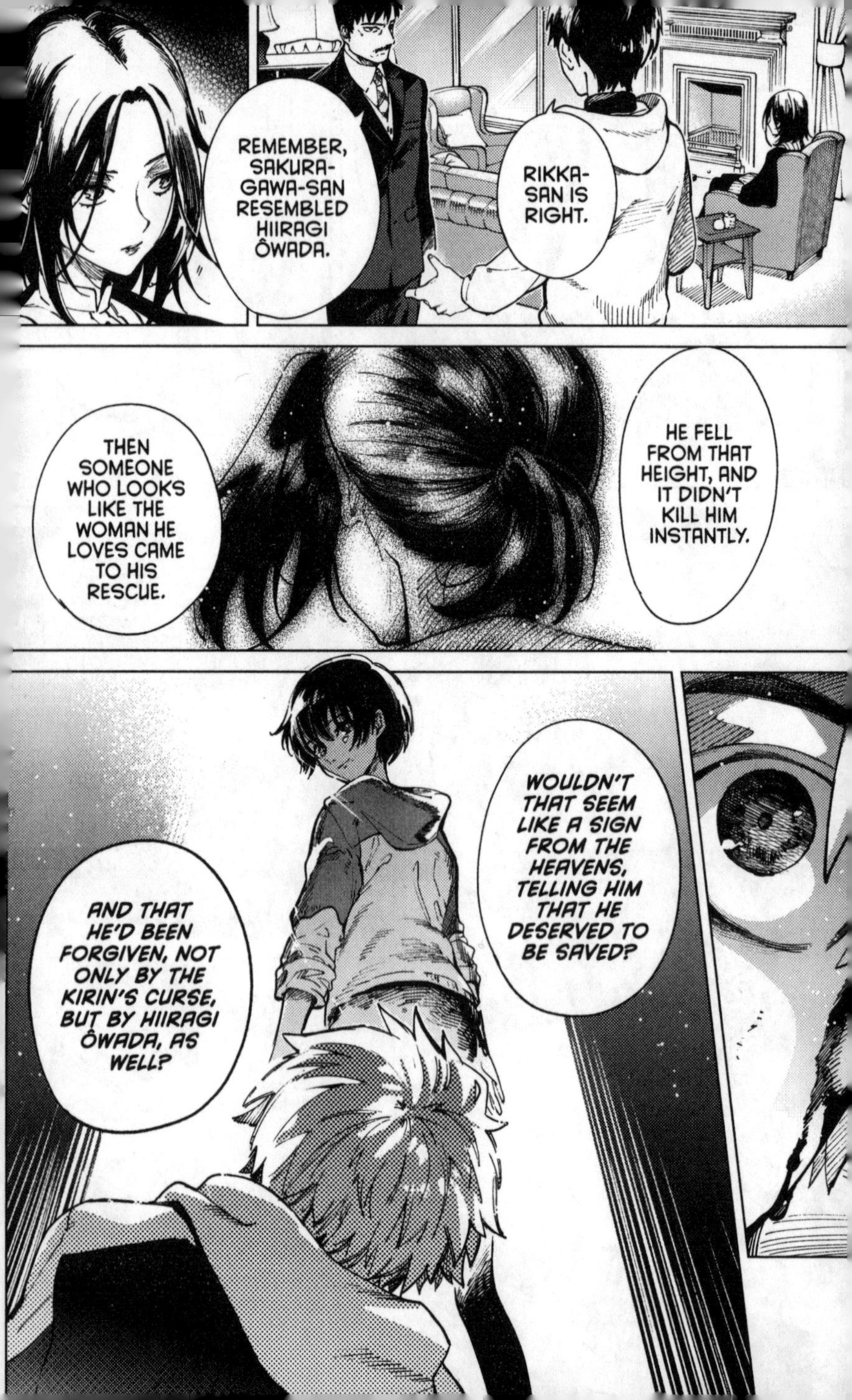
RIKKA-SAN IS RIGHT.
REMEMBER, SAKURA-GAWA-SAN RESEMBLED HIIRAGI ÔWADA.
HE FELL FROM THAT HEIGHT, AND IT DIDN'T KILL HIM INSTANTLY.
THEN SOMEONE WHO LOOKS LIKE THE WOMAN HE LOVES CAME TO HIS RESCUE.
WOULDN'T THAT SEEM LIKE A SIGN FROM THE HEAVENS, TELLING HIM THAT HE DESERVED TO BE SAVED?
AND THAT HE'D BEEN FORGIVEN, NOT ONLY BY THE KIRIN'S CURSE, BUT BY HIIRAGI ÔWADA, AS WELL?

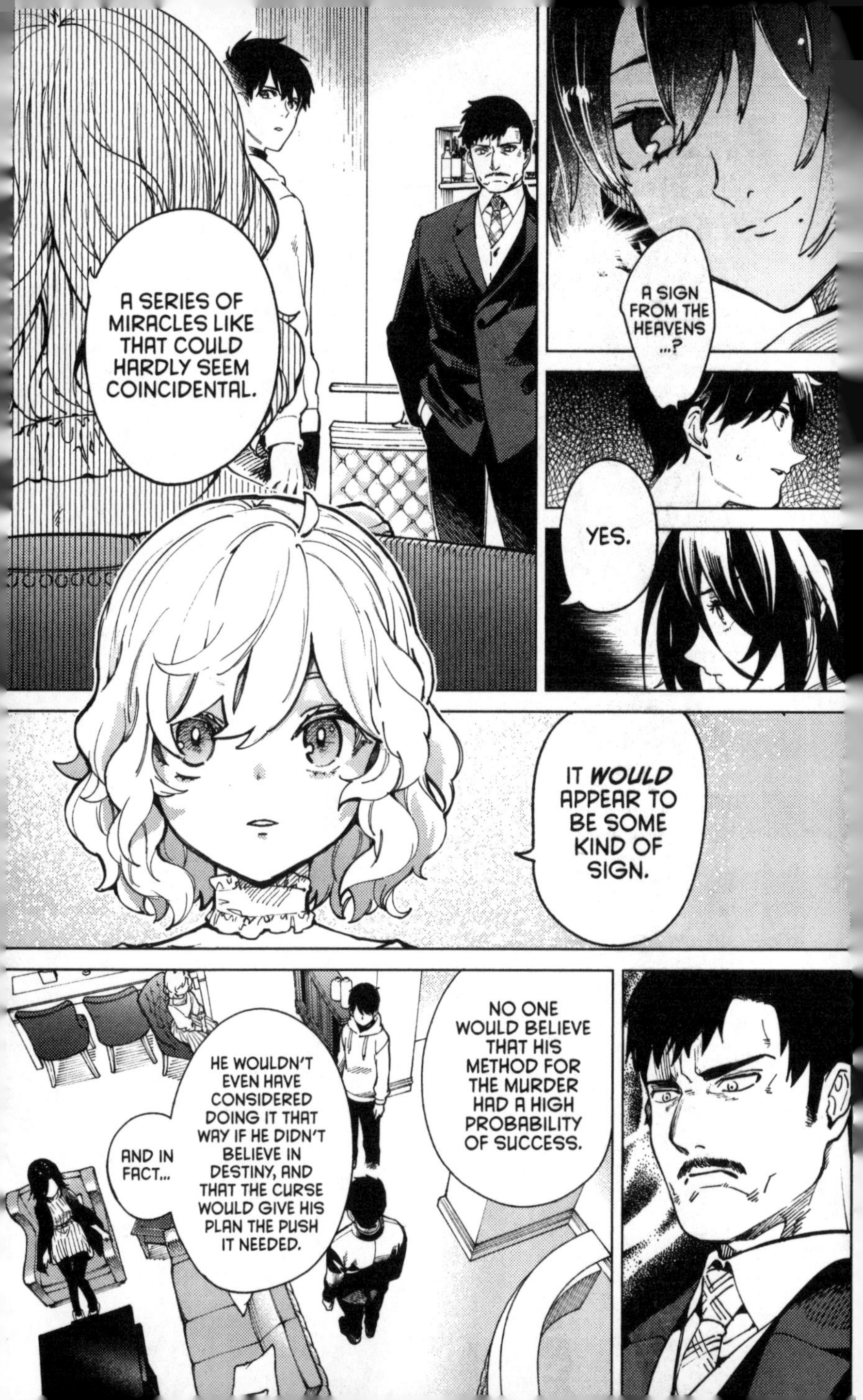
A SERIES OF MIRACLES LIKE THAT COULD HARDLY SEEM COINCIDENTAL.
IT *WOULD* APPEAR TO BE SOME KIND OF SIGN.
A SIGN FROM THE HEAVENS ...?
YES.
NO ONE WOULD BELIEVE THAT HIS METHOD FOR THE MURDER HAD A HIGH PROBABILITY OF SUCCESS.
AND IN FACT...
HE WOULDN'T EVEN HAVE CONSIDERED DOING IT THAT WAY IF HE DIDN'T BELIEVE IN DESTINY, AND THAT THE CURSE WOULD GIVE HIS PLAN THE PUSH IT NEEDED.

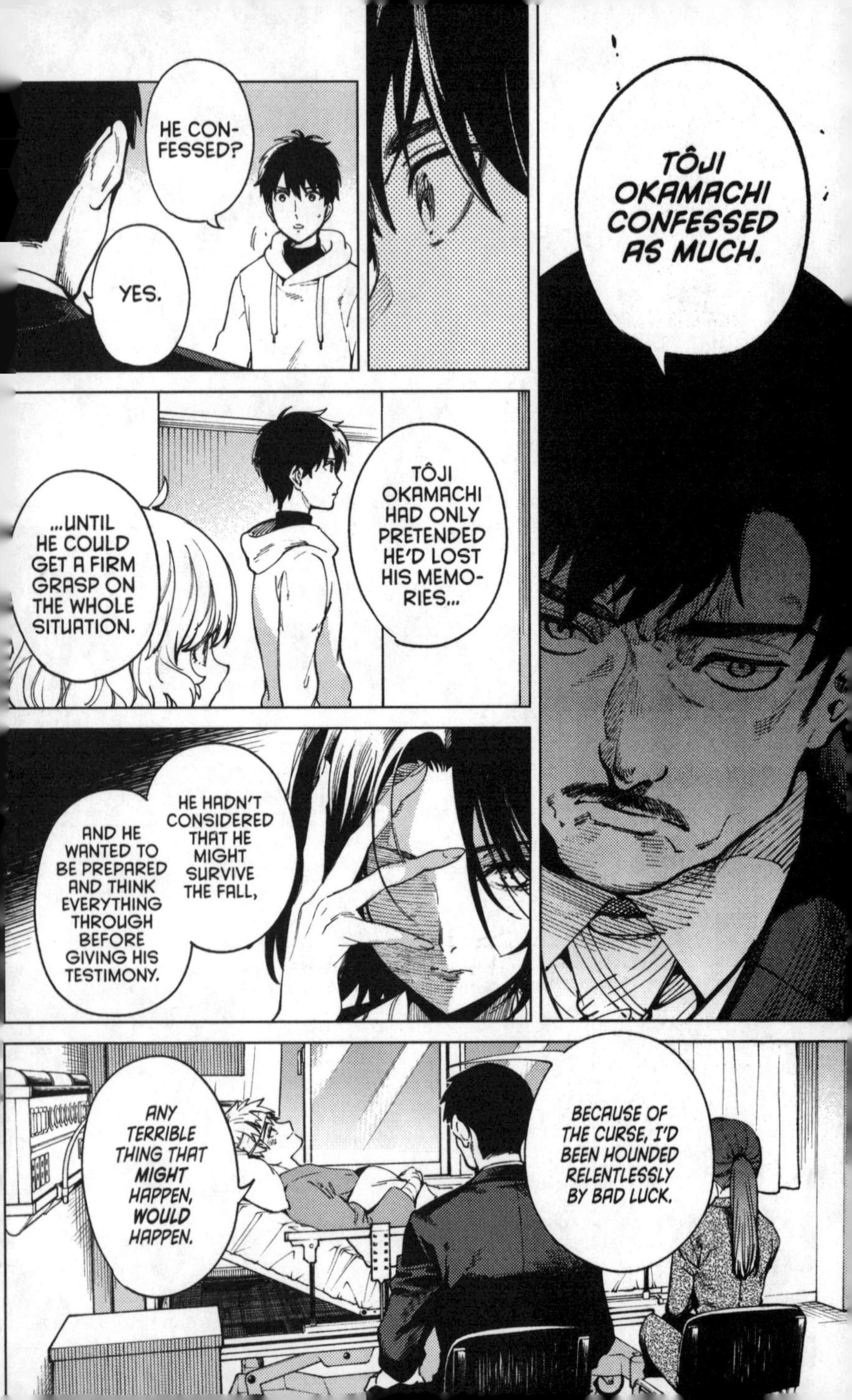
TÔJI OKAMACHI CONFESSED AS MUCH.
HE CON-FESSED?
YES.
TÔJI OKAMACHI HAD ONLY PRETENDED HE'D LOST HIS MEMO-RIES...
...UNTIL HE COULD GET A FIRM GRASP ON THE WHOLE SITUATION.
HE HADN'T CONSIDERED THAT HE MIGHT SURVIVE THE FALL,
AND HE WANTED TO BE PREPARED AND THINK EVERYTHING THROUGH BEFORE GIVING HIS TESTIMONY.
BECAUSE OF THE CURSE, I'D BEEN HOUNDED RELENTLESSLY BY BAD LUCK.
ANY TERRIBLE THING THAT MIGHT HAPPEN, WOULD HAPPEN.

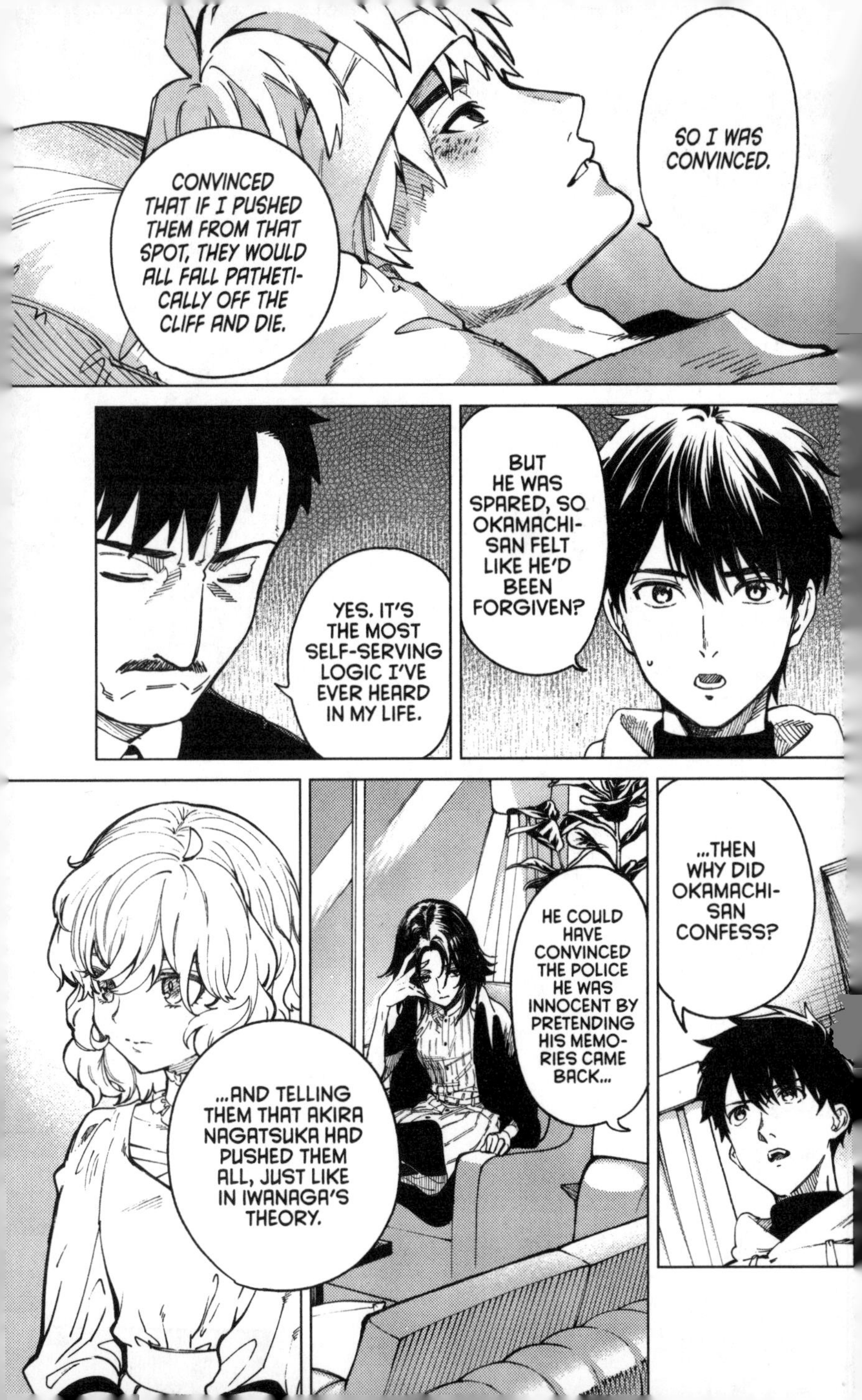
SO I WAS CONVINCED.
CONVINCED THAT IF I PUSHED THEM FROM THAT SPOT, THEY WOULD ALL FALL PATHETICALLY OFF THE CLIFF AND DIE.
BUT HE WAS SPARED, SO OKAMACHI-SAN FELT LIKE HE'D BEEN FORGIVEN?
YES. IT'S THE MOST SELF-SERVING LOGIC I'VE EVER HEARD IN MY LIFE.
...THEN WHY DID OKAMACHI-SAN CONFESS?
HE COULD HAVE CONVINCED THE POLICE HE WAS INNOCENT BY PRETENDING HIS MEMORIES CAME BACK...
...AND TELLING THEM THAT AKIRA NAGATSUKA HAD PUSHED THEM ALL, JUST LIKE IN IWANAGA'S THEORY.

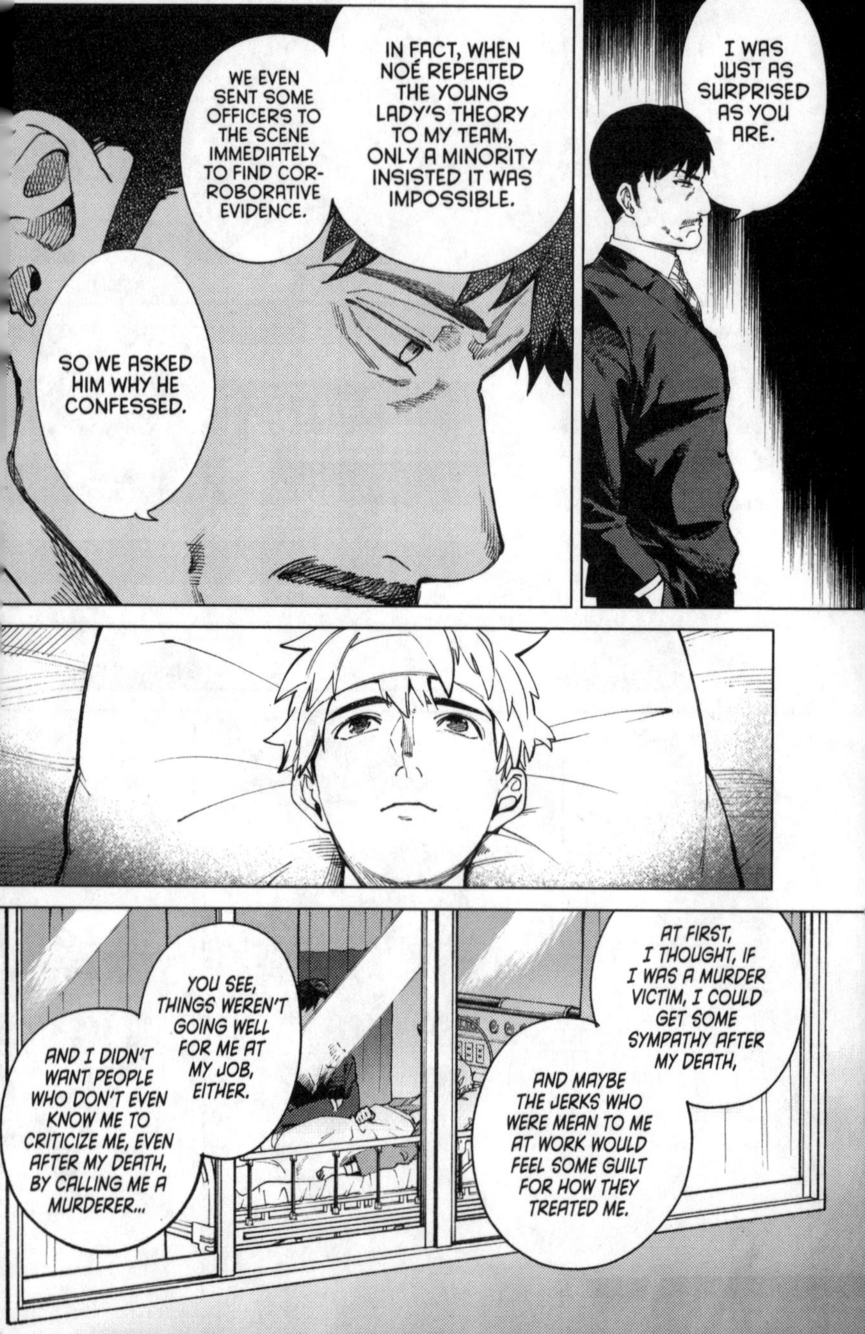
I WAS JUST AS SURPRISED AS YOU ARE.
IN FACT, WHEN NOÉ REPEATED THE YOUNG LADY'S THEORY TO MY TEAM, ONLY A MINORITY INSISTED IT WAS IMPOSSIBLE.
WE EVEN SENT SOME OFFICERS TO THE SCENE IMMEDIATELY TO FIND COR-ROBORATIVE EVIDENCE.
SO WE ASKED HIM WHY HE CONFESSED.
AT FIRST, I THOUGHT, IF I WAS A MURDER VICTIM, I COULD GET SOME SYMPATHY AFTER MY DEATH,
AND MAYBE THE JERKS WHO WERE MEAN TO ME AT WORK WOULD FEEL SOME GUILT FOR HOW THEY TREATED ME.
YOU SEE, THINGS WEREN'T GOING WELL FOR ME AT MY JOB, EITHER.
AND I DIDN'T WANT PEOPLE WHO DON'T EVEN KNOW ME TO CRITICIZE ME, EVEN AFTER MY DEATH, BY CALLING ME A MURDERER...

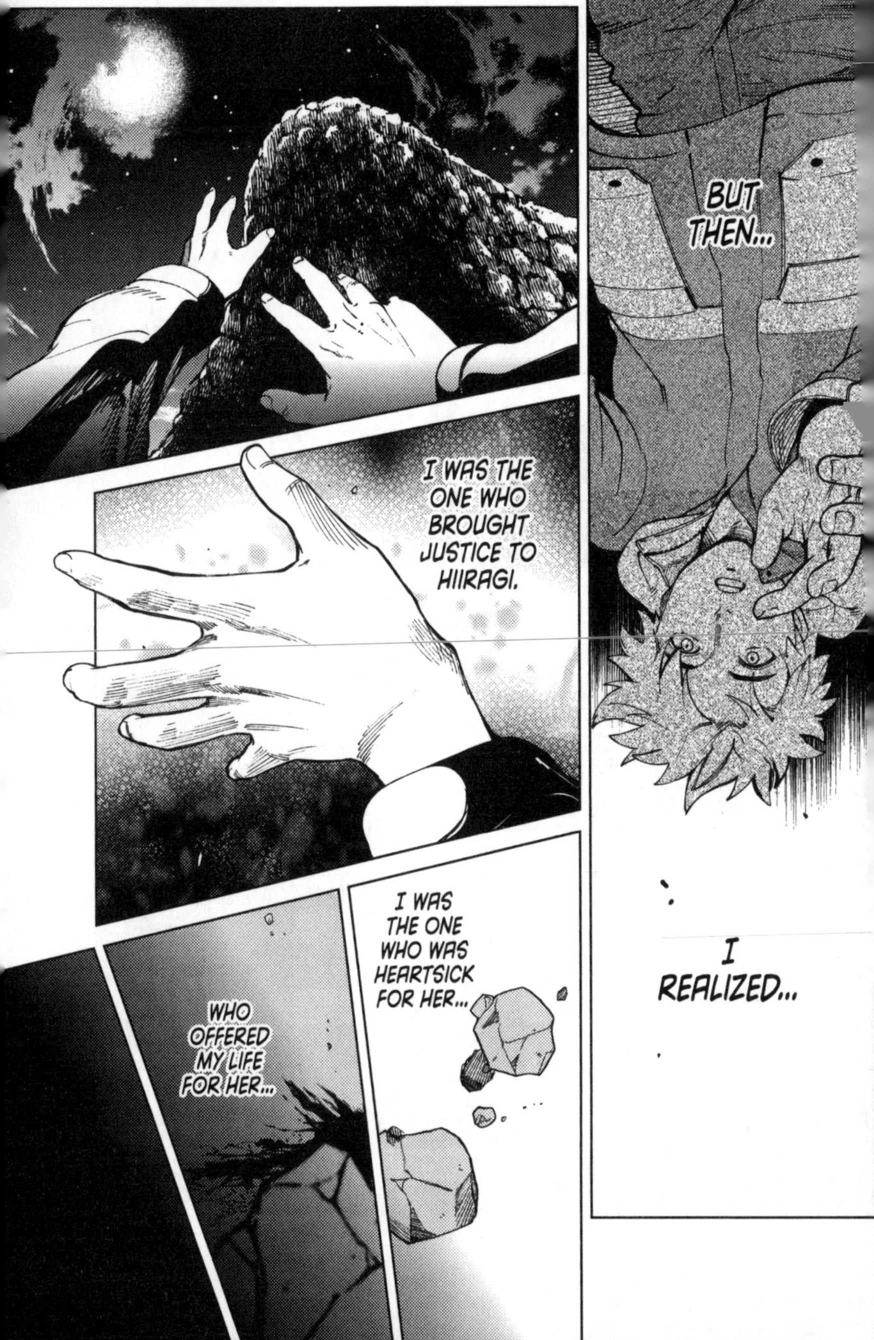
BUT THEN...
I REALIZED...
I WAS THE ONE WHO BROUGHT JUSTICE TO HIIRAGI.
I WAS THE ONE WHO WAS HEARTSICK FOR HER...
WHO OFFERED MY LIFE FOR HER...

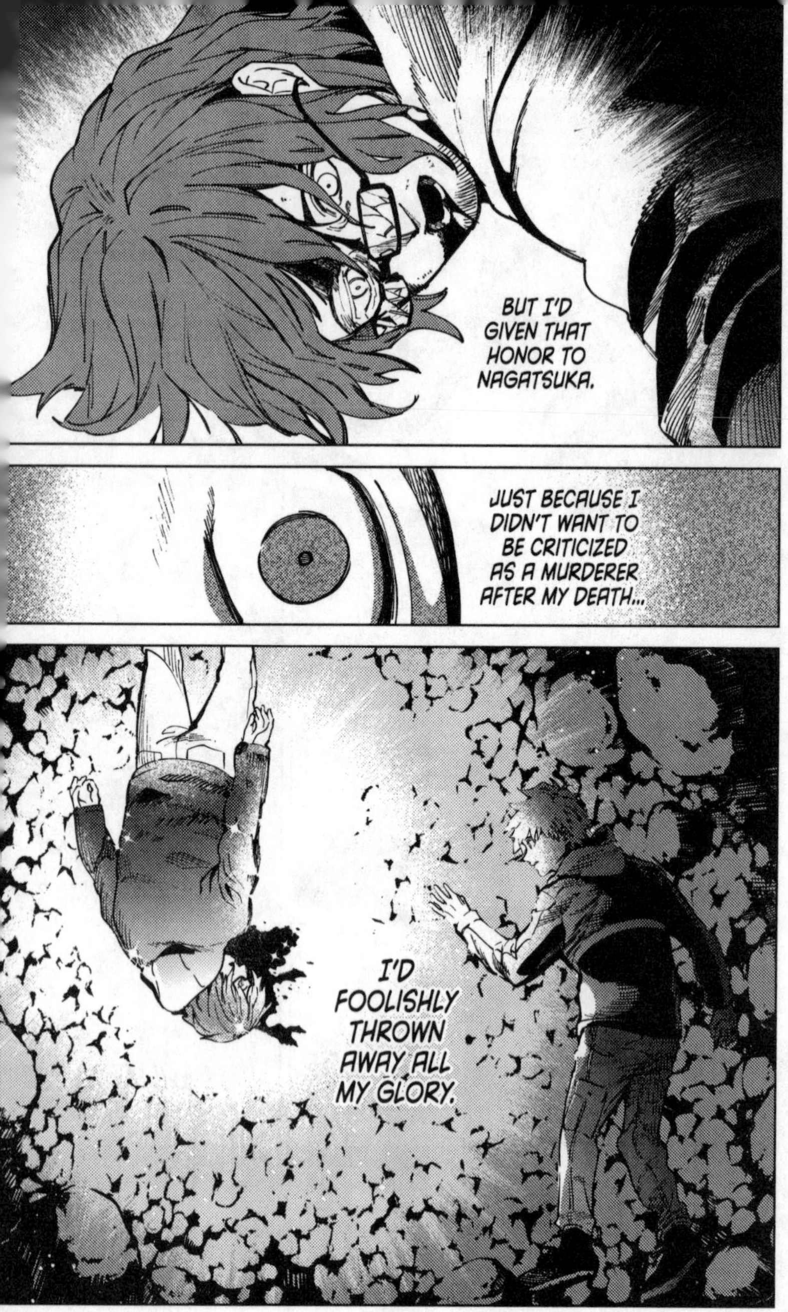
BUT I'D GIVEN THAT HONOR TO NAGATSUKA.
JUST BECAUSE I DIDN'T WANT TO BE CRITICIZED AS A MURDERER AFTER MY DEATH...
I'D FOOLISHLY THROWN AWAY ALL MY GLORY.

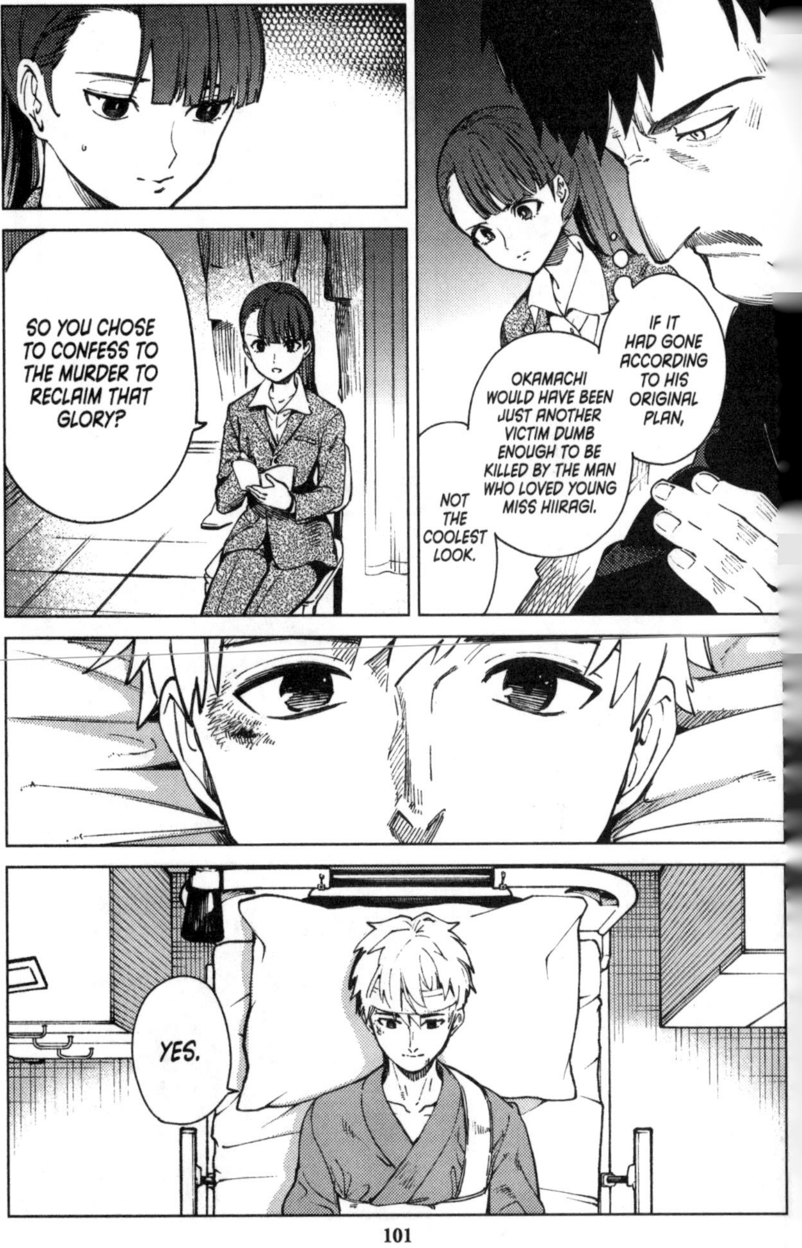
IF IT HAD GONE ACCORDING TO HIS ORIGINAL PLAN,
OKAMACHI WOULD HAVE BEEN JUST ANOTHER VICTIM DUMB ENOUGH TO BE KILLED BY THE MAN WHO LOVED YOUNG MISS HIIRAGI.
NOT THE COOLEST LOOK.
SO YOU CHOSE TO CONFESS TO THE MURDER TO RECLAIM THAT GLORY?
YES.

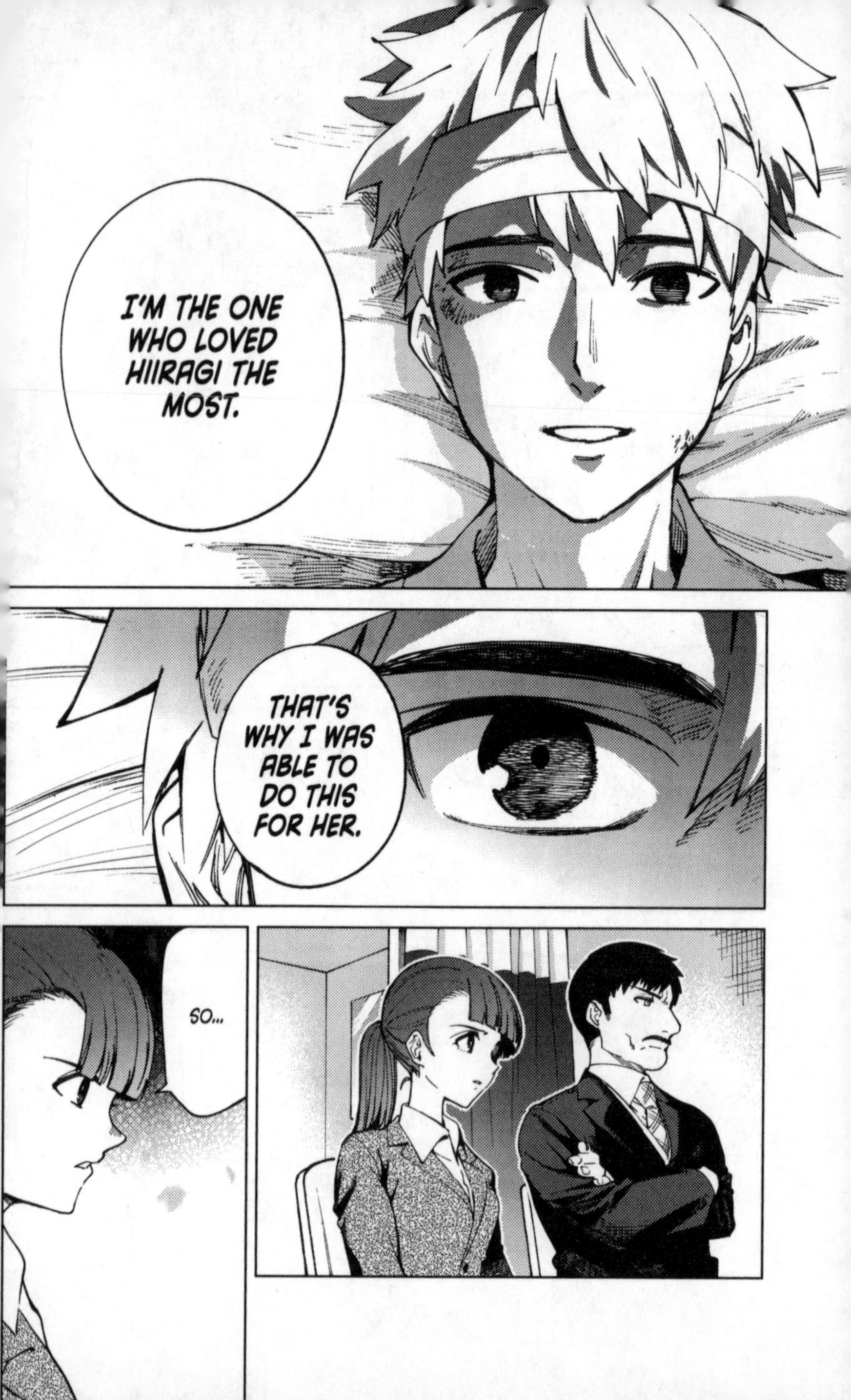
I'M THE ONE WHO LOVED HIIRAGI THE MOST.
THAT'S WHY I WAS ABLE TO DO THIS FOR HER.
SO...

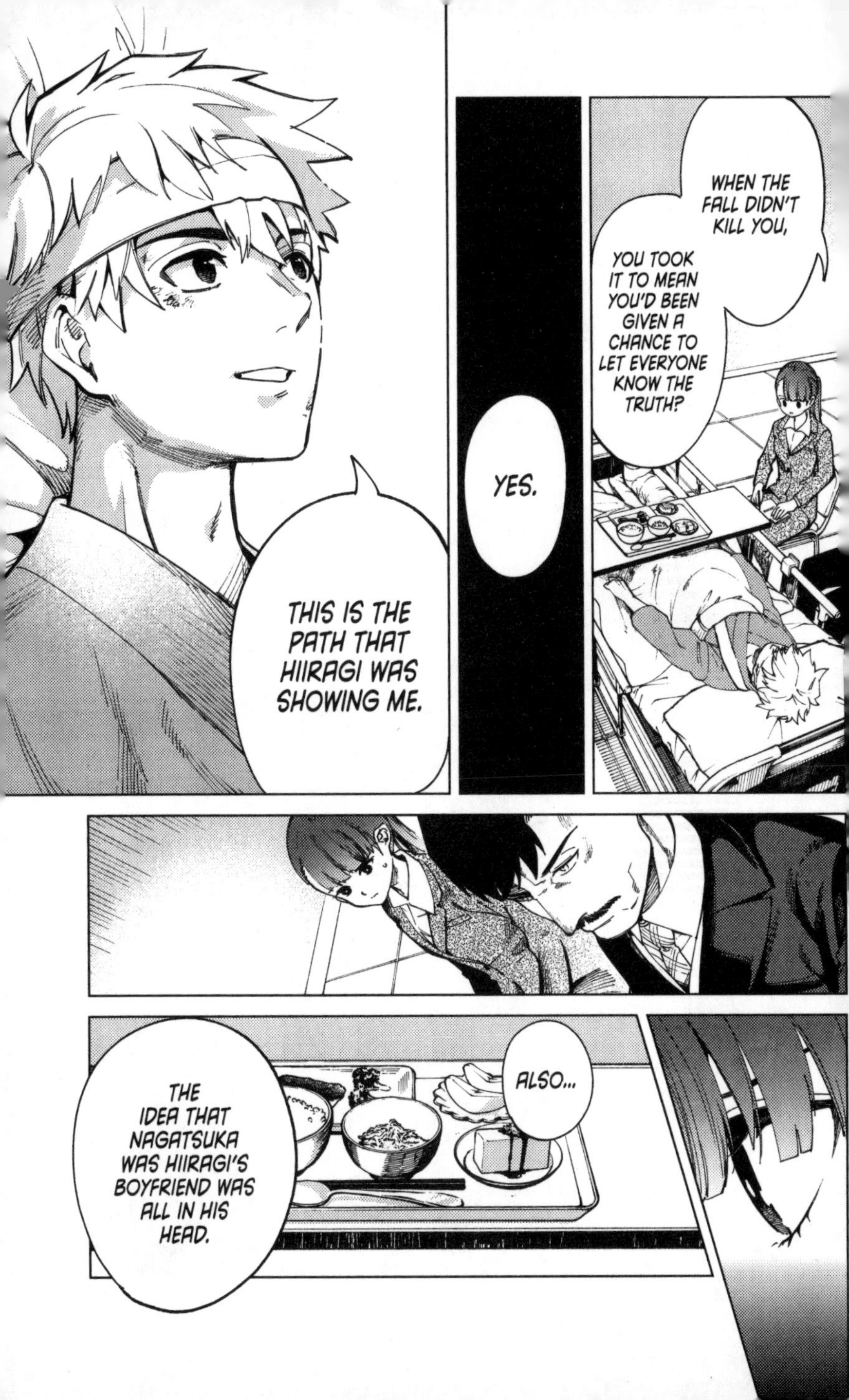
WHEN THE FALL DIDN'T KILL YOU,
YOU TOOK IT TO MEAN YOU'D BEEN GIVEN A CHANCE TO LET EVERYONE KNOW THE TRUTH?
YES.
THIS IS THE PATH THAT HIIRAGI WAS SHOWING ME.
ALSO...
THE IDEA THAT NAGATSUKA WAS HIIRAGI'S BOYFRIEND WAS ALL IN HIS HEAD.

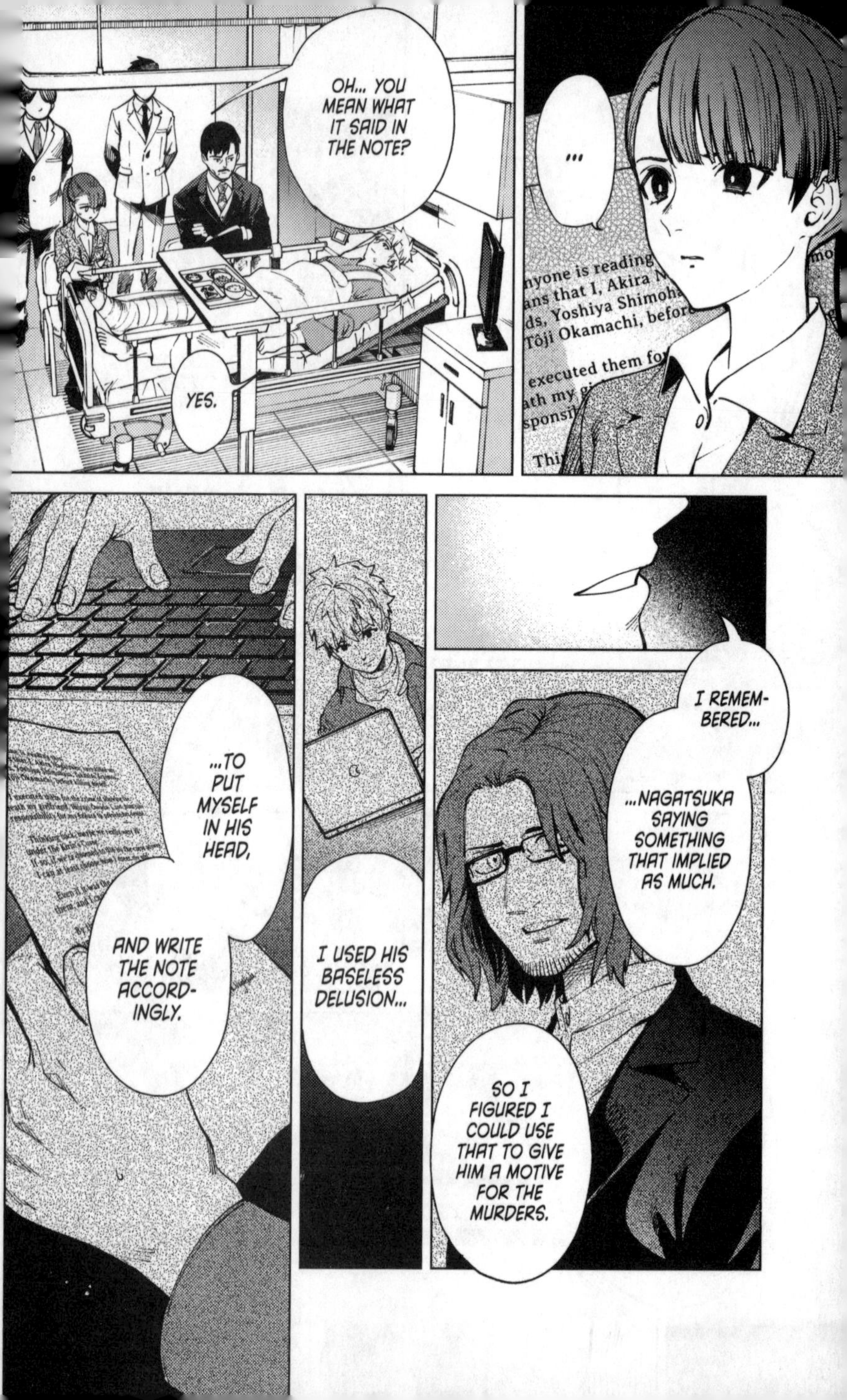
...
nyone is reading
ans that I, Akira N
ds, Yoshiya Shimoha
Tôji Okamachi, befor
executed them fo
ath my g
sponsi
Thi
OH... YOU MEAN WHAT IT SAID IN THE NOTE?
YES.
I REMEMBERED...
...NAGATSUKA SAYING SOMETHING THAT IMPLIED AS MUCH.
SO I FIGURED I COULD USE THAT TO GIVE HIM A MOTIVE FOR THE MURDERS.
I USED HIS BASELESS DELUSION...
...TO PUT MYSELF IN HIS HEAD,
AND WRITE THE NOTE ACCORDINGLY.

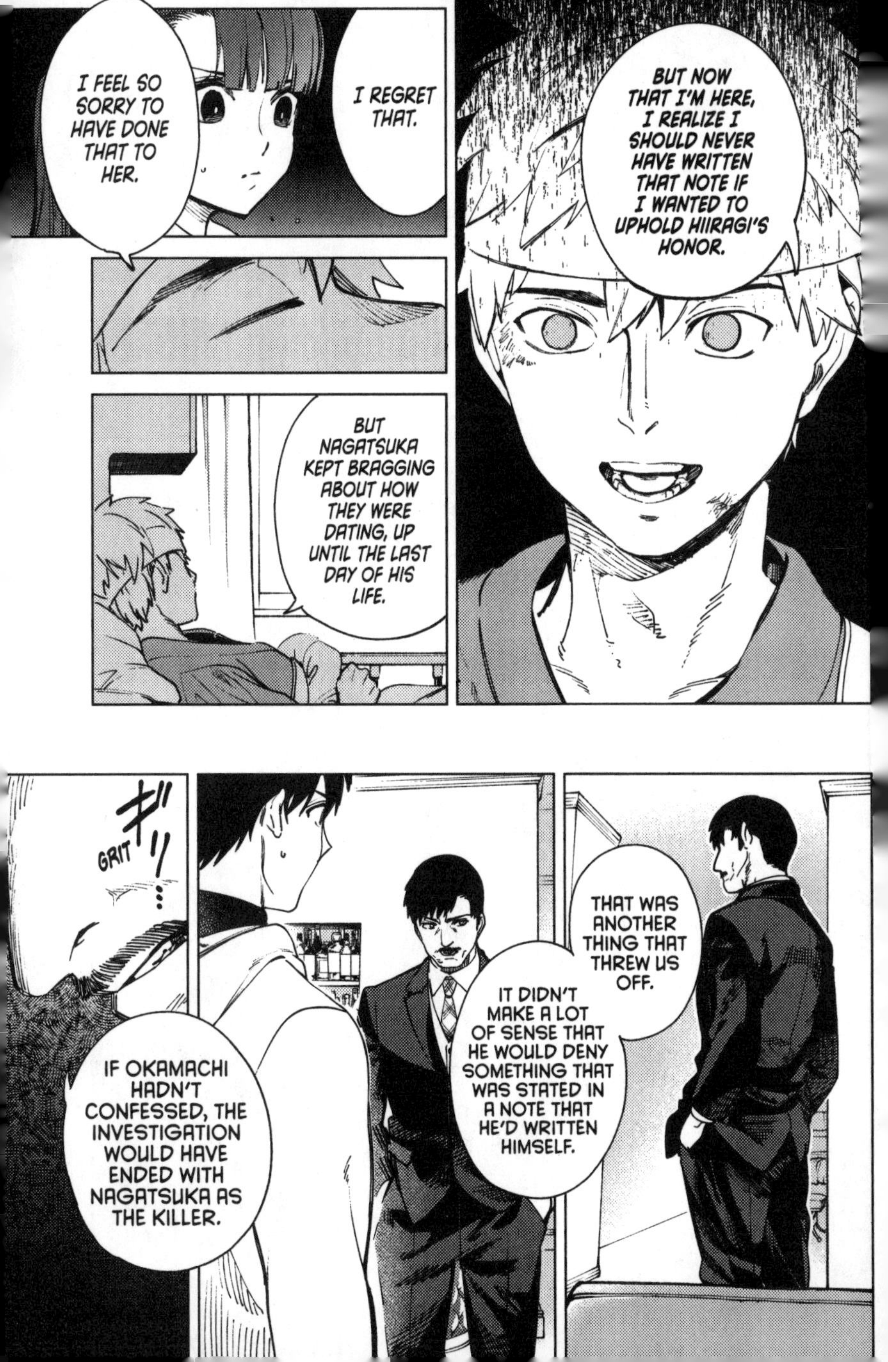
BUT NOW THAT I'M HERE, I REALIZE I SHOULD NEVER HAVE WRITTEN THAT NOTE IF I WANTED TO UPHOLD HIIRAGI'S HONOR.
I REGRET THAT.
I FEEL SO SORRY TO HAVE DONE THAT TO HER.
BUT NAGATSUKA KEPT BRAGGING ABOUT HOW THEY WERE DATING, UP UNTIL THE LAST DAY OF HIS LIFE.
THAT WAS ANOTHER THING THAT THREW US OFF.
IT DIDN'T MAKE A LOT OF SENSE THAT HE WOULD DENY SOMETHING THAT WAS STATED IN A NOTE THAT HE'D WRITTEN HIMSELF.
IF OKAMACHI HADN'T CONFESSED, THE INVESTIGATION WOULD HAVE ENDED WITH NAGATSUKA AS THE KILLER.
ギリ
GRIT
...

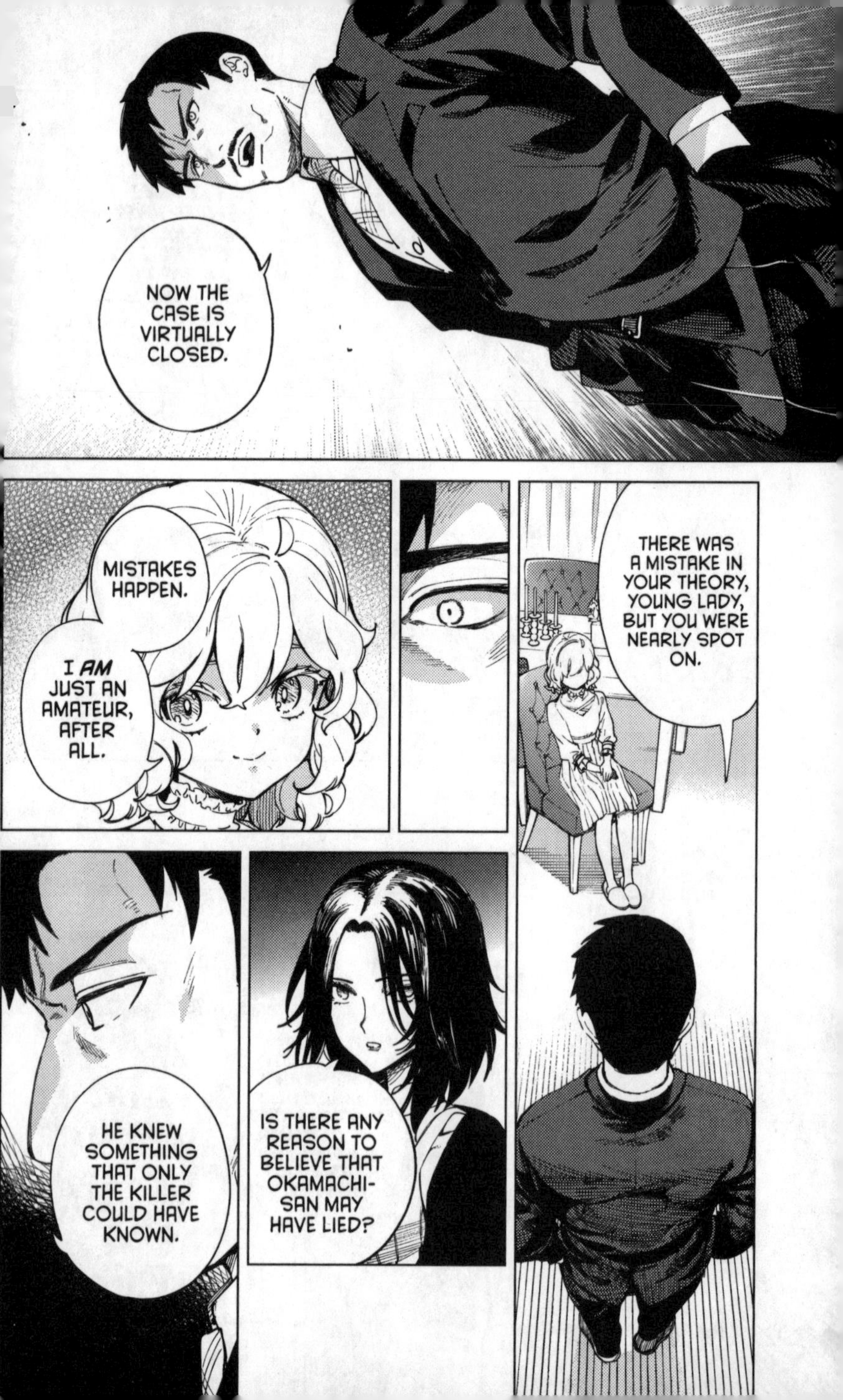
NOW THE CASE IS VIRTUALLY CLOSED.
THERE WAS A MISTAKE IN YOUR THEORY, YOUNG LADY, BUT YOU WERE NEARLY SPOT ON.
MISTAKES HAPPEN.
I *AM* JUST AN AMATEUR, AFTER ALL.
IS THERE ANY REASON TO BELIEVE THAT OKAMACHI-SAN MAY HAVE LIED?
HE KNEW SOMETHING THAT ONLY THE KILLER COULD HAVE KNOWN.

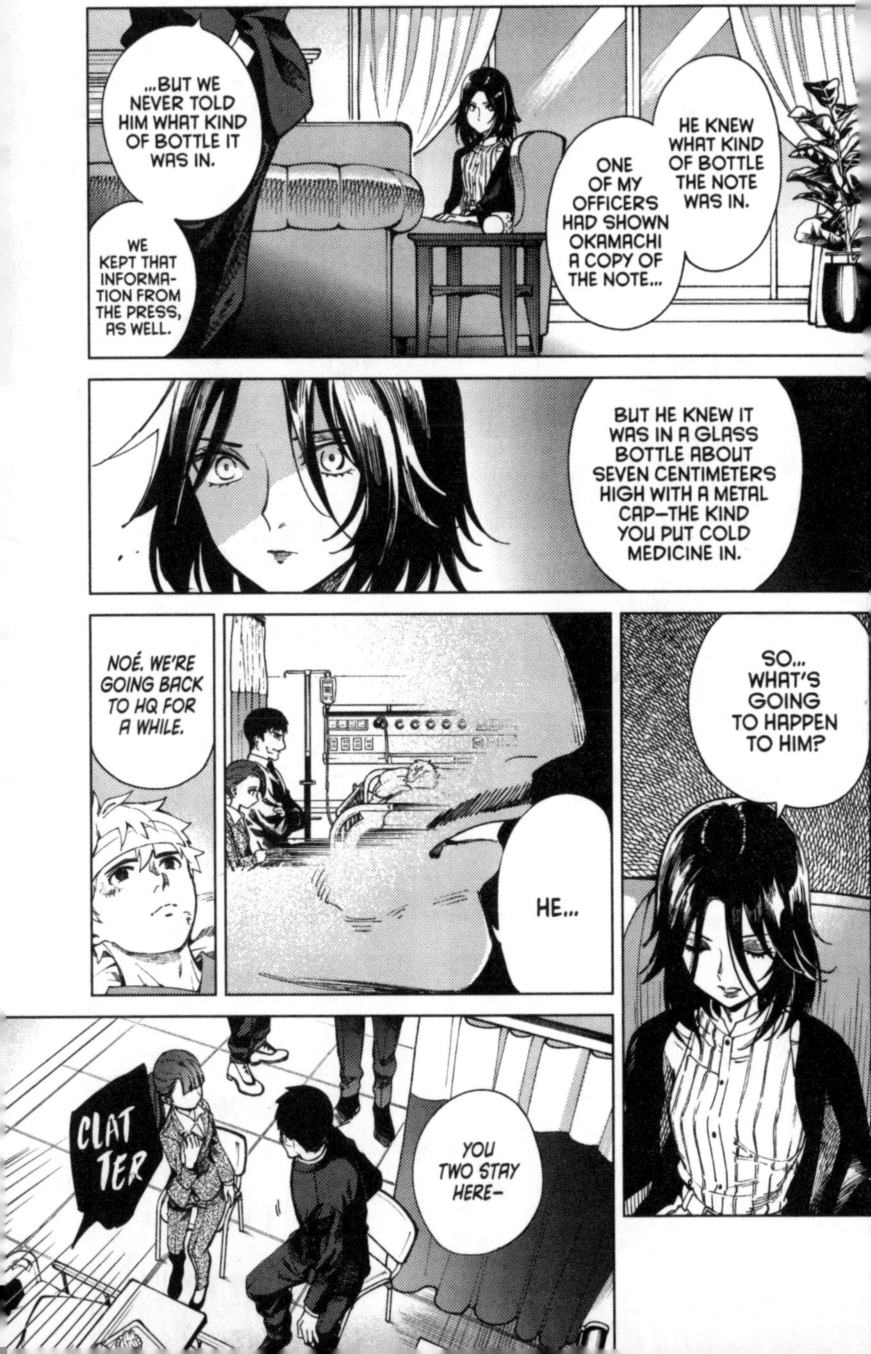
HE KNEW WHAT KIND OF BOTTLE THE NOTE WAS IN.
ONE OF MY OFFICERS HAD SHOWN OKAMACHI A COPY OF THE NOTE...
...BUT WE NEVER TOLD HIM WHAT KIND OF BOTTLE IT WAS IN.
WE KEPT THAT INFORMATION FROM THE PRESS, AS WELL.
BUT HE KNEW IT WAS IN A GLASS BOTTLE ABOUT SEVEN CENTIMETERS HIGH WITH A METAL CAP—THE KIND YOU PUT COLD MEDICINE IN.
SO... WHAT'S GOING TO HAPPEN TO HIM?
HE...
NOÉ. WE'RE GOING BACK TO HQ FOR A WHILE.
YOU TWO STAY HERE-
CLATTER

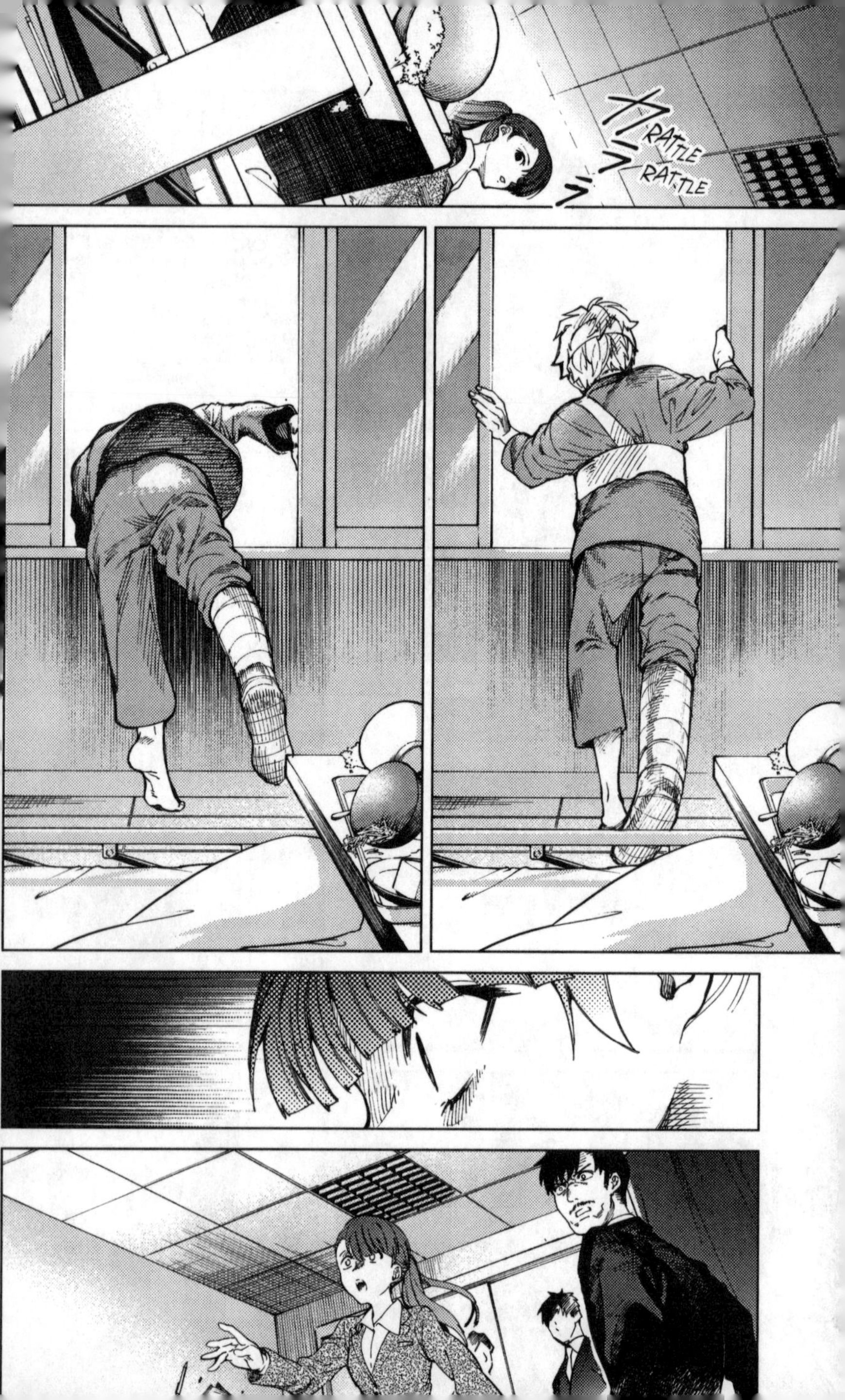
カラララ
RATTLE
RATTLE

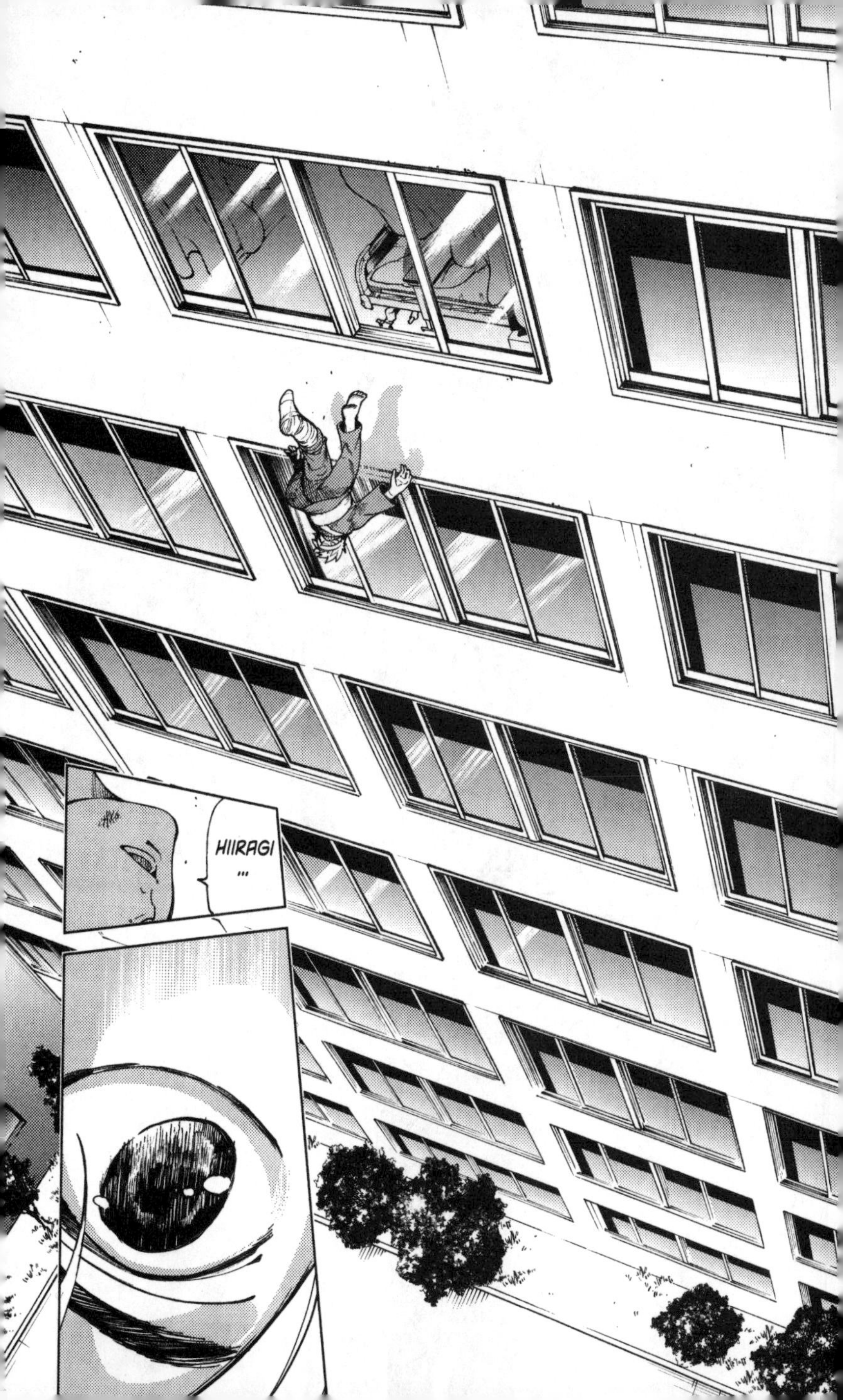
HIIRAGI
...

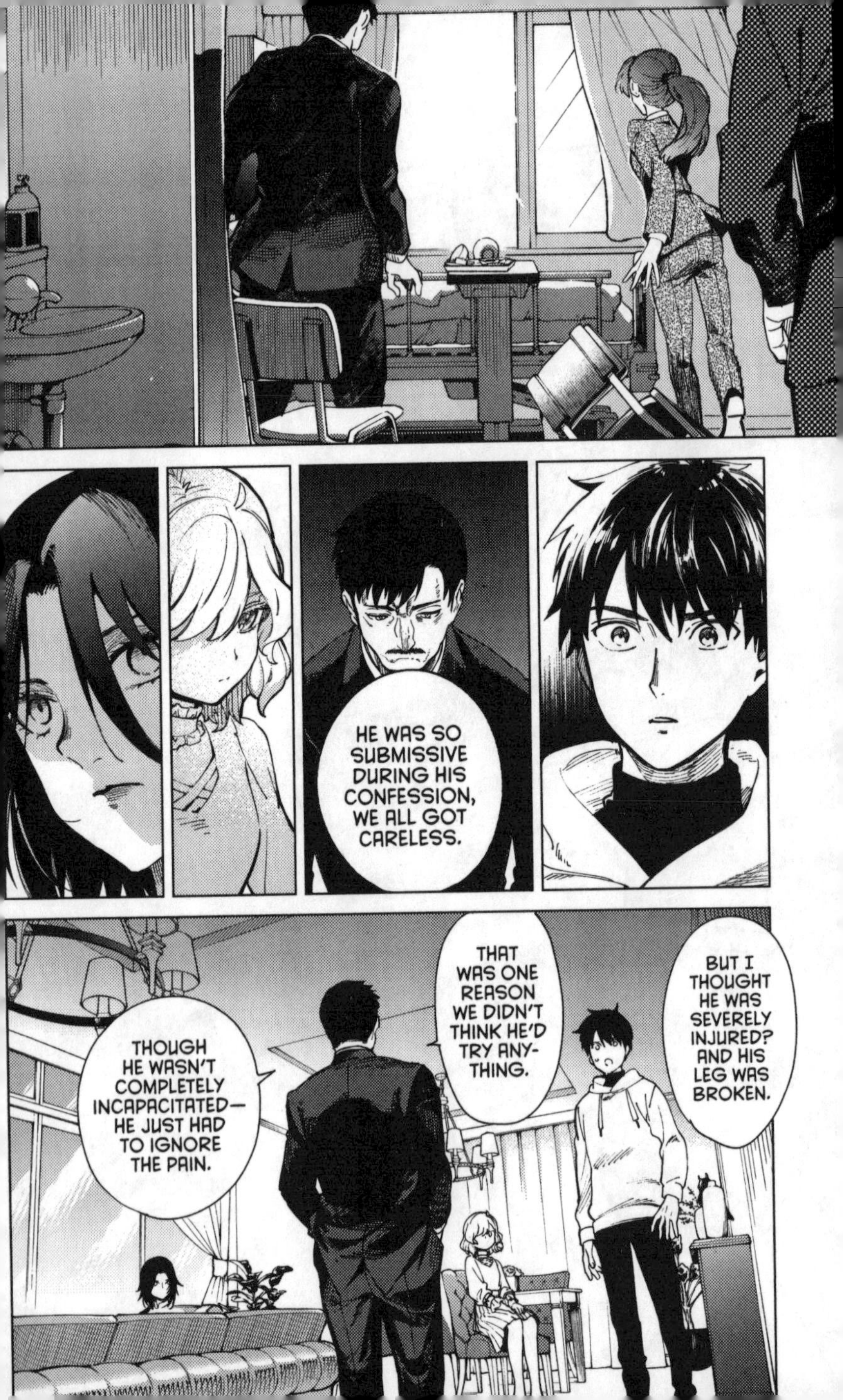
HE WAS SO SUBMISSIVE DURING HIS CONFESSION, WE ALL GOT CARELESS.
BUT I THOUGHT HE WAS SEVERELY INJURED? AND HIS LEG WAS BROKEN.
THAT WAS ONE REASON WE DIDN'T THINK HE'D TRY ANY-THING.
THOUGH HE WASN'T COMPLETELY INCAPACITATED— HE JUST HAD TO IGNORE THE PAIN.

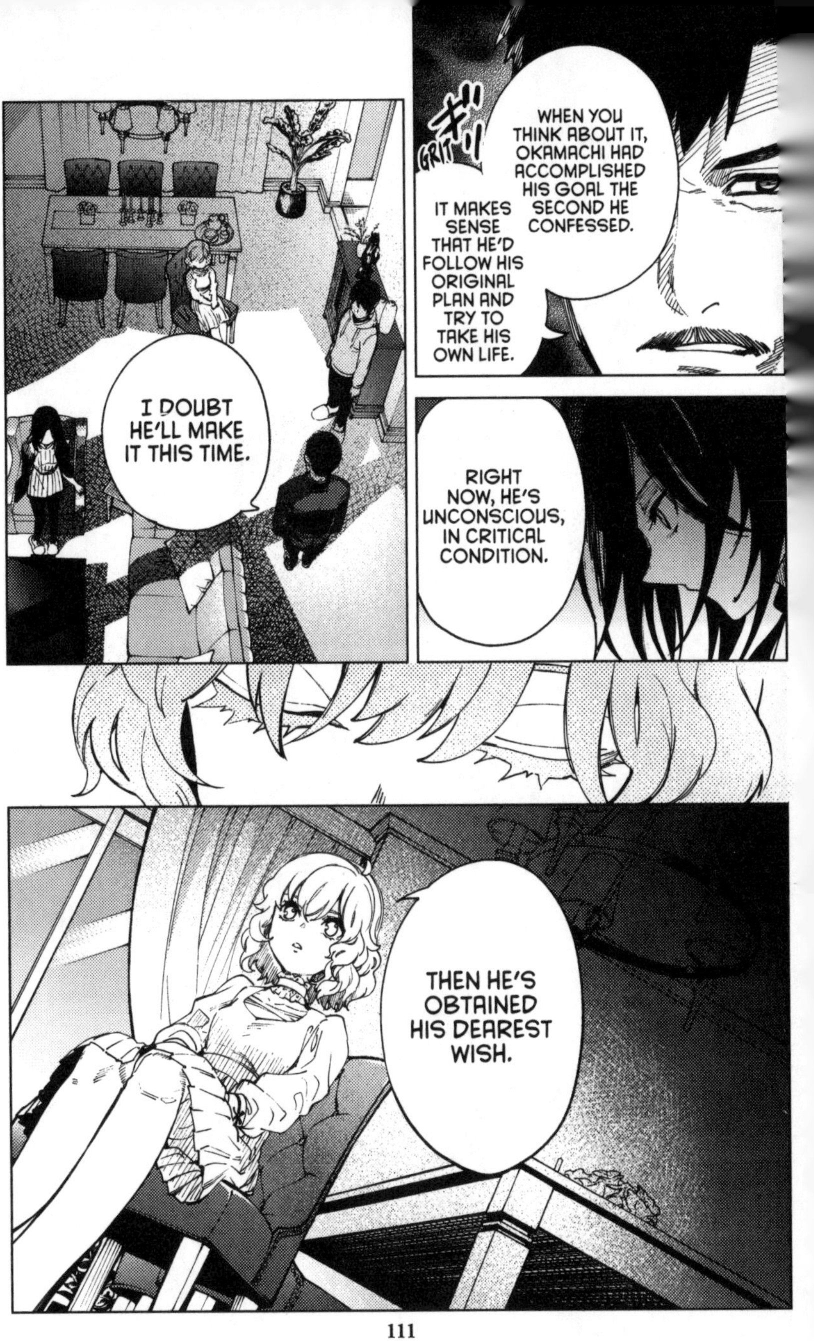
ギリ
GRIT
WHEN YOU THINK ABOUT IT, OKAMACHI HAD ACCOMPLISHED HIS GOAL THE SECOND HE CONFESSED.
IT MAKES SENSE THAT HE'D FOLLOW HIS ORIGINAL PLAN AND TRY TO TAKE HIS OWN LIFE.
RIGHT NOW, HE'S UNCONSCIOUS, IN CRITICAL CONDITION.
I DOUBT HE'LL MAKE IT THIS TIME.
THEN HE'S OBTAINED HIS DEAREST WISH.

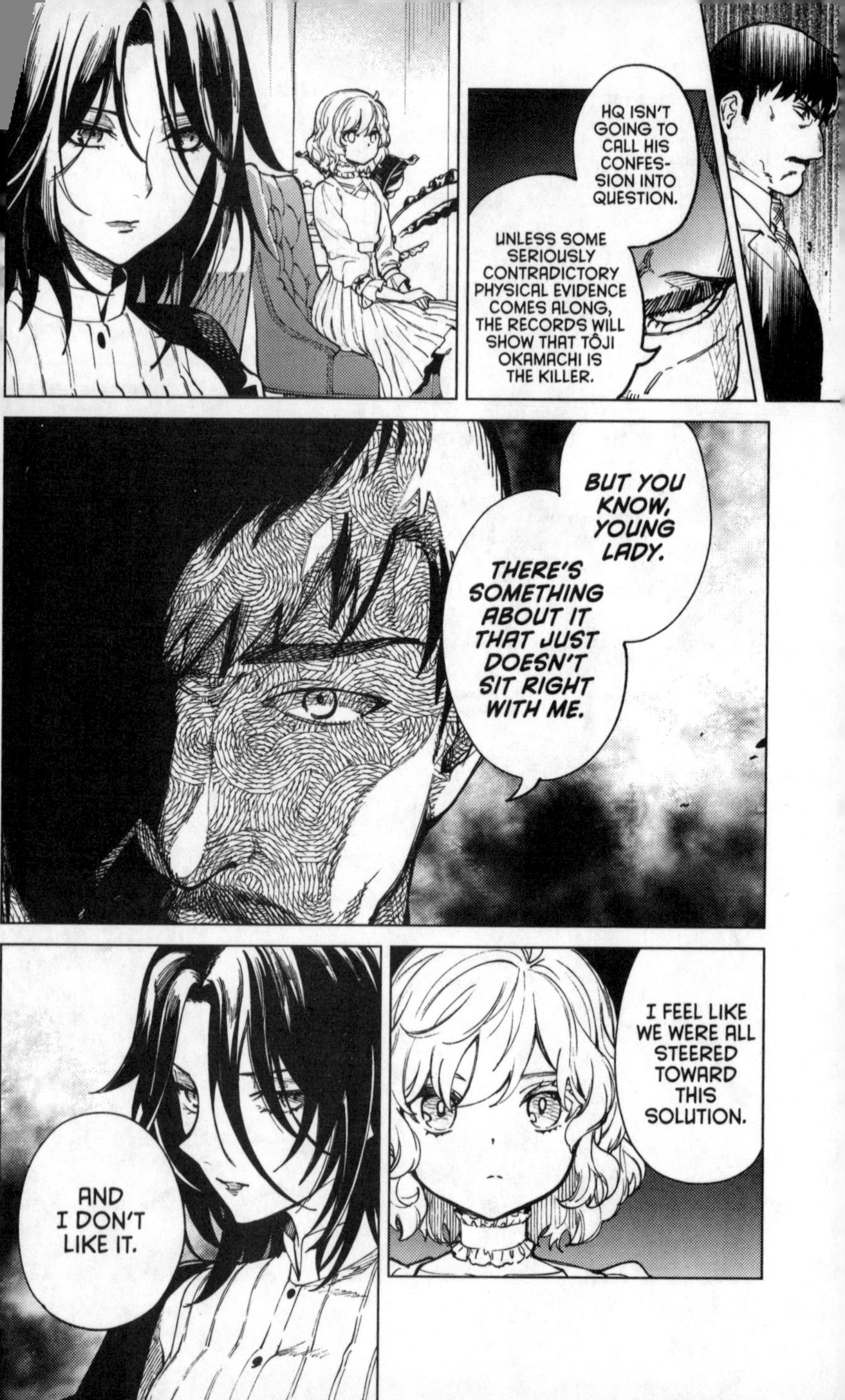
HQ ISN'T GOING TO CALL HIS CONFESSION INTO QUESTION.
UNLESS SOME SERIOUSLY CONTRADICTORY PHYSICAL EVIDENCE COMES ALONG, THE RECORDS WILL SHOW THAT TÔJI OKAMACHI IS THE KILLER.
BUT YOU KNOW, YOUNG LADY.
THERE'S SOMETHING ABOUT IT THAT JUST DOESN'T SIT RIGHT WITH ME.
I FEEL LIKE WE WERE ALL STEERED TOWARD THIS SOLUTION.
AND I DON'T LIKE IT.

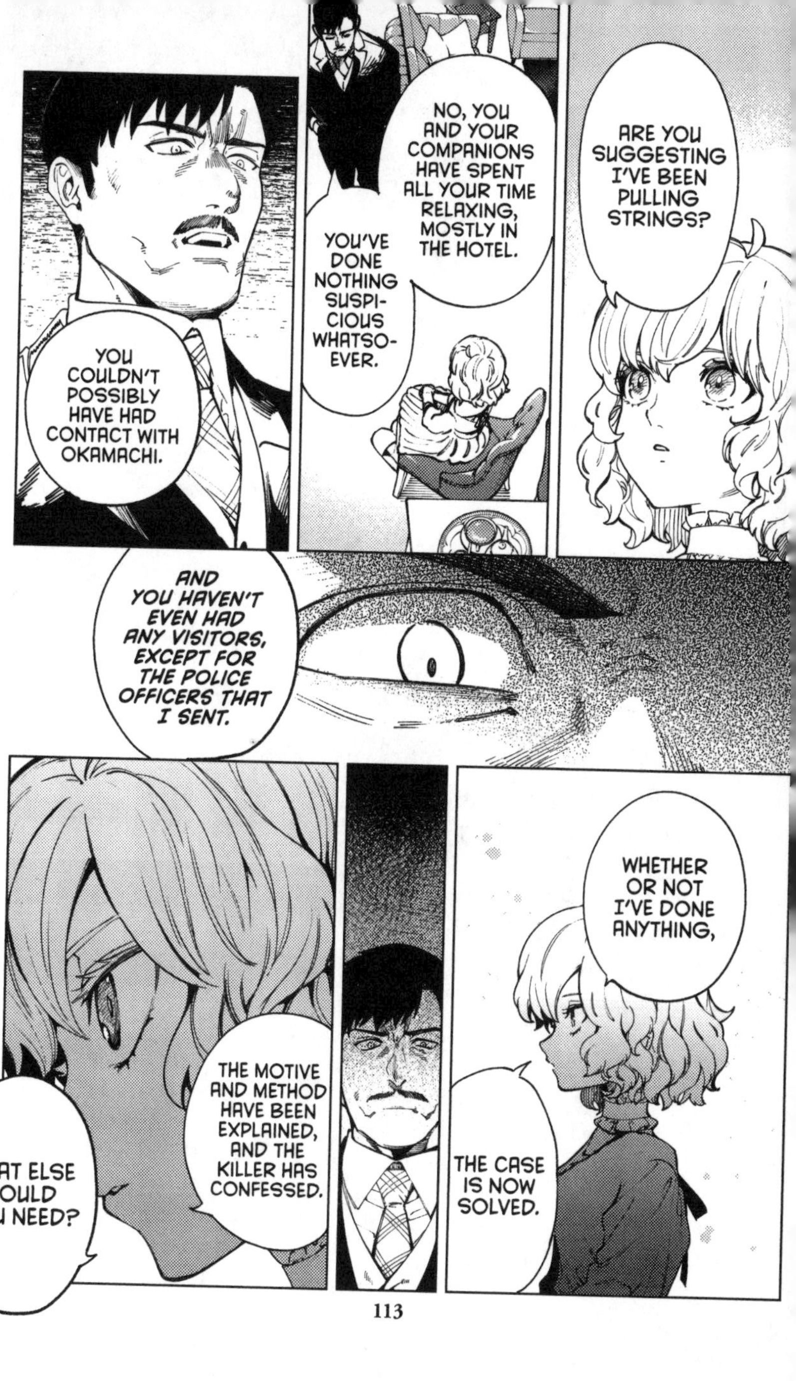
ARE YOU SUGGESTING I'VE BEEN PULLING STRINGS?
NO, YOU AND YOUR COMPANIONS HAVE SPENT ALL YOUR TIME RELAXING, MOSTLY IN THE HOTEL.
YOU'VE DONE NOTHING SUSPICIOUS WHATSOEVER.
YOU COULDN'T POSSIBLY HAVE HAD CONTACT WITH OKAMACHI.
AND YOU HAVEN'T EVEN HAD ANY VISITORS, EXCEPT FOR THE POLICE OFFICERS THAT I SENT.
WHETHER OR NOT I'VE DONE ANYTHING,
THE CASE IS NOW SOLVED.
THE MOTIVE AND METHOD HAVE BEEN EXPLAINED, AND THE KILLER HAS CONFESSED.
WHAT ELSE COULD YOU NEED?

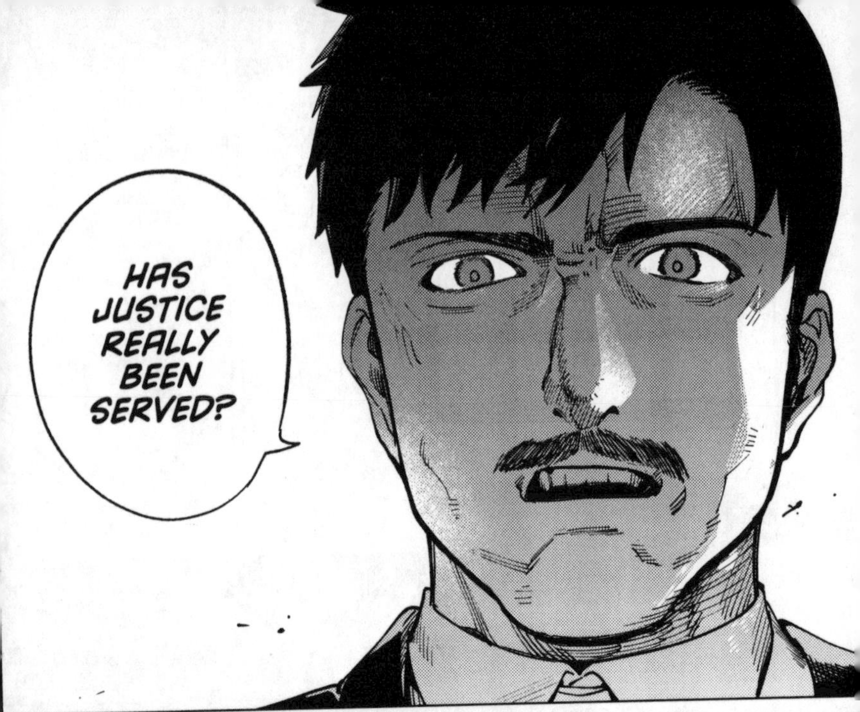
HAS JUSTICE REALLY BEEN SERVED?
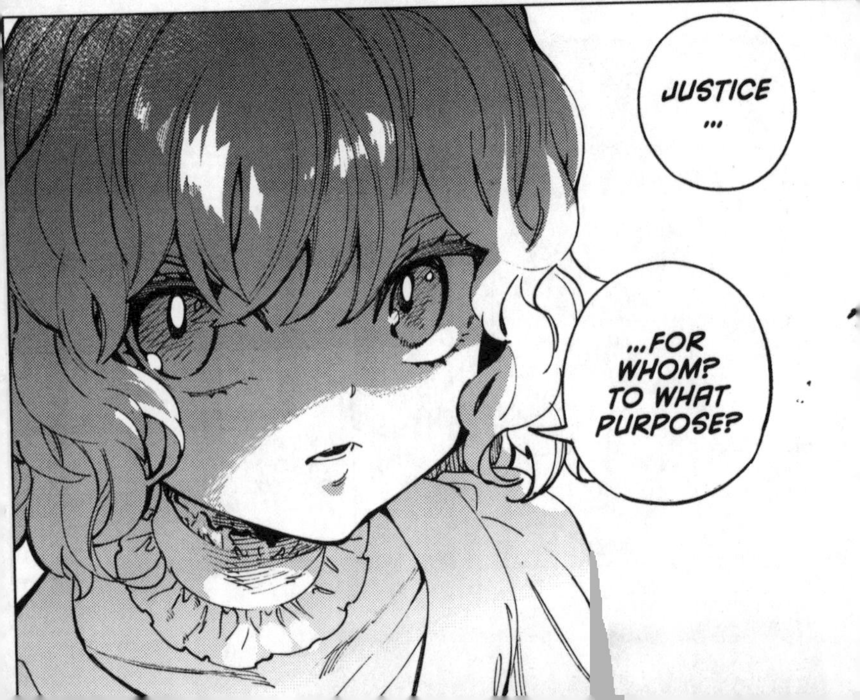
JUSTICE ...
...FOR WHOM? TO WHAT PURPOSE?

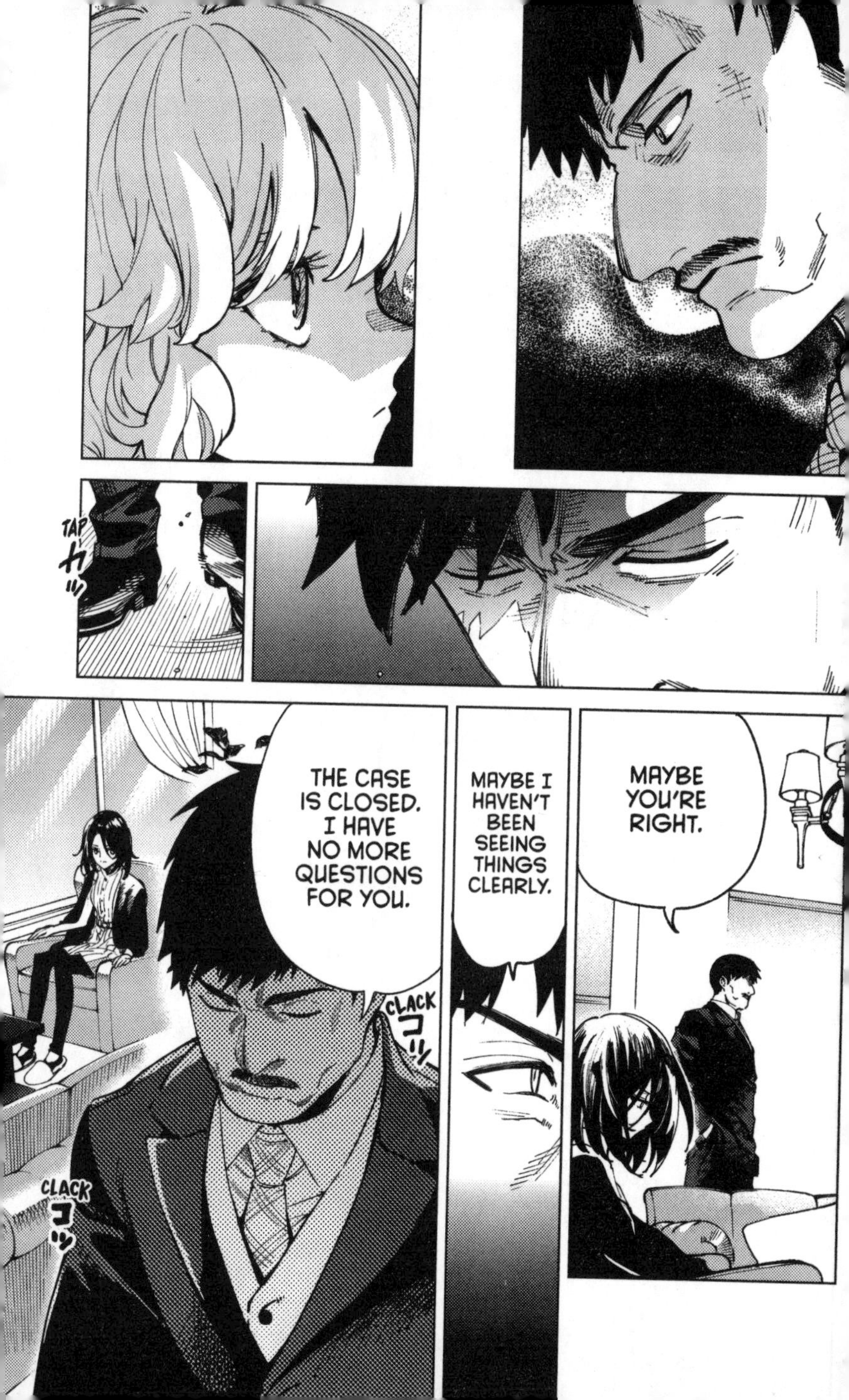
TAP
MAYBE YOU'RE RIGHT.
MAYBE I HAVEN'T BEEN SEEING THINGS CLEARLY.
THE CASE IS CLOSED. I HAVE NO MORE QUESTIONS FOR YOU.
CLACK
CLACK

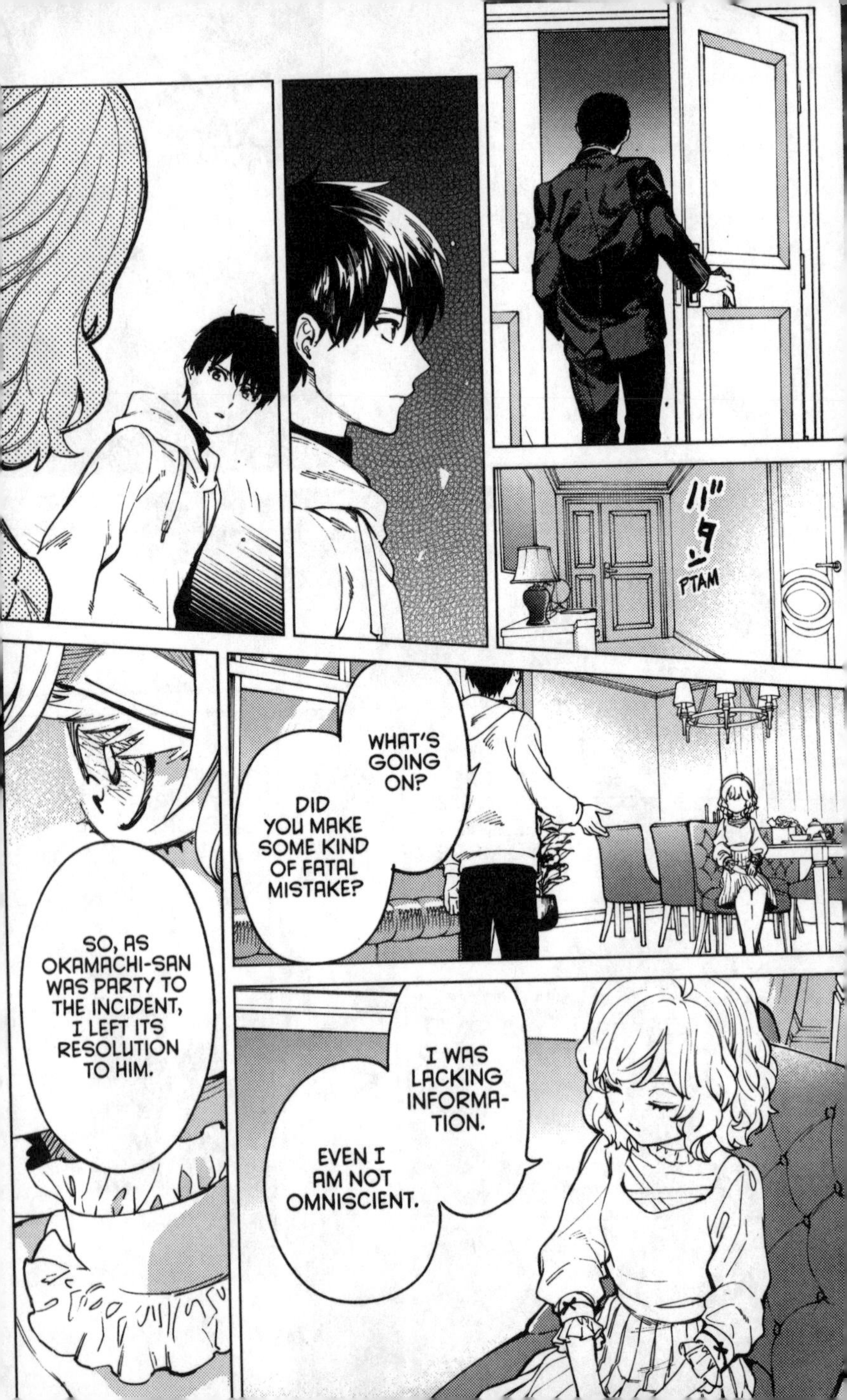
バタン
PTAM
WHAT'S GOING ON?
DID YOU MAKE SOME KIND OF FATAL MISTAKE?
I WAS LACKING INFORMA-TION.
EVEN I AM NOT OMNISCIENT.
SO, AS OKAMACHI-SAN WAS PARTY TO THE INCIDENT, I LEFT ITS RESOLUTION TO HIM.

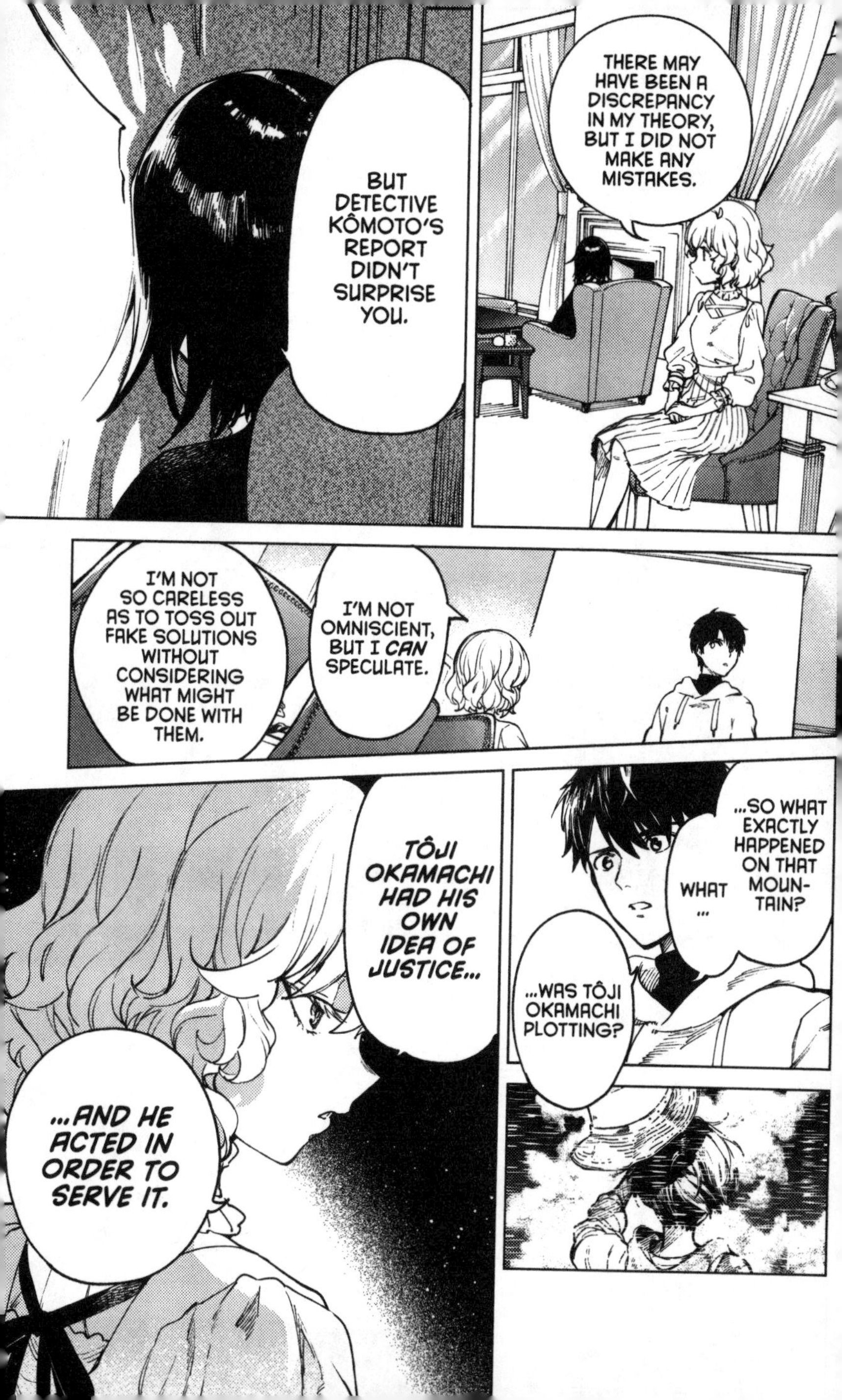
THERE MAY HAVE BEEN A DISCREPANCY IN MY THEORY, BUT I DID NOT MAKE ANY MISTAKES.
BUT DETECTIVE KÔMOTO'S REPORT DIDN'T SURPRISE YOU.
I'M NOT OMNISCIENT, BUT I *CAN* SPECULATE.
I'M NOT SO CARELESS AS TO TOSS OUT FAKE SOLUTIONS WITHOUT CONSIDERING WHAT MIGHT BE DONE WITH THEM.
...SO WHAT EXACTLY HAPPENED ON THAT MOUNTAIN?
WHAT ...
...WAS TÔJI OKAMACHI PLOTTING?
TÔJI OKAMACHI HAD HIS OWN IDEA OF JUSTICE...
...AND HE ACTED IN ORDER TO SERVE IT.

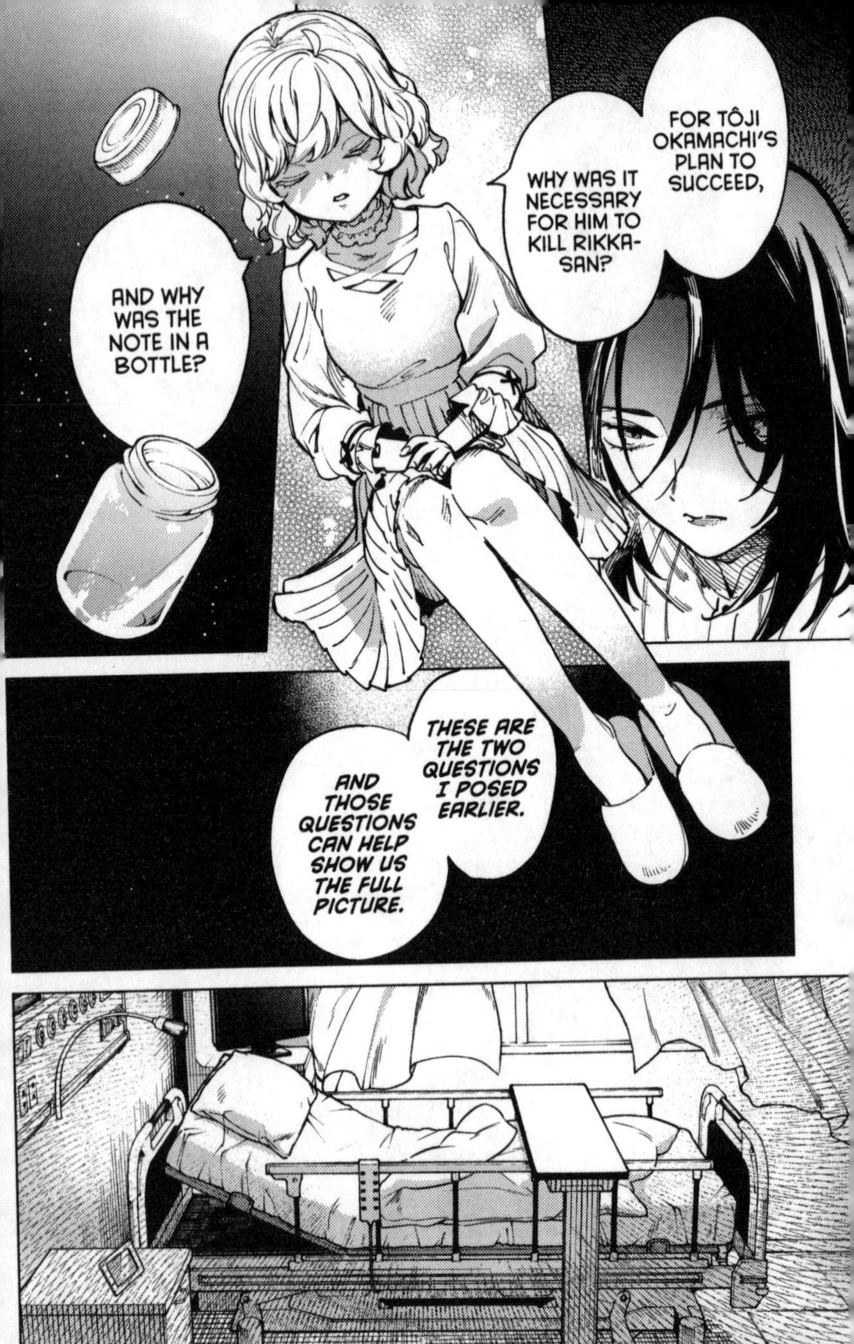
FOR TÔJI OKAMACHI'S PLAN TO SUCCEED,
WHY WAS IT NECESSARY FOR HIM TO KILL RIKKA-SAN?
AND WHY WAS THE NOTE IN A BOTTLE?
THESE ARE THE TWO QUESTIONS I POSED EARLIER.
AND THOSE QUESTIONS CAN HELP SHOW US THE FULL PICTURE.

IN/SPECTRE

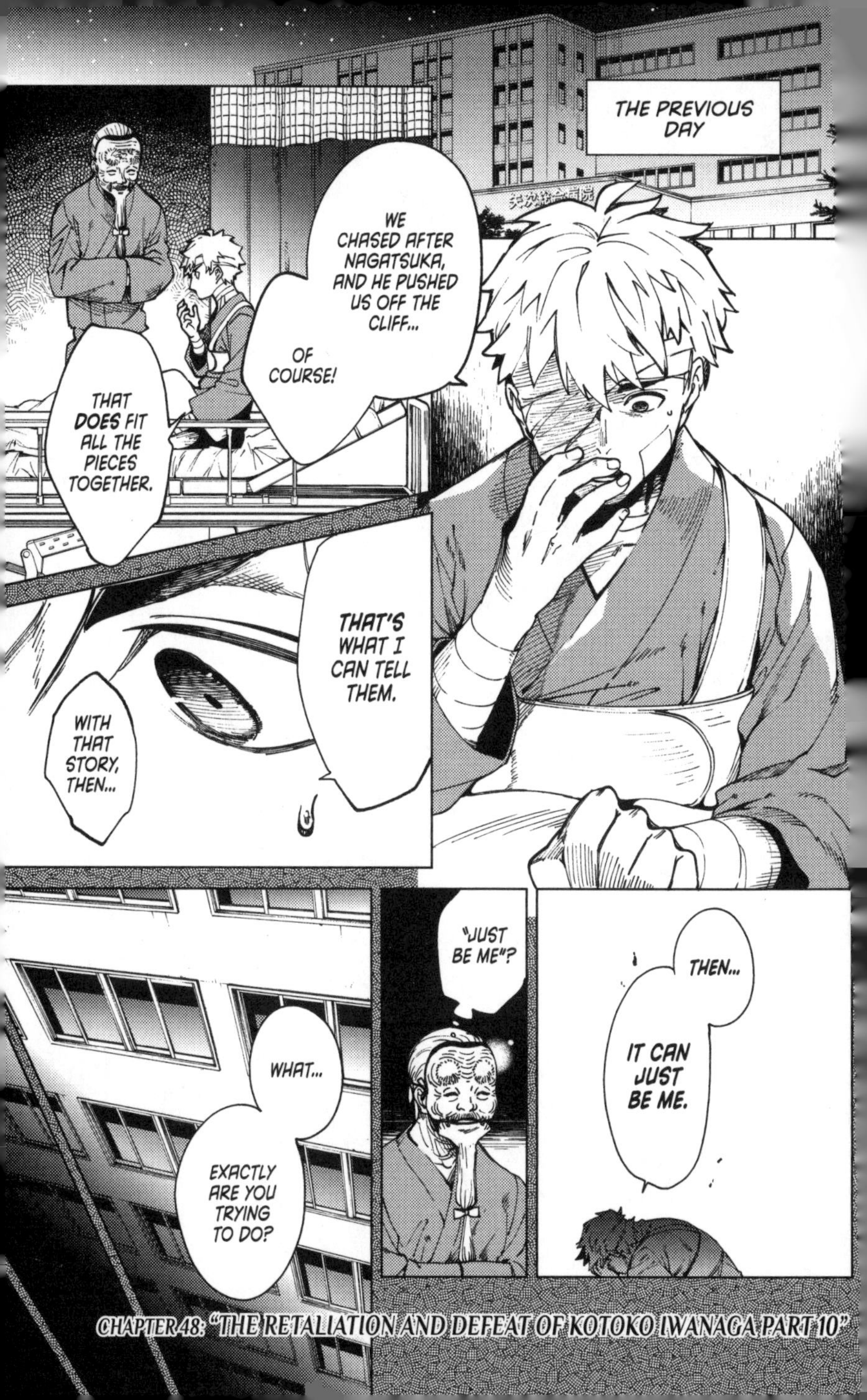
THE PREVIOUS DAY
WE CHASED AFTER NAGATSUKA, AND HE PUSHED US OFF THE CLIFF...
OF COURSE!
THAT **DOES** FIT ALL THE PIECES TOGETHER.
THAT'S WHAT I CAN TELL THEM.
WITH THAT STORY, THEN...
THEN...
IT CAN JUST BE ME.
"JUST BE ME"?
WHAT...
EXACTLY ARE YOU TRYING TO DO?
CHAPTER 48: "THE RETALIATION AND DEFEAT OF KOTOKO IWANAGA PART 10"

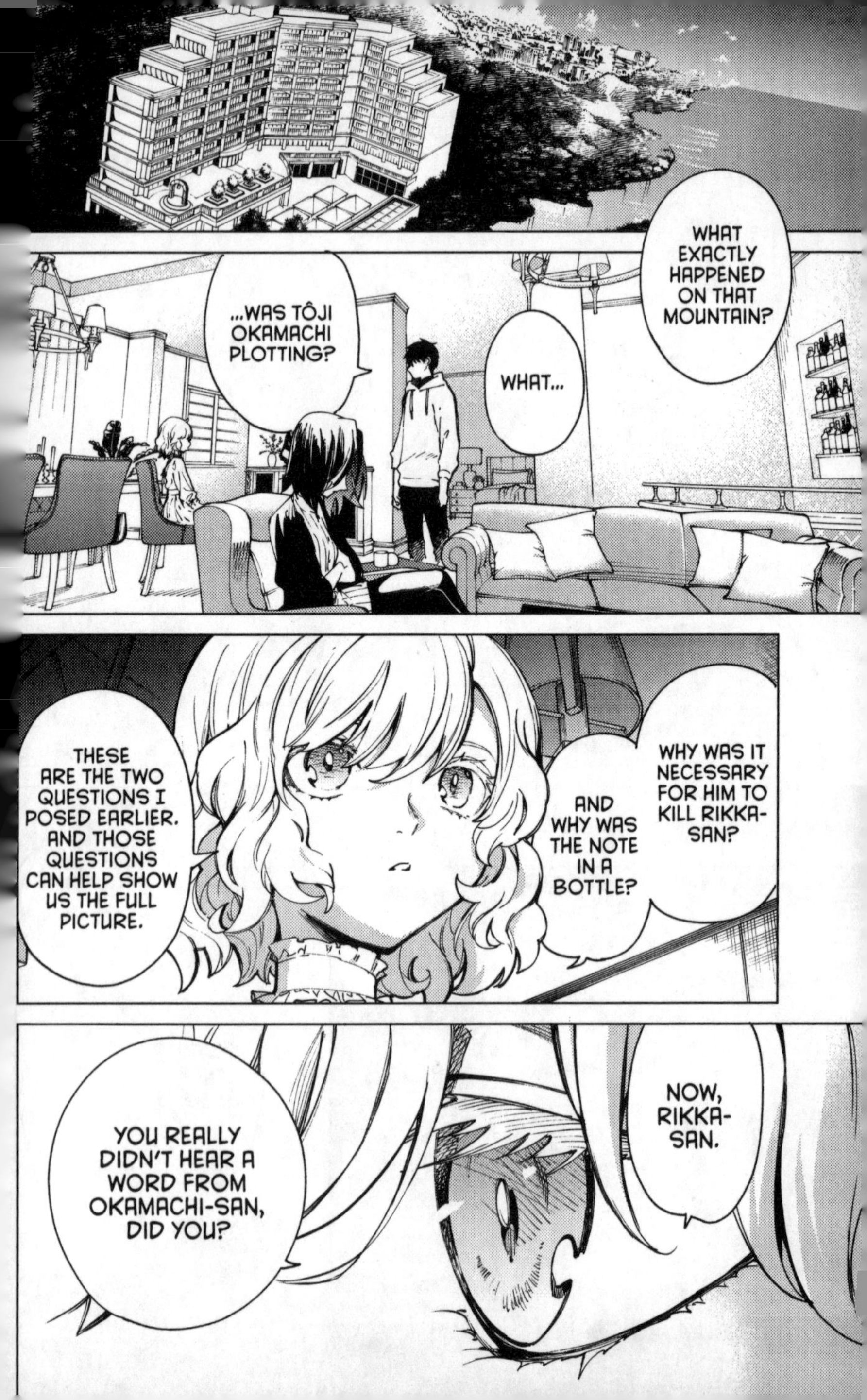
WHAT EXACTLY HAPPENED ON THAT MOUNTAIN?
WHAT...
...WAS TÔJI OKAMACHI PLOTTING?
WHY WAS IT NECESSARY FOR HIM TO KILL RIKKA-SAN?
AND WHY WAS THE NOTE IN A BOTTLE?
THESE ARE THE TWO QUESTIONS I POSED EARLIER. AND THOSE QUESTIONS CAN HELP SHOW US THE FULL PICTURE.
NOW, RIKKA-SAN.
YOU REALLY DIDN'T HEAR A WORD FROM OKAMACHI-SAN, DID YOU?

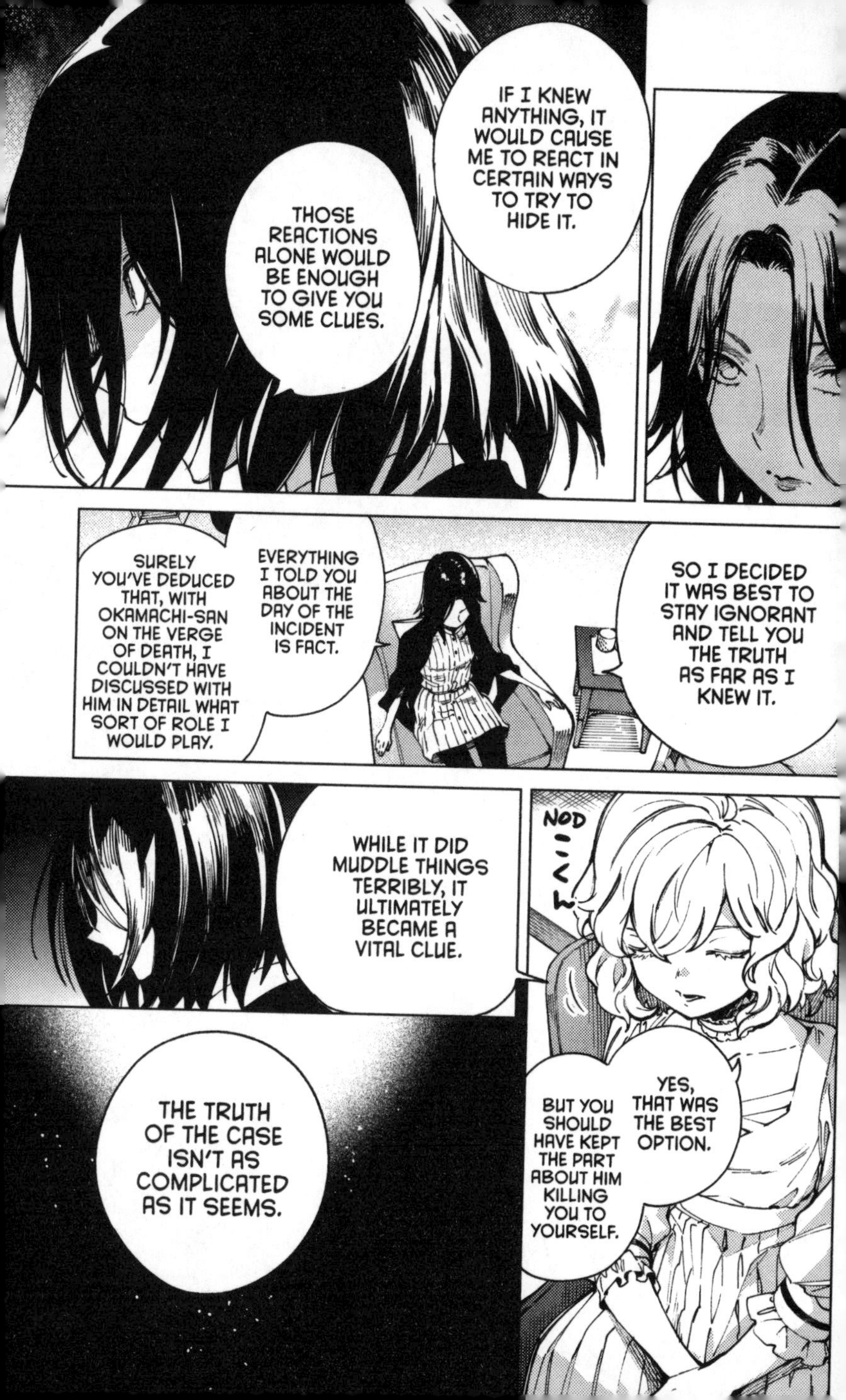
IF I KNEW ANYTHING, IT WOULD CAUSE ME TO REACT IN CERTAIN WAYS TO TRY TO HIDE IT.
THOSE REACTIONS ALONE WOULD BE ENOUGH TO GIVE YOU SOME CLUES.
SO I DECIDED IT WAS BEST TO STAY IGNORANT AND TELL YOU THE TRUTH AS FAR AS I KNEW IT.
EVERYTHING I TOLD YOU ABOUT THE DAY OF THE INCIDENT IS FACT.
SURELY YOU'VE DEDUCED THAT, WITH OKAMACHI-SAN ON THE VERGE OF DEATH, I COULDN'T HAVE DISCUSSED WITH HIM IN DETAIL WHAT SORT OF ROLE I WOULD PLAY.
NOD
YES, THAT WAS THE BEST OPTION.
BUT YOU SHOULD HAVE KEPT THE PART ABOUT HIM KILLING YOU TO YOURSELF.
WHILE IT DID MUDDLE THINGS TERRIBLY, IT ULTIMATELY BECAME A VITAL CLUE.
THE TRUTH OF THE CASE ISN'T AS COMPLICATED AS IT SEEMS.

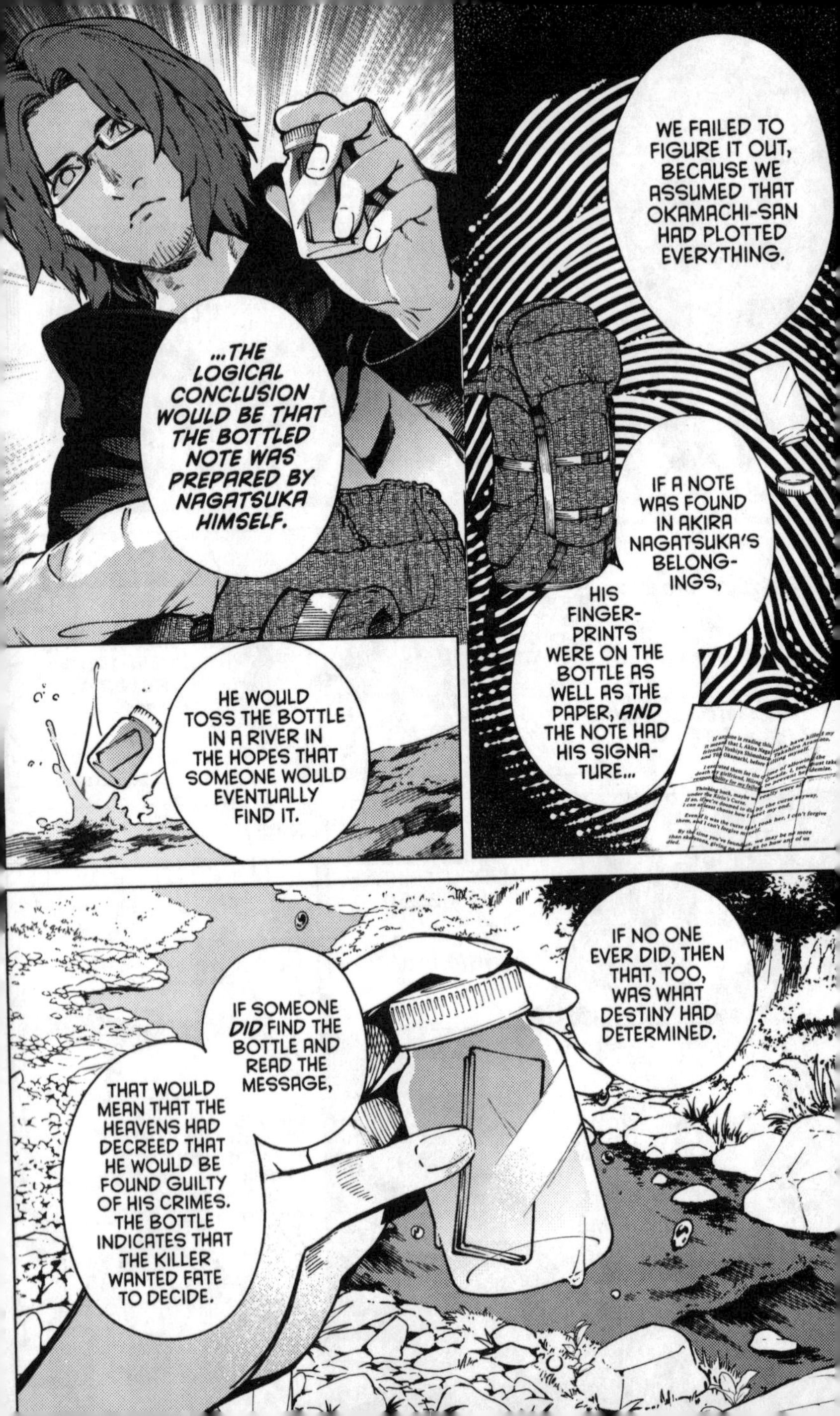
WE FAILED TO FIGURE IT OUT, BECAUSE WE ASSUMED THAT OKAMACHI-SAN HAD PLOTTED EVERYTHING.
IF A NOTE WAS FOUND IN AKIRA NAGATSUKA'S BELONGINGS,
HIS FINGERPRINTS WERE ON THE BOTTLE AS WELL AS THE PAPER, *AND* THE NOTE HAD HIS SIGNATURE...
...THE LOGICAL CONCLUSION WOULD BE THAT THE BOTTLED NOTE WAS PREPARED BY NAGATSUKA HIMSELF.
HE WOULD TOSS THE BOTTLE IN A RIVER IN THE HOPES THAT SOMEONE WOULD EVENTUALLY FIND IT.
IF NO ONE EVER DID, THEN THAT, TOO, WAS WHAT DESTINY HAD DETERMINED.
IF SOMEONE *DID* FIND THE BOTTLE AND READ THE MESSAGE,
THAT WOULD MEAN THAT THE HEAVENS HAD DECREED THAT HE WOULD BE FOUND GUILTY OF HIS CRIMES. THE BOTTLE INDICATES THAT THE KILLER WANTED FATE TO DECIDE.

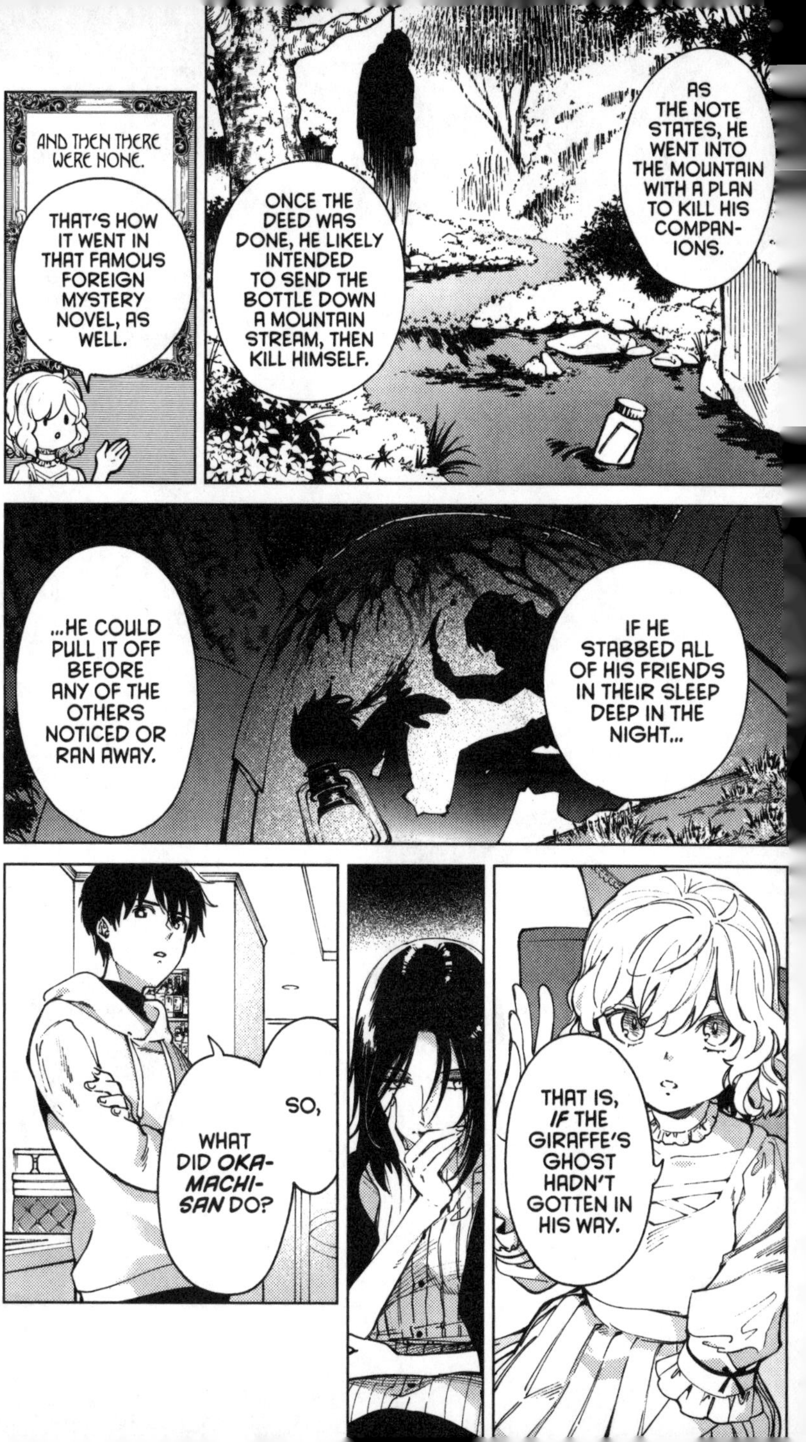
AS THE NOTE STATES, HE WENT INTO THE MOUNTAIN WITH A PLAN TO KILL HIS COMPANIONS.
ONCE THE DEED WAS DONE, HE LIKELY INTENDED TO SEND THE BOTTLE DOWN A MOUNTAIN STREAM, THEN KILL HIMSELF.
AND THEN THERE WERE NONE.
THAT'S HOW IT WENT IN THAT FAMOUS FOREIGN MYSTERY NOVEL, AS WELL.
IF HE STABBED ALL OF HIS FRIENDS IN THEIR SLEEP DEEP IN THE NIGHT...
...HE COULD PULL IT OFF BEFORE ANY OF THE OTHERS NOTICED OR RAN AWAY.
THAT IS, *IF* THE GIRAFFE'S GHOST HADN'T GOTTEN IN HIS WAY.
SO,
WHAT DID *OKAMACHI-SAN* DO?

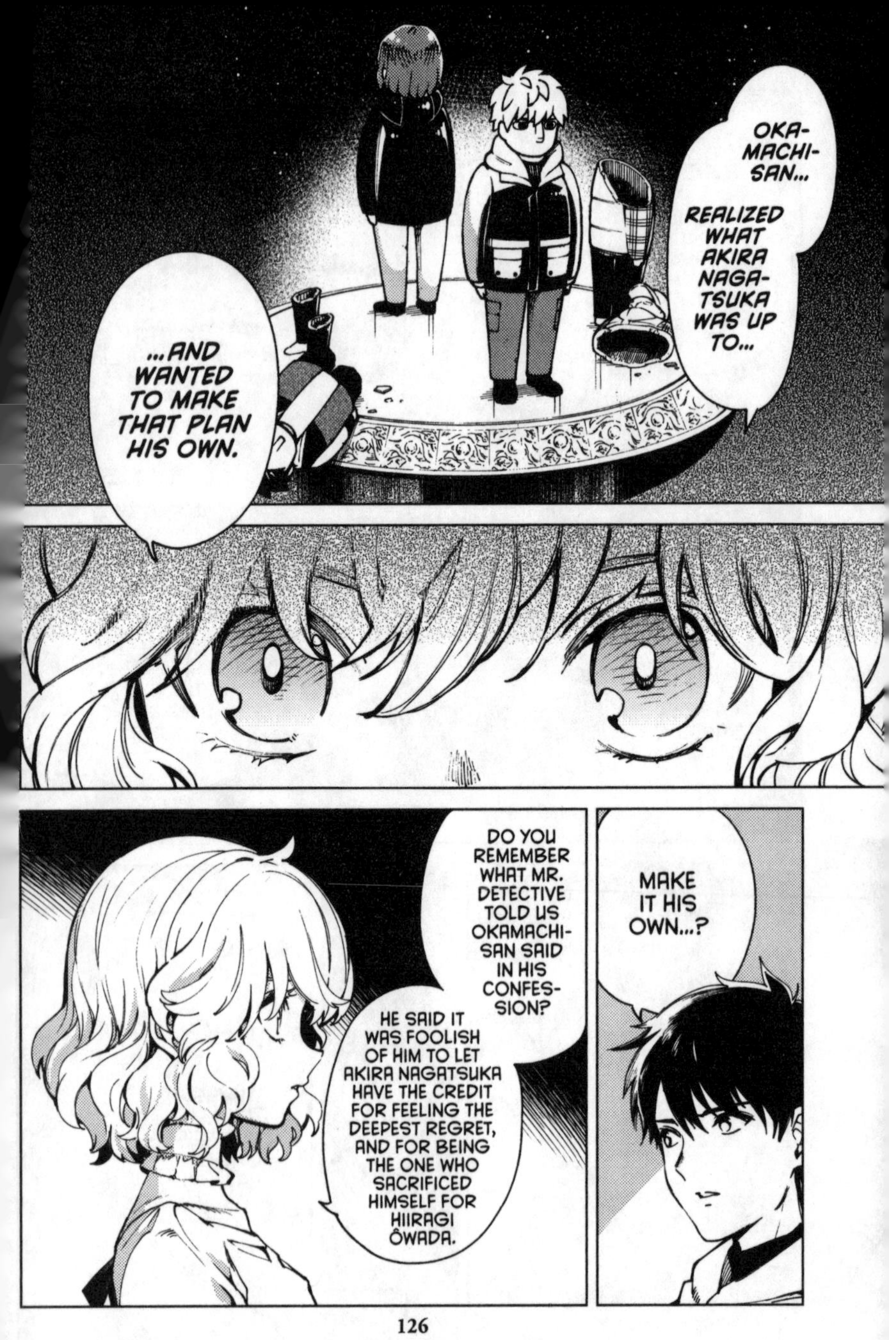
OKA-MACHI-SAN... REALIZED WHAT AKIRA NAGA-TSUKA WAS UP TO...
...AND WANTED TO MAKE THAT PLAN HIS OWN.
MAKE IT HIS OWN...?
DO YOU REMEMBER WHAT MR. DETECTIVE TOLD US OKAMACHI-SAN SAID IN HIS CONFES-SION?
HE SAID IT WAS FOOLISH OF HIM TO LET AKIRA NAGATSUKA HAVE THE CREDIT FOR FEELING THE DEEPEST REGRET, AND FOR BEING THE ONE WHO SACRIFICED HIMSELF FOR HIIRAGI ÔWADA.

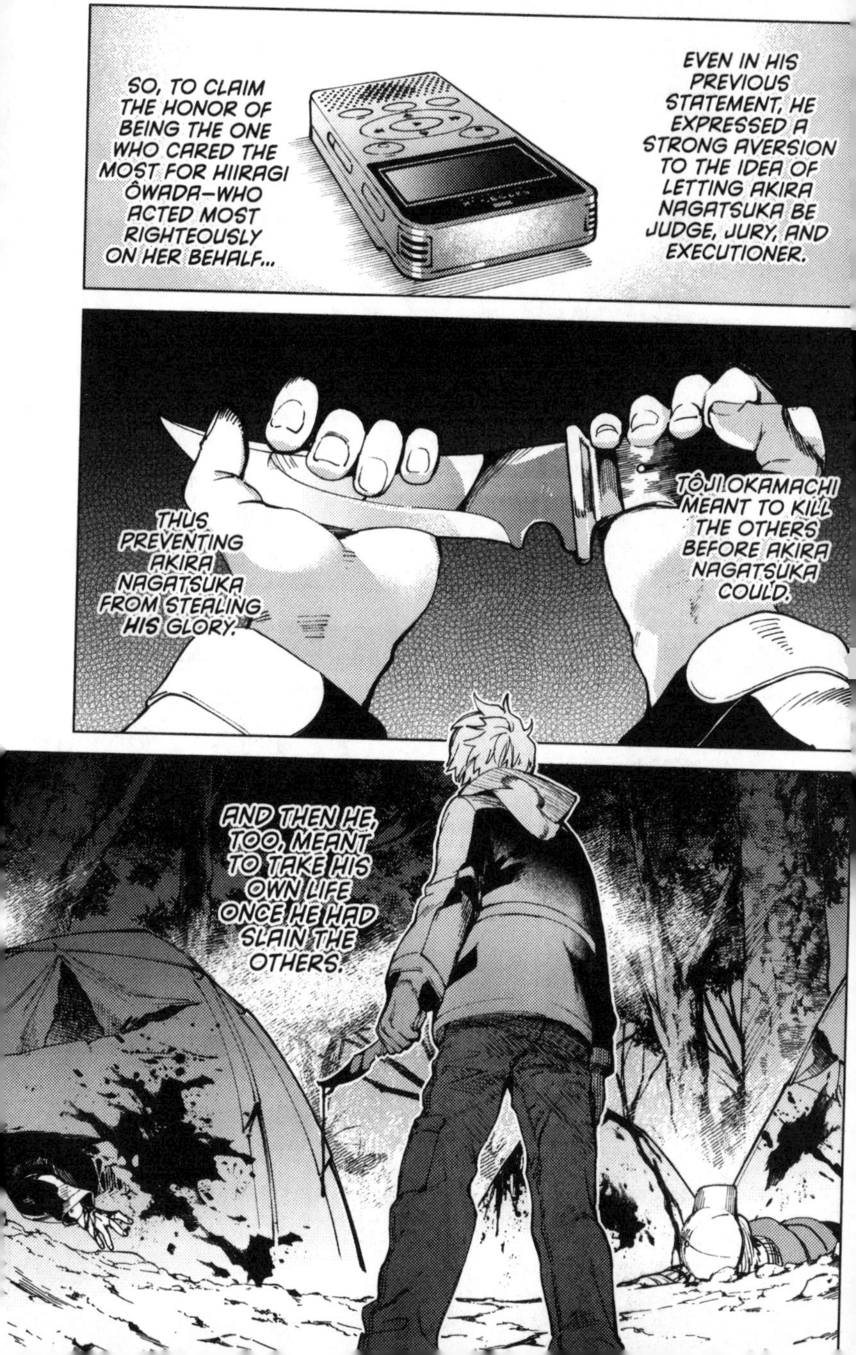
EVEN IN HIS PREVIOUS STATEMENT, HE EXPRESSED A STRONG AVERSION TO THE IDEA OF LETTING AKIRA NAGATSUKA BE JUDGE, JURY, AND EXECUTIONER.
SO, TO CLAIM THE HONOR OF BEING THE ONE WHO CARED THE MOST FOR HIIRAGI ÔWADA—WHO ACTED MOST RIGHTEOUSLY ON HER BEHALF...
TÔJI OKAMACHI MEANT TO KILL THE OTHERS BEFORE AKIRA NAGATSUKA COULD.
THUS PREVENTING AKIRA NAGATSUKA FROM STEALING HIS GLORY.
AND THEN HE, TOO, MEANT TO TAKE HIS OWN LIFE ONCE HE HAD SLAIN THE OTHERS.

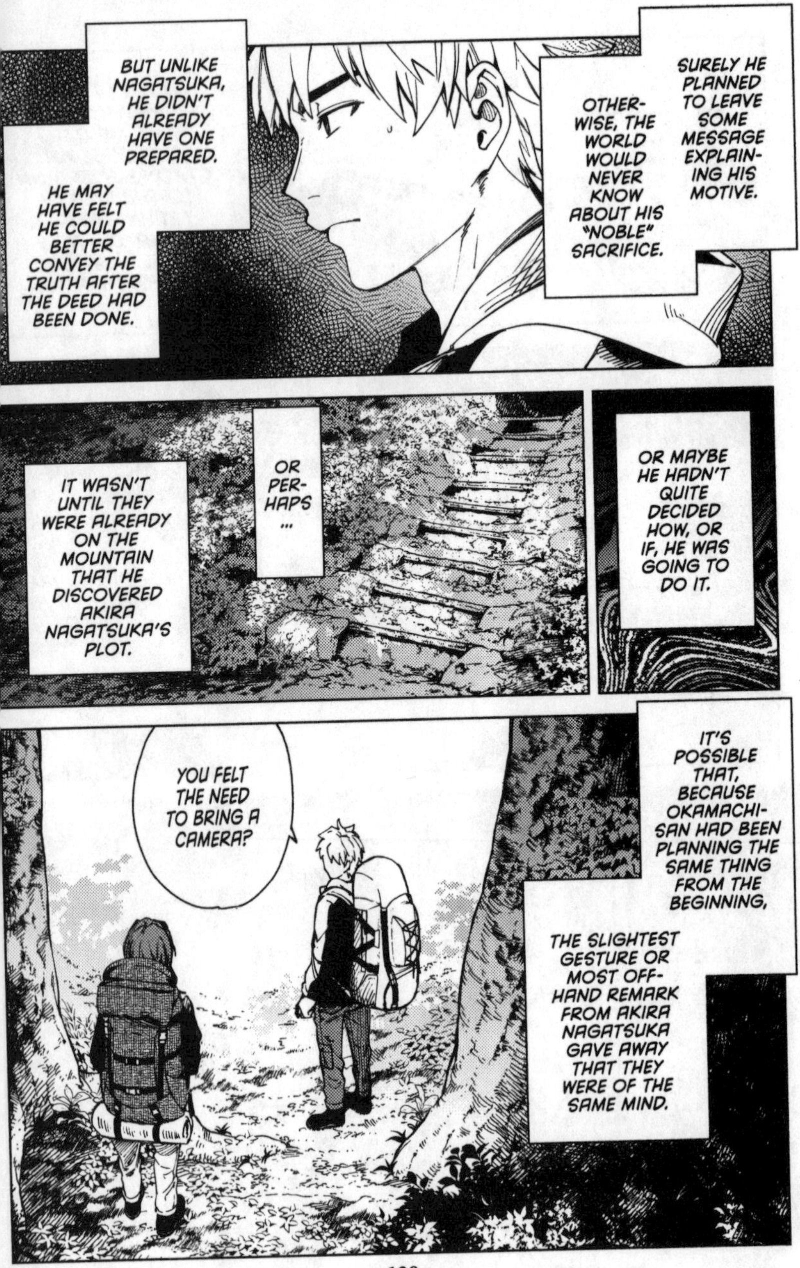
SURELY HE PLANNED TO LEAVE SOME MESSAGE EXPLAINING HIS MOTIVE.
OTHERWISE, THE WORLD WOULD NEVER KNOW ABOUT HIS "NOBLE" SACRIFICE.
BUT UNLIKE NAGATSUKA, HE DIDN'T ALREADY HAVE ONE PREPARED.
HE MAY HAVE FELT HE COULD BETTER CONVEY THE TRUTH AFTER THE DEED HAD BEEN DONE.
OR MAYBE HE HADN'T QUITE DECIDED HOW, OR IF, HE WAS GOING TO DO IT.
OR PERHAPS...
IT WASN'T UNTIL THEY WERE ALREADY ON THE MOUNTAIN THAT HE DISCOVERED AKIRA NAGATSUKA'S PLOT.
IT'S POSSIBLE THAT, BECAUSE OKAMACHI-SAN HAD BEEN PLANNING THE SAME THING FROM THE BEGINNING,
THE SLIGHTEST GESTURE OR MOST OFF-HAND REMARK FROM AKIRA NAGATSUKA GAVE AWAY THAT THEY WERE OF THE SAME MIND.
YOU FELT THE NEED TO BRING A CAMERA?

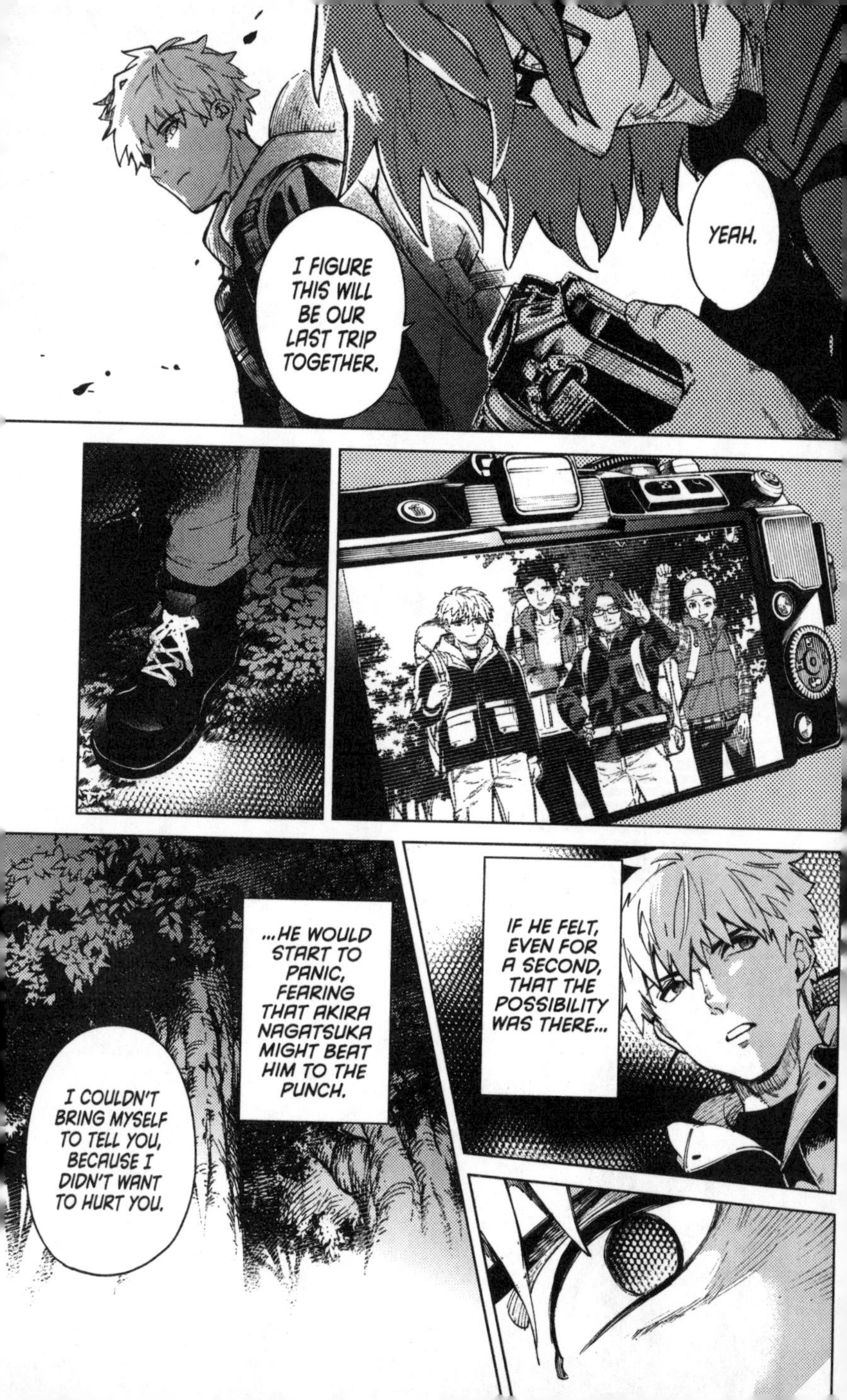
YEAH.
I FIGURE THIS WILL BE OUR LAST TRIP TOGETHER.
IF HE FELT, EVEN FOR A SECOND, THAT THE POSSIBILITY WAS THERE...
...HE WOULD START TO PANIC, FEARING THAT AKIRA NAGATSUKA MIGHT BEAT HIM TO THE PUNCH.
I COULDN'T BRING MYSELF TO TELL YOU, BECAUSE I DIDN'T WANT TO HURT YOU.

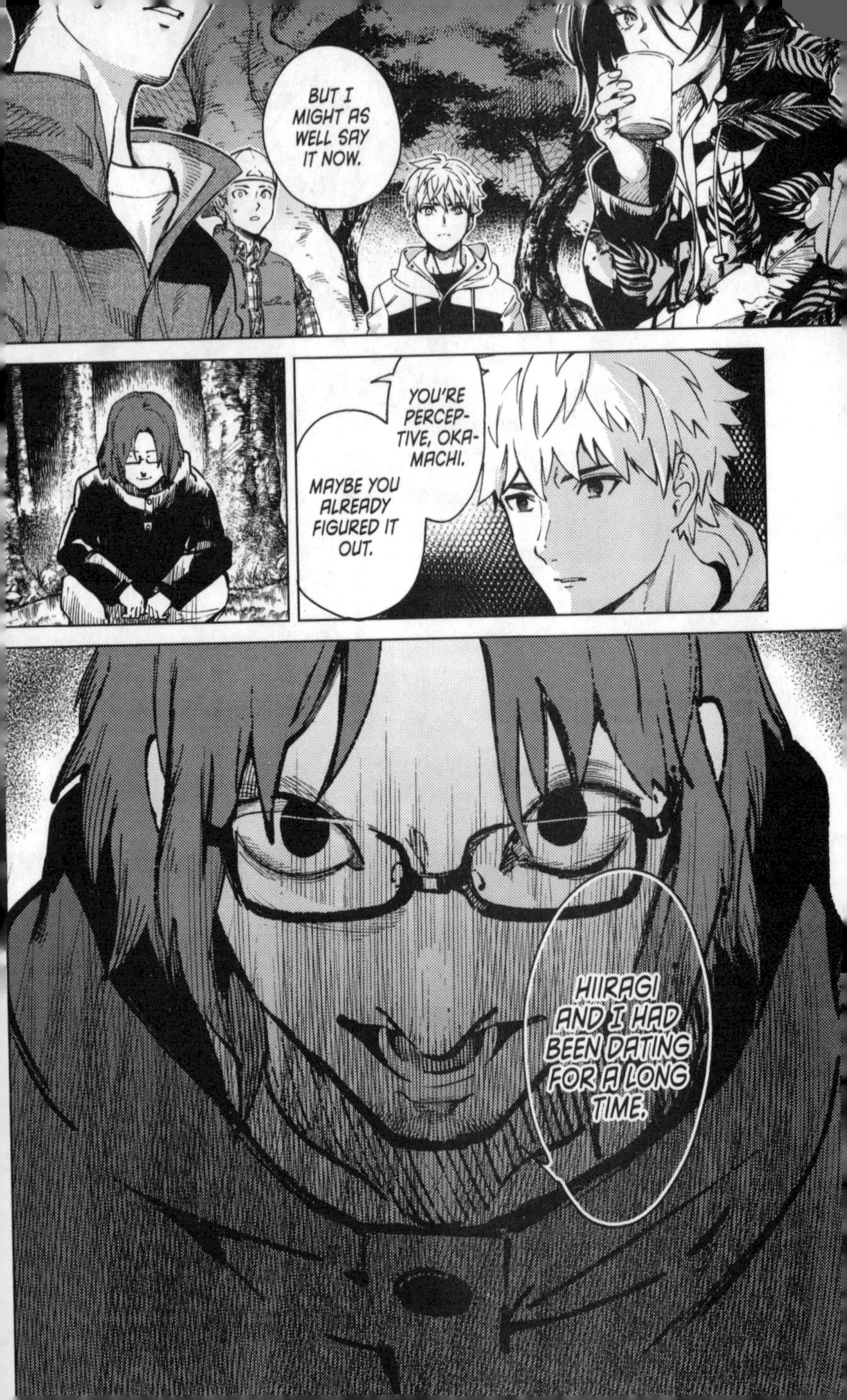
BUT I MIGHT AS WELL SAY IT NOW.
YOU'RE PERCEPTIVE, OKAMACHI.
MAYBE YOU ALREADY FIGURED IT OUT.
HIIRAGI AND I HAD BEEN DATING FOR A LONG TIME.

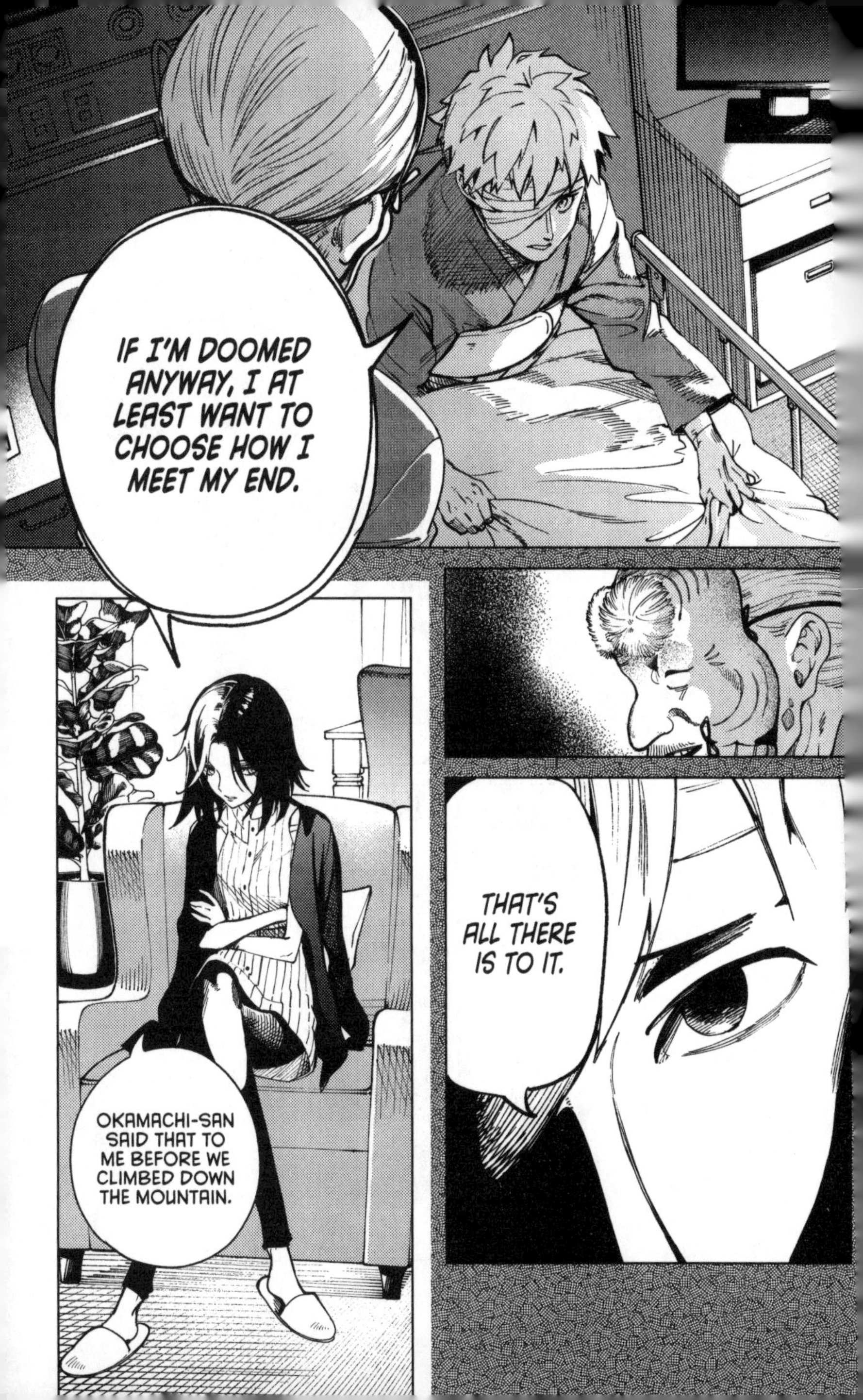
IF I'M DOOMED ANYWAY, I AT LEAST WANT TO CHOOSE HOW I MEET MY END.
THAT'S ALL THERE IS TO IT.
OKAMACHI-SAN SAID THAT TO ME BEFORE WE CLIMBED DOWN THE MOUNTAIN.

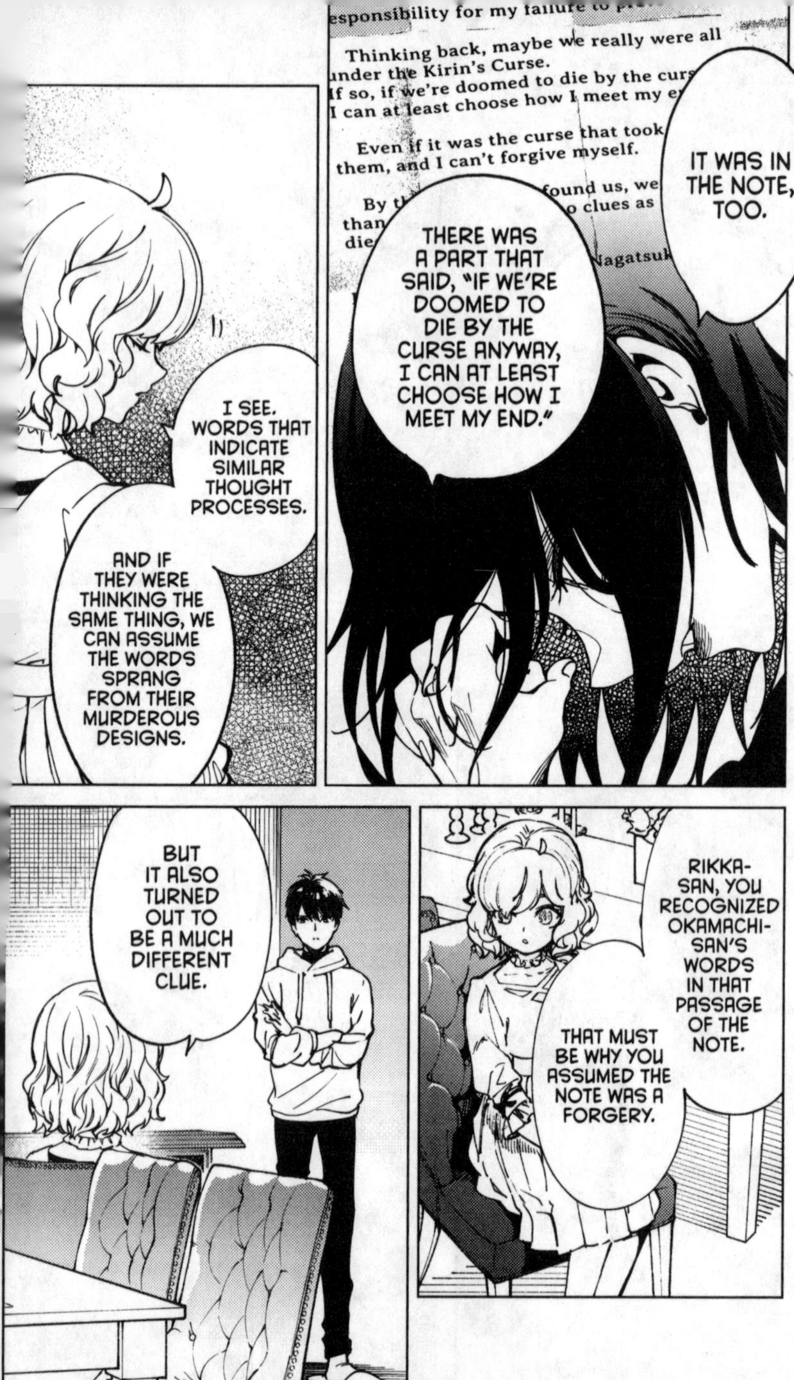
esponsibility for my failure to pr
Thinking back, maybe we really were all under the Kirin's Curse.
If so, if we're doomed to die by the curs
I can at least choose how I meet my e
Even if it was the curse that took
them, and I can't forgive myself.
found us, we
o clues as
Nagatsuk
IT WAS IN THE NOTE, TOO.
THERE WAS A PART THAT SAID, "IF WE'RE DOOMED TO DIE BY THE CURSE ANYWAY, I CAN AT LEAST CHOOSE HOW I MEET MY END."
I SEE. WORDS THAT INDICATE SIMILAR THOUGHT PROCESSES.
AND IF THEY WERE THINKING THE SAME THING, WE CAN ASSUME THE WORDS SPRANG FROM THEIR MURDEROUS DESIGNS.
RIKKA-SAN, YOU RECOGNIZED OKAMACHI-SAN'S WORDS IN THAT PASSAGE OF THE NOTE.
THAT MUST BE WHY YOU ASSUMED THE NOTE WAS A FORGERY.
BUT IT ALSO TURNED OUT TO BE A MUCH DIFFERENT CLUE.

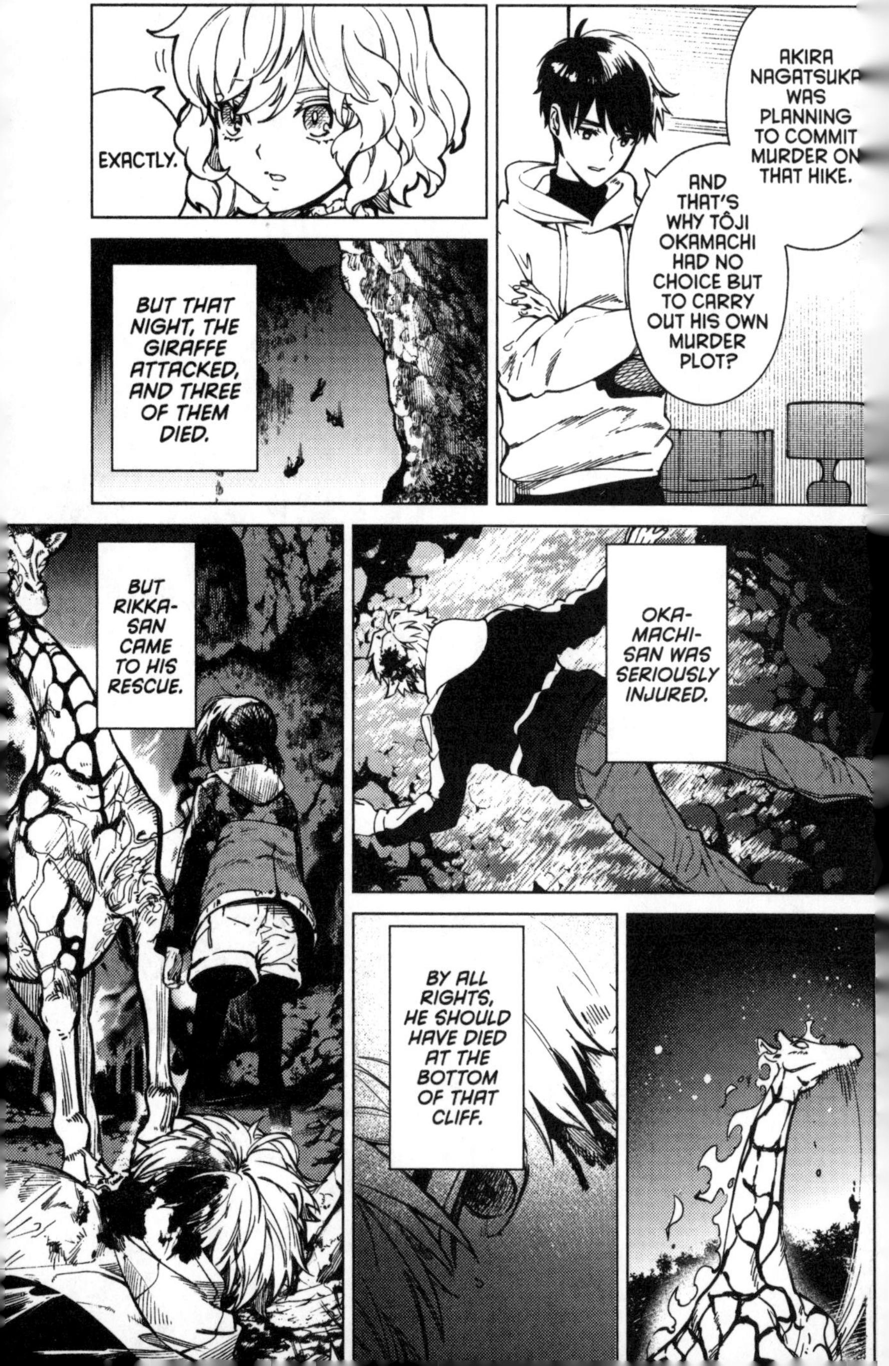
AKIRA NAGATSUKA WAS PLANNING TO COMMIT MURDER ON THAT HIKE.
AND THAT'S WHY TÔJI OKAMACHI HAD NO CHOICE BUT TO CARRY OUT HIS OWN MURDER PLOT?
EXACTLY.
BUT THAT NIGHT, THE GIRAFFE ATTACKED, AND THREE OF THEM DIED.
OKA-MACHI-SAN WAS SERIOUSLY INJURED.
BY ALL RIGHTS, HE SHOULD HAVE DIED AT THE BOTTOM OF THAT CLIFF.
BUT RIKKA-SAN CAME TO HIS RESCUE.

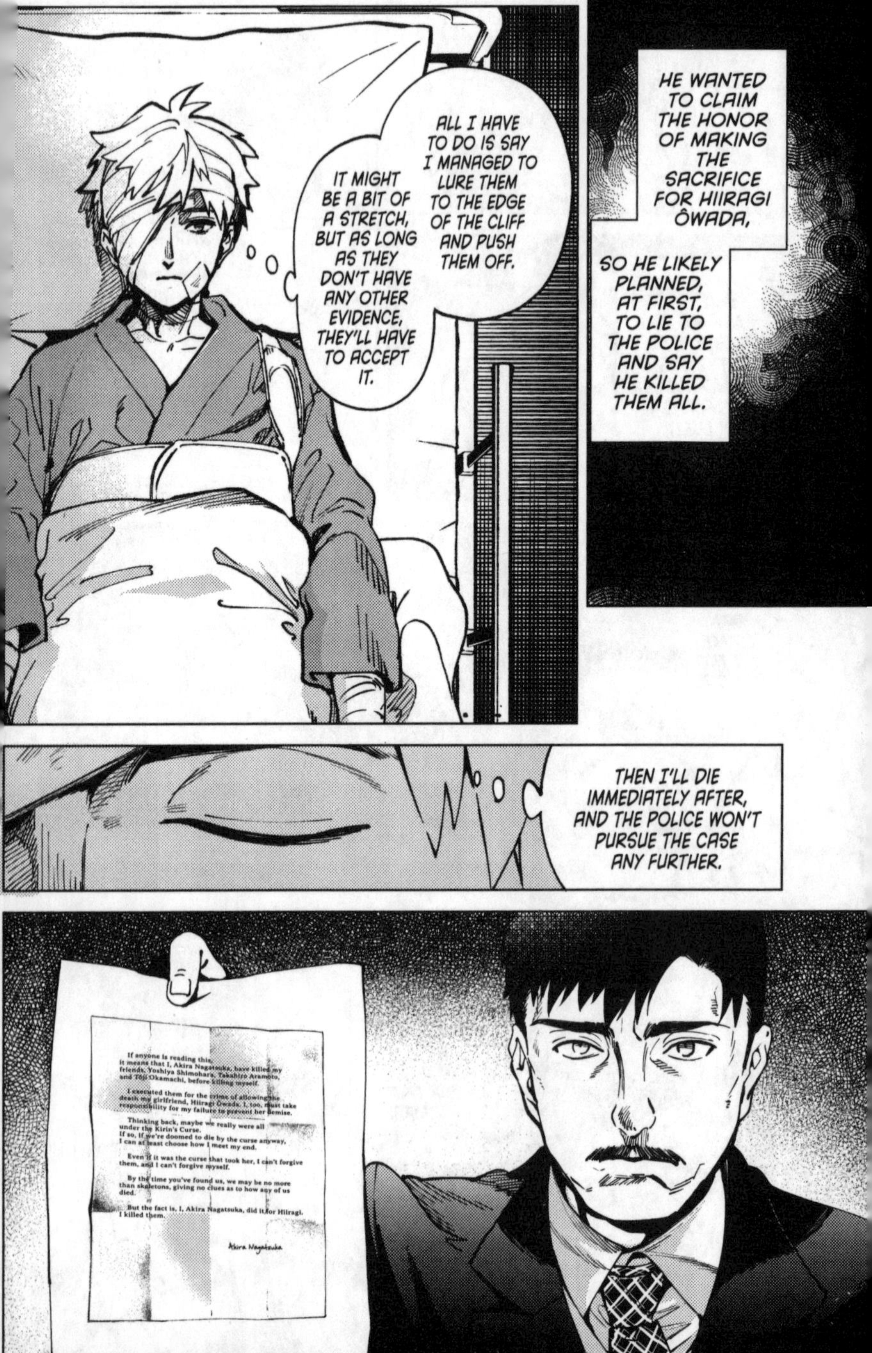
HE WANTED TO CLAIM THE HONOR OF MAKING THE SACRIFICE FOR HIIRAGI ÔWADA,
SO HE LIKELY PLANNED, AT FIRST, TO LIE TO THE POLICE AND SAY HE KILLED THEM ALL.
ALL I HAVE TO DO IS SAY I MANAGED TO LURE THEM TO THE EDGE OF THE CLIFF AND PUSH THEM OFF.
IT MIGHT BE A BIT OF A STRETCH, BUT AS LONG AS THEY DON'T HAVE ANY OTHER EVIDENCE, THEY'LL HAVE TO ACCEPT IT.
THEN I'LL DIE IMMEDIATELY AFTER, AND THE POLICE WON'T PURSUE THE CASE ANY FURTHER.
If anyone is reading this, it means that I, Akira Nagatsuka, have killed my friends, Yoshiya Shimohara, Takahiro Aramoto, and Tôji Okamachi, before killing myself.
I executed them for the crime of allowing the death my girlfriend, Hiiragi Ôwada. I, too, must take responsibility for my failure to prevent her demise.
Thinking back, maybe we really were all under the Kirin's Curse.
If so, if we're doomed to die by the curse anyway, I can at least choose how I meet my end.
Even if it was the curse that took her, I can't forgive them, and I can't forgive myself.
By the time you've found us, we may be no more than skeletons, giving no clues as to how any of us died.
But the fact is, I, Akira Nagatsuka, did it for Hiiragi. I killed them.
Akira Nagatsuka

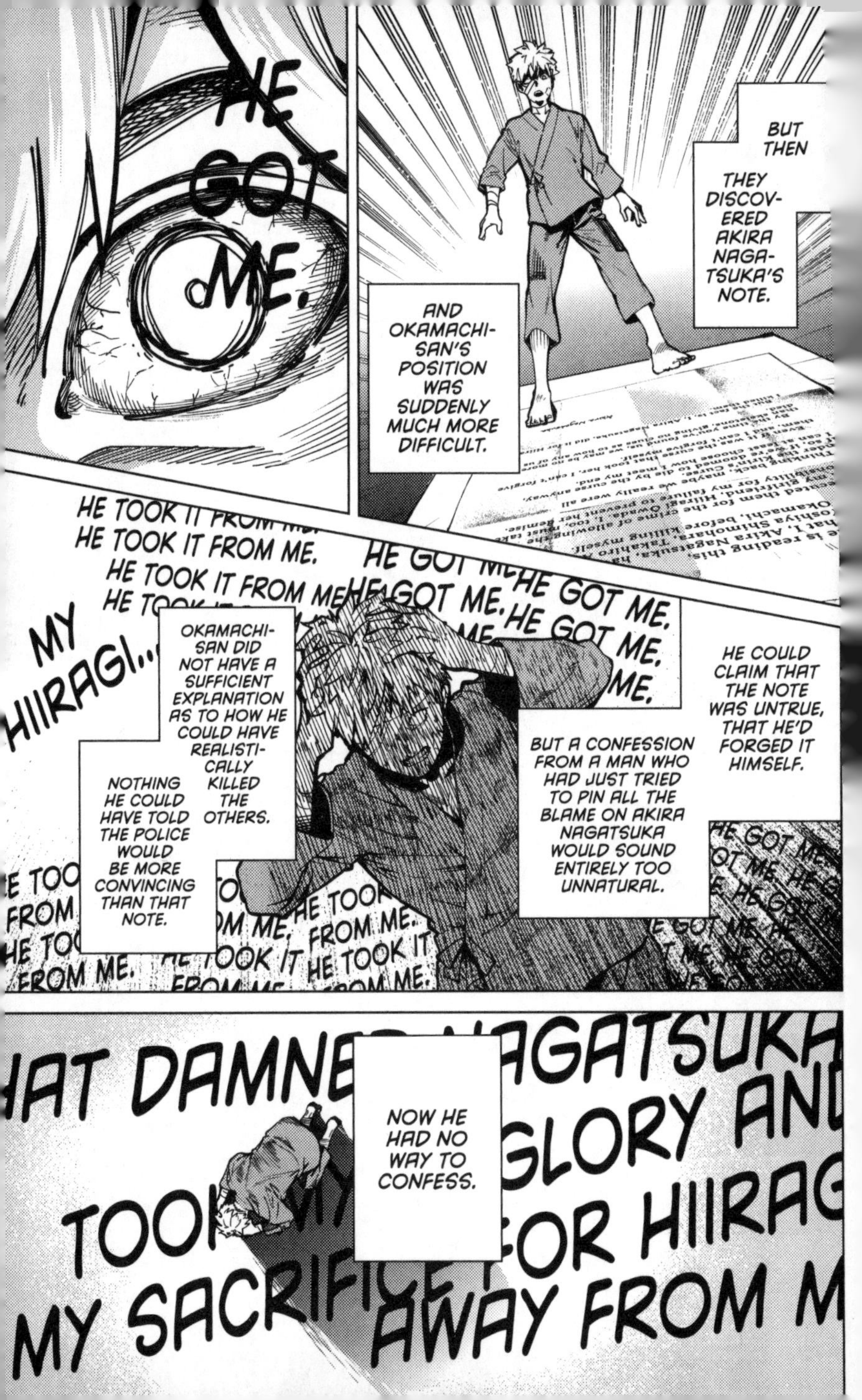
BUT THEN
THEY DISCOVERED AKIRA NAGATSUKA'S NOTE.
AND OKAMACHI-SAN'S POSITION WAS SUDDENLY MUCH MORE DIFFICULT.
HE GOT ME.
HE COULD CLAIM THAT THE NOTE WAS UNTRUE, THAT HE'D FORGED IT HIMSELF.
BUT A CONFESSION FROM A MAN WHO HAD JUST TRIED TO PIN ALL THE BLAME ON AKIRA NAGATSUKA WOULD SOUND ENTIRELY TOO UNNATURAL.
HE GOT ME. HE GOT ME. HE GOT ME.
HE TOOK IT FROM ME.
HE TOOK IT FROM ME.
MY HIIRAGI...
OKAMACHI-SAN DID NOT HAVE A SUFFICIENT EXPLANATION AS TO HOW HE COULD HAVE REALISTICALLY KILLED THE OTHERS.
NOTHING HE COULD HAVE TOLD THE POLICE WOULD BE MORE CONVINCING THAN THAT NOTE.
HE TOOK IT FROM ME. HE TOOK IT FROM ME.
NOW HE HAD NO WAY TO CONFESS.
HAT DAMNE
AGATSUKA
GLORY AN
TOO
FOR HIIRAG
MY SACRIFICE
AWAY FROM M

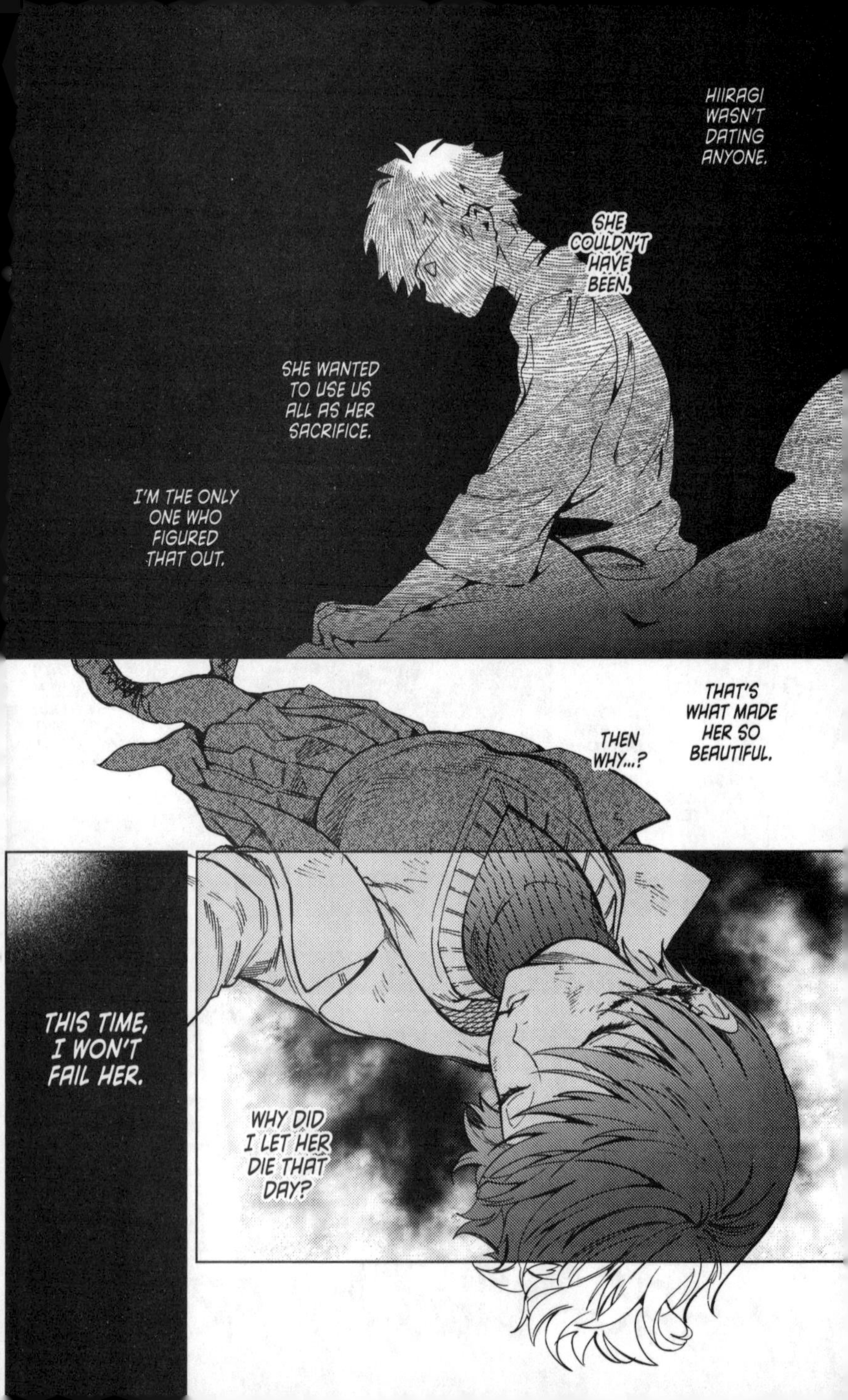
HIIRAGI WASN'T DATING ANYONE.
SHE COULDN'T HAVE BEEN.
SHE WANTED TO USE US ALL AS HER SACRIFICE.
I'M THE ONLY ONE WHO FIGURED THAT OUT.
THAT'S WHAT MADE HER SO BEAUTIFUL.
THEN WHY...?
WHY DID I LET HER DIE THAT DAY?
THIS TIME, I WON'T FAIL HER.

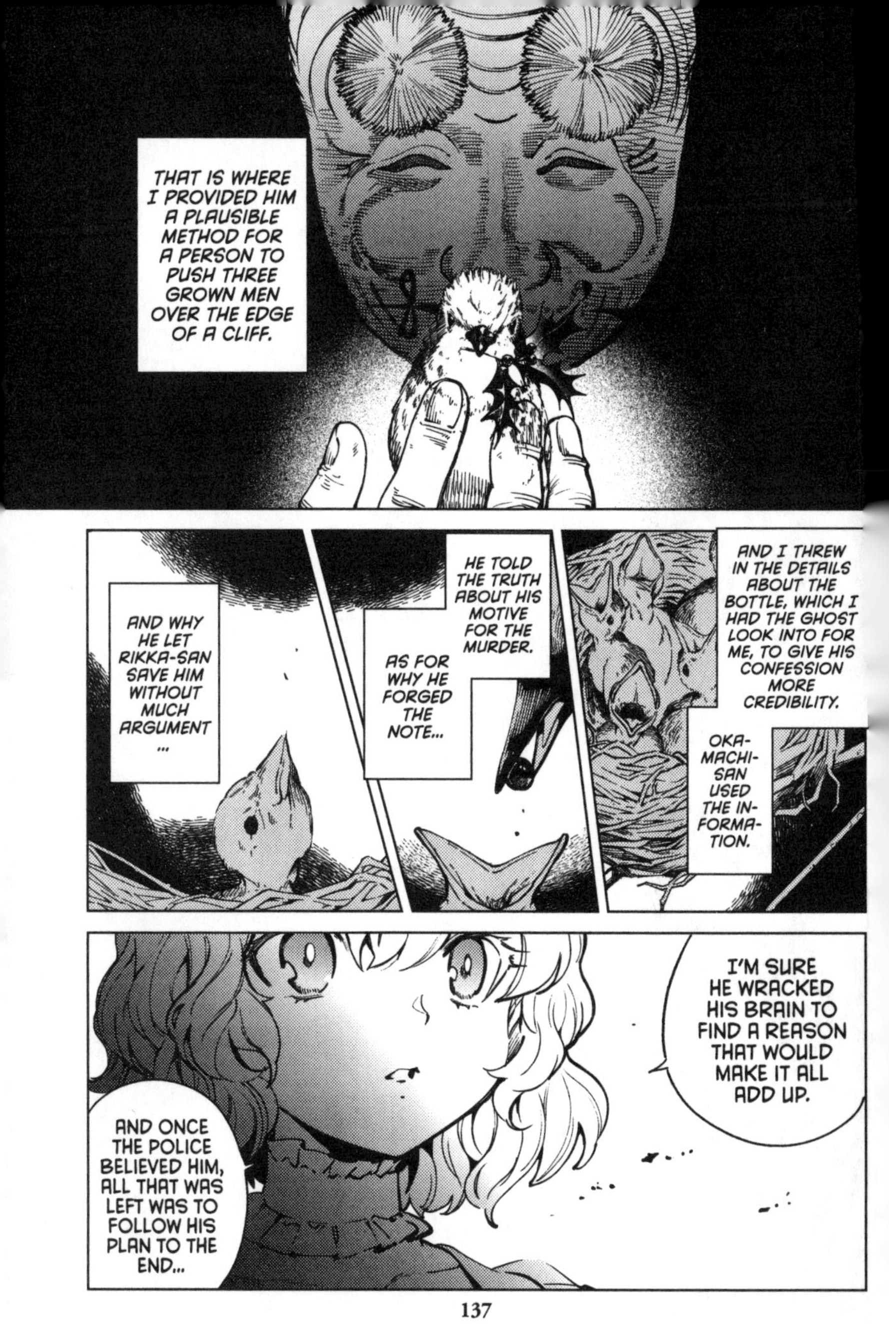
THAT IS WHERE I PROVIDED HIM A PLAUSIBLE METHOD FOR A PERSON TO PUSH THREE GROWN MEN OVER THE EDGE OF A CLIFF.
AND I THREW IN THE DETAILS ABOUT THE BOTTLE, WHICH I HAD THE GHOST LOOK INTO FOR ME, TO GIVE HIS CONFESSION MORE CREDIBILITY.
OKAMACHI-SAN USED THE INFORMATION.
HE TOLD THE TRUTH ABOUT HIS MOTIVE FOR THE MURDER.
AS FOR WHY HE FORGED THE NOTE...
AND WHY HE LET RIKKA-SAN SAVE HIM WITHOUT MUCH ARGUMENT...
I'M SURE HE WRACKED HIS BRAIN TO FIND A REASON THAT WOULD MAKE IT ALL ADD UP.
AND ONCE THE POLICE BELIEVED HIM, ALL THAT WAS LEFT WAS TO FOLLOW HIS PLAN TO THE END...

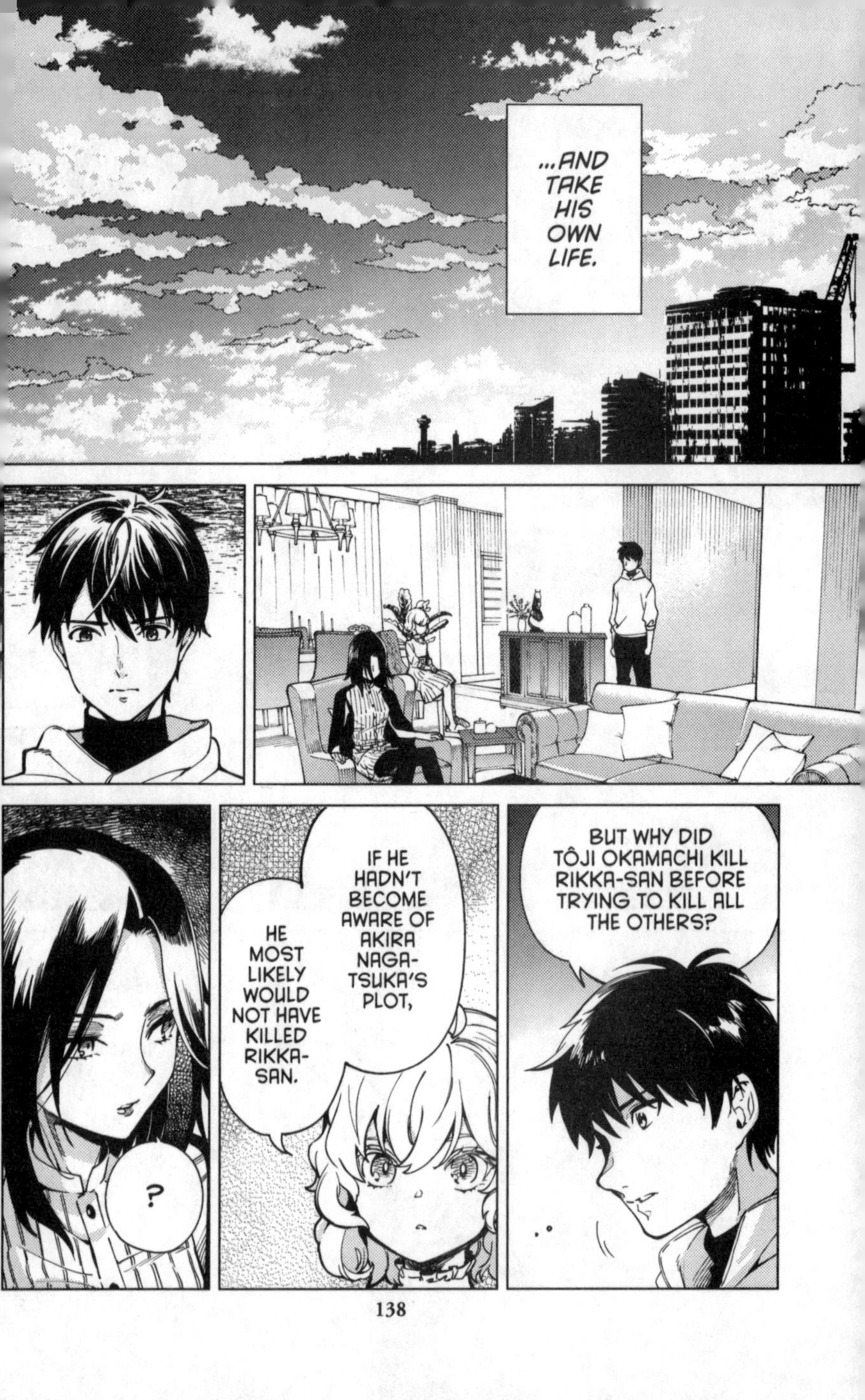
...AND TAKE HIS OWN LIFE.
BUT WHY DID TÔJI OKAMACHI KILL RIKKA-SAN BEFORE TRYING TO KILL ALL THE OTHERS?
IF HE HADN'T BECOME AWARE OF AKIRA NAGA-TSUKA'S PLOT,
HE MOST LIKELY WOULD NOT HAVE KILLED RIKKA-SAN.
?

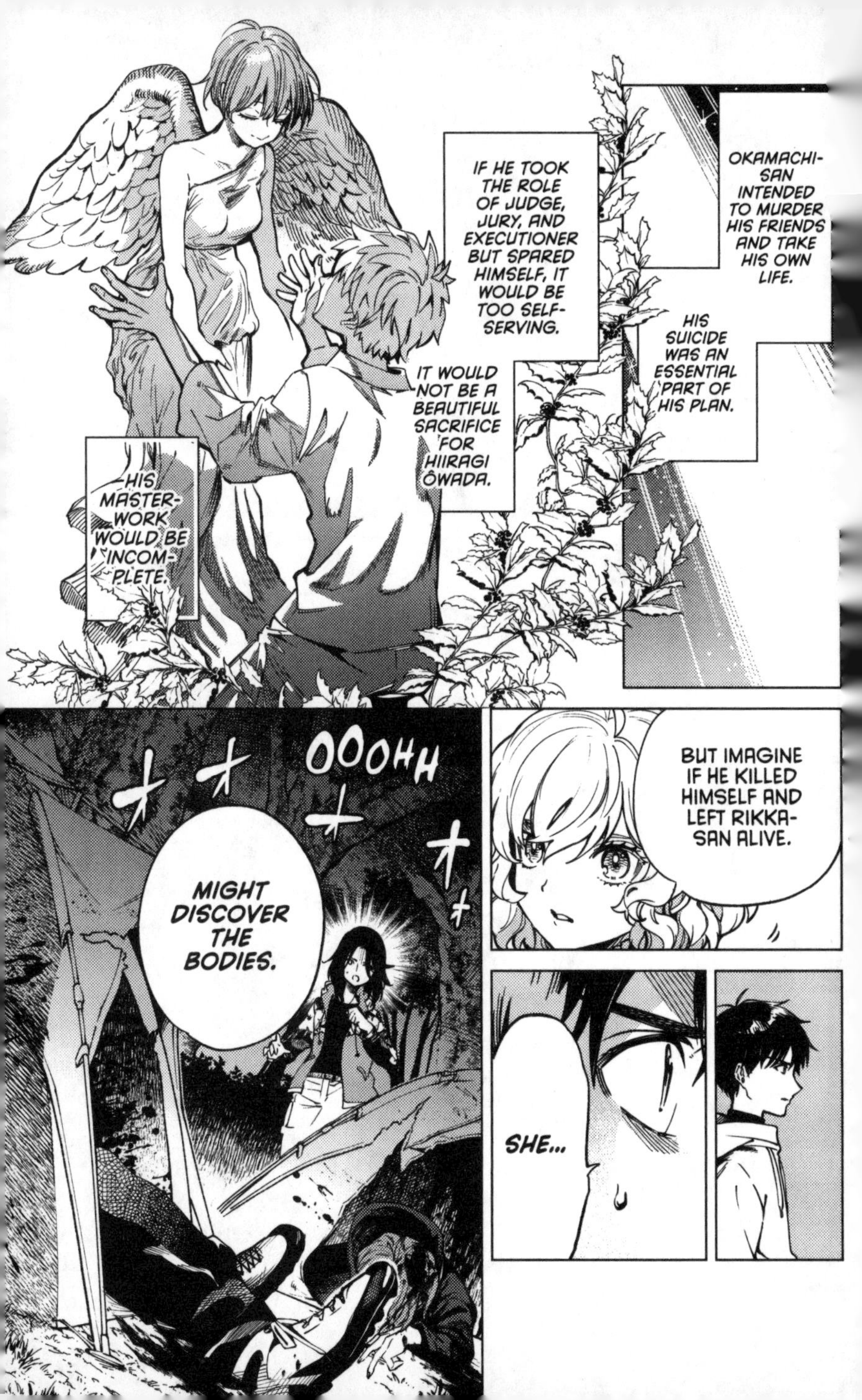
OKAMACHI-SAN INTENDED TO MURDER HIS FRIENDS AND TAKE HIS OWN LIFE.
HIS SUICIDE WAS AN ESSENTIAL PART OF HIS PLAN.
IF HE TOOK THE ROLE OF JUDGE, JURY, AND EXECUTIONER BUT SPARED HIMSELF, IT WOULD BE TOO SELF-SERVING.
IT WOULD NOT BE A BEAUTIFUL SACRIFICE FOR HIIRAGI ÔWADA.
HIS MASTER-WORK WOULD BE INCOM-PLETE.
BUT IMAGINE IF HE KILLED HIMSELF AND LEFT RIKKA-SAN ALIVE.
SHE...
OOOHH
MIGHT DISCOVER THE BODIES.

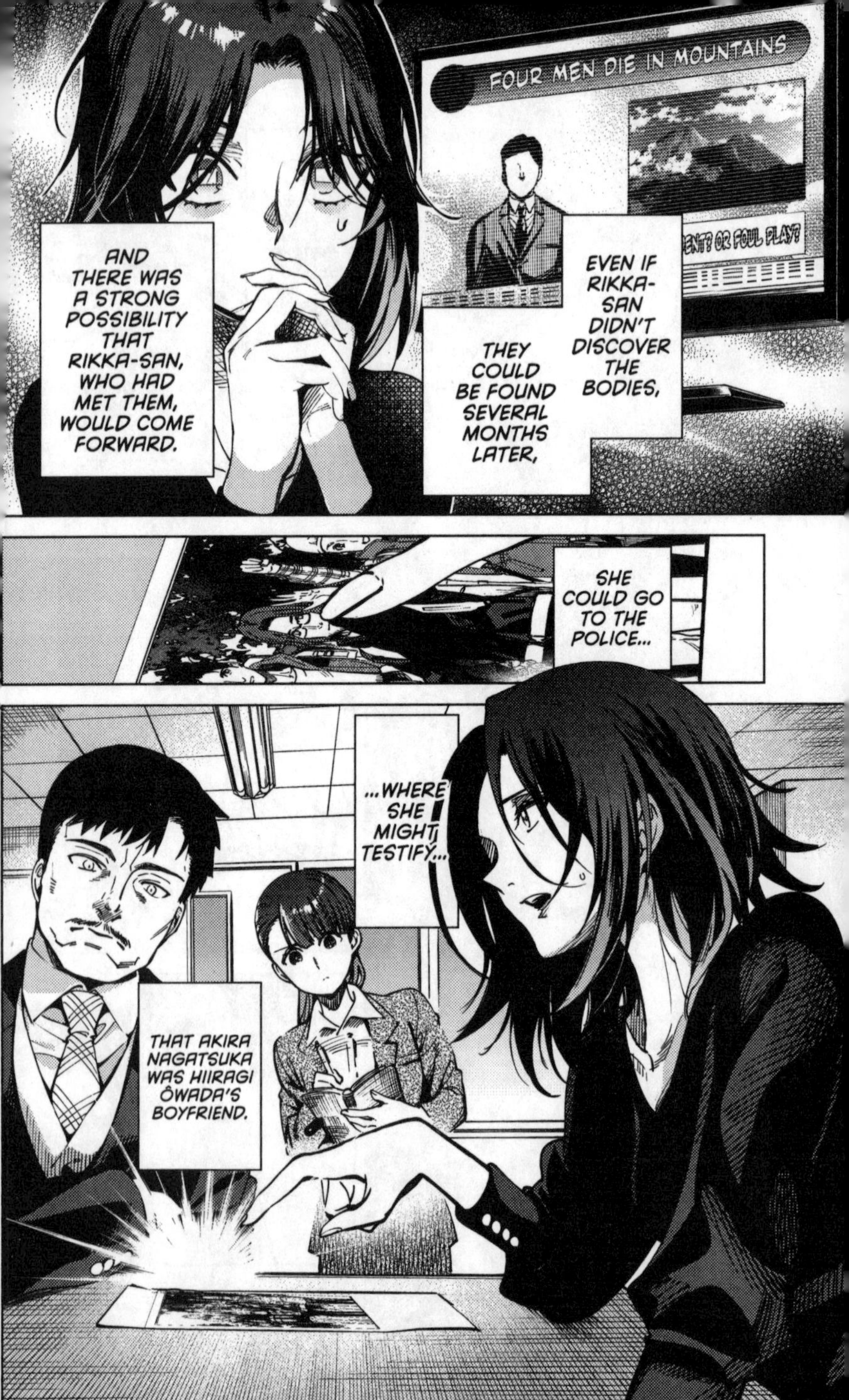
FOUR MEN DIE IN MOUNTAINS
EVEN IF RIKKA-SAN DIDN'T DISCOVER THE BODIES,
THEY COULD BE FOUND SEVERAL MONTHS LATER,
AND THERE WAS A STRONG POSSIBILITY THAT RIKKA-SAN, WHO HAD MET THEM, WOULD COME FORWARD.
SHE COULD GO TO THE POLICE...
...WHERE SHE MIGHT TESTIFY...
THAT AKIRA NAGATSUKA WAS HIIRAGI ÔWADA'S BOYFRIEND.

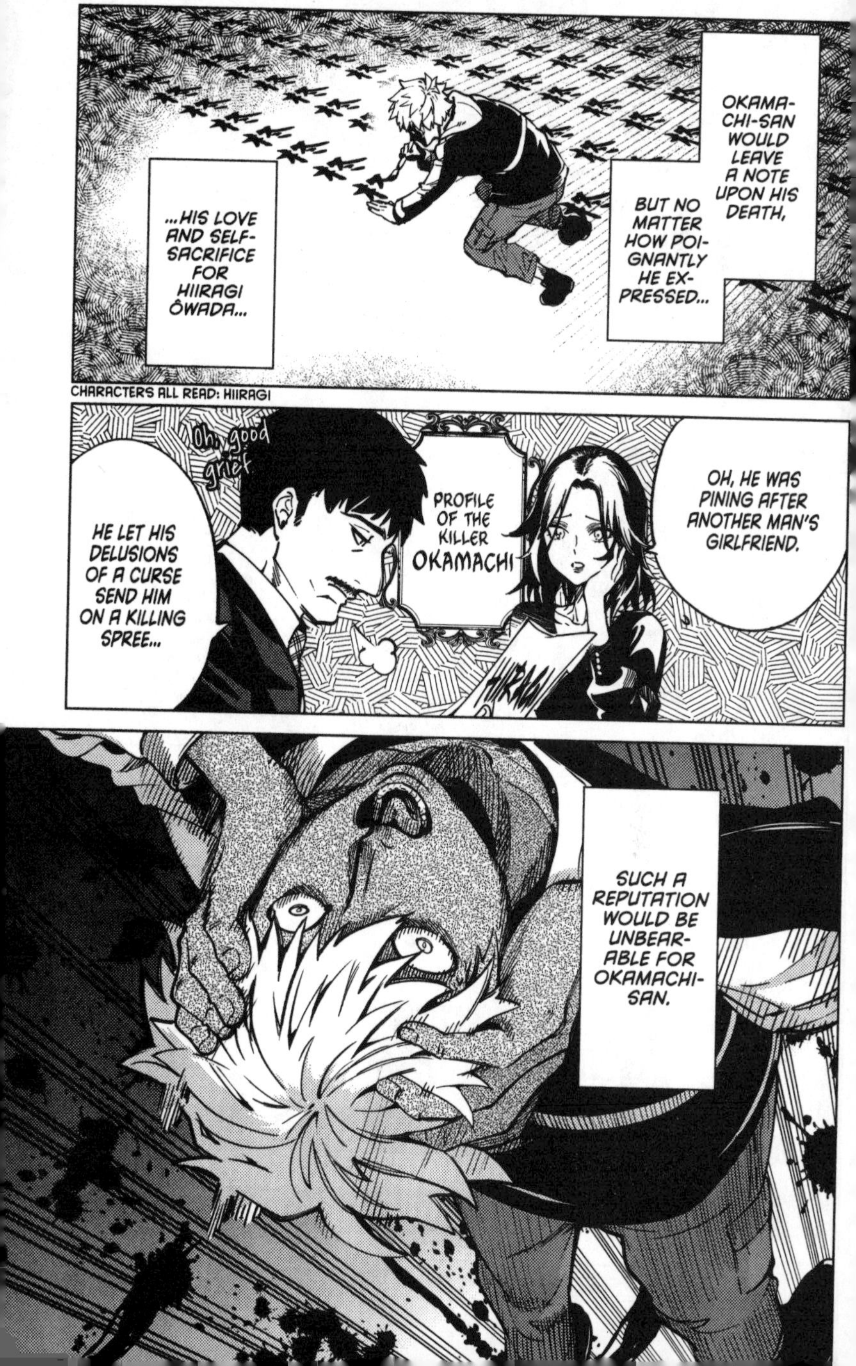
OKAMACHI-SAN WOULD LEAVE A NOTE UPON HIS DEATH,
BUT NO MATTER HOW POIGNANTLY HE EXPRESSED...
...HIS LOVE AND SELF-SACRIFICE FOR HIIRAGI ÔWADA...
CHARACTERS ALL READ: HIIRAGI
OH, HE WAS PINING AFTER ANOTHER MAN'S GIRLFRIEND.
PROFILE OF THE KILLER OKAMACHI
HIIRAGI
Oh, good grief
HE LET HIS DELUSIONS OF A CURSE SEND HIM ON A KILLING SPREE...
SUCH A REPUTATION WOULD BE UNBEARABLE FOR OKAMACHI-SAN.

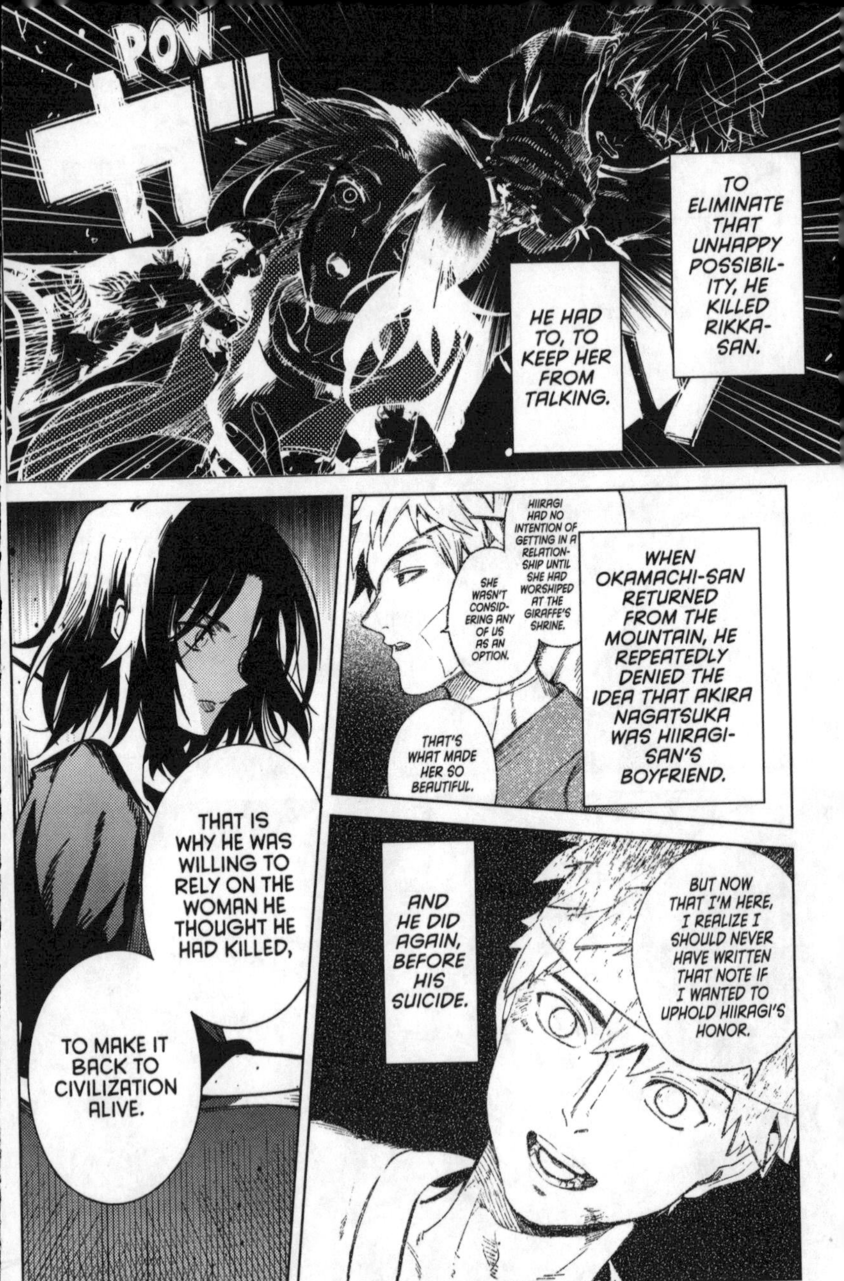
POW
ッ‼
TO ELIMINATE THAT UNHAPPY POSSIBILITY, HE KILLED RIKKA-SAN.
HE HAD TO, TO KEEP HER FROM TALKING.
WHEN OKAMACHI-SAN RETURNED FROM THE MOUNTAIN, HE REPEATEDLY DENIED THE IDEA THAT AKIRA NAGATSUKA WAS HIIRAGI-SAN'S BOYFRIEND.
HIIRAGI HAD NO INTENTION OF GETTING IN A RELATIONSHIP UNTIL SHE HAD WORSHIPED AT THE GIRAFFE'S SHRINE.
SHE WASN'T CONSIDERING ANY OF US AS AN OPTION.
THAT'S WHAT MADE HER SO BEAUTIFUL.
BUT NOW THAT I'M HERE, I REALIZE I SHOULD NEVER HAVE WRITTEN THAT NOTE IF I WANTED TO UPHOLD HIIRAGI'S HONOR.
AND HE DID AGAIN, BEFORE HIS SUICIDE.
THAT IS WHY HE WAS WILLING TO RELY ON THE WOMAN HE THOUGHT HE HAD KILLED,
TO MAKE IT BACK TO CIVILIZATION ALIVE.

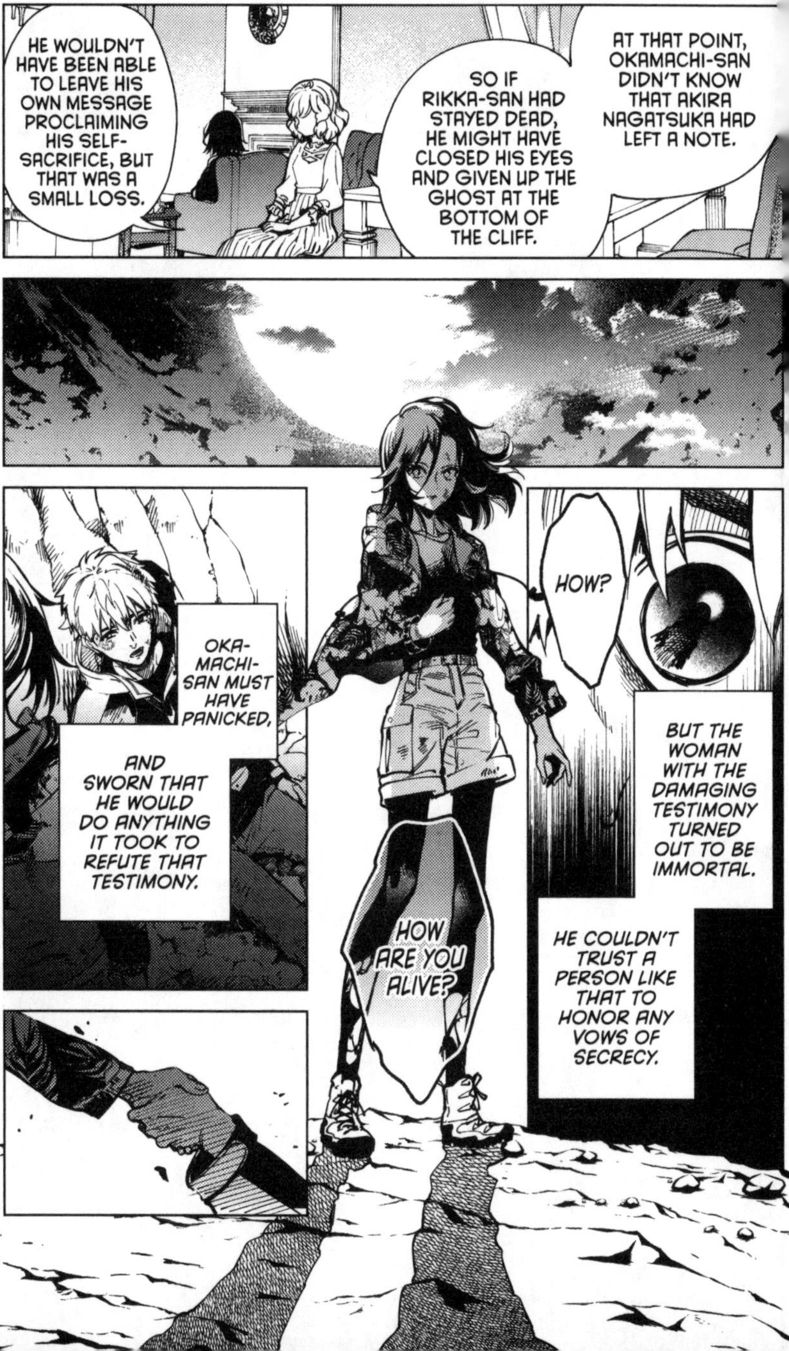
AT THAT POINT, OKAMACHI-SAN DIDN'T KNOW THAT AKIRA NAGATSUKA HAD LEFT A NOTE.
SO IF RIKKA-SAN HAD STAYED DEAD, HE MIGHT HAVE CLOSED HIS EYES AND GIVEN UP THE GHOST AT THE BOTTOM OF THE CLIFF.
HE WOULDN'T HAVE BEEN ABLE TO LEAVE HIS OWN MESSAGE PROCLAIMING HIS SELF-SACRIFICE, BUT THAT WAS A SMALL LOSS.
OKA-MACHI-SAN MUST HAVE PANICKED,
AND SWORN THAT HE WOULD DO ANYTHING IT TOOK TO REFUTE THAT TESTIMONY.
HOW?
BUT THE WOMAN WITH THE DAMAGING TESTIMONY TURNED OUT TO BE IMMORTAL.
HE COULDN'T TRUST A PERSON LIKE THAT TO HONOR ANY VOWS OF SECRECY.
HOW ARE YOU ALIVE?

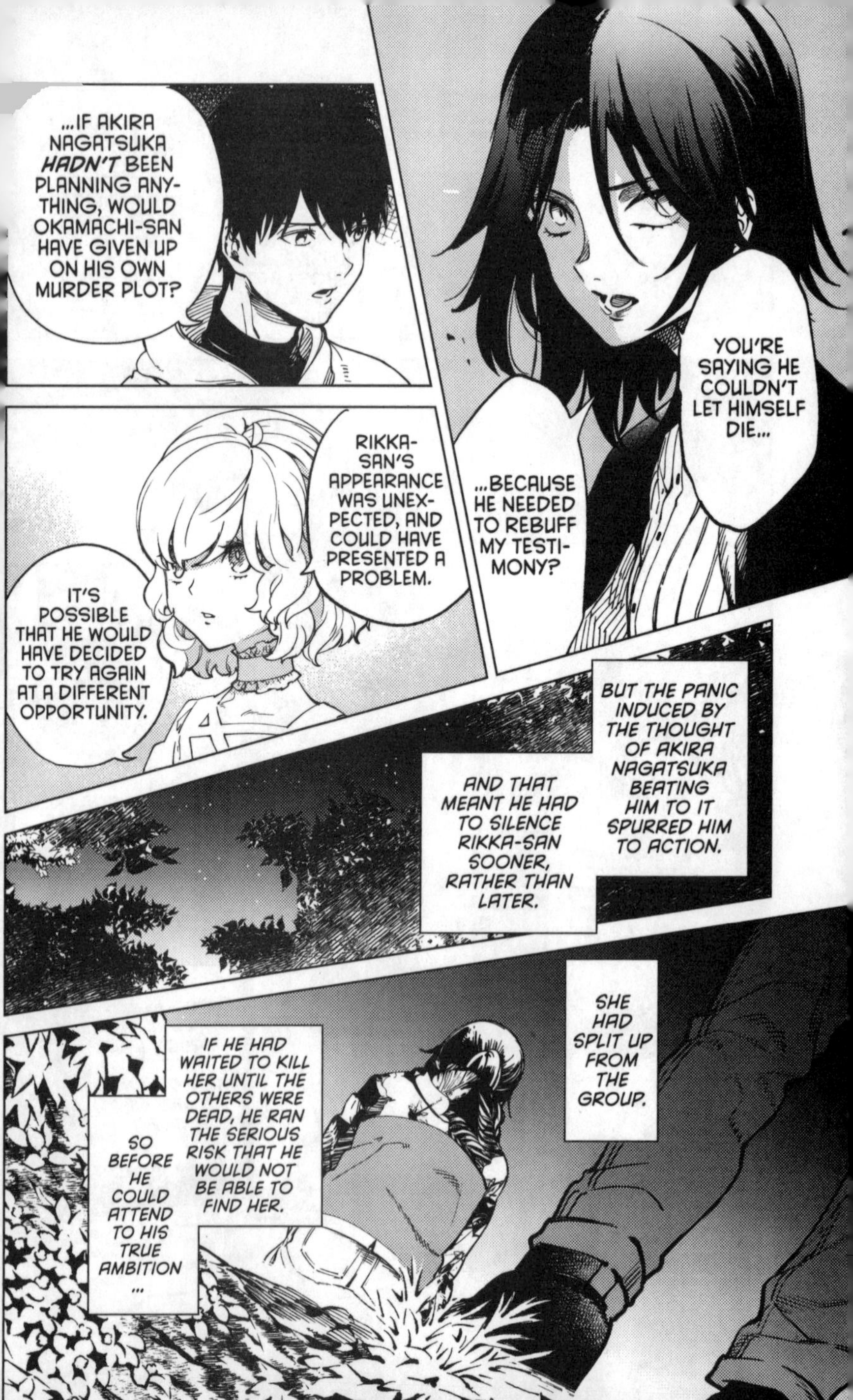
YOU'RE SAYING HE COULDN'T LET HIMSELF DIE...
...BECAUSE HE NEEDED TO REBUFF MY TESTIMONY?
...IF AKIRA NAGATSUKA *HADN'T* BEEN PLANNING ANYTHING, WOULD OKAMACHI-SAN HAVE GIVEN UP ON HIS OWN MURDER PLOT?
RIKKA-SAN'S APPEARANCE WAS UNEXPECTED, AND COULD HAVE PRESENTED A PROBLEM.
IT'S POSSIBLE THAT HE WOULD HAVE DECIDED TO TRY AGAIN AT A DIFFERENT OPPORTUNITY.
BUT THE PANIC INDUCED BY THE THOUGHT OF AKIRA NAGATSUKA BEATING HIM TO IT SPURRED HIM TO ACTION.
AND THAT MEANT HE HAD TO SILENCE RIKKA-SAN SOONER, RATHER THAN LATER.
SHE HAD SPLIT UP FROM THE GROUP.
IF HE HAD WAITED TO KILL HER UNTIL THE OTHERS WERE DEAD, HE RAN THE SERIOUS RISK THAT HE WOULD NOT BE ABLE TO FIND HER.
SO BEFORE HE COULD ATTEND TO HIS TRUE AMBITION...

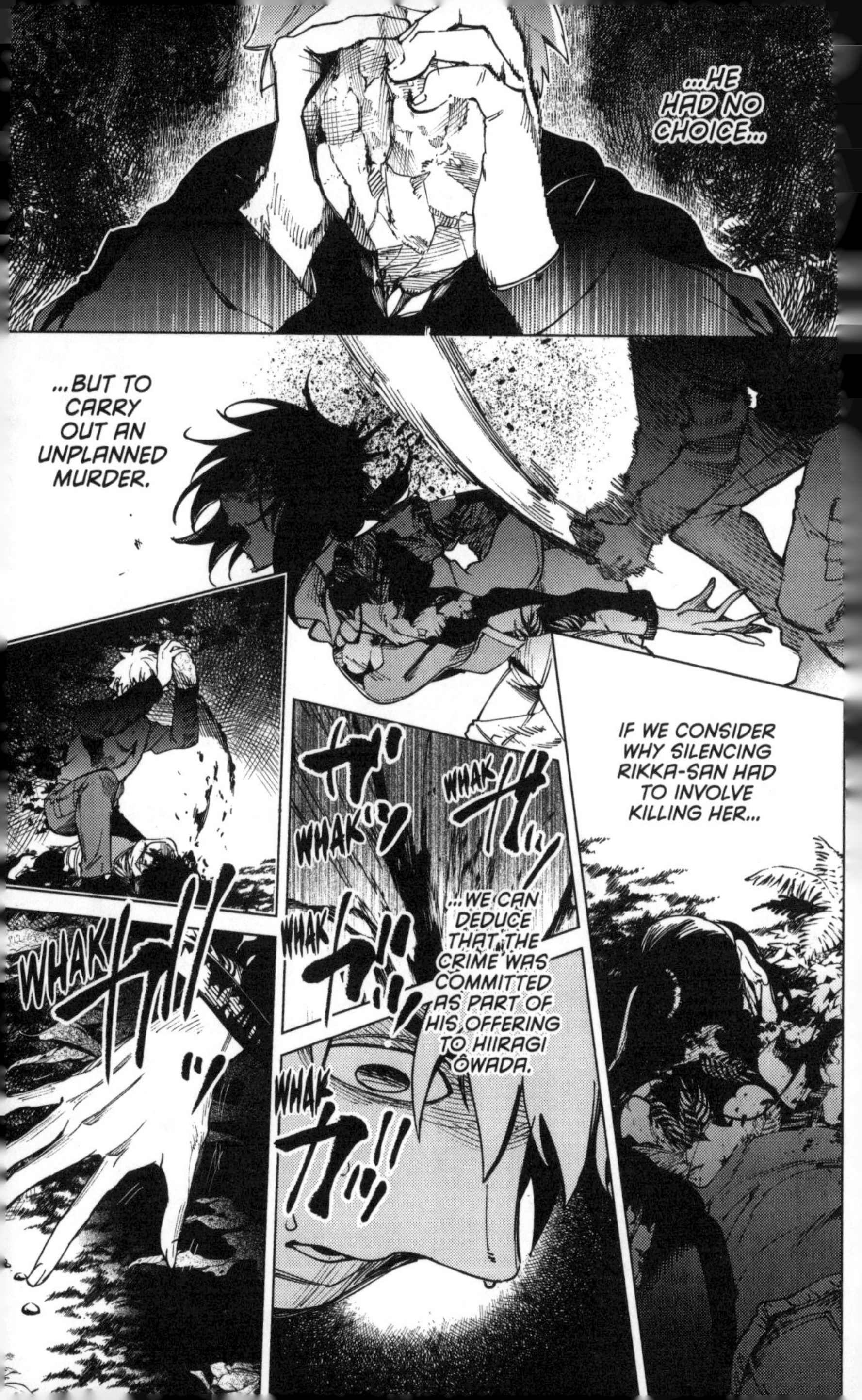
...HE HAD NO CHOICE...
...BUT TO CARRY OUT AN UNPLANNED MURDER.
IF WE CONSIDER WHY SILENCING RIKKA-SAN HAD TO INVOLVE KILLING HER...
WHAK
WHAK
WHAK
...WE CAN DEDUCE THAT THE CRIME WAS COMMITTED AS PART OF HIS OFFERING TO HIIRAGI ŌWADA.
WHAK
WHAK

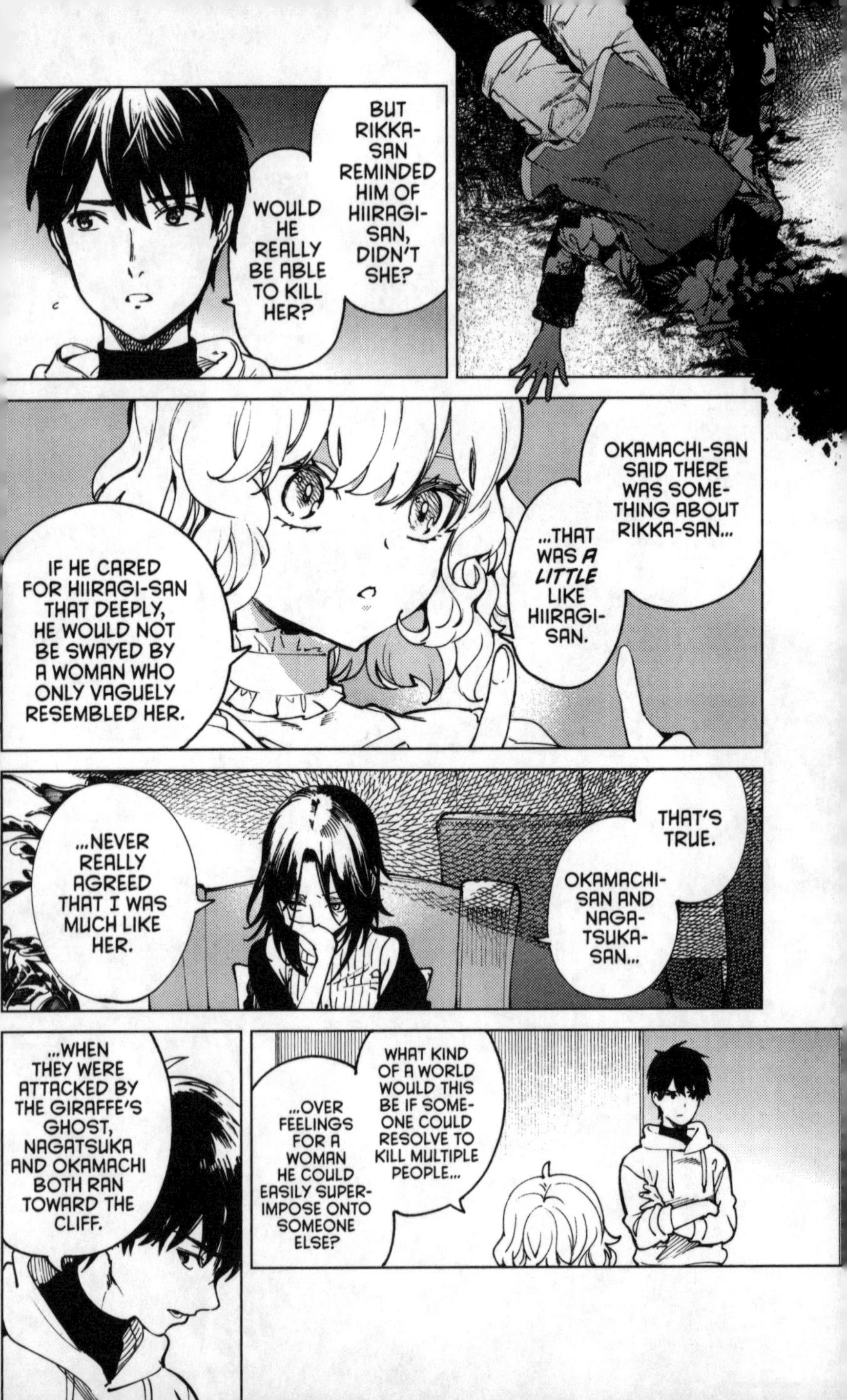
BUT RIKKA-SAN REMINDED HIM OF HIIRAGI-SAN, DIDN'T SHE?
WOULD HE REALLY BE ABLE TO KILL HER?
OKAMACHI-SAN SAID THERE WAS SOMETHING ABOUT RIKKA-SAN...
...THAT WAS *A LITTLE* LIKE HIIRAGI-SAN.
IF HE CARED FOR HIIRAGI-SAN THAT DEEPLY, HE WOULD NOT BE SWAYED BY A WOMAN WHO ONLY VAGUELY RESEMBLED HER.
THAT'S TRUE.
OKAMACHI-SAN AND NAGATSUKA-SAN...
...NEVER REALLY AGREED THAT I WAS MUCH LIKE HER.
WHAT KIND OF A WORLD WOULD THIS BE IF SOMEONE COULD RESOLVE TO KILL MULTIPLE PEOPLE...
...OVER FEELINGS FOR A WOMAN HE COULD EASILY SUPERIMPOSE ONTO SOMEONE ELSE?
...WHEN THEY WERE ATTACKED BY THE GIRAFFE'S GHOST, NAGATSUKA AND OKAMACHI BOTH RAN TOWARD THE CLIFF.

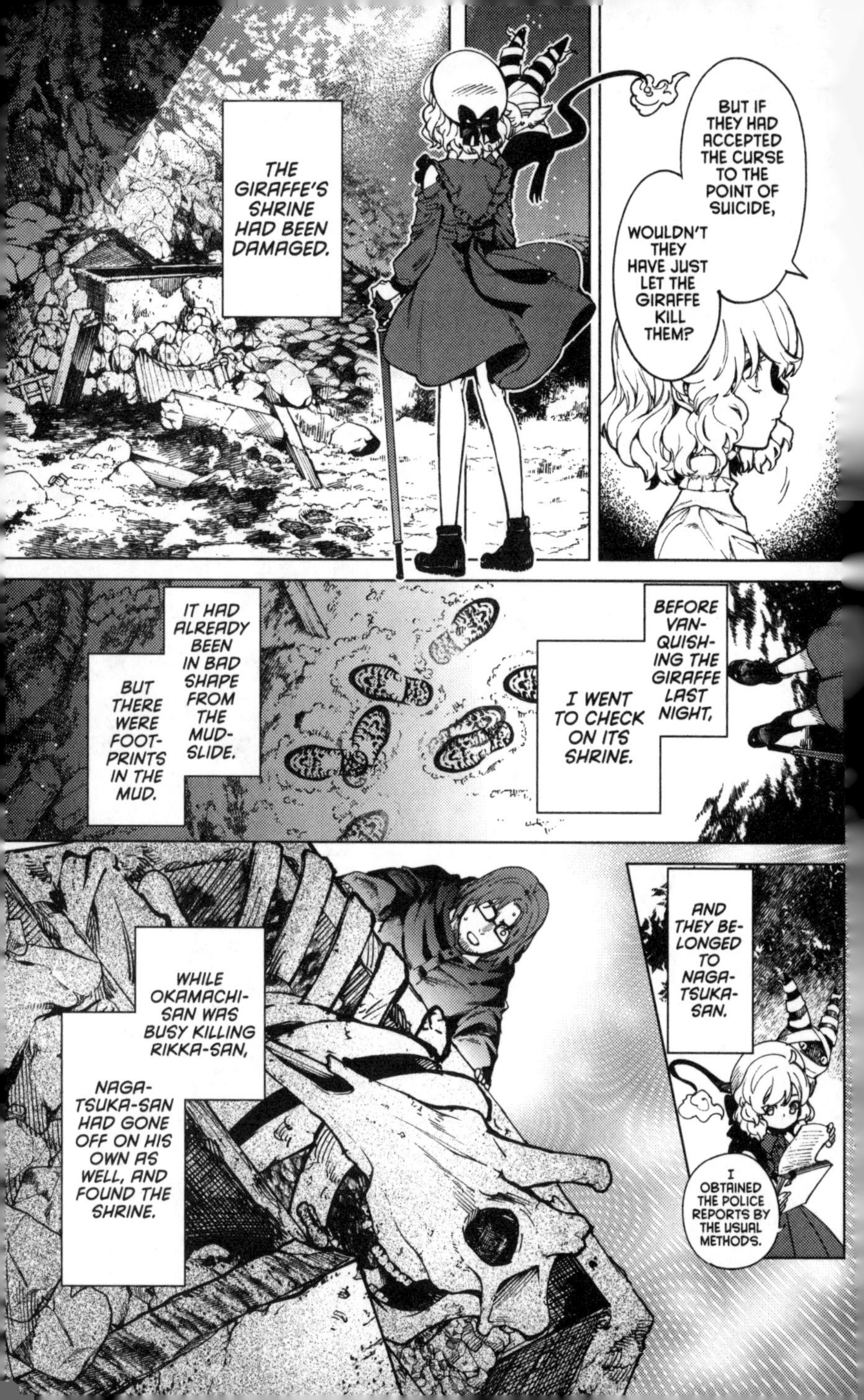
BUT IF THEY HAD ACCEPTED THE CURSE TO THE POINT OF SUICIDE, WOULDN'T THEY HAVE JUST LET THE GIRAFFE KILL THEM?
THE GIRAFFE'S SHRINE HAD BEEN DAMAGED.
BEFORE VAN-QUISH-ING THE GIRAFFE LAST NIGHT,
I WENT TO CHECK ON ITS SHRINE.
IT HAD ALREADY BEEN IN BAD SHAPE FROM THE MUD-SLIDE.
BUT THERE WERE FOOT-PRINTS IN THE MUD.
AND THEY BE-LONGED TO NAGA-TSUKA-SAN.
I OBTAINED THE POLICE REPORTS BY THE USUAL METHODS.
WHILE OKAMACHI-SAN WAS BUSY KILLING RIKKA-SAN,
NAGA-TSUKA-SAN HAD GONE OFF ON HIS OWN AS WELL, AND FOUND THE SHRINE.

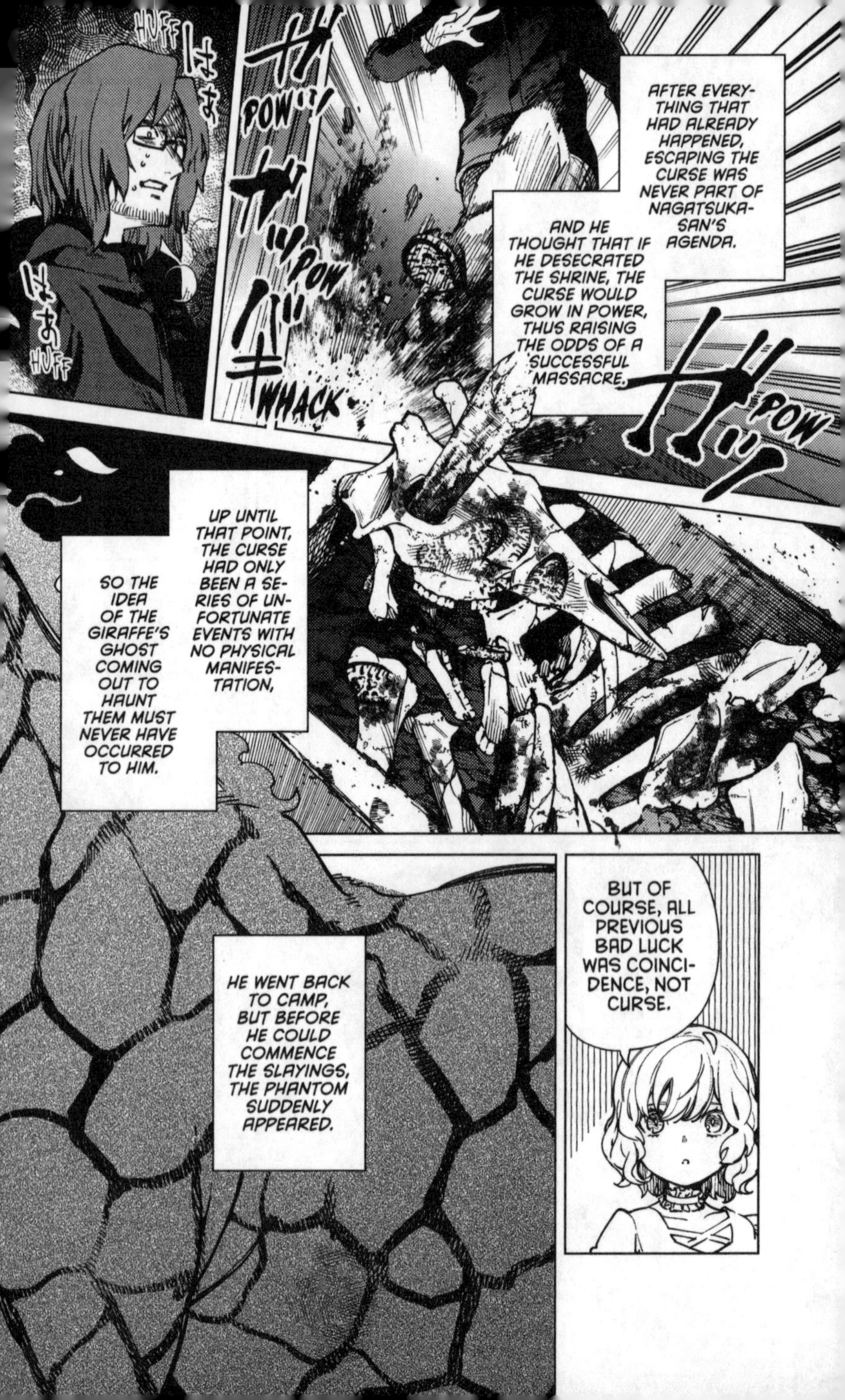
AFTER EVERYTHING THAT HAD ALREADY HAPPENED, ESCAPING THE CURSE WAS NEVER PART OF NAGATSUKA-SAN'S AGENDA.
AND HE THOUGHT THAT IF HE DESECRATED THE SHRINE, THE CURSE WOULD GROW IN POWER, THUS RAISING THE ODDS OF A SUCCESSFUL MASSACRE.
POW
POW!!
POW
WHACK
HUFF
HUFF
UP UNTIL THAT POINT, THE CURSE HAD ONLY BEEN A SERIES OF UNFORTUNATE EVENTS WITH NO PHYSICAL MANIFESTATION,
SO THE IDEA OF THE GIRAFFE'S GHOST COMING OUT TO HAUNT THEM MUST NEVER HAVE OCCURRED TO HIM.
BUT OF COURSE, ALL PREVIOUS BAD LUCK WAS COINCIDENCE, NOT CURSE.
HE WENT BACK TO CAMP, BUT BEFORE HE COULD COMMENCE THE SLAYINGS, THE PHANTOM SUDDENLY APPEARED.

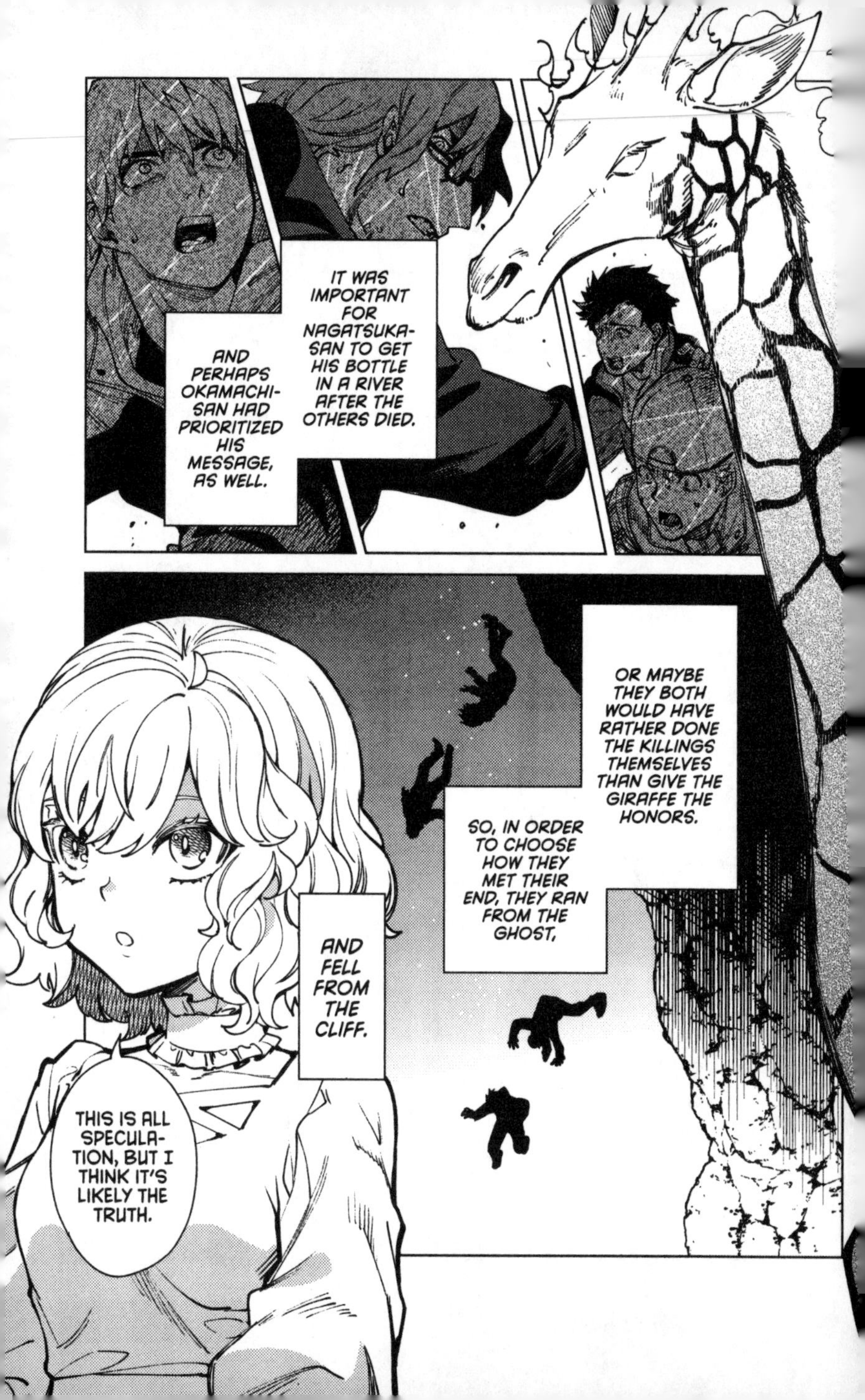
IT WAS IMPORTANT FOR NAGATSUKA-SAN TO GET HIS BOTTLE IN A RIVER AFTER THE OTHERS DIED.
AND PERHAPS OKAMACHI-SAN HAD PRIORITIZED HIS MESSAGE, AS WELL.
OR MAYBE THEY BOTH WOULD HAVE RATHER DONE THE KILLINGS THEMSELVES THAN GIVE THE GIRAFFE THE HONORS.
SO, IN ORDER TO CHOOSE HOW THEY MET THEIR END, THEY RAN FROM THE GHOST,
AND FELL FROM THE CLIFF.
THIS IS ALL SPECULATION, BUT I THINK IT'S LIKELY THE TRUTH.

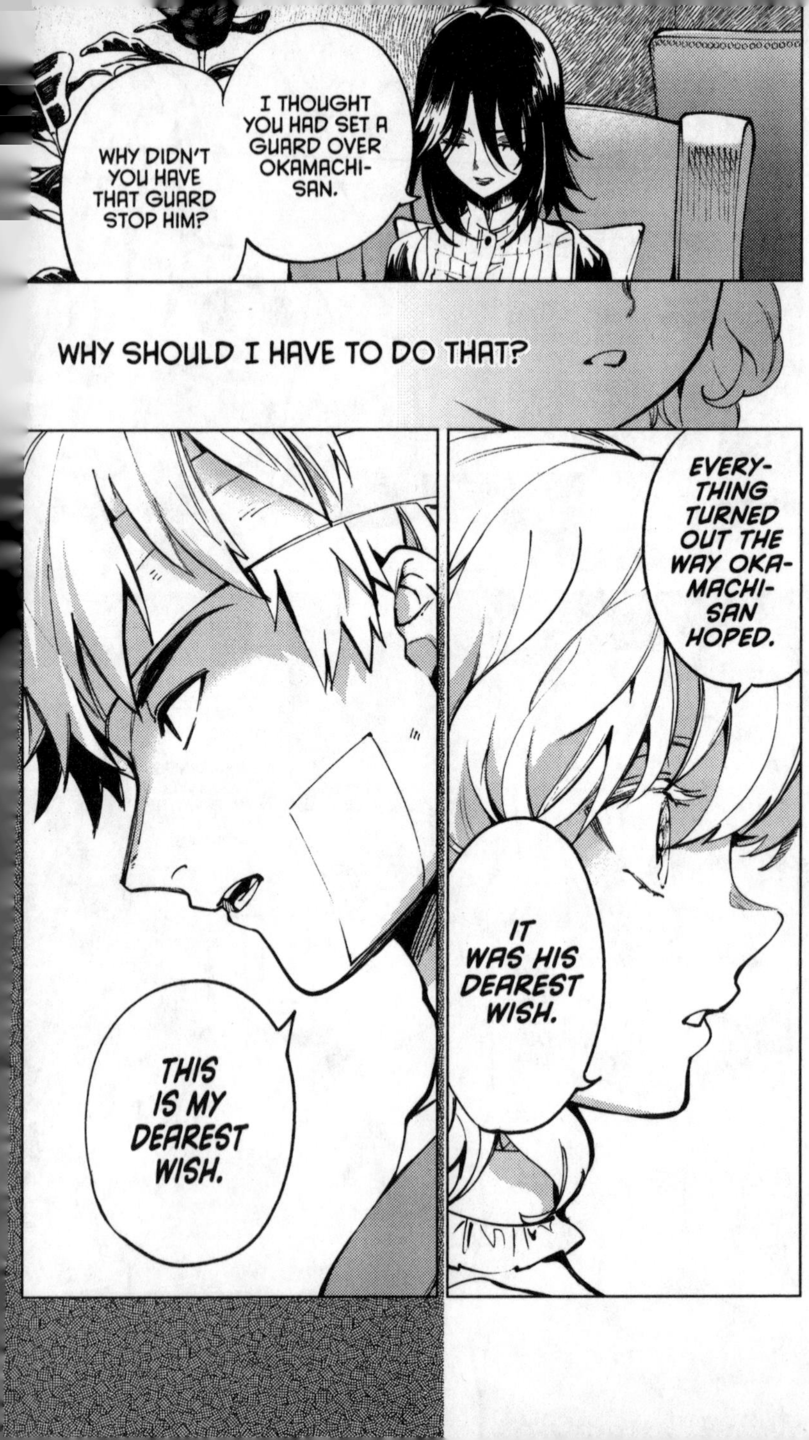
I THOUGHT YOU HAD SET A GUARD OVER OKAMACHI-SAN.
WHY DIDN'T YOU HAVE THAT GUARD STOP HIM?
WHY SHOULD I HAVE TO DO THAT?
EVERYTHING TURNED OUT THE WAY OKAMACHI-SAN HOPED.
IT WAS HIS DEAREST WISH.
THIS IS MY DEAREST WISH.

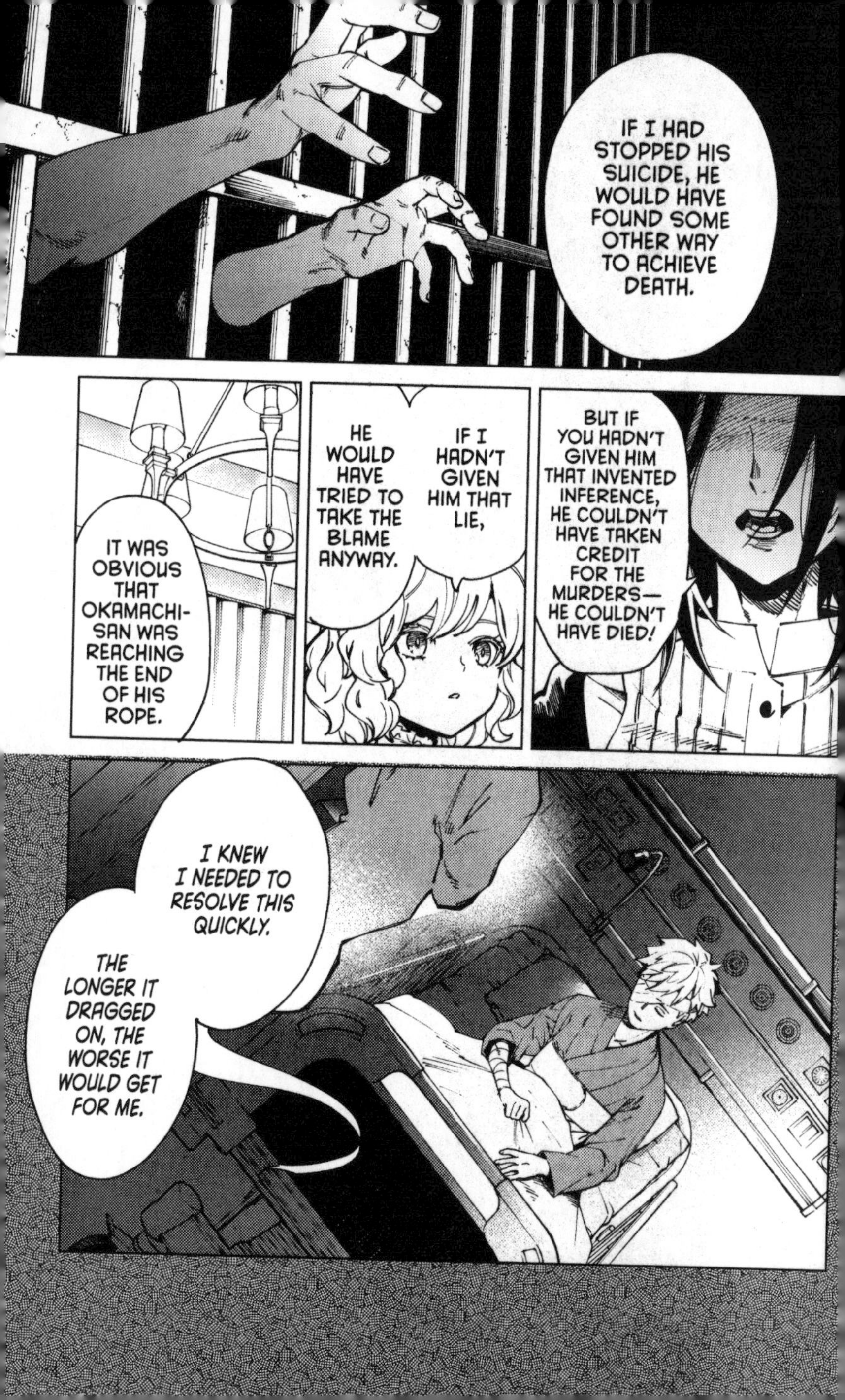
IF I HAD STOPPED HIS SUICIDE, HE WOULD HAVE FOUND SOME OTHER WAY TO ACHIEVE DEATH.
BUT IF YOU HADN'T GIVEN HIM THAT INVENTED INFERENCE, HE COULDN'T HAVE TAKEN CREDIT FOR THE MURDERS—HE COULDN'T HAVE DIED!
IF I HADN'T GIVEN HIM THAT LIE,
HE WOULD HAVE TRIED TO TAKE THE BLAME ANYWAY.
IT WAS OBVIOUS THAT OKAMACHI-SAN WAS REACHING THE END OF HIS ROPE.
I KNEW I NEEDED TO RESOLVE THIS QUICKLY.
THE LONGER IT DRAGGED ON, THE WORSE IT WOULD GET FOR ME.

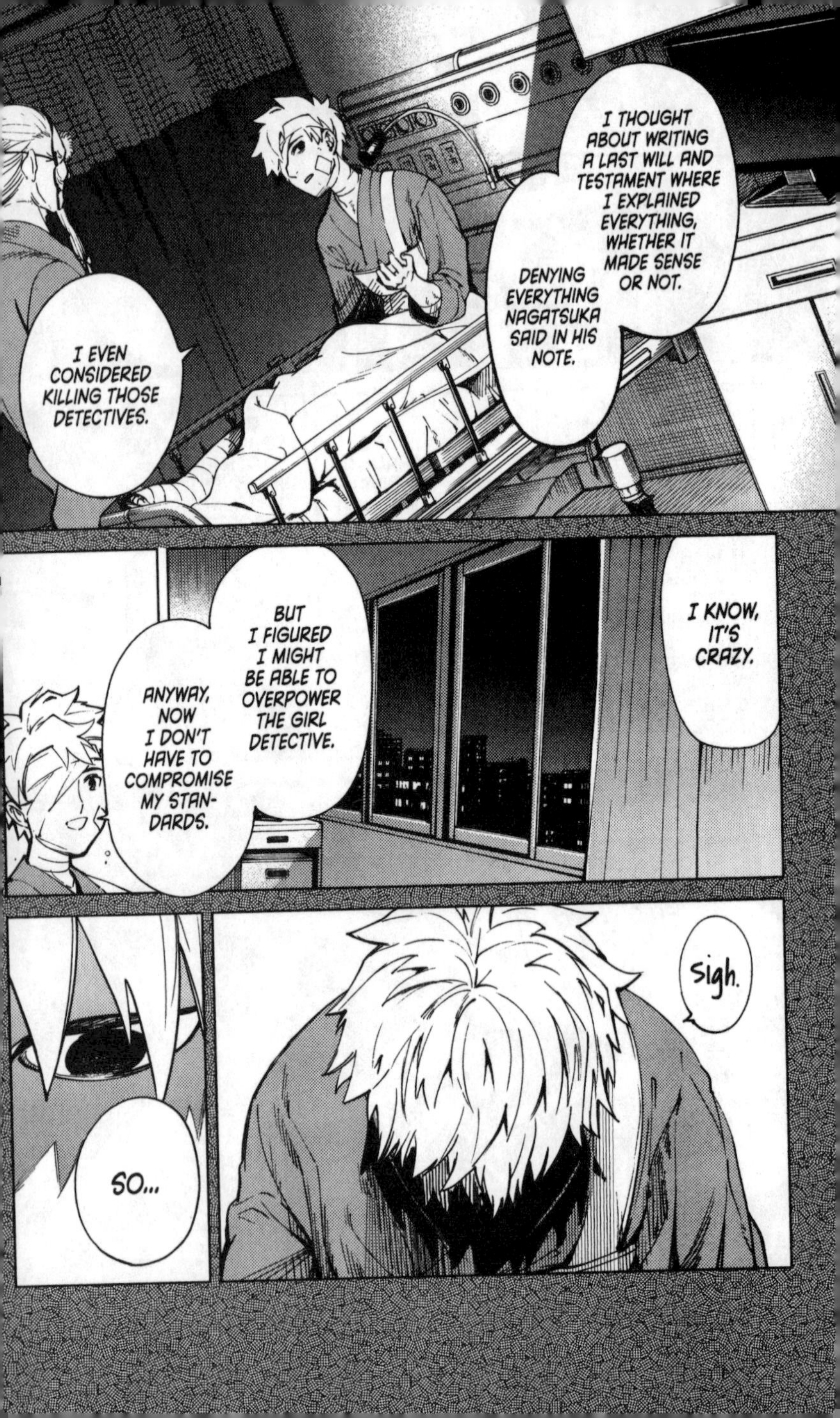
I THOUGHT ABOUT WRITING A LAST WILL AND TESTAMENT WHERE I EXPLAINED EVERYTHING, WHETHER IT MADE SENSE OR NOT.
DENYING EVERYTHING NAGATSUKA SAID IN HIS NOTE.
I EVEN CONSIDERED KILLING THOSE DETECTIVES.
I KNOW, IT'S CRAZY.
BUT I FIGURED I MIGHT BE ABLE TO OVERPOWER THE GIRL DETECTIVE.
ANYWAY, NOW I DON'T HAVE TO COMPROMISE MY STAN-DARDS.
Sigh.
SO...

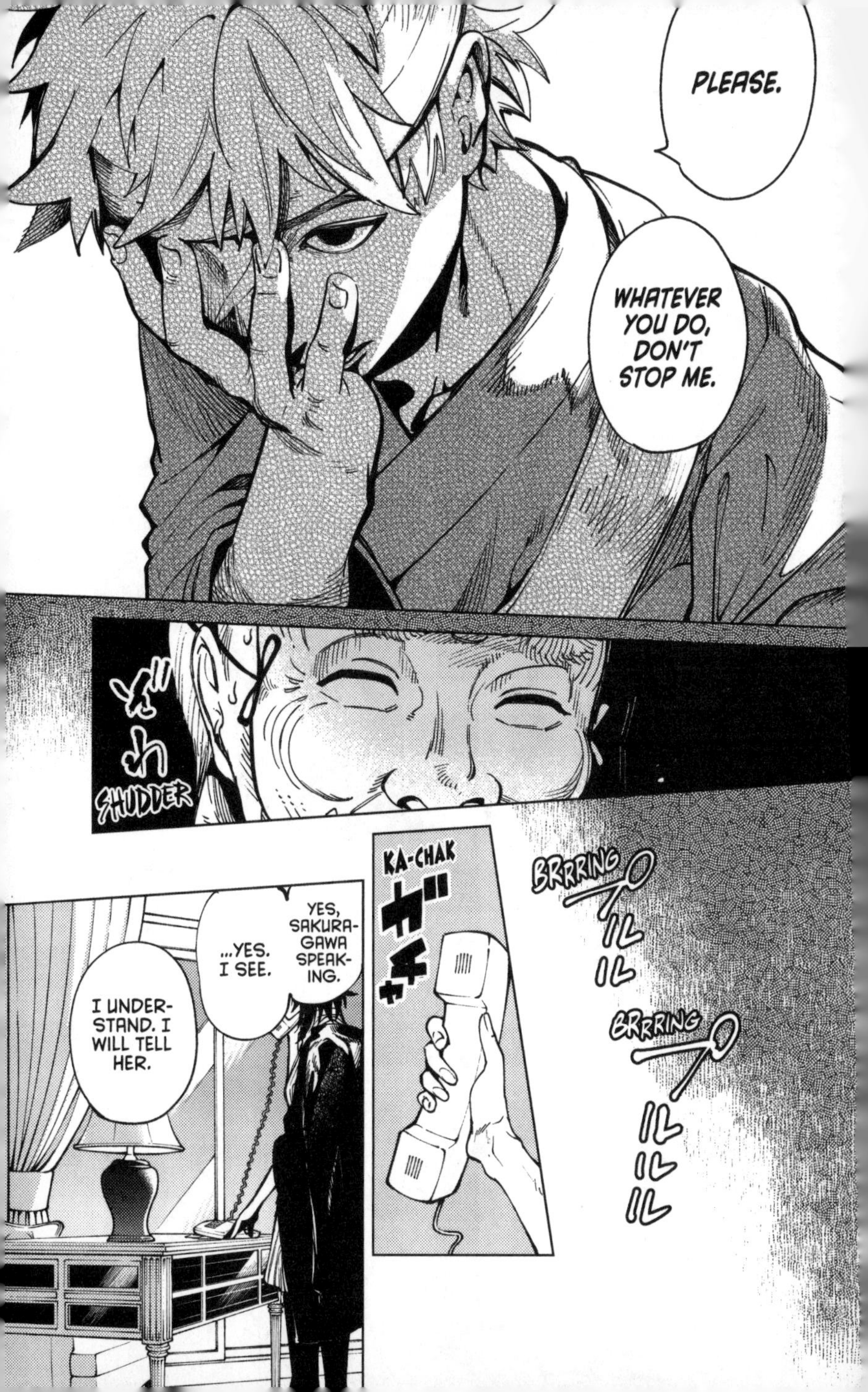
PLEASE.
WHATEVER YOU DO, DON'T STOP ME.
SHUDDER
BRRRING
BRRRING
KA-CHAK
YES, SAKURA-GAWA SPEAK-ING.
...YES. I SEE.
I UNDER-STAND. I WILL TELL HER.

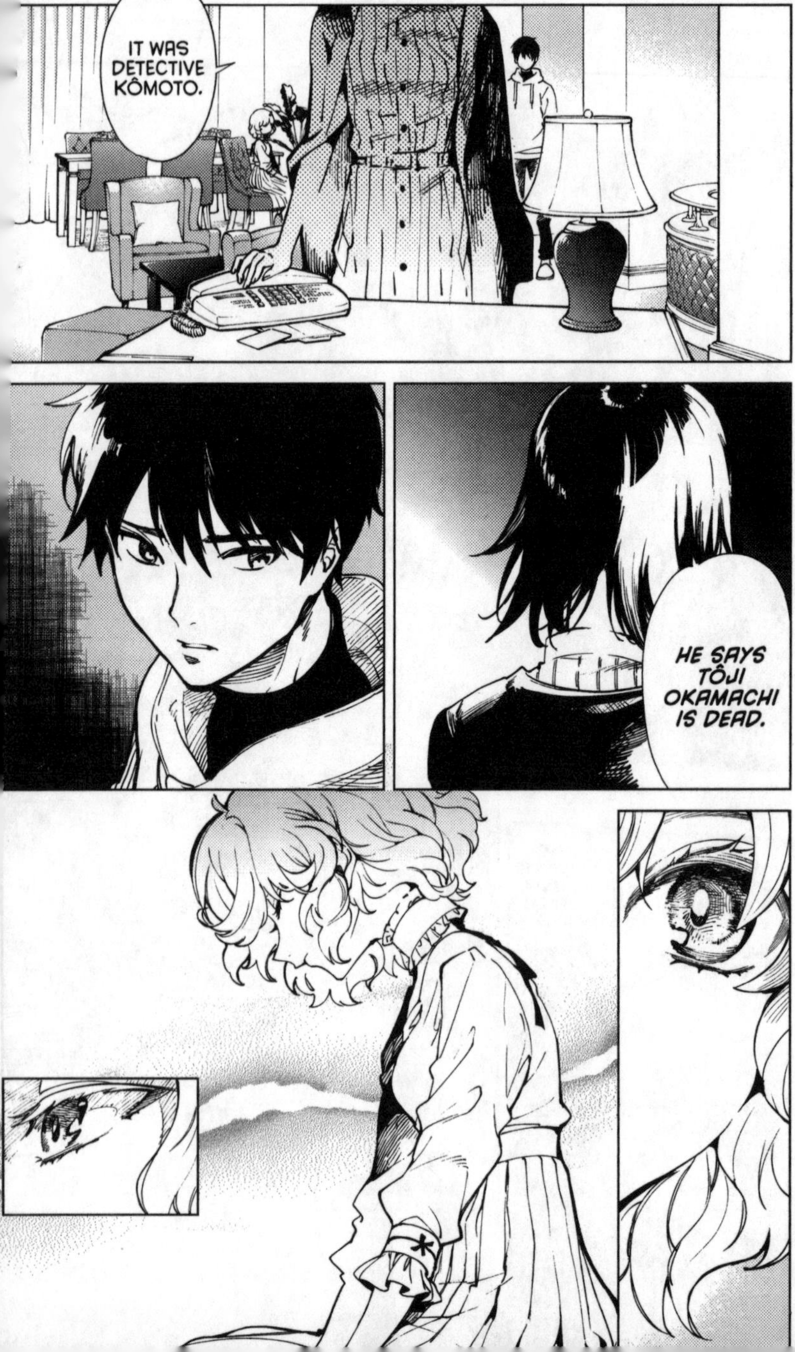
IT WAS DETECTIVE KÔMOTO.
HE SAYS TÔJI OKAMACHI IS DEAD.

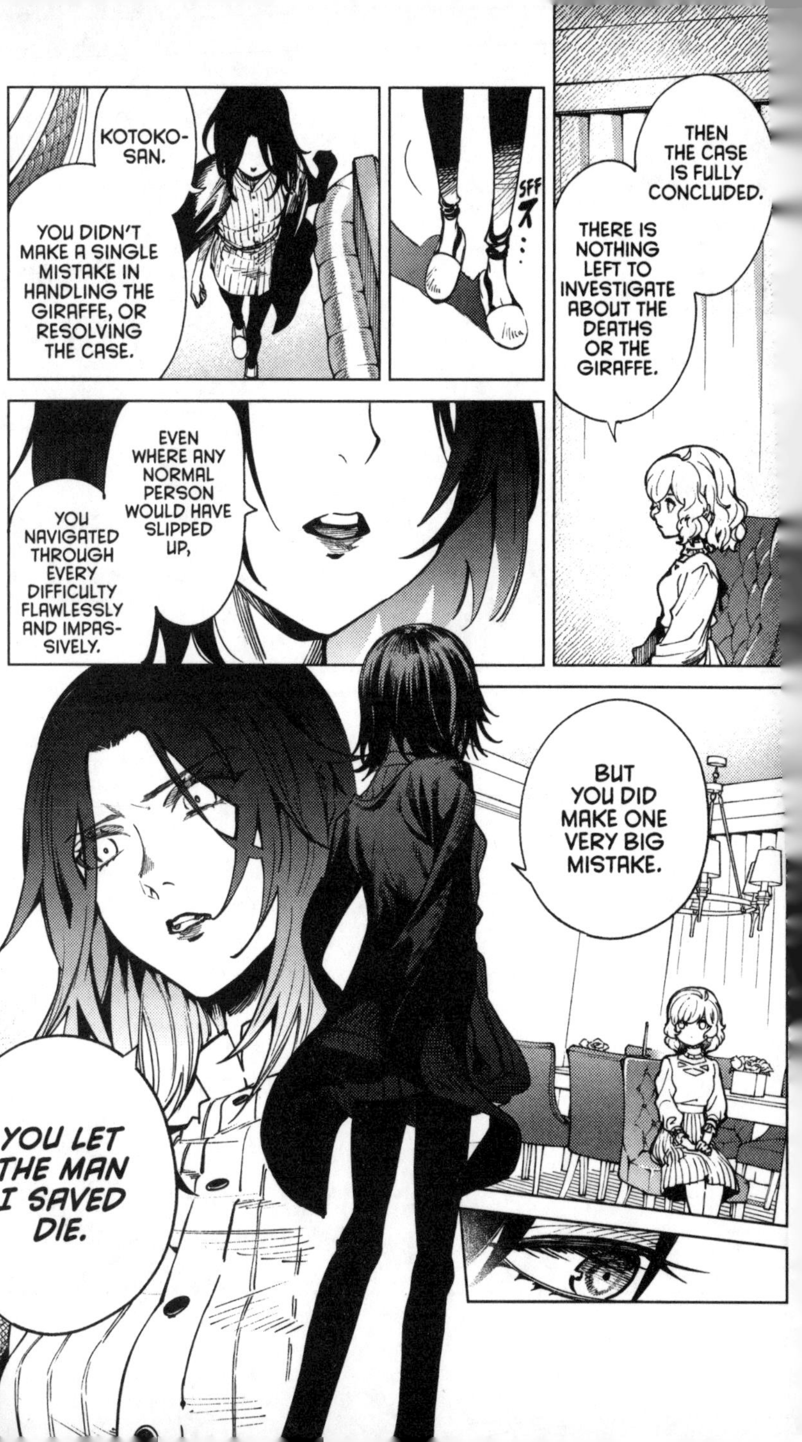
THEN THE CASE IS FULLY CONCLUDED.
THERE IS NOTHING LEFT TO INVESTIGATE ABOUT THE DEATHS OR THE GIRAFFE.
SFF
KOTOKO-SAN.
YOU DIDN'T MAKE A SINGLE MISTAKE IN HANDLING THE GIRAFFE, OR RESOLVING THE CASE.
EVEN WHERE ANY NORMAL PERSON WOULD HAVE SLIPPED UP,
YOU NAVIGATED THROUGH EVERY DIFFICULTY FLAWLESSLY AND IMPASSIVELY.
BUT YOU DID MAKE ONE VERY BIG MISTAKE.
YOU LET THE MAN I SAVED DIE.

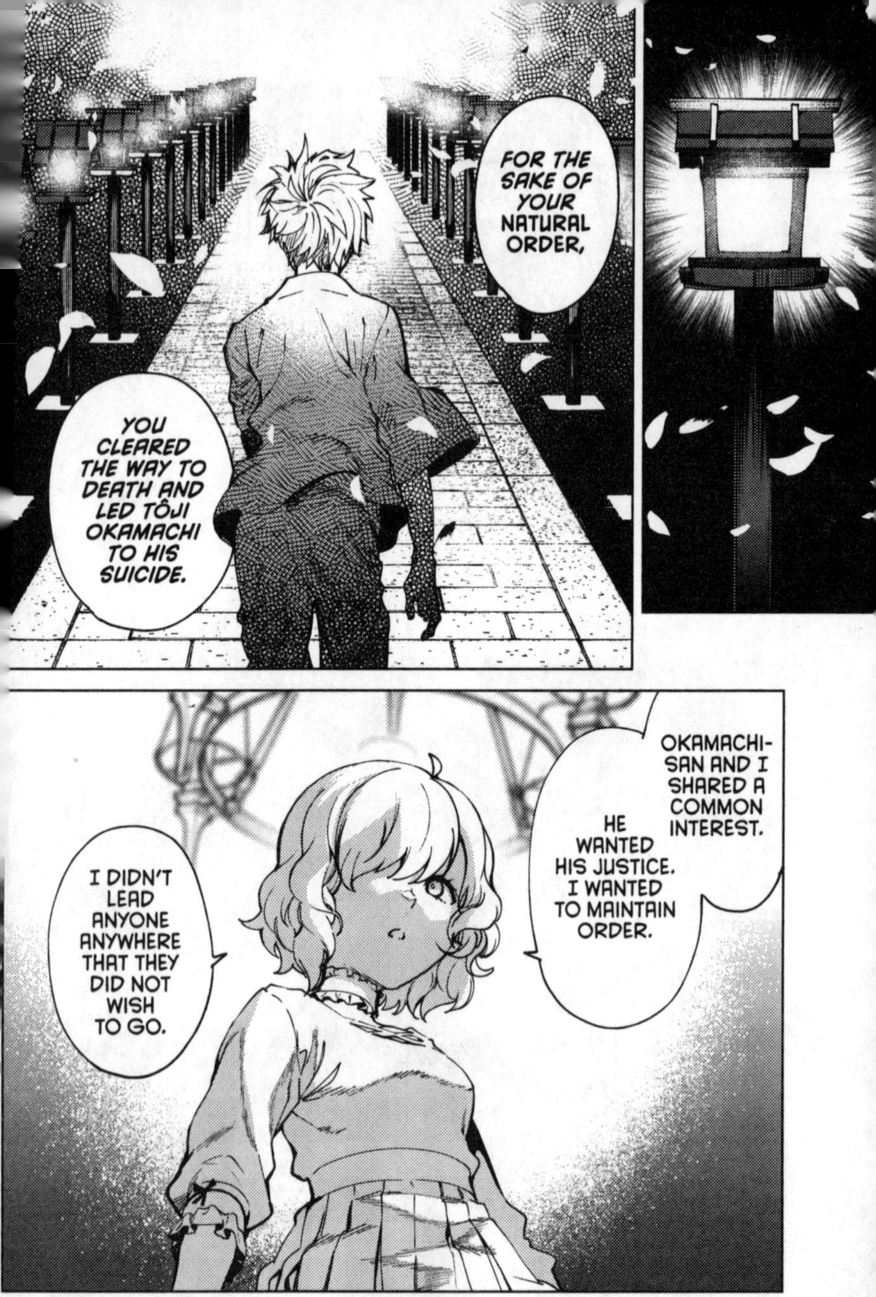
FOR THE SAKE OF YOUR NATURAL ORDER,
YOU CLEARED THE WAY TO DEATH AND LED TÔJI OKAMACHI TO HIS SUICIDE.
OKAMACHI-SAN AND I SHARED A COMMON INTEREST.
HE WANTED HIS JUSTICE. I WANTED TO MAINTAIN ORDER.
I DIDN'T LEAD ANYONE ANYWHERE THAT THEY DID NOT WISH TO GO.

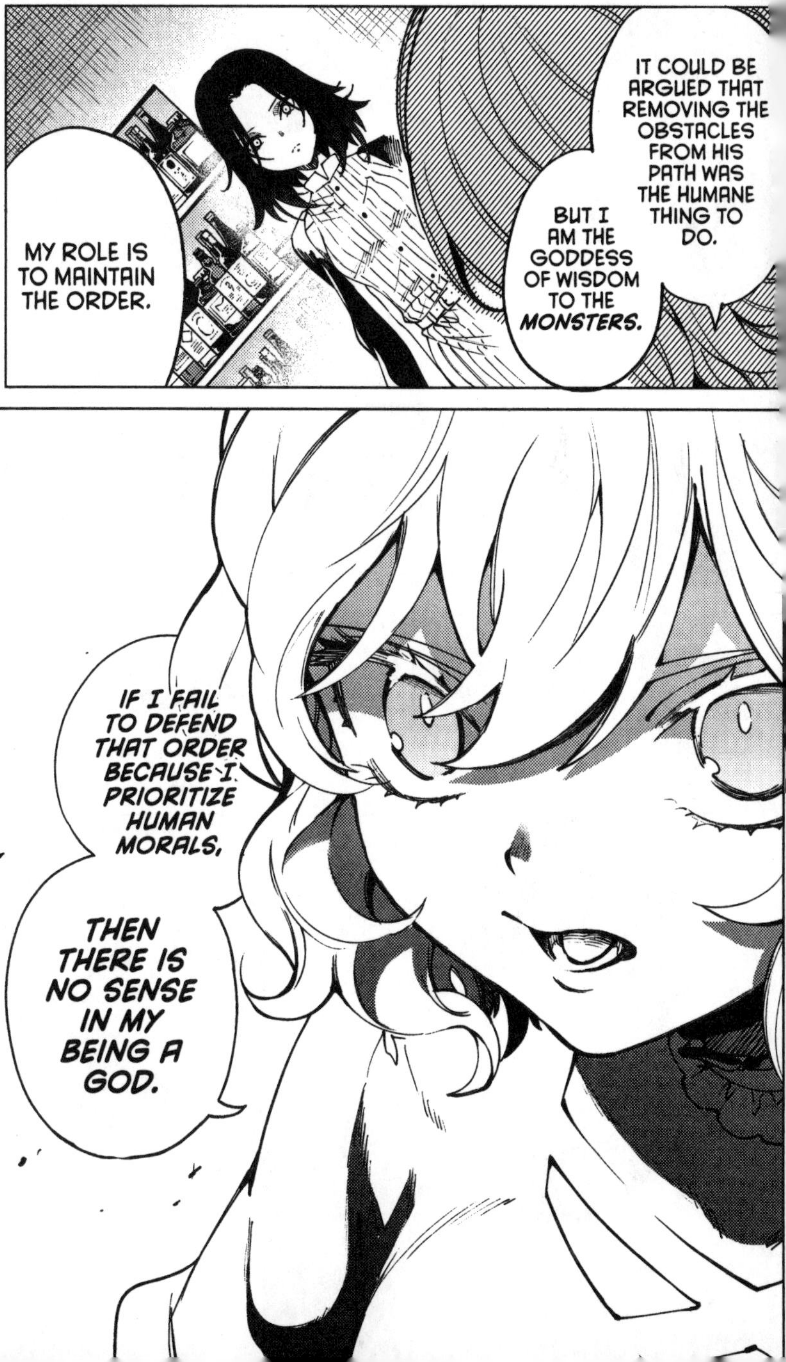
IT COULD BE ARGUED THAT REMOVING THE OBSTACLES FROM HIS PATH WAS THE HUMANE THING TO DO.
BUT I AM THE GODDESS OF WISDOM TO THE *MONSTERS.*
MY ROLE IS TO MAINTAIN THE ORDER.
IF I FAIL TO DEFEND THAT ORDER BECAUSE I PRIORITIZE HUMAN MORALS,
THEN THERE IS NO SENSE IN MY BEING A GOD.

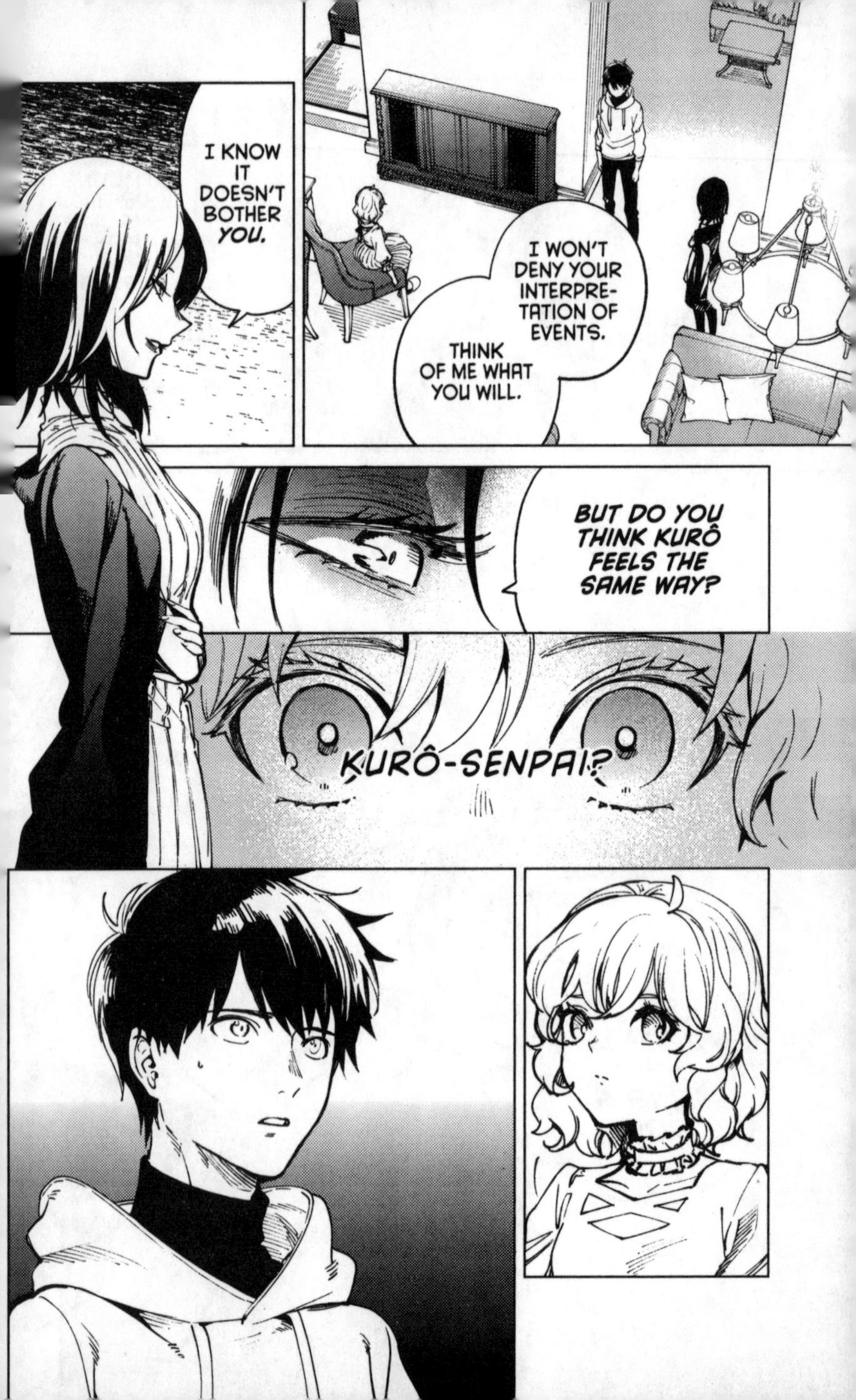
I WON'T DENY YOUR INTERPRETATION OF EVENTS.
THINK OF ME WHAT YOU WILL.
I KNOW IT DOESN'T BOTHER *YOU.*
BUT DO YOU THINK KURÔ FEELS THE SAME WAY?
KURÔ-SENPAI?

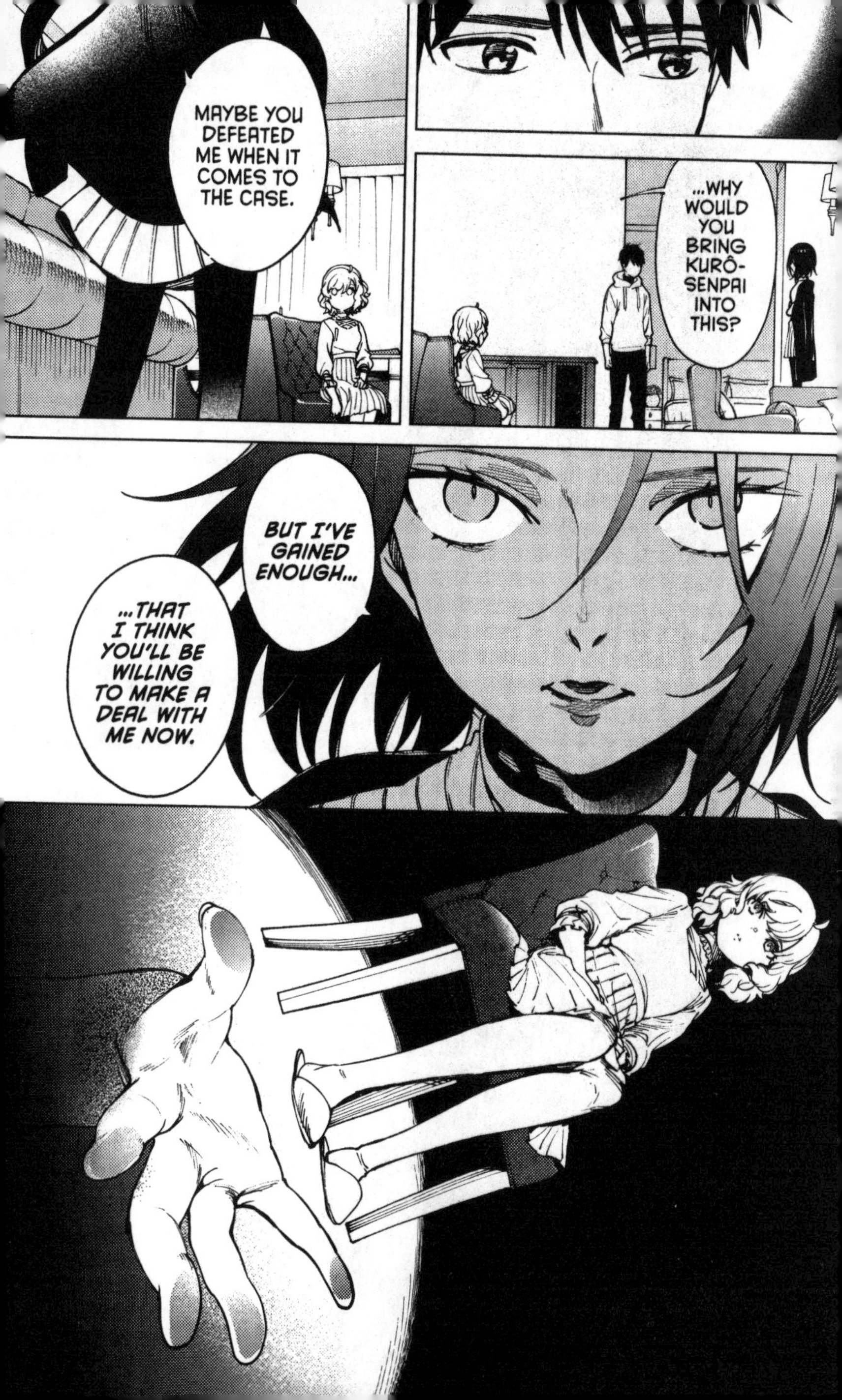
...WHY WOULD YOU BRING KURÔ-SENPAI INTO THIS?
MAYBE YOU DEFEATED ME WHEN IT COMES TO THE CASE.
BUT I'VE GAINED ENOUGH...
...THAT I THINK YOU'LL BE WILLING TO MAKE A DEAL WITH ME NOW.

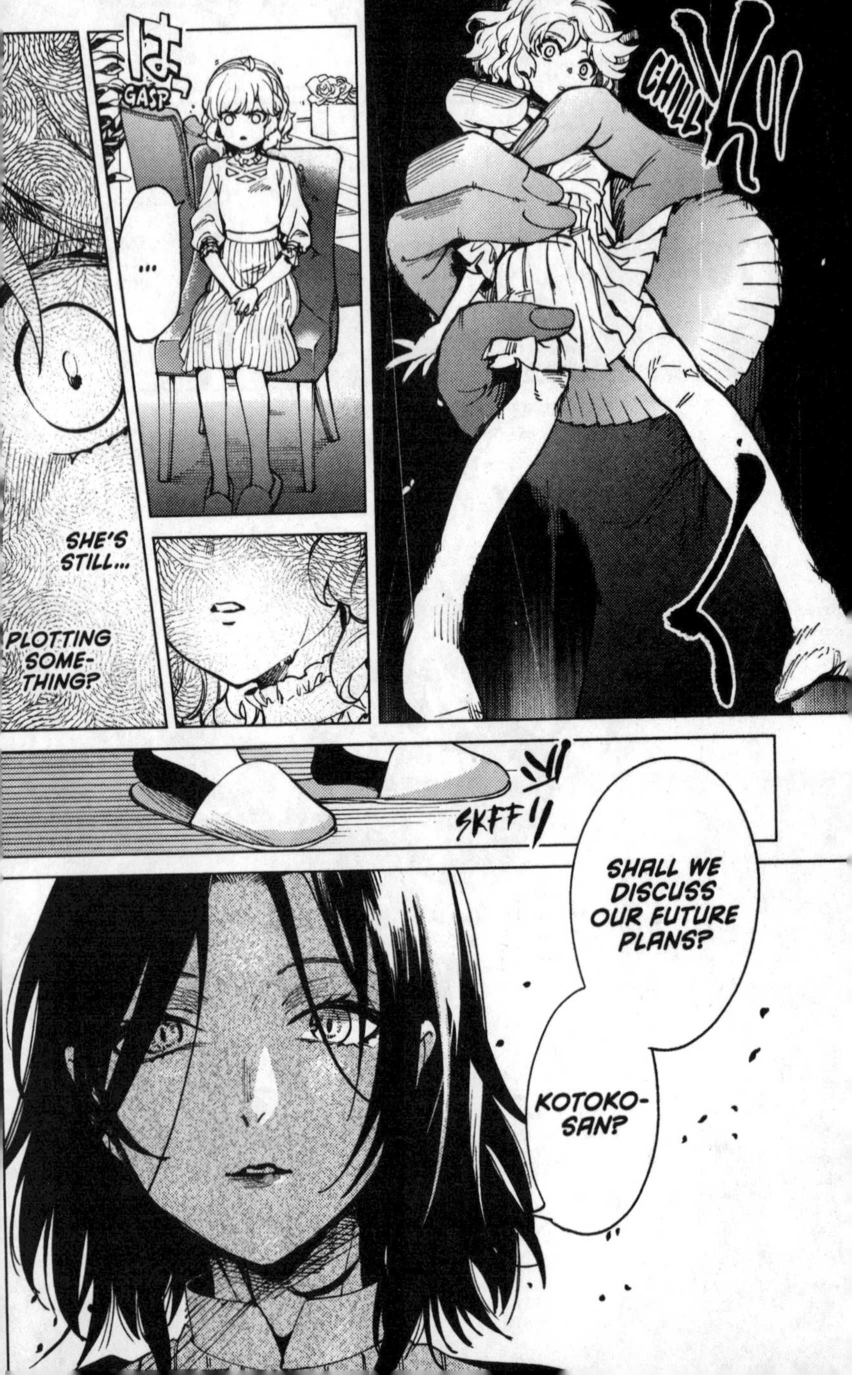
CHILL
はっ
GASP
...
SHE'S STILL...
PLOTTING SOME-THING?
SKFF
SHALL WE DISCUSS OUR FUTURE PLANS?
KOTOKO-SAN?

IN/SPECTRE

CHAPTER 49: "THE RETALIATION AND DEFEAT OF KOTOKO IWANAGA PART 11"

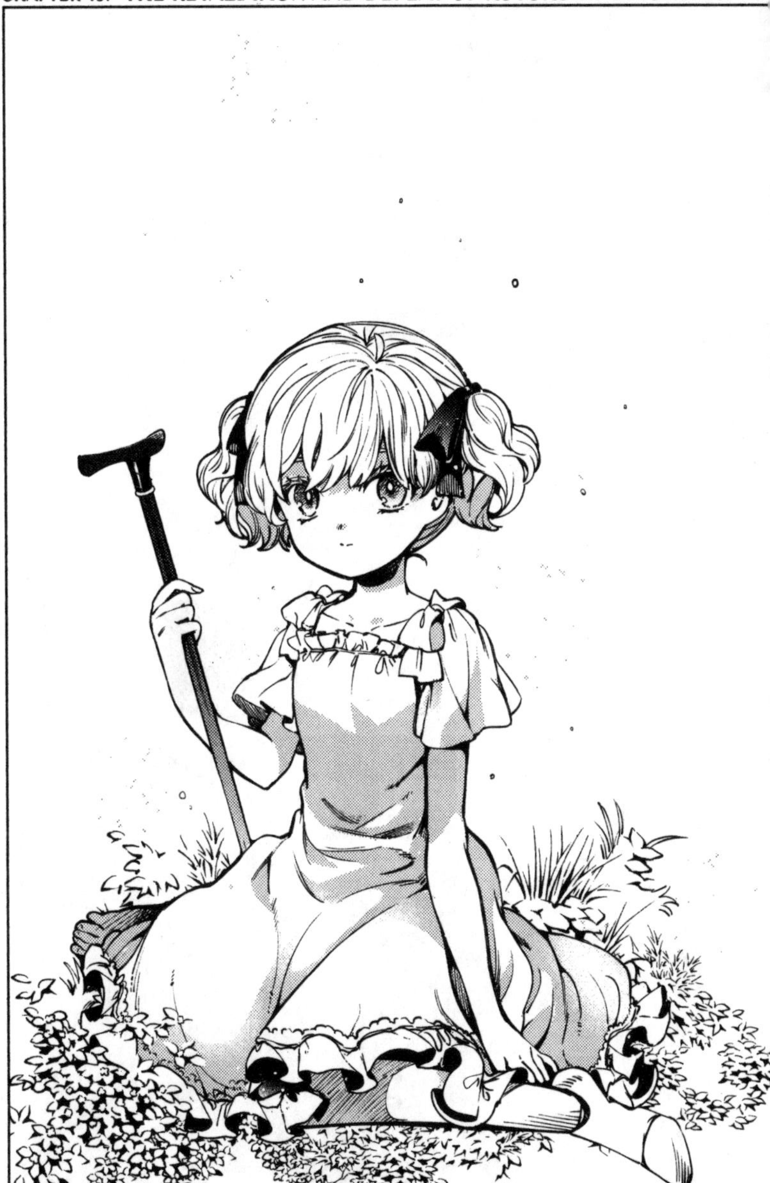

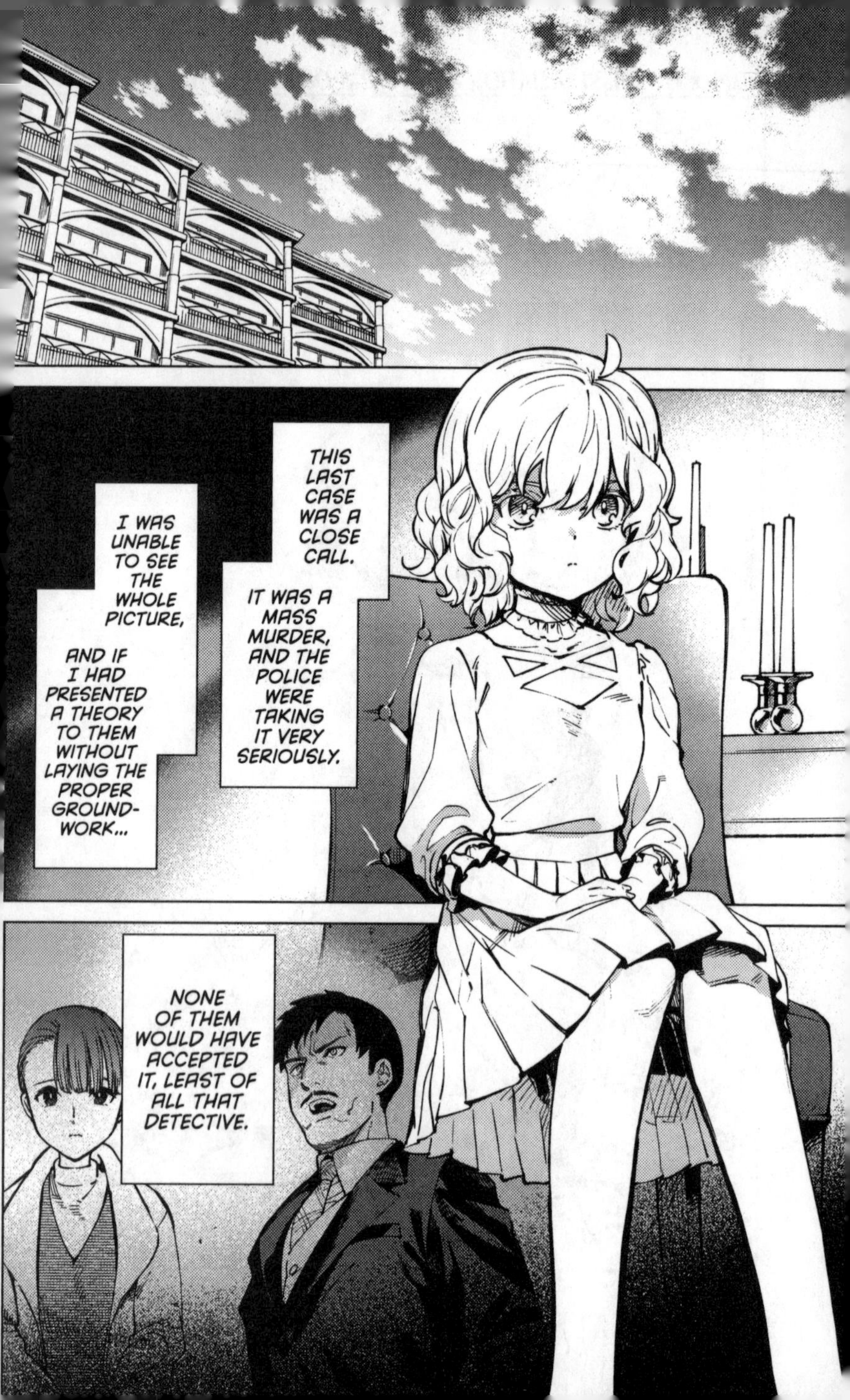
THIS LAST CASE WAS A CLOSE CALL.
IT WAS A MASS MURDER, AND THE POLICE WERE TAKING IT VERY SERIOUSLY.
I WAS UNABLE TO SEE THE WHOLE PICTURE,
AND IF I HAD PRESENTED A THEORY TO THEM WITHOUT LAYING THE PROPER GROUND-WORK...
NONE OF THEM WOULD HAVE ACCEPTED IT, LEAST OF ALL THAT DETECTIVE.

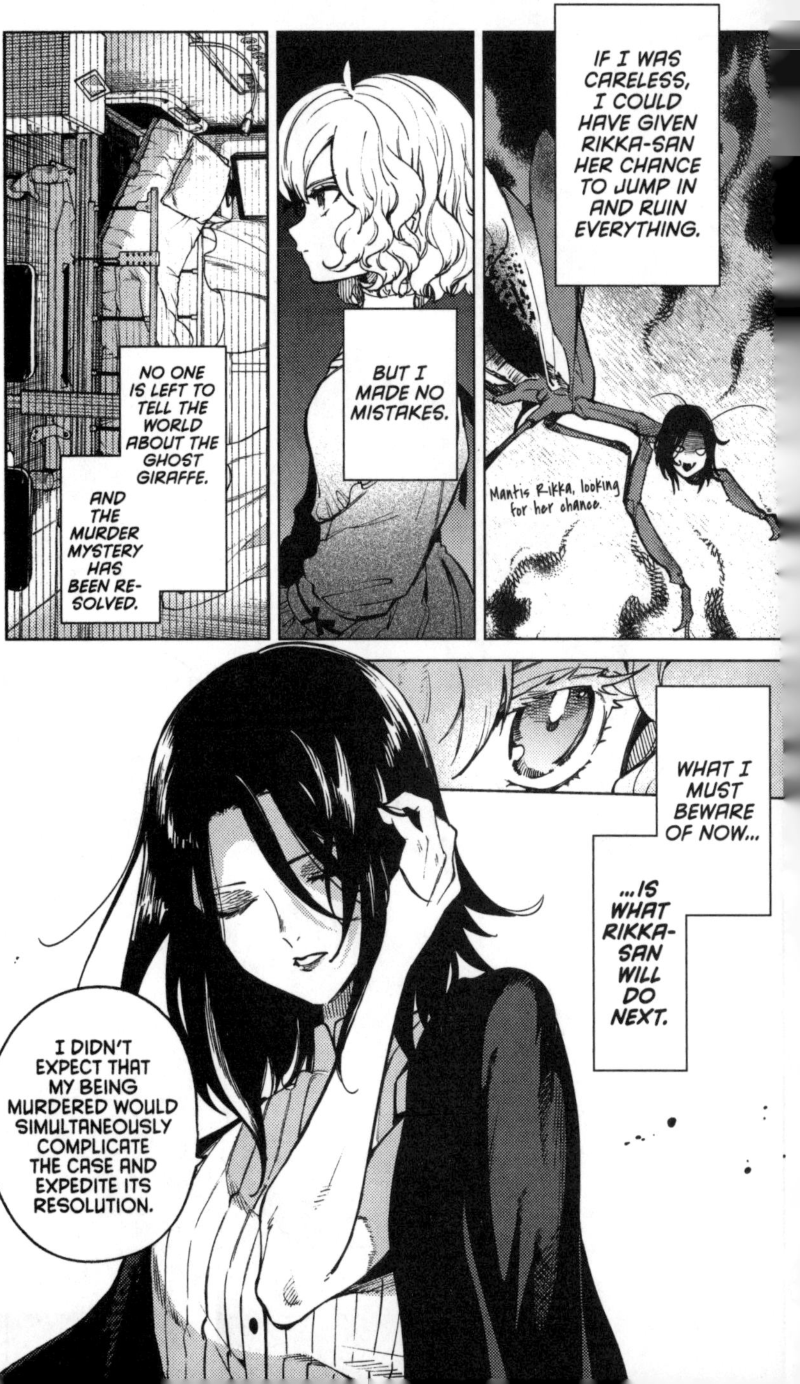
IF I WAS CARELESS, I COULD HAVE GIVEN RIKKA-SAN HER CHANCE TO JUMP IN AND RUIN EVERYTHING.
Mantis Rikka, looking for her chance.
BUT I MADE NO MISTAKES.
NO ONE IS LEFT TO TELL THE WORLD ABOUT THE GHOST GIRAFFE.
AND THE MURDER MYSTERY HAS BEEN RE-SOLVED.
WHAT I MUST BEWARE OF NOW...
...IS WHAT RIKKA-SAN WILL DO NEXT.
I DIDN'T EXPECT THAT MY BEING MURDERED WOULD SIMULTANEOUSLY COMPLICATE THE CASE AND EXPEDITE ITS RESOLUTION.

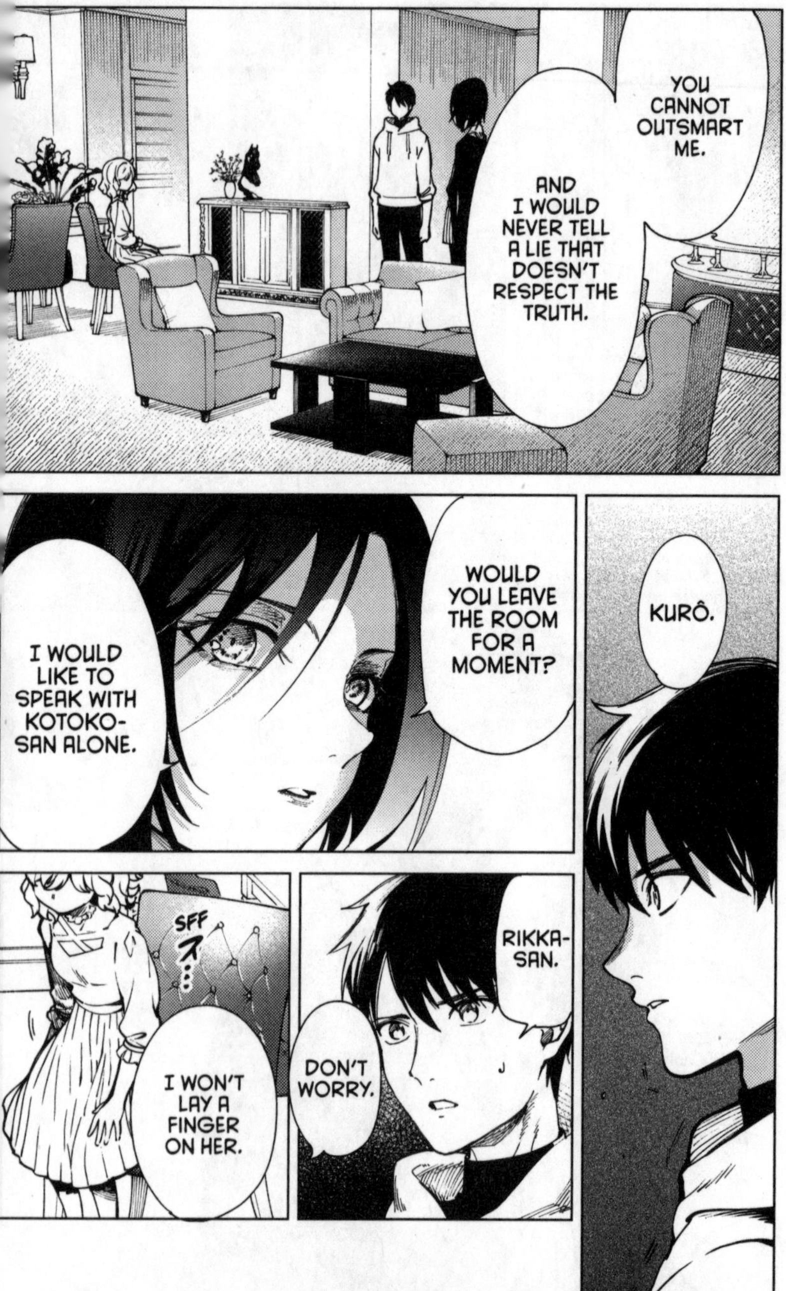
YOU CANNOT OUTSMART ME.
AND I WOULD NEVER TELL A LIE THAT DOESN'T RESPECT THE TRUTH.
KURÔ.
WOULD YOU LEAVE THE ROOM FOR A MOMENT?
I WOULD LIKE TO SPEAK WITH KOTOKO-SAN ALONE.
RIKKA-SAN.
DON'T WORRY.
SFF
I WON'T LAY A FINGER ON HER.

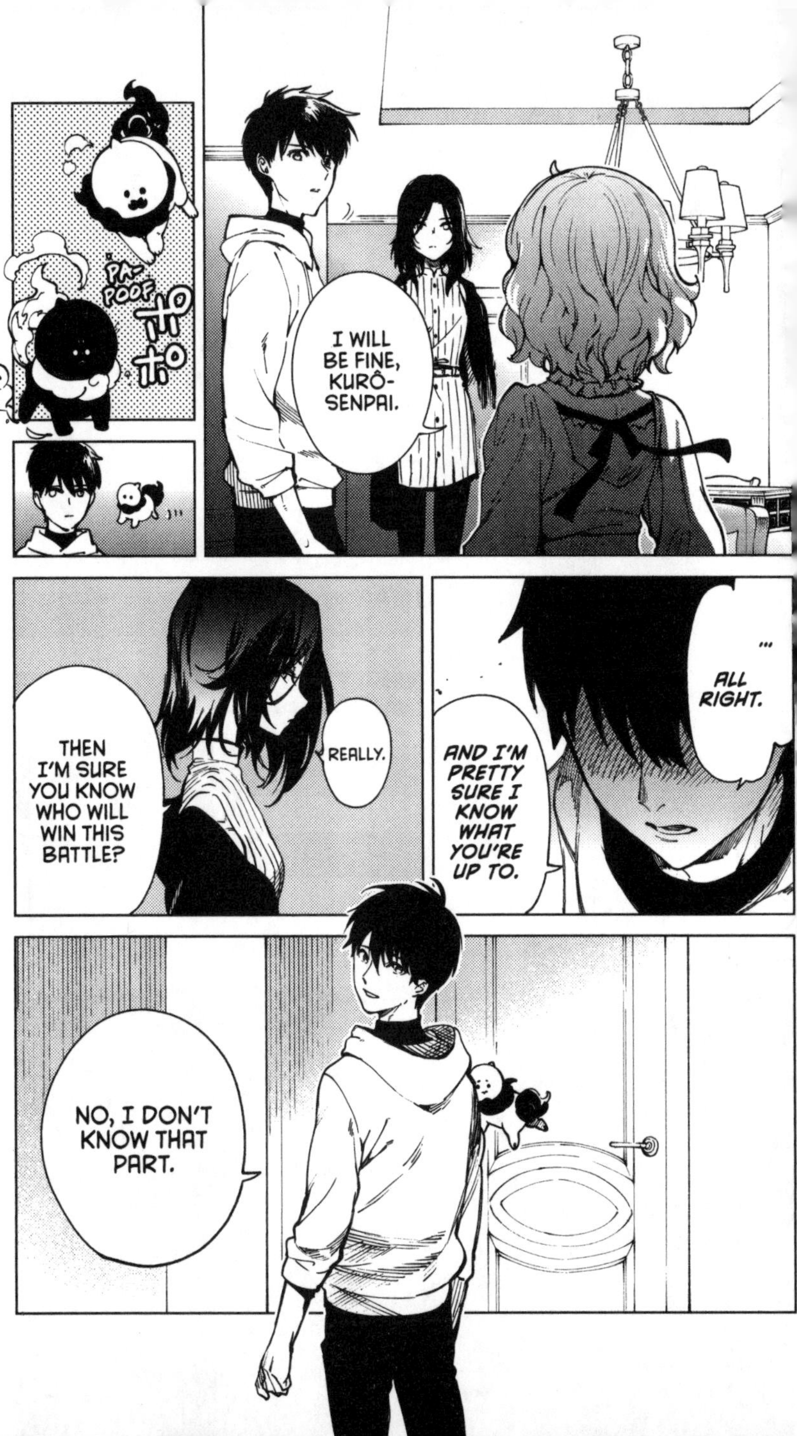
I WILL BE FINE, KURÔ-SENPAI.
PA-POOF
...
ALL RIGHT.
AND I'M PRETTY SURE I KNOW WHAT YOU'RE UP TO.
REALLY.
THEN I'M SURE YOU KNOW WHO WILL WIN THIS BATTLE?
NO, I DON'T KNOW THAT PART.

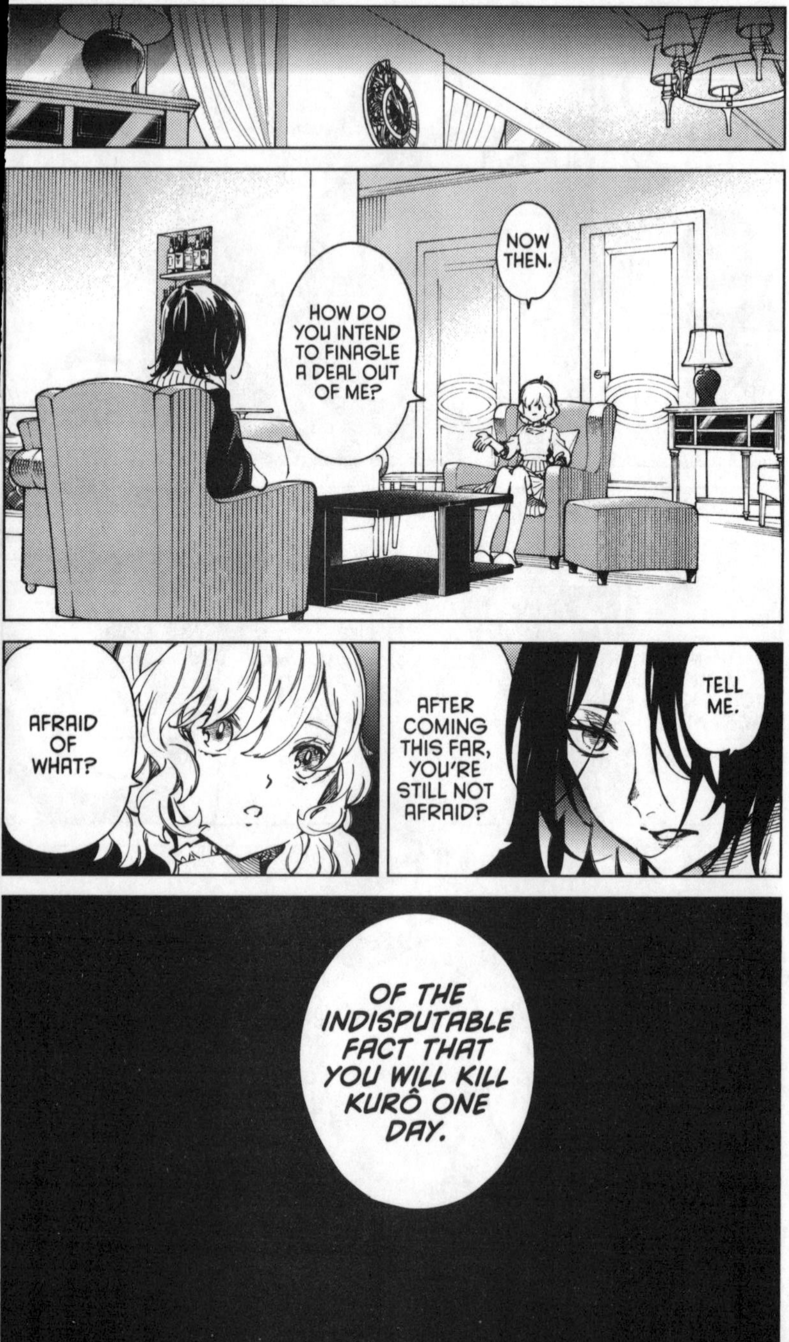
NOW THEN.
HOW DO YOU INTEND TO FINAGLE A DEAL OUT OF ME?
TELL ME.
AFTER COMING THIS FAR, YOU'RE STILL NOT AFRAID?
AFRAID OF WHAT?
OF THE INDISPUTABLE FACT THAT YOU WILL KILL KURÔ ONE DAY.

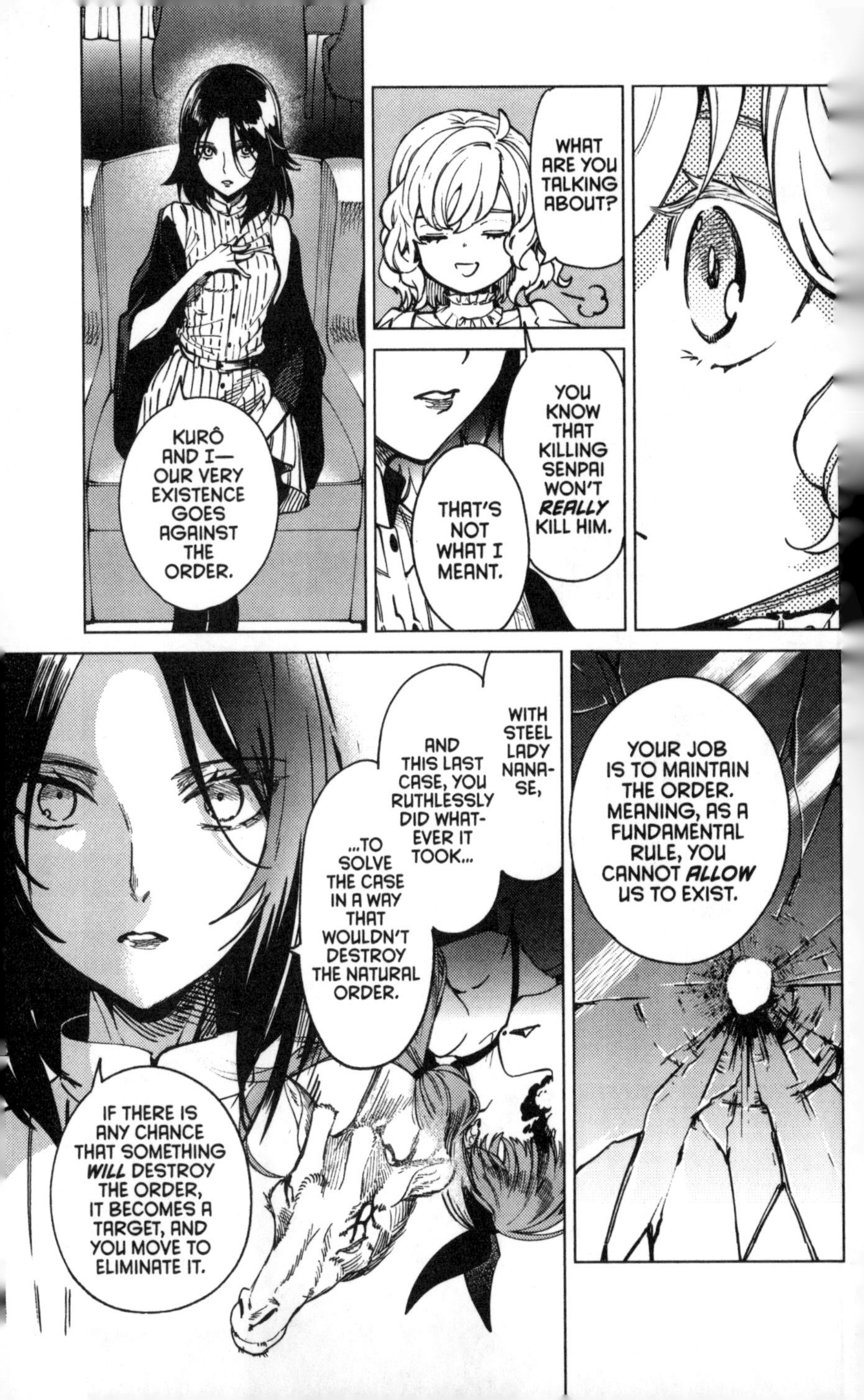
WHAT ARE YOU TALKING ABOUT?
YOU KNOW THAT KILLING SENPAI WON'T *REALLY* KILL HIM.
THAT'S NOT WHAT I MEANT.
KURÔ AND I— OUR VERY EXISTENCE GOES AGAINST THE ORDER.
YOUR JOB IS TO MAINTAIN THE ORDER. MEANING, AS A FUNDAMENTAL RULE, YOU CANNOT *ALLOW* US TO EXIST.
WITH STEEL LADY NANA-SE,
AND THIS LAST CASE, YOU RUTHLESSLY DID WHATEVER IT TOOK...
...TO SOLVE THE CASE IN A WAY THAT WOULDN'T DESTROY THE NATURAL ORDER.
IF THERE IS ANY CHANCE THAT SOMETHING *WILL* DESTROY THE ORDER, IT BECOMES A TARGET, AND YOU MOVE TO ELIMINATE IT.

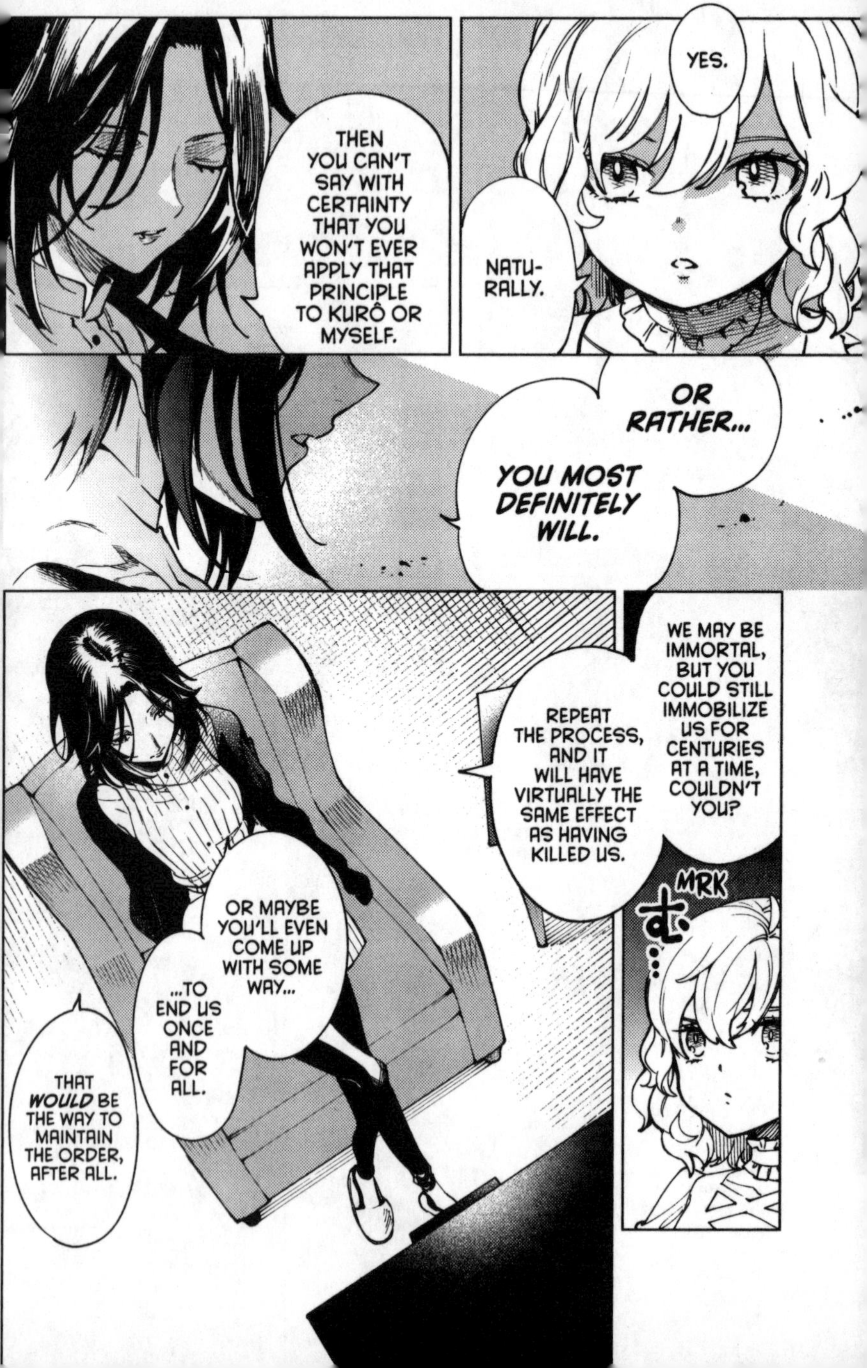
YES.
NATU-RALLY.
THEN YOU CAN'T SAY WITH CERTAINTY THAT YOU WON'T EVER APPLY THAT PRINCIPLE TO KURÔ OR MYSELF.
OR RATHER...
YOU MOST DEFINITELY WILL.
WE MAY BE IMMORTAL, BUT YOU COULD STILL IMMOBILIZE US FOR CENTURIES AT A TIME, COULDN'T YOU?
REPEAT THE PROCESS, AND IT WILL HAVE VIRTUALLY THE SAME EFFECT AS HAVING KILLED US.
MRK
む…
OR MAYBE YOU'LL EVEN COME UP WITH SOME WAY...
...TO END US ONCE AND FOR ALL.
THAT *WOULD* BE THE WAY TO MAINTAIN THE ORDER, AFTER ALL.

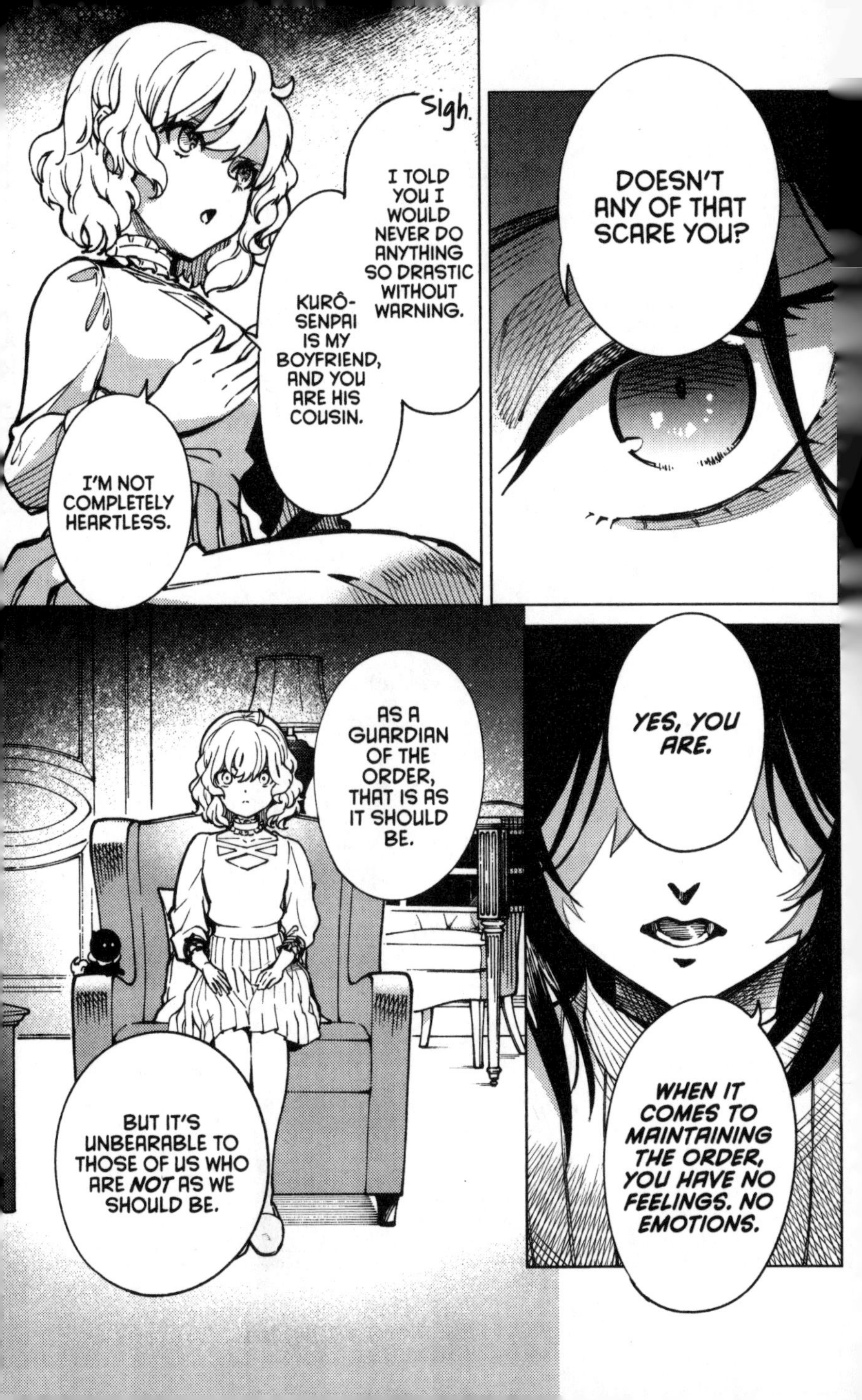
DOESN'T ANY OF THAT SCARE YOU?
Sigh.
I TOLD YOU I WOULD NEVER DO ANYTHING SO DRASTIC WITHOUT WARNING.
KURÔ-SENPAI IS MY BOYFRIEND, AND YOU ARE HIS COUSIN.
I'M NOT COMPLETELY HEARTLESS.
YES, YOU ARE.
WHEN IT COMES TO MAINTAINING THE ORDER, YOU HAVE NO FEELINGS. NO EMOTIONS.
AS A GUARDIAN OF THE ORDER, THAT IS AS IT SHOULD BE.
BUT IT'S UNBEARABLE TO THOSE OF US WHO ARE NOT AS WE SHOULD BE.

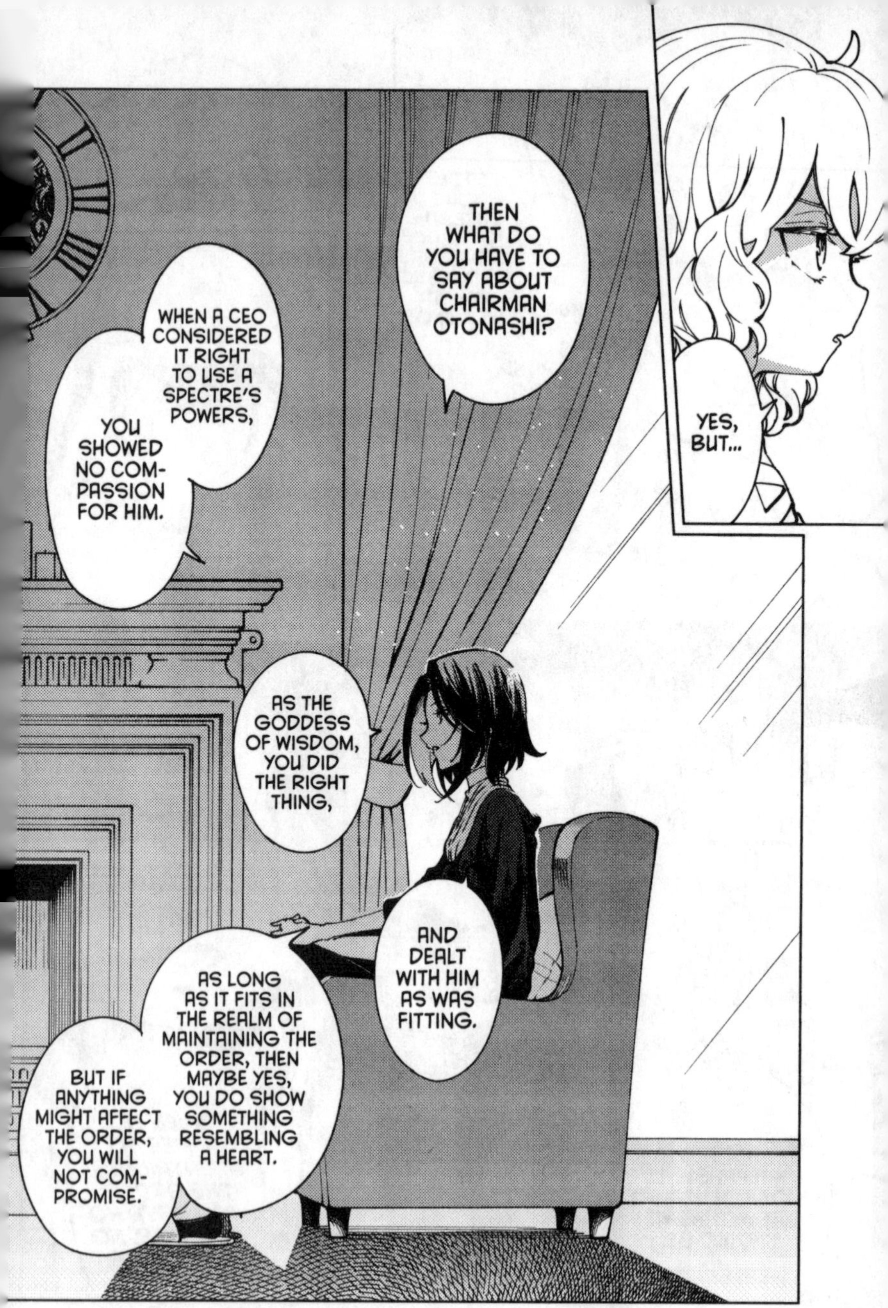
YES, BUT...
THEN WHAT DO YOU HAVE TO SAY ABOUT CHAIRMAN OTONASHI?
WHEN A CEO CONSIDERED IT RIGHT TO USE A SPECTRE'S POWERS,
YOU SHOWED NO COMPASSION FOR HIM.
AS THE GODDESS OF WISDOM, YOU DID THE RIGHT THING,
AND DEALT WITH HIM AS WAS FITTING.
AS LONG AS IT FITS IN THE REALM OF MAINTAINING THE ORDER, THEN MAYBE YES, YOU DO SHOW SOMETHING RESEMBLING A HEART.
BUT IF ANYTHING MIGHT AFFECT THE ORDER, YOU WILL NOT COMPROMISE.

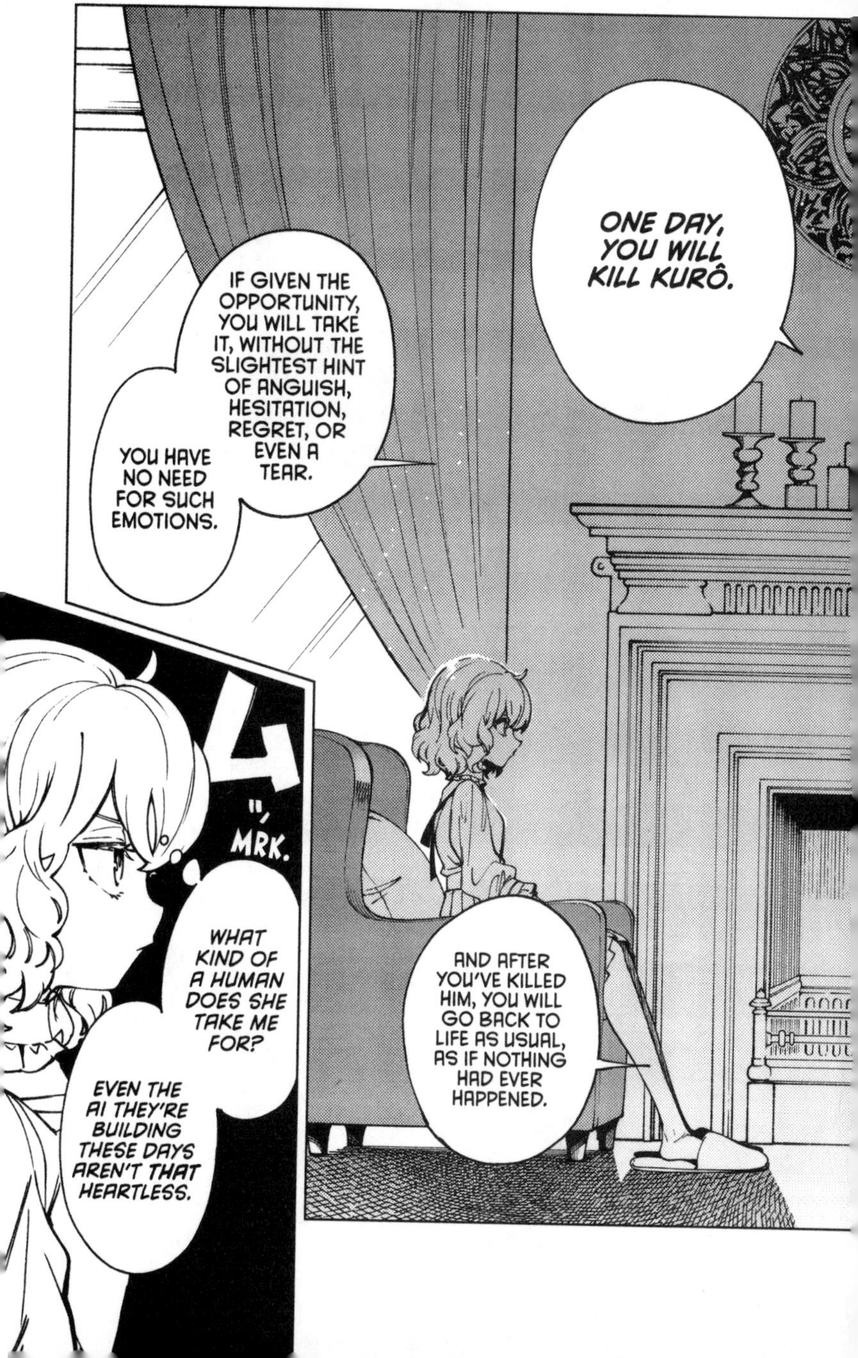
ONE DAY, YOU WILL KILL KURÔ.
IF GIVEN THE OPPORTUNITY, YOU WILL TAKE IT, WITHOUT THE SLIGHTEST HINT OF ANGUISH, HESITATION, REGRET, OR EVEN A TEAR.
YOU HAVE NO NEED FOR SUCH EMOTIONS.
AND AFTER YOU'VE KILLED HIM, YOU WILL GO BACK TO LIFE AS USUAL, AS IF NOTHING HAD EVER HAPPENED.
MRK.
WHAT KIND OF A HUMAN DOES SHE TAKE ME FOR?
EVEN THE AI THEY'RE BUILDING THESE DAYS AREN'T THAT HEARTLESS.

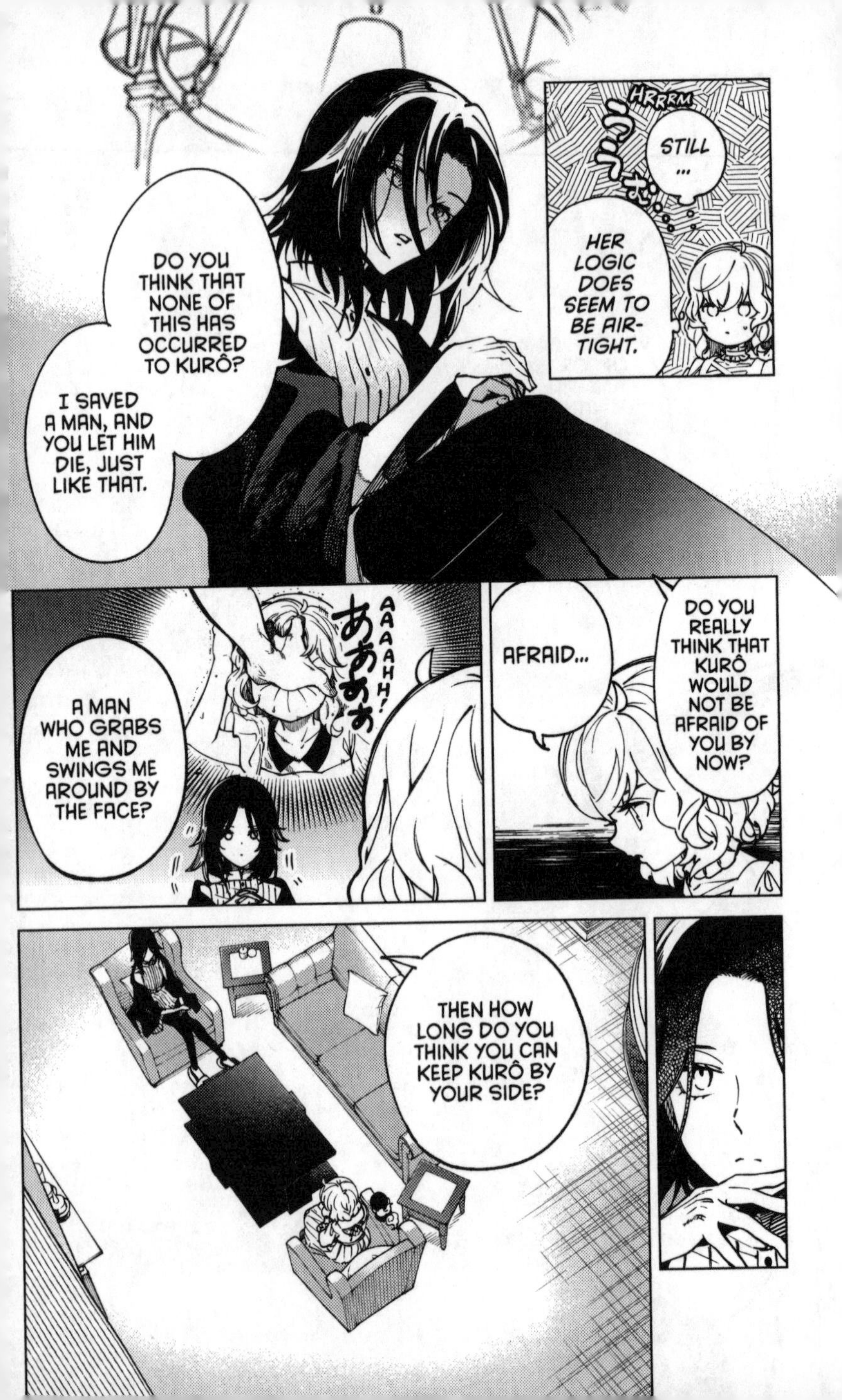
HRRRM
STILL ...
HER LOGIC DOES SEEM TO BE AIR-TIGHT.
DO YOU THINK THAT NONE OF THIS HAS OCCURRED TO KURÔ?
I SAVED A MAN, AND YOU LET HIM DIE, JUST LIKE THAT.
DO YOU REALLY THINK THAT KURÔ WOULD NOT BE AFRAID OF YOU BY NOW?
AFRAID...
AAAAHH!
A MAN WHO GRABS ME AND SWINGS ME AROUND BY THE FACE?
THEN HOW LONG DO YOU THINK YOU CAN KEEP KURÔ BY YOUR SIDE?

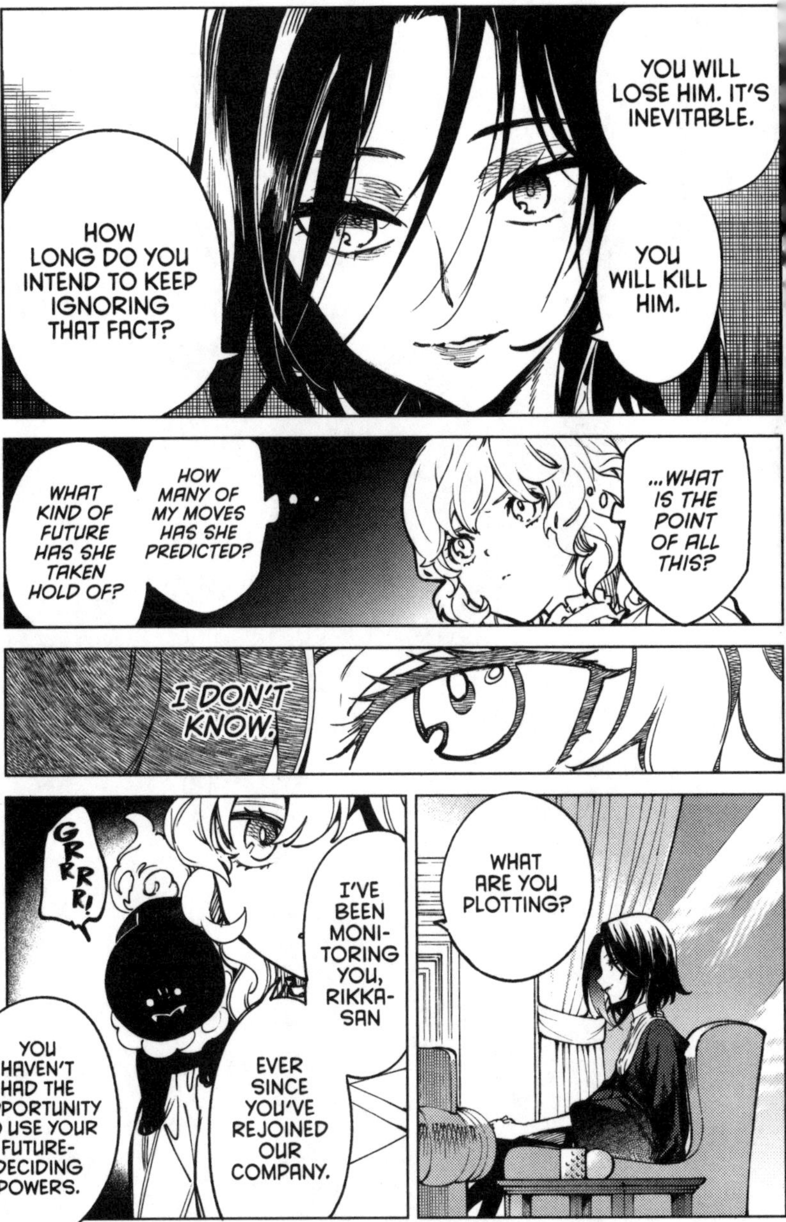
YOU WILL LOSE HIM. IT'S INEVITABLE.
YOU WILL KILL HIM.
HOW LONG DO YOU INTEND TO KEEP IGNORING THAT FACT?
...WHAT IS THE POINT OF ALL THIS?
HOW MANY OF MY MOVES HAS SHE PREDICTED?
WHAT KIND OF FUTURE HAS SHE TAKEN HOLD OF?
I DON'T KNOW.
WHAT ARE YOU PLOTTING?
I'VE BEEN MONI-TORING YOU, RIKKA-SAN
EVER SINCE YOU'VE REJOINED OUR COMPANY.
GRRRR!
YOU HAVEN'T HAD THE OPPORTUNITY TO USE YOUR FUTURE-DECIDING POWERS.

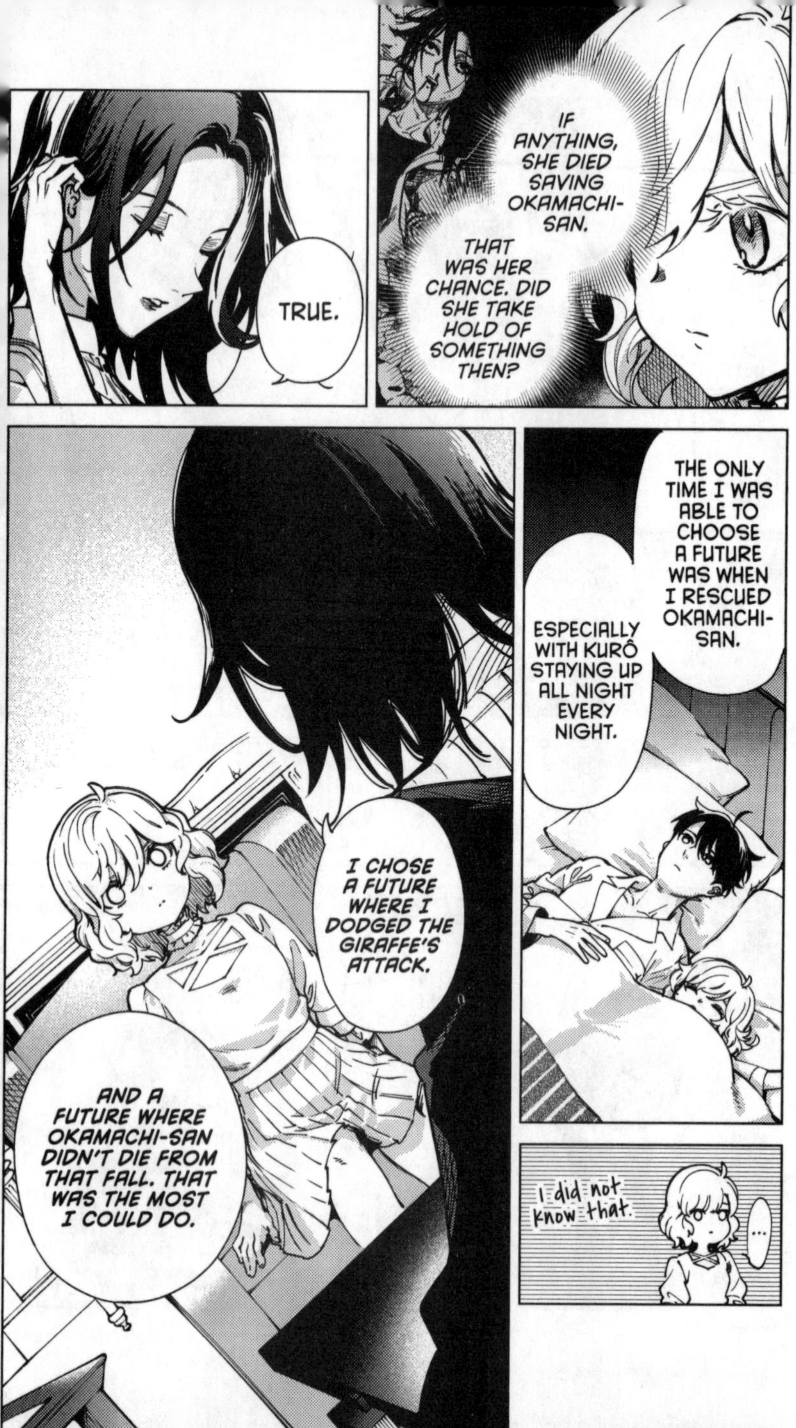
IF ANYTHING, SHE DIED SAVING OKAMACHI-SAN.
THAT WAS HER CHANCE. DID SHE TAKE HOLD OF SOMETHING THEN?
TRUE.
THE ONLY TIME I WAS ABLE TO CHOOSE A FUTURE WAS WHEN I RESCUED OKAMACHI-SAN.
ESPECIALLY WITH KURÔ STAYING UP ALL NIGHT EVERY NIGHT.
...
I did not know that.
I CHOSE A FUTURE WHERE I DODGED THE GIRAFFE'S ATTACK.
AND A FUTURE WHERE OKAMACHI-SAN DIDN'T DIE FROM THAT FALL. THAT WAS THE MOST I COULD DO.

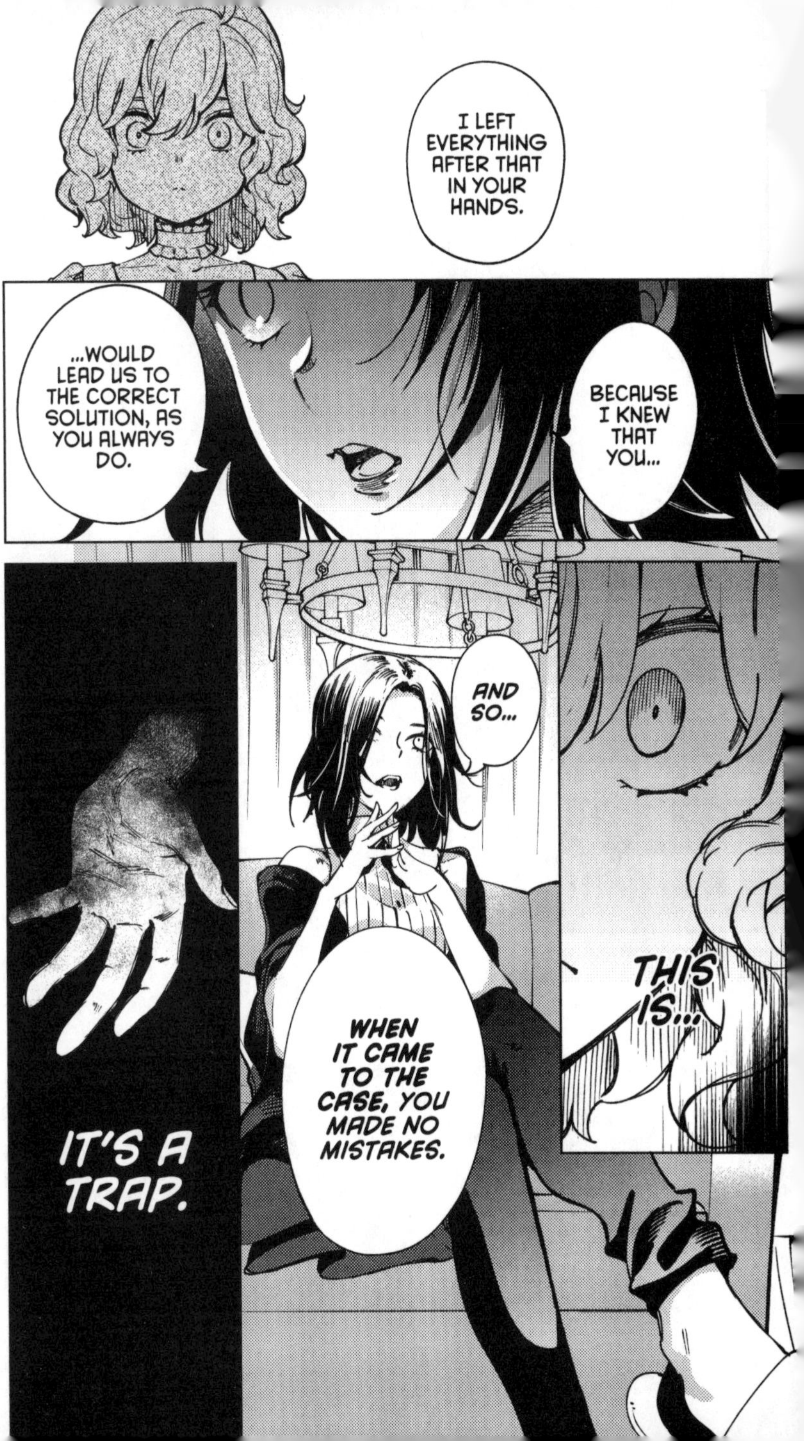
I LEFT EVERYTHING AFTER THAT IN YOUR HANDS.
BECAUSE I KNEW THAT YOU...
...WOULD LEAD US TO THE CORRECT SOLUTION, AS YOU ALWAYS DO.
THIS IS...
AND SO...
WHEN IT CAME TO THE CASE, YOU MADE NO MISTAKES.
IT'S A TRAP.

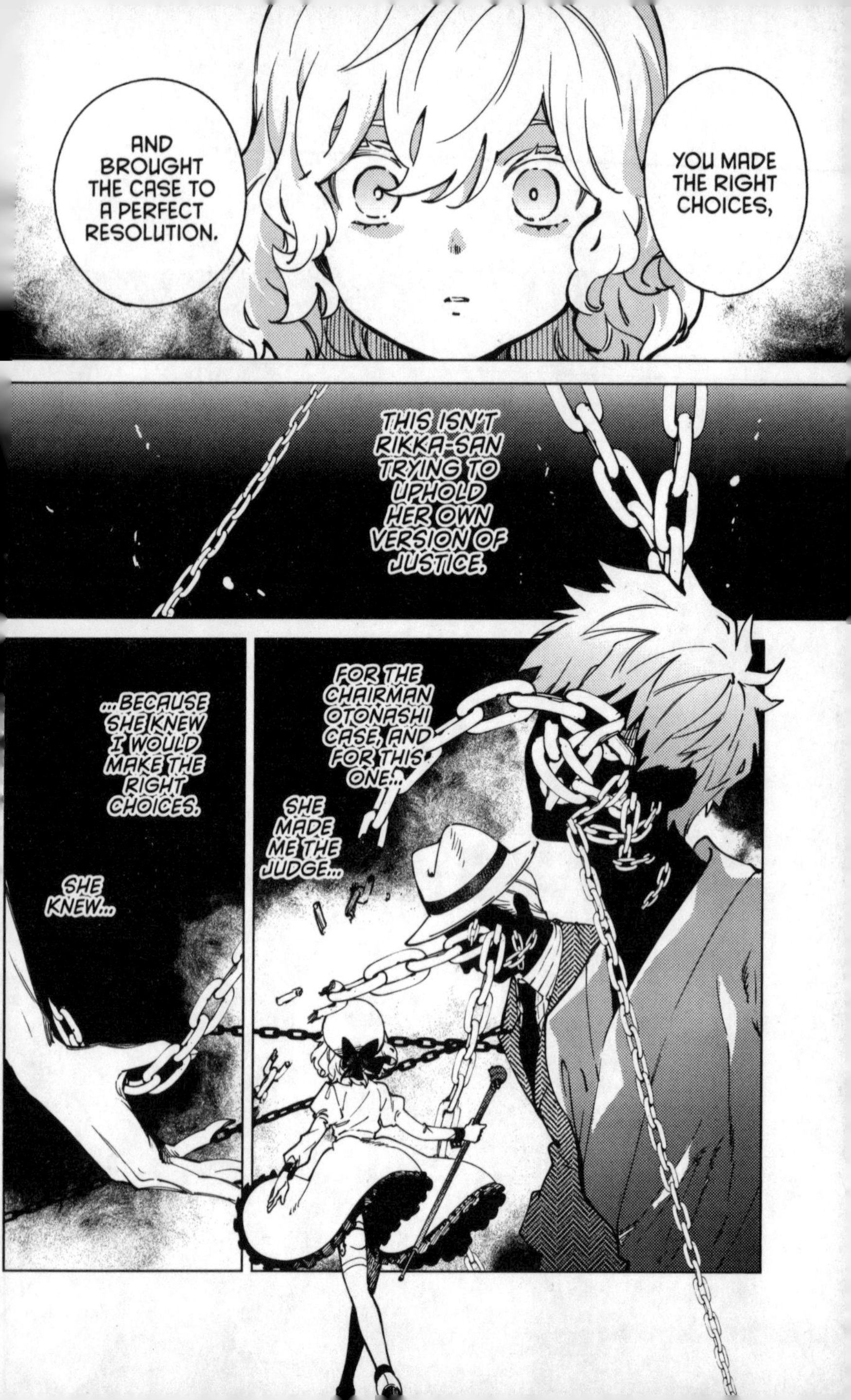
YOU MADE THE RIGHT CHOICES,
AND BROUGHT THE CASE TO A PERFECT RESOLUTION.
THIS ISN'T RIKKA-SAN TRYING TO UPHOLD HER OWN VERSION OF JUSTICE.
FOR THE CHAIRMAN OTONASHI CASE, AND FOR THIS ONE...
SHE MADE ME THE JUDGE...
...BECAUSE SHE KNEW I WOULD MAKE THE RIGHT CHOICES.
SHE KNEW...

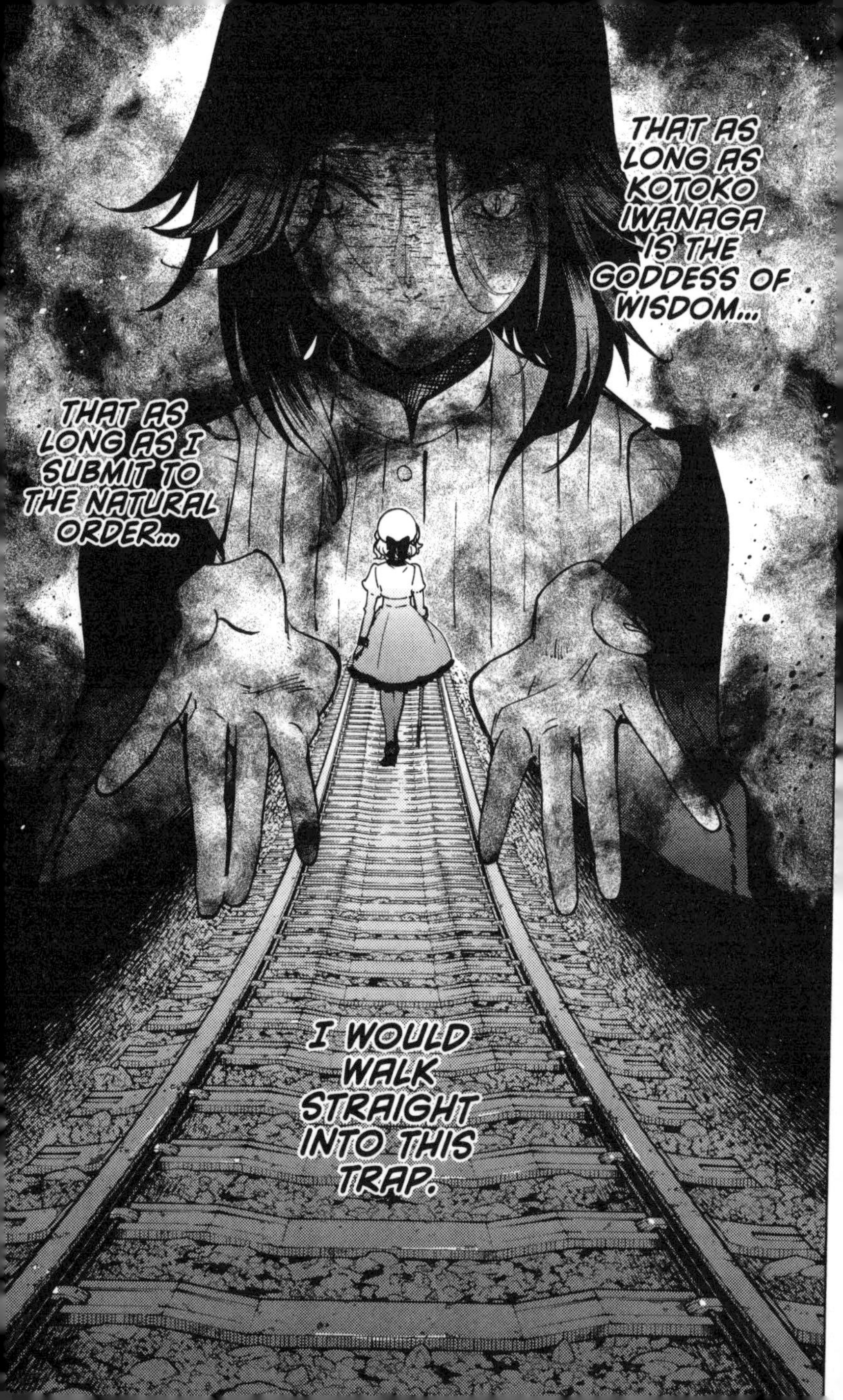
THAT AS LONG AS KOTOKO IWANAGA IS THE GODDESS OF WISDOM...
THAT AS LONG AS I SUBMIT TO THE NATURAL ORDER...
I WOULD WALK STRAIGHT INTO THIS TRAP.

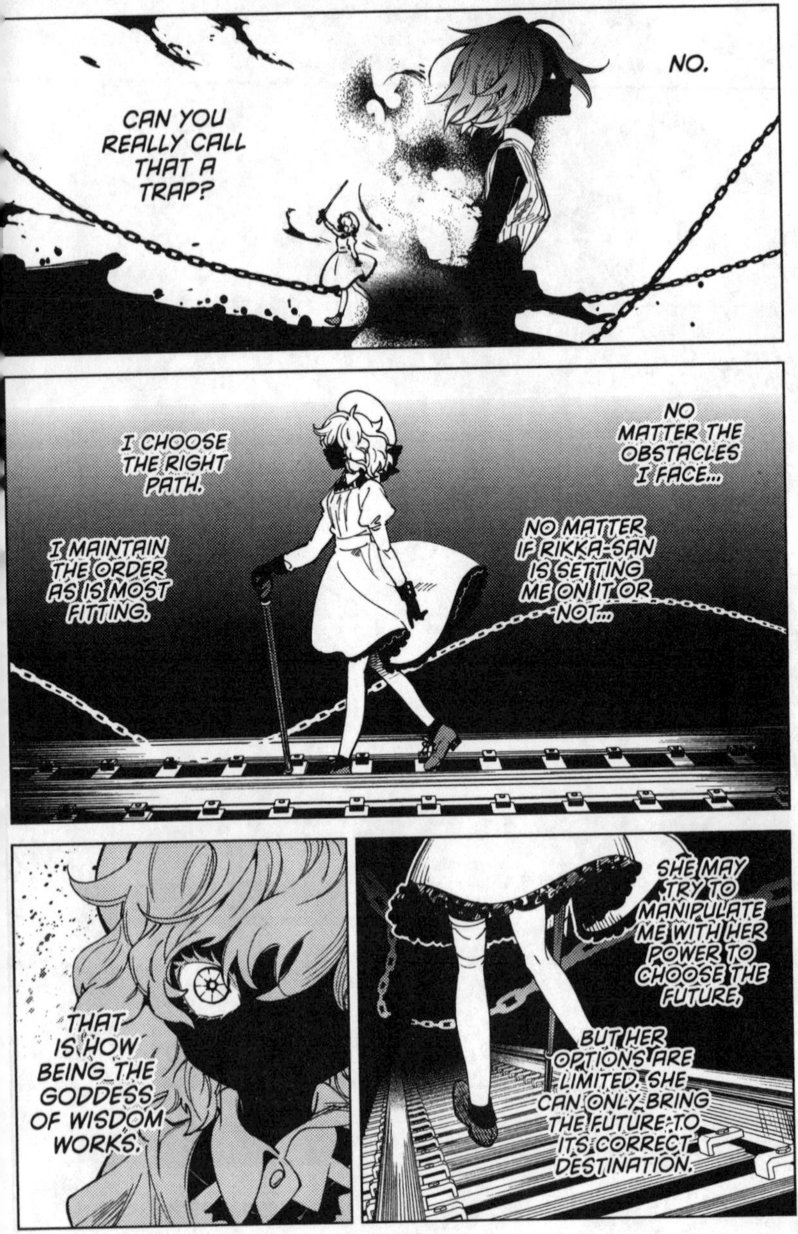
NO.
CAN YOU REALLY CALL THAT A TRAP?
NO MATTER THE OBSTACLES I FACE...
NO MATTER IF RIKKA-SAN IS SETTING ME ON IT OR NOT...
I CHOOSE THE RIGHT PATH.
I MAINTAIN THE ORDER AS IS MOST FITTING.
SHE MAY TRY TO MANIPULATE ME WITH HER POWER TO CHOOSE THE FUTURE,
BUT HER OPTIONS ARE LIMITED. SHE CAN ONLY BRING THE FUTURE TO ITS CORRECT DESTINATION.
THAT IS HOW BEING THE GODDESS OF WISDOM WORKS.

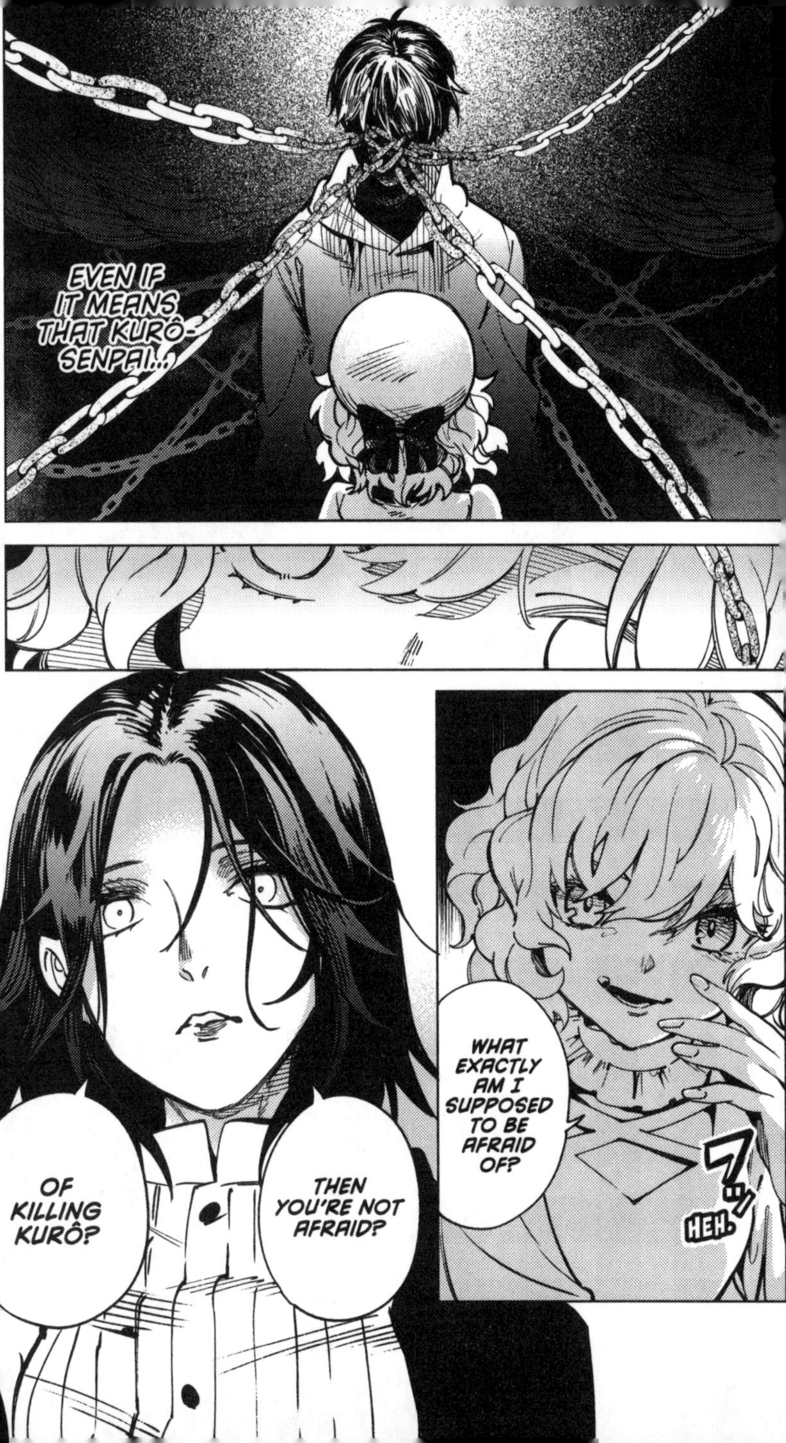
EVEN IF IT MEANS THAT KURÔ-SENPAI...
WHAT EXACTLY AM I SUPPOSED TO BE AFRAID OF?
HEH.
THEN YOU'RE NOT AFRAID?
OF KILLING KURÔ?

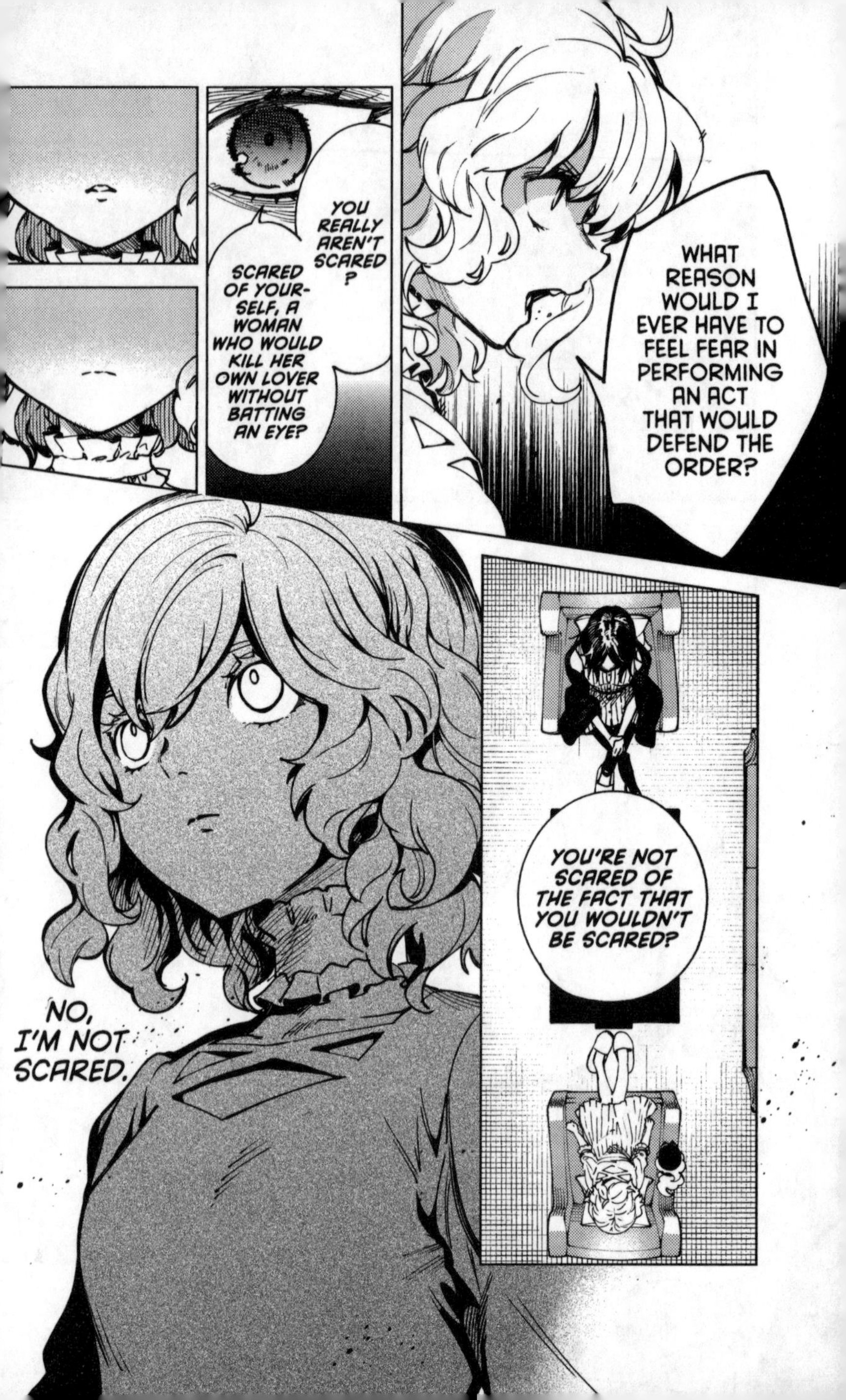
WHAT REASON WOULD I EVER HAVE TO FEEL FEAR IN PERFORMING AN ACT THAT WOULD DEFEND THE ORDER?
YOU REALLY AREN'T SCARED?
SCARED OF YOURSELF, A WOMAN WHO WOULD KILL HER OWN LOVER WITHOUT BATTING AN EYE?
YOU'RE NOT SCARED OF THE FACT THAT YOU WOULDN'T BE SCARED?
NO, I'M NOT SCARED.

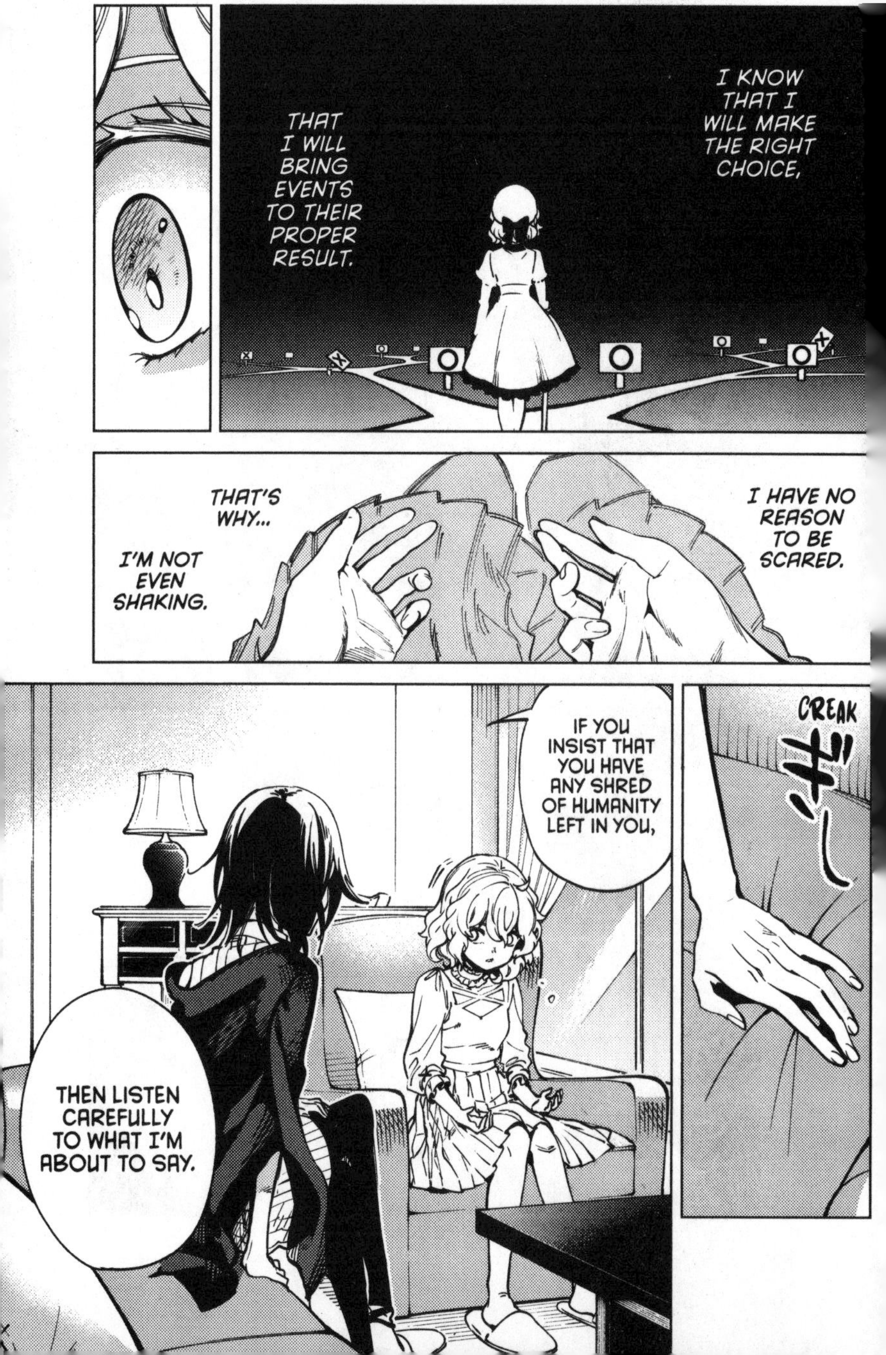
I KNOW THAT I WILL MAKE THE RIGHT CHOICE,
THAT I WILL BRING EVENTS TO THEIR PROPER RESULT.
I HAVE NO REASON TO BE SCARED.
THAT'S WHY...
I'M NOT EVEN SHAKING.
CREAK
IF YOU INSIST THAT YOU HAVE ANY SHRED OF HUMANITY LEFT IN YOU,
THEN LISTEN CAREFULLY TO WHAT I'M ABOUT TO SAY.

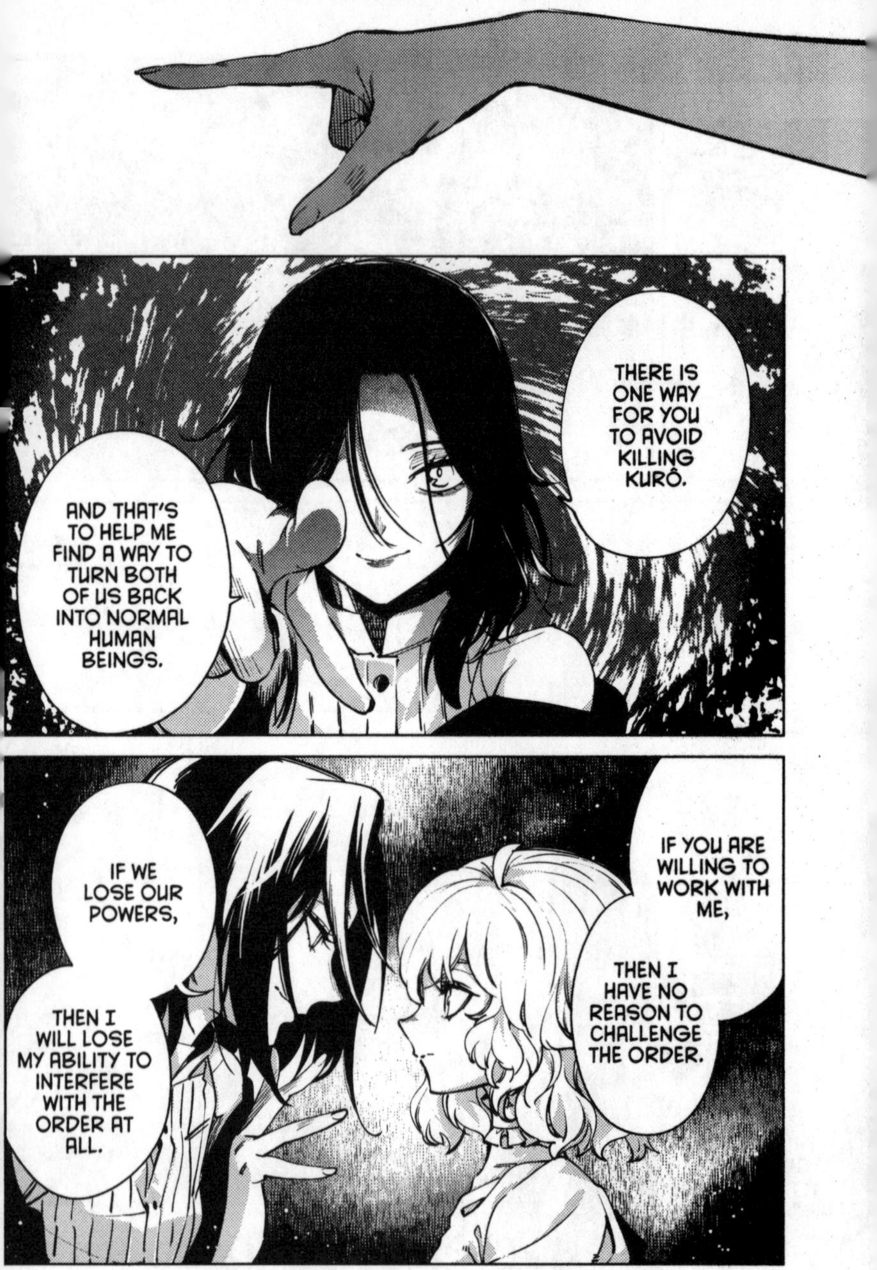
THERE IS ONE WAY FOR YOU TO AVOID KILLING KURÔ.
AND THAT'S TO HELP ME FIND A WAY TO TURN BOTH OF US BACK INTO NORMAL HUMAN BEINGS.
IF YOU ARE WILLING TO WORK WITH ME,
THEN I HAVE NO REASON TO CHALLENGE THE ORDER.
IF WE LOSE OUR POWERS,
THEN I WILL LOSE MY ABILITY TO INTERFERE WITH THE ORDER AT ALL.

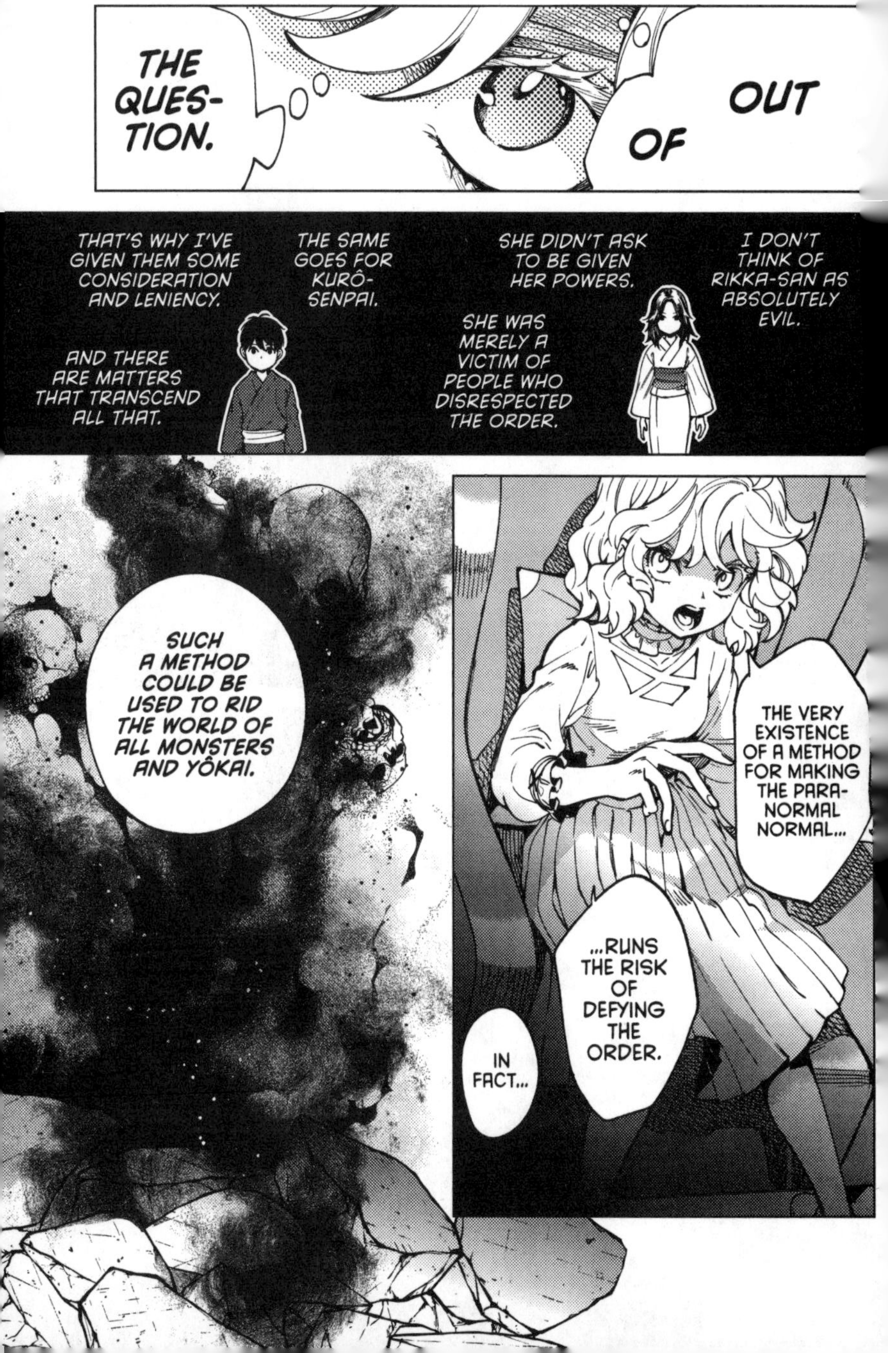
OUT OF
THE QUES-TION.
I DON'T THINK OF RIKKA-SAN AS ABSOLUTELY EVIL.
SHE DIDN'T ASK TO BE GIVEN HER POWERS.
SHE WAS MERELY A VICTIM OF PEOPLE WHO DISRESPECTED THE ORDER.
THE SAME GOES FOR KURÔ-SENPAI.
THAT'S WHY I'VE GIVEN THEM SOME CONSIDERATION AND LENIENCY.
AND THERE ARE MATTERS THAT TRANSCEND ALL THAT.
THE VERY EXISTENCE OF A METHOD FOR MAKING THE PARA-NORMAL NORMAL...
...RUNS THE RISK OF DEFYING THE ORDER.
IN FACT...
SUCH A METHOD COULD BE USED TO RID THE WORLD OF ALL MONSTERS AND YÔKAI.

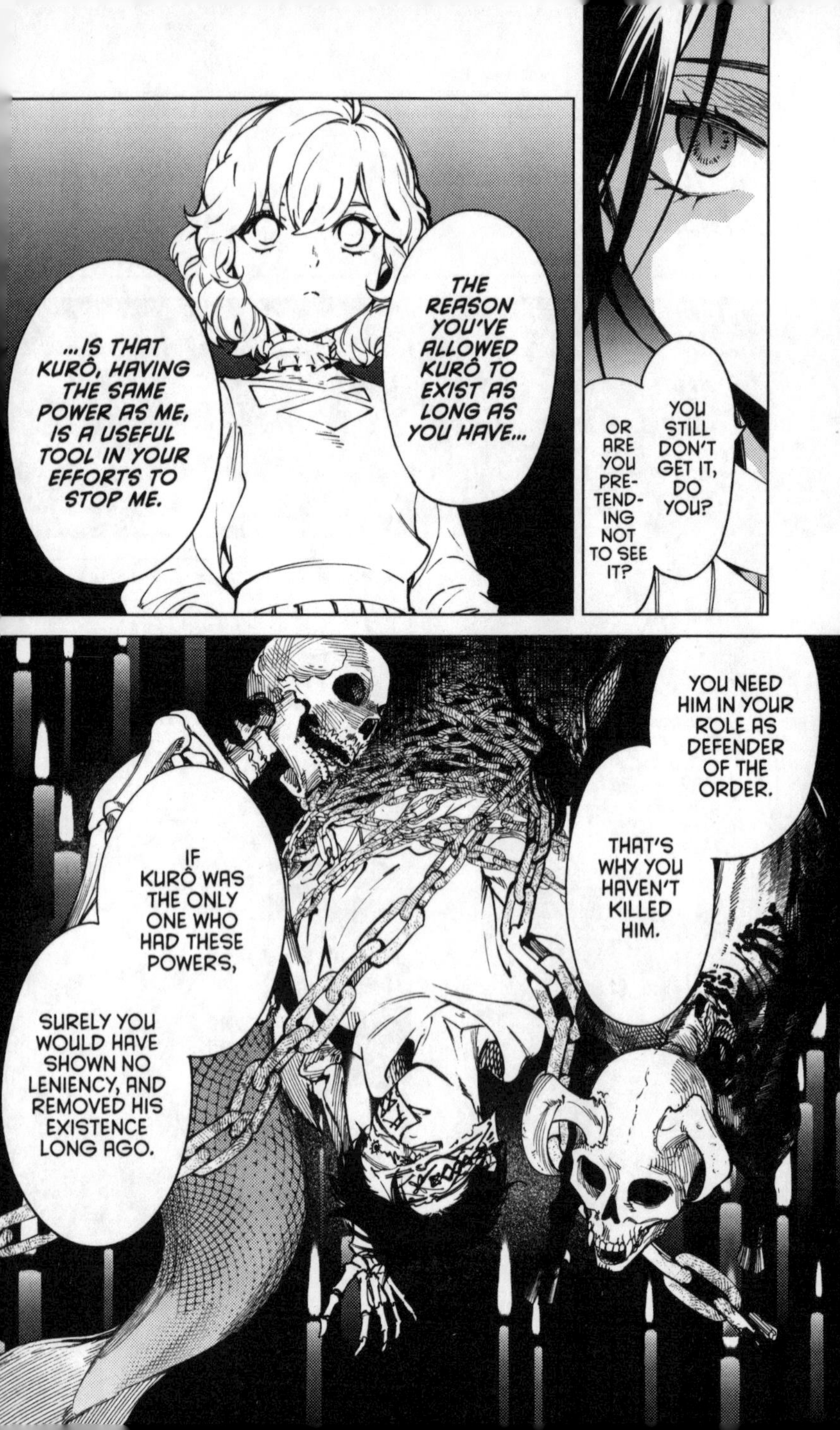
YOU STILL DON'T GET IT, DO YOU?
OR ARE YOU PRE-TEND-ING NOT TO SEE IT?
THE REASON YOU'VE ALLOWED KURÔ TO EXIST AS LONG AS YOU HAVE...
...IS THAT KURÔ, HAVING THE SAME POWER AS ME, IS A USEFUL TOOL IN YOUR EFFORTS TO STOP ME.
YOU NEED HIM IN YOUR ROLE AS DEFENDER OF THE ORDER.
THAT'S WHY YOU HAVEN'T KILLED HIM.
IF KURÔ WAS THE ONLY ONE WHO HAD THESE POWERS,
SURELY YOU WOULD HAVE SHOWN NO LENIENCY, AND REMOVED HIS EXISTENCE LONG AGO.

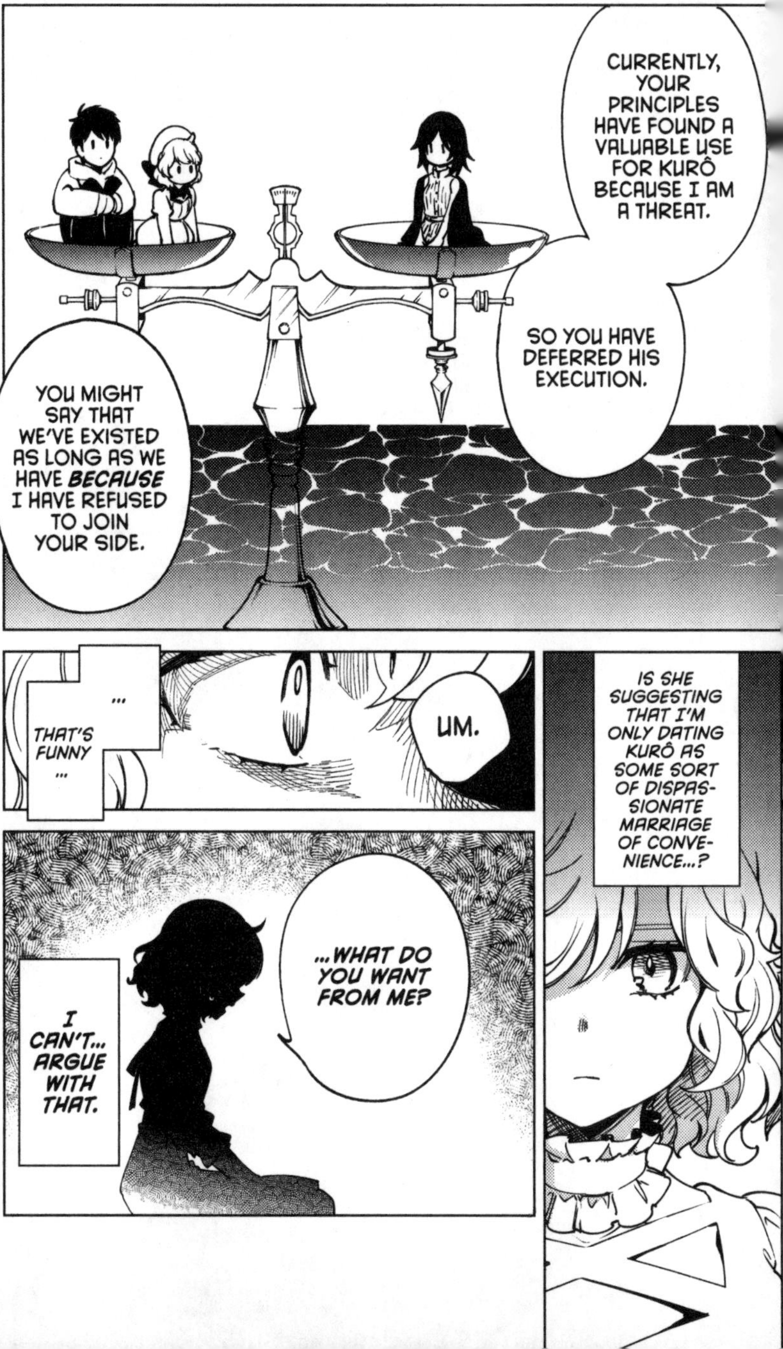
CURRENTLY, YOUR PRINCIPLES HAVE FOUND A VALUABLE USE FOR KURÔ BECAUSE I AM A THREAT.
SO YOU HAVE DEFERRED HIS EXECUTION.
YOU MIGHT SAY THAT WE'VE EXISTED AS LONG AS WE HAVE *BECAUSE* I HAVE REFUSED TO JOIN YOUR SIDE.
IS SHE SUGGESTING THAT I'M ONLY DATING KURÔ AS SOME SORT OF DISPAS-SIONATE MARRIAGE OF CONVE-NIENCE...?
UM.
...
THAT'S FUNNY ...
...WHAT DO YOU WANT FROM ME?
I CAN'T... ARGUE WITH THAT.

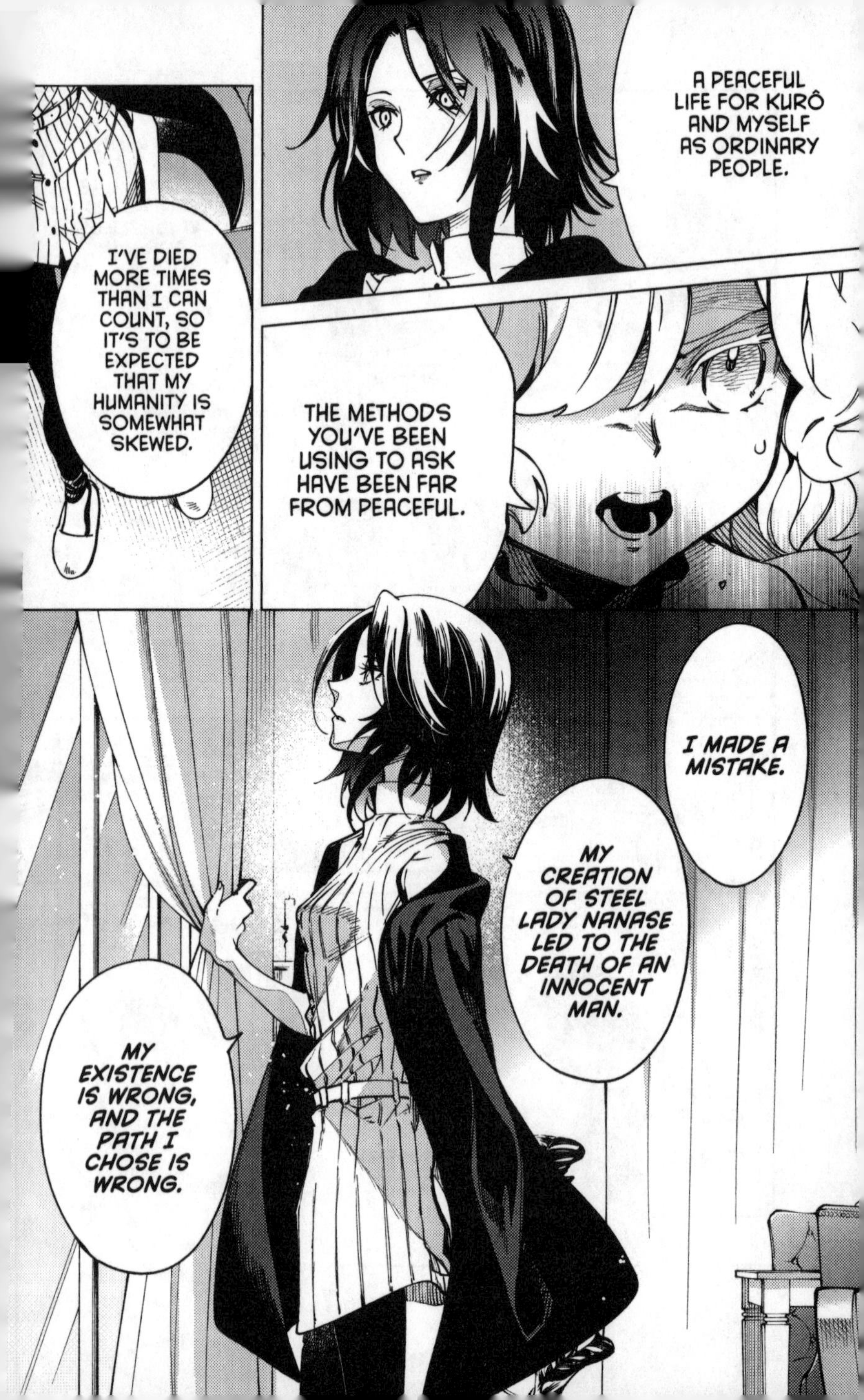
A PEACEFUL LIFE FOR KURÔ AND MYSELF AS ORDINARY PEOPLE.
THE METHODS YOU'VE BEEN USING TO ASK HAVE BEEN FAR FROM PEACEFUL.
I'VE DIED MORE TIMES THAN I CAN COUNT, SO IT'S TO BE EXPECTED THAT MY HUMANITY IS SOMEWHAT SKEWED.
I MADE A MISTAKE.
MY CREATION OF STEEL LADY NANASE LED TO THE DEATH OF AN INNOCENT MAN.
MY EXISTENCE IS WRONG, AND THE PATH I CHOSE IS WRONG.

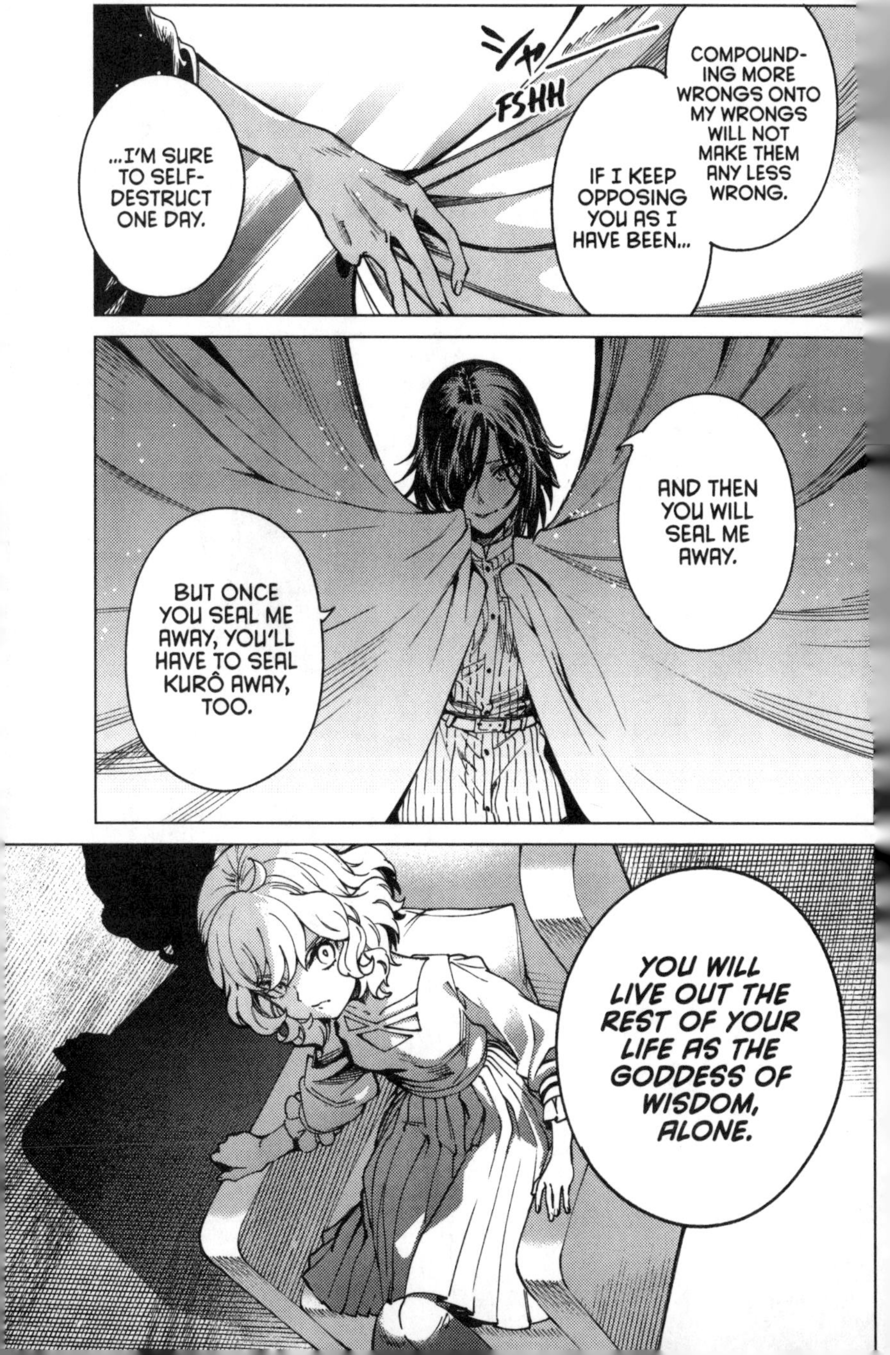
COMPOUNDING MORE WRONGS ONTO MY WRONGS WILL NOT MAKE THEM ANY LESS WRONG.
FSHH
IF I KEEP OPPOSING YOU AS I HAVE BEEN...
...I'M SURE TO SELF-DESTRUCT ONE DAY.
AND THEN YOU WILL SEAL ME AWAY.
BUT ONCE YOU SEAL ME AWAY, YOU'LL HAVE TO SEAL KURÔ AWAY, TOO.
YOU WILL LIVE OUT THE REST OF YOUR LIFE AS THE GODDESS OF WISDOM, ALONE.

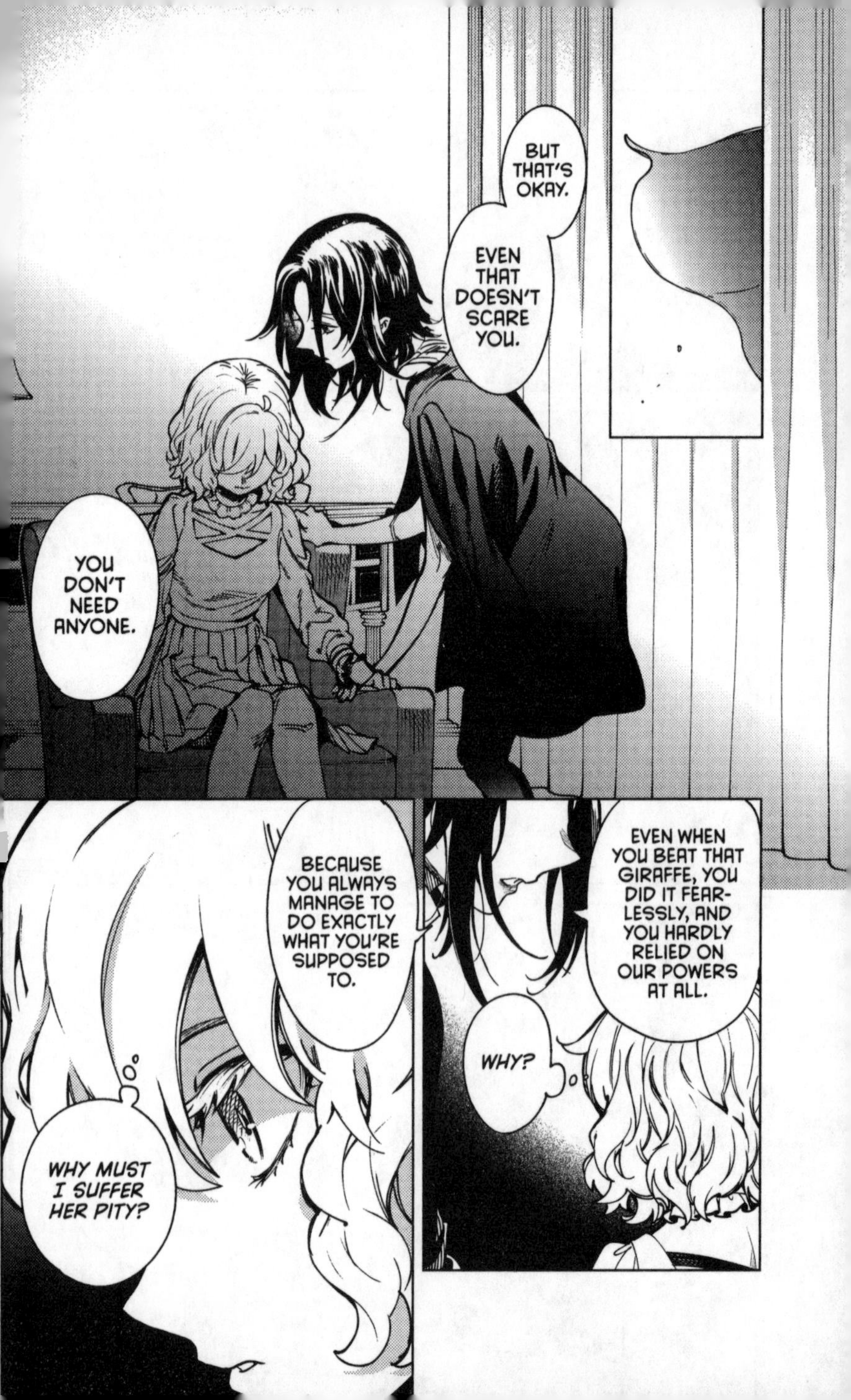
BUT THAT'S OKAY.
EVEN THAT DOESN'T SCARE YOU.
YOU DON'T NEED ANYONE.
EVEN WHEN YOU BEAT THAT GIRAFFE, YOU DID IT FEAR-LESSLY, AND YOU HARDLY RELIED ON OUR POWERS AT ALL.
WHY?
BECAUSE YOU ALWAYS MANAGE TO DO EXACTLY WHAT YOU'RE SUPPOSED TO.
WHY MUST I SUFFER HER PITY?

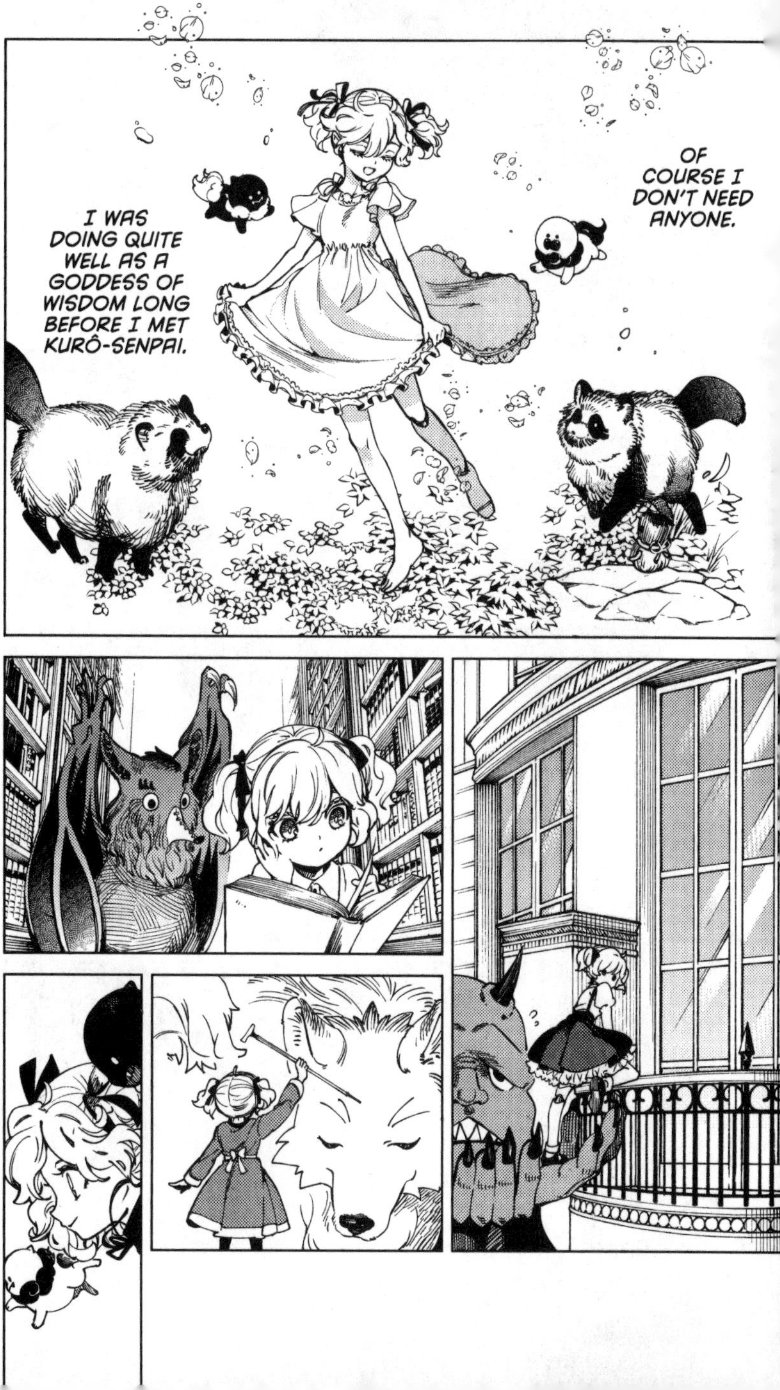
OF COURSE I DON'T NEED ANYONE.
I WAS DOING QUITE WELL AS A GODDESS OF WISDOM LONG BEFORE I MET KURÔ-SENPAI.

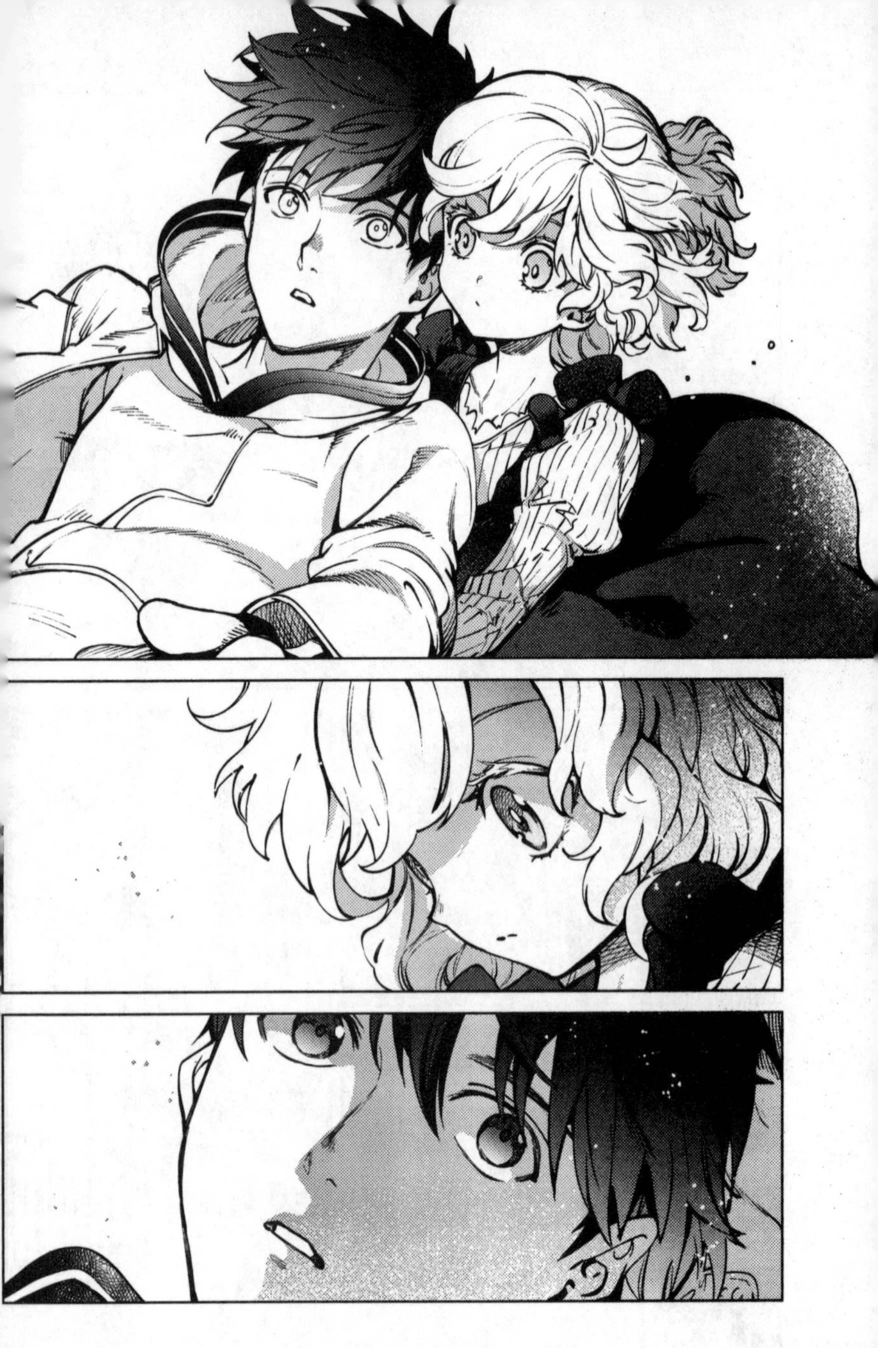

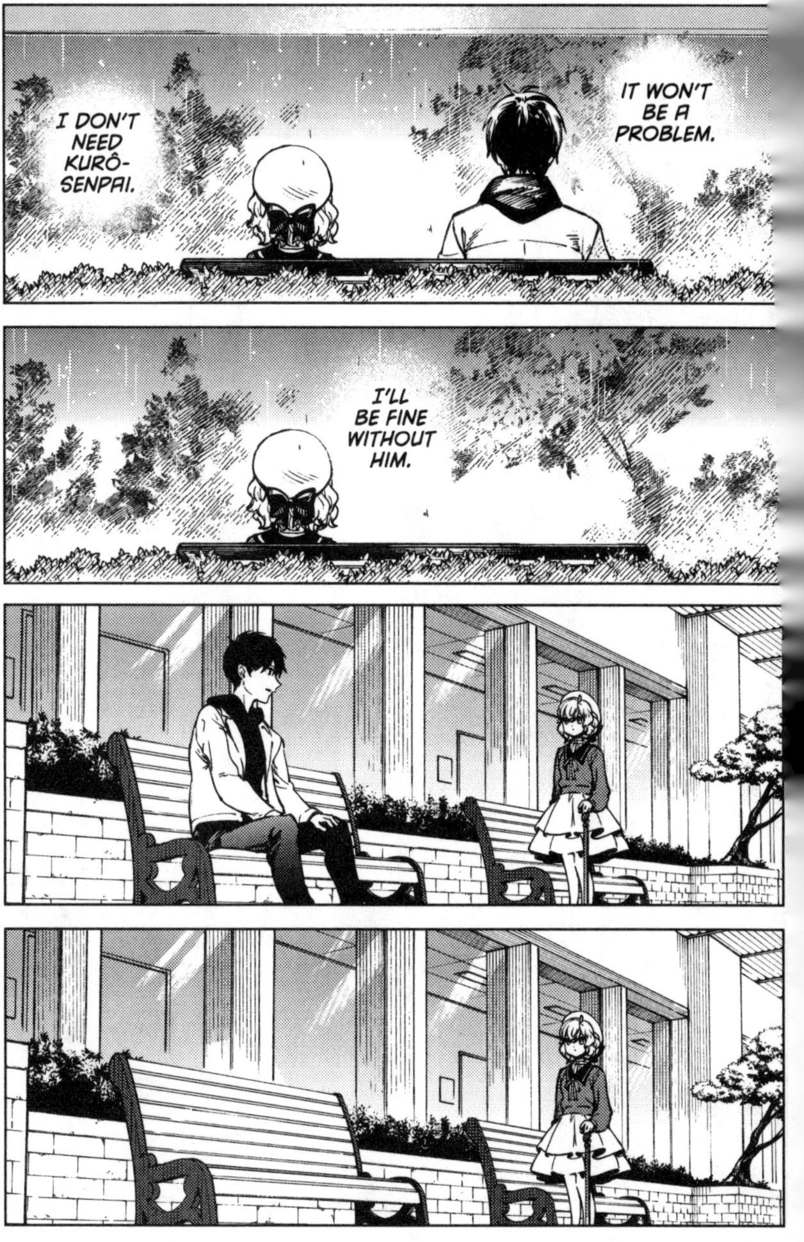
IT WON'T BE A PROBLEM.
I DON'T NEED KURÔ-SENPAI.
I'LL BE FINE WITHOUT HIM.

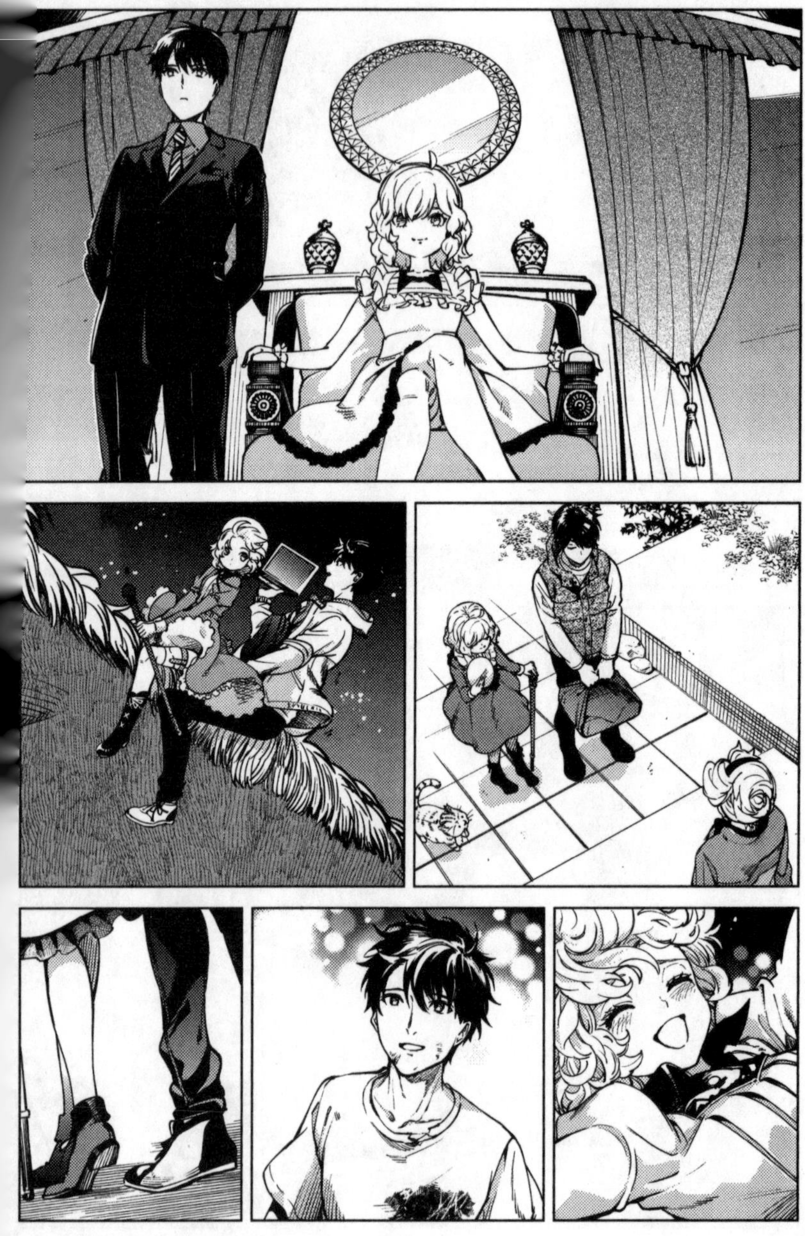

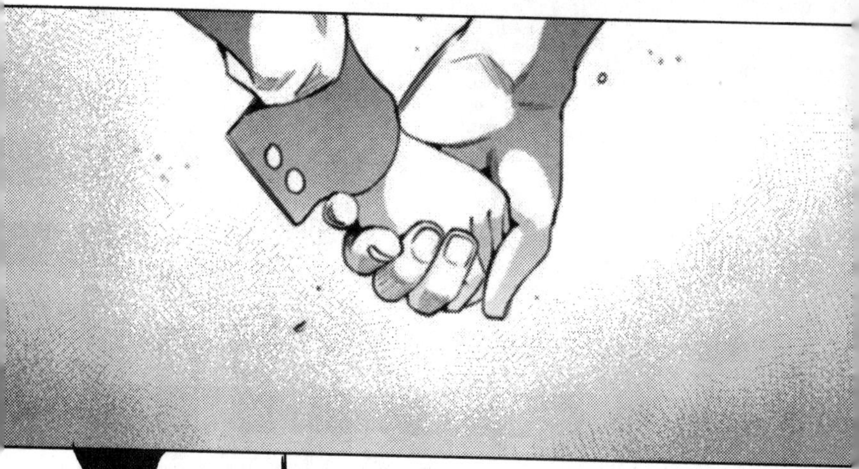
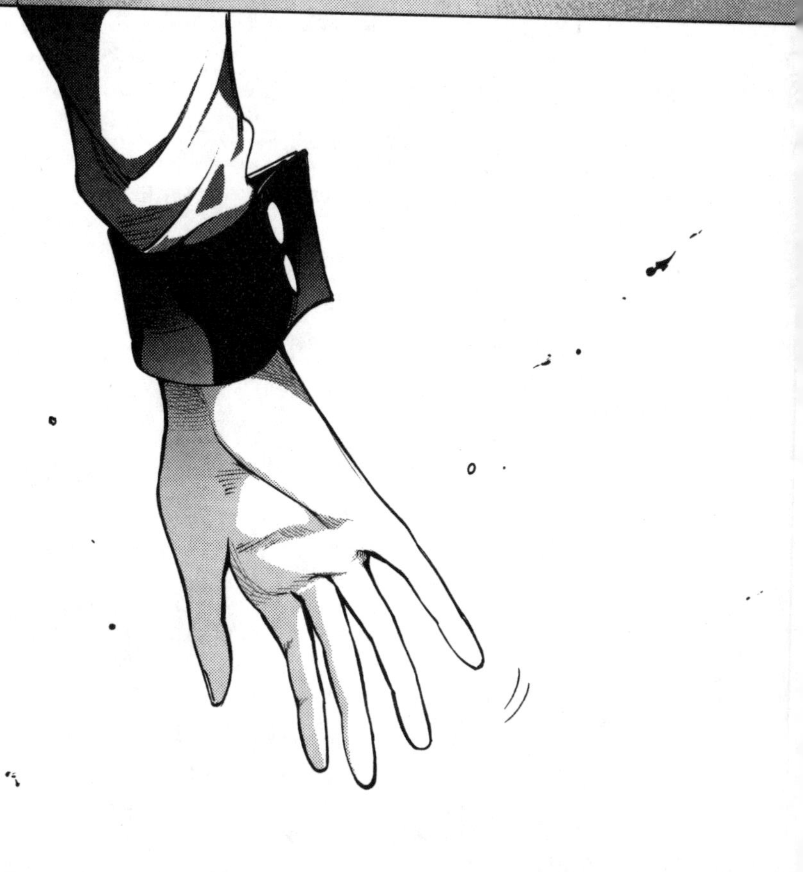

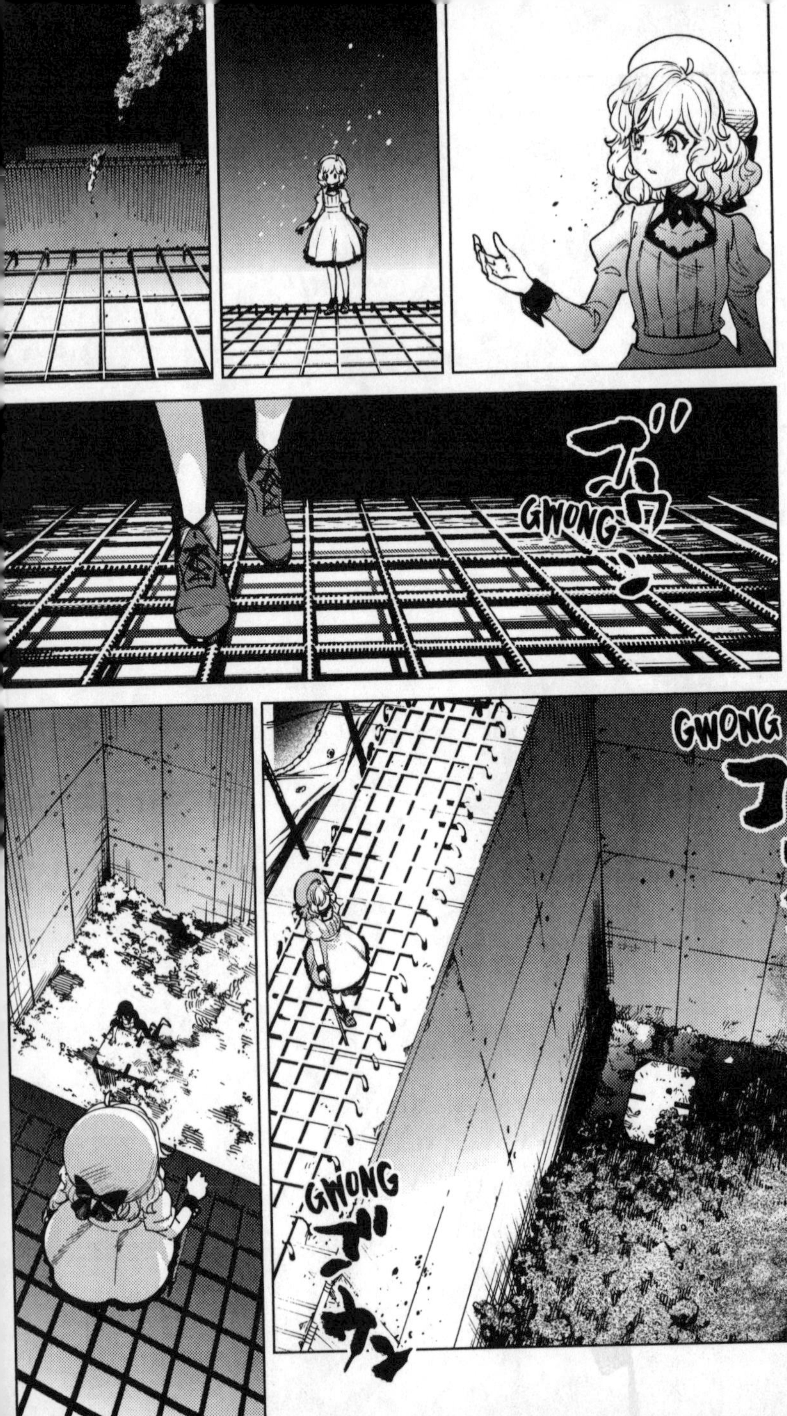
GWONG
GWONG
ブゥン
GWONG

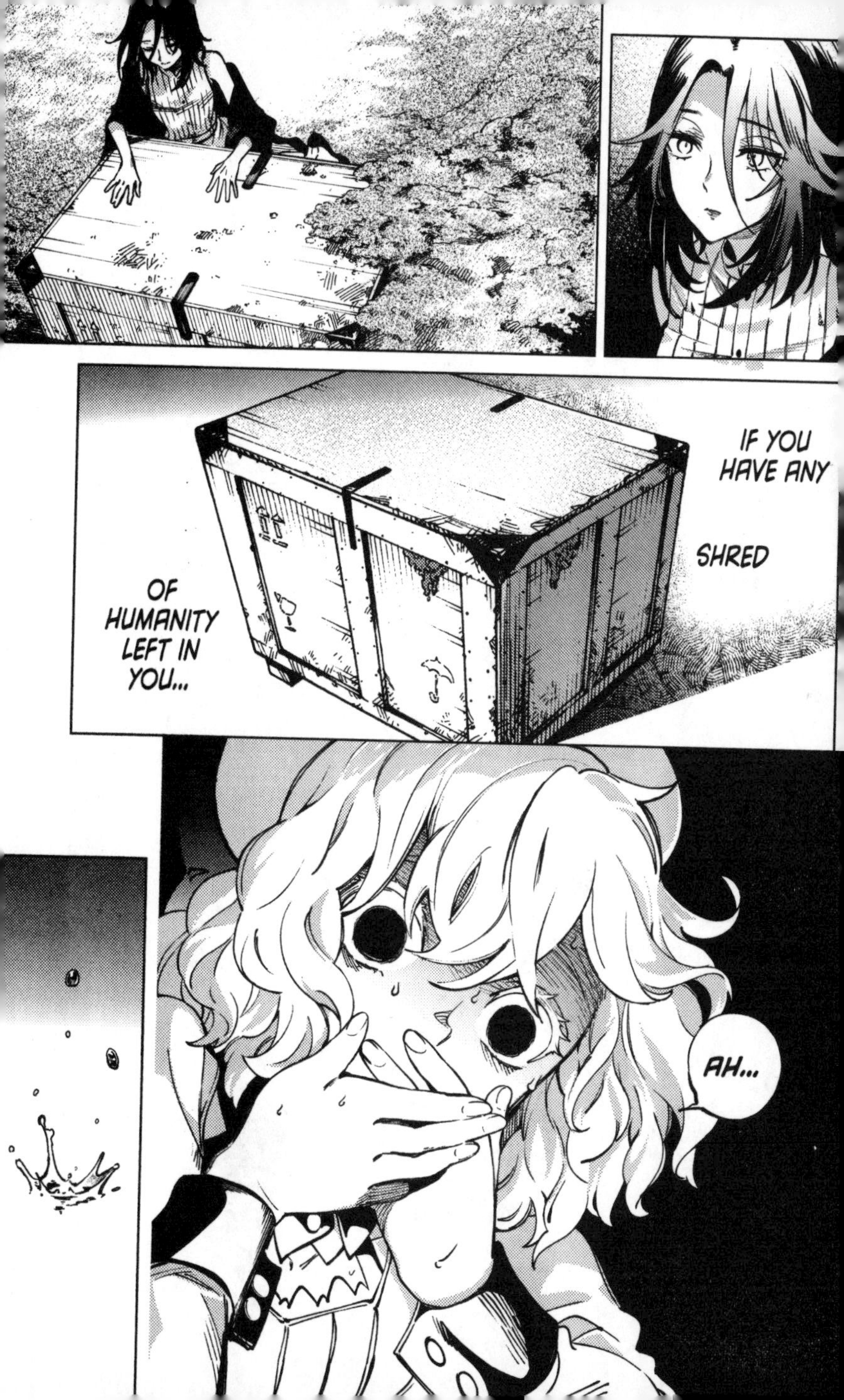
IF YOU HAVE ANY
SHRED
OF HUMANITY LEFT IN YOU...
AH...

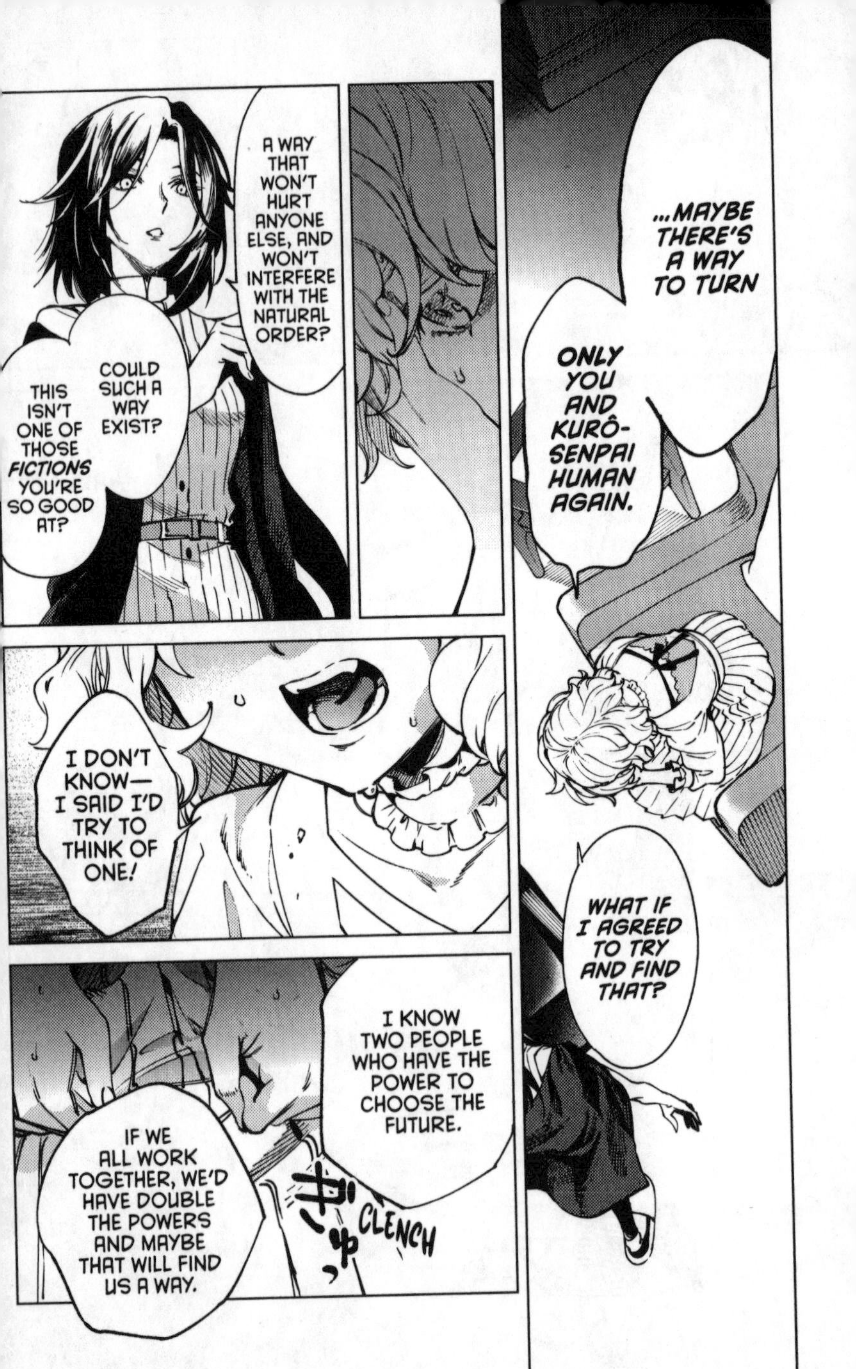
...MAYBE THERE'S A WAY TO TURN
ONLY YOU AND KURÔ-SENPAI HUMAN AGAIN.
WHAT IF I AGREED TO TRY AND FIND THAT?
A WAY THAT WON'T HURT ANYONE ELSE, AND WON'T INTERFERE WITH THE NATURAL ORDER?
COULD SUCH A WAY EXIST?
THIS ISN'T ONE OF THOSE *FICTIONS* YOU'RE SO GOOD AT?
I DON'T KNOW— I SAID I'D TRY TO THINK OF ONE!
I KNOW TWO PEOPLE WHO HAVE THE POWER TO CHOOSE THE FUTURE.
IF WE ALL WORK TOGETHER, WE'D HAVE DOUBLE THE POWERS AND MAYBE THAT WILL FIND US A WAY.
CLENCH

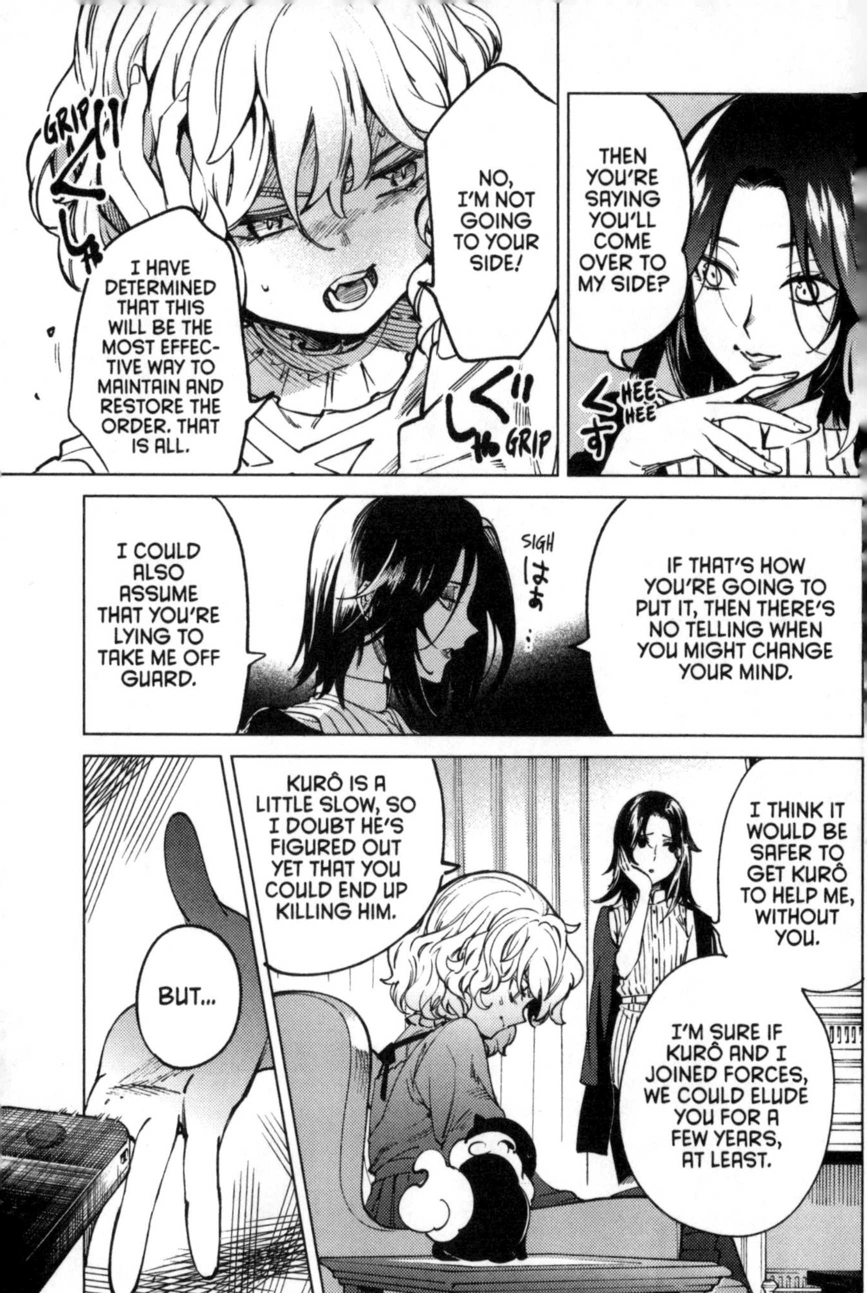
THEN YOU'RE SAYING YOU'LL COME OVER TO MY SIDE?
HEE HEE
NO, I'M NOT GOING TO YOUR SIDE!
GRIP
GRIP
I HAVE DETERMINED THAT THIS WILL BE THE MOST EFFECTIVE WAY TO MAINTAIN AND RESTORE THE ORDER. THAT IS ALL.
IF THAT'S HOW YOU'RE GOING TO PUT IT, THEN THERE'S NO TELLING WHEN YOU MIGHT CHANGE YOUR MIND.
SIGH
I COULD ALSO ASSUME THAT YOU'RE LYING TO TAKE ME OFF GUARD.
I THINK IT WOULD BE SAFER TO GET KURÔ TO HELP ME, WITHOUT YOU.
I'M SURE IF KURÔ AND I JOINED FORCES, WE COULD ELUDE YOU FOR A FEW YEARS, AT LEAST.
KURÔ IS A LITTLE SLOW, SO I DOUBT HE'S FIGURED OUT YET THAT YOU COULD END UP KILLING HIM.
BUT...

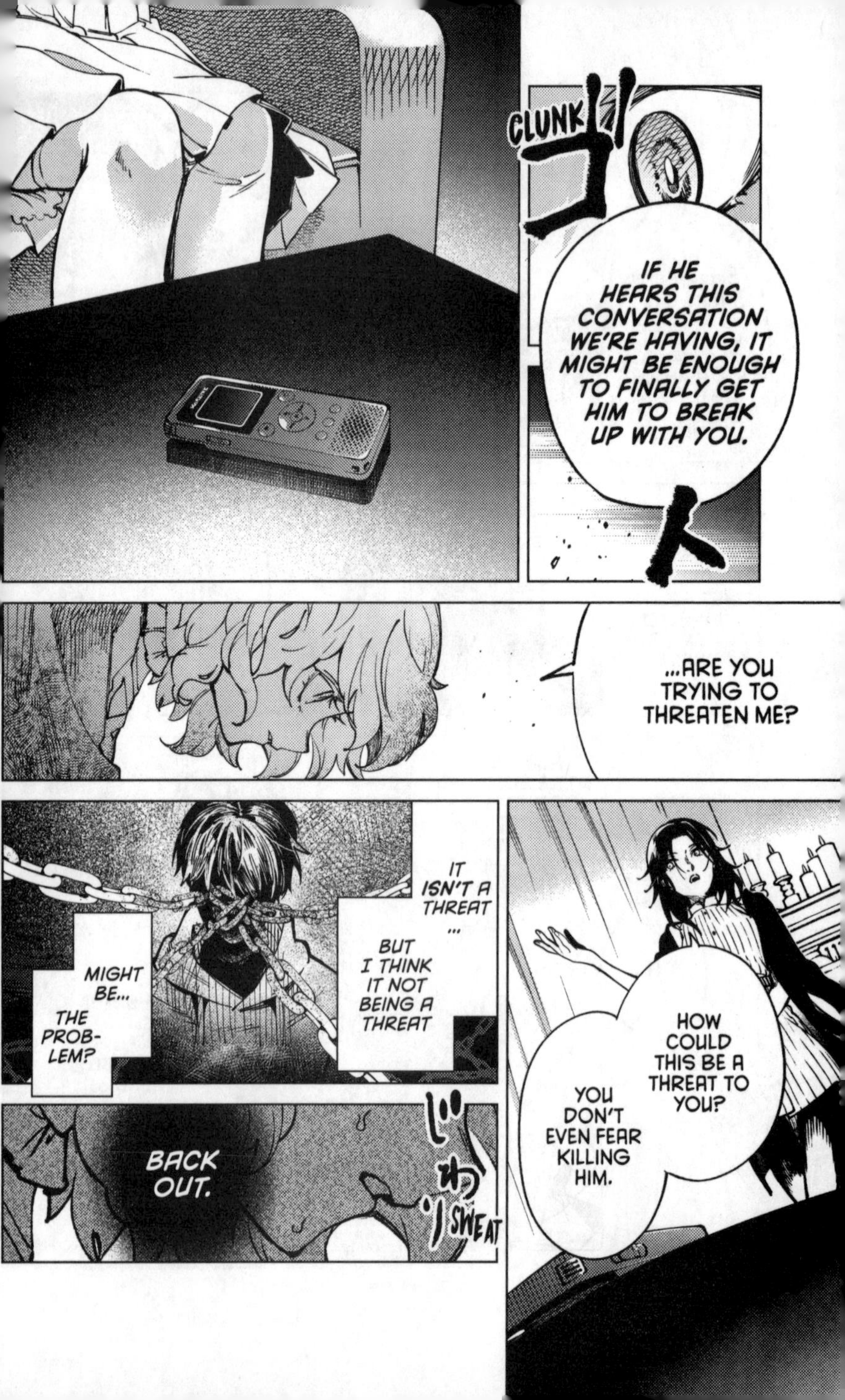
CLUNK
IF HE HEARS THIS CONVERSATION WE'RE HAVING, IT MIGHT BE ENOUGH TO FINALLY GET HIM TO BREAK UP WITH YOU.
...ARE YOU TRYING TO THREATEN ME?
HOW COULD THIS BE A THREAT TO YOU?
YOU DON'T EVEN FEAR KILLING HIM.
IT ISN'T A THREAT...
BUT I THINK IT NOT BEING A THREAT
MIGHT BE... THE PROB-LEM?
BACK OUT.
SWEAT

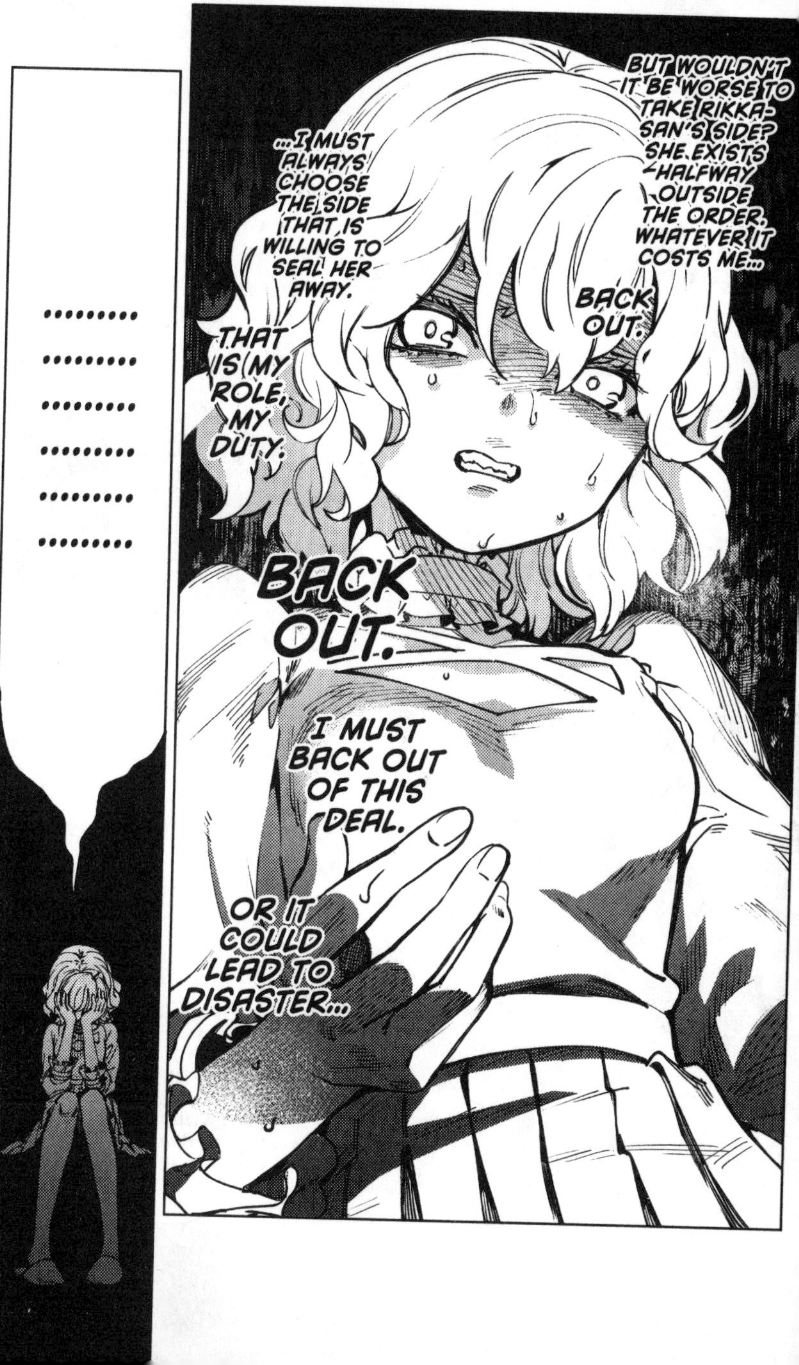
BUT WOULDN'T IT BE WORSE TO TAKE RIKKA-SAN'S SIDE? SHE EXISTS HALFWAY OUTSIDE THE ORDER. WHATEVER IT COSTS ME...
...I MUST ALWAYS CHOOSE THE SIDE THAT IS WILLING TO SEAL HER AWAY.
BACK OUT.
THAT IS MY ROLE, MY DUTY.
BACK OUT.
I MUST BACK OUT OF THIS DEAL.
OR IT COULD LEAD TO DISASTER...
....
....
....
....
....
....

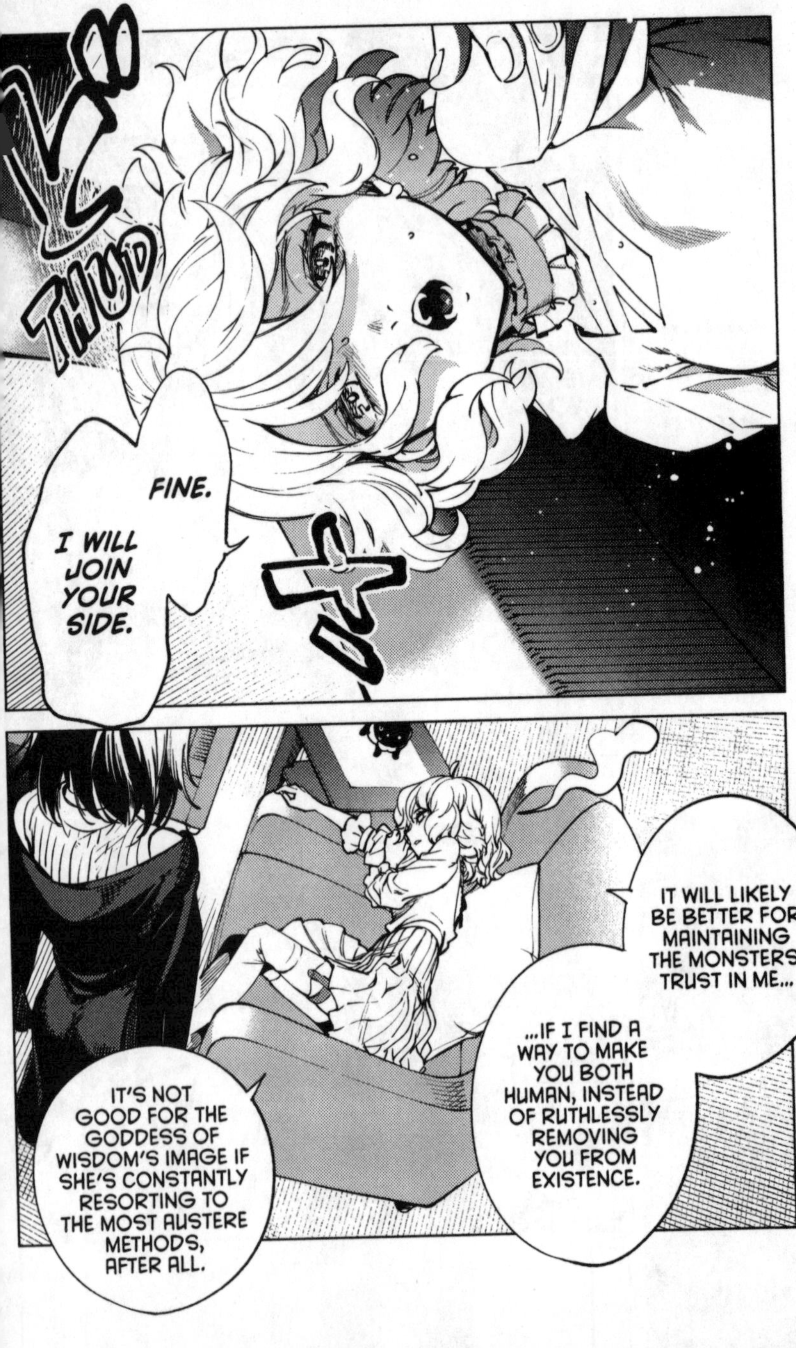
THUD
FINE.
I WILL JOIN YOUR SIDE.
IT WILL LIKELY BE BETTER FOR MAINTAINING THE MONSTERS' TRUST IN ME...
...IF I FIND A WAY TO MAKE YOU BOTH HUMAN, INSTEAD OF RUTHLESSLY REMOVING YOU FROM EXISTENCE.
IT'S NOT GOOD FOR THE GODDESS OF WISDOM'S IMAGE IF SHE'S CONSTANTLY RESORTING TO THE MOST AUSTERE METHODS, AFTER ALL.

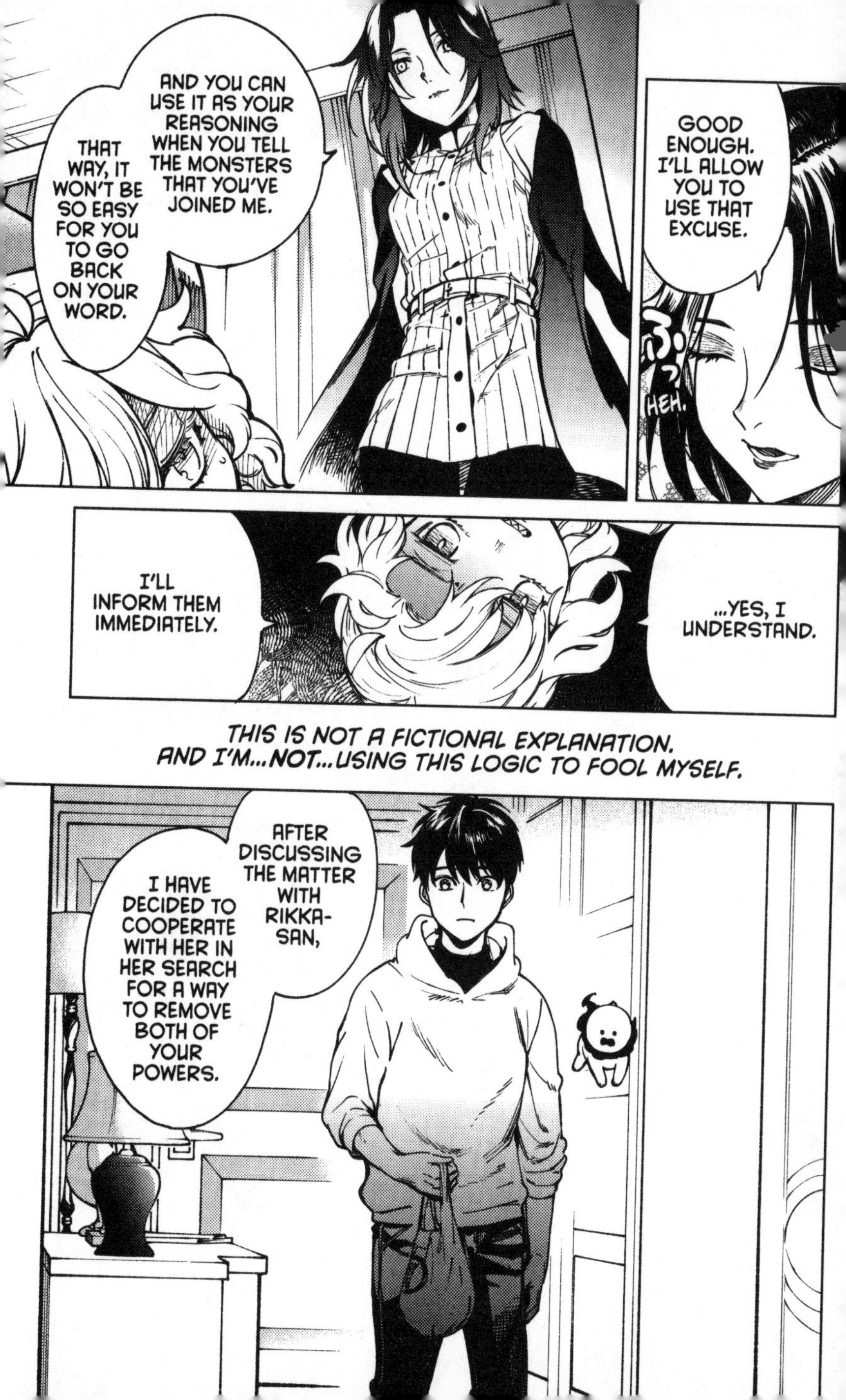
GOOD ENOUGH. I'LL ALLOW YOU TO USE THAT EXCUSE.
ふっ
HEH.
AND YOU CAN USE IT AS YOUR REASONING WHEN YOU TELL THE MONSTERS THAT YOU'VE JOINED ME.
THAT WAY, IT WON'T BE SO EASY FOR YOU TO GO BACK ON YOUR WORD.
...YES, I UNDERSTAND.
I'LL INFORM THEM IMMEDIATELY.
THIS IS NOT A FICTIONAL EXPLANATION. AND I'M...NOT...USING THIS LOGIC TO FOOL MYSELF.
AFTER DISCUSSING THE MATTER WITH RIKKA-SAN,
I HAVE DECIDED TO COOPERATE WITH HER IN HER SEARCH FOR A WAY TO REMOVE BOTH OF YOUR POWERS.

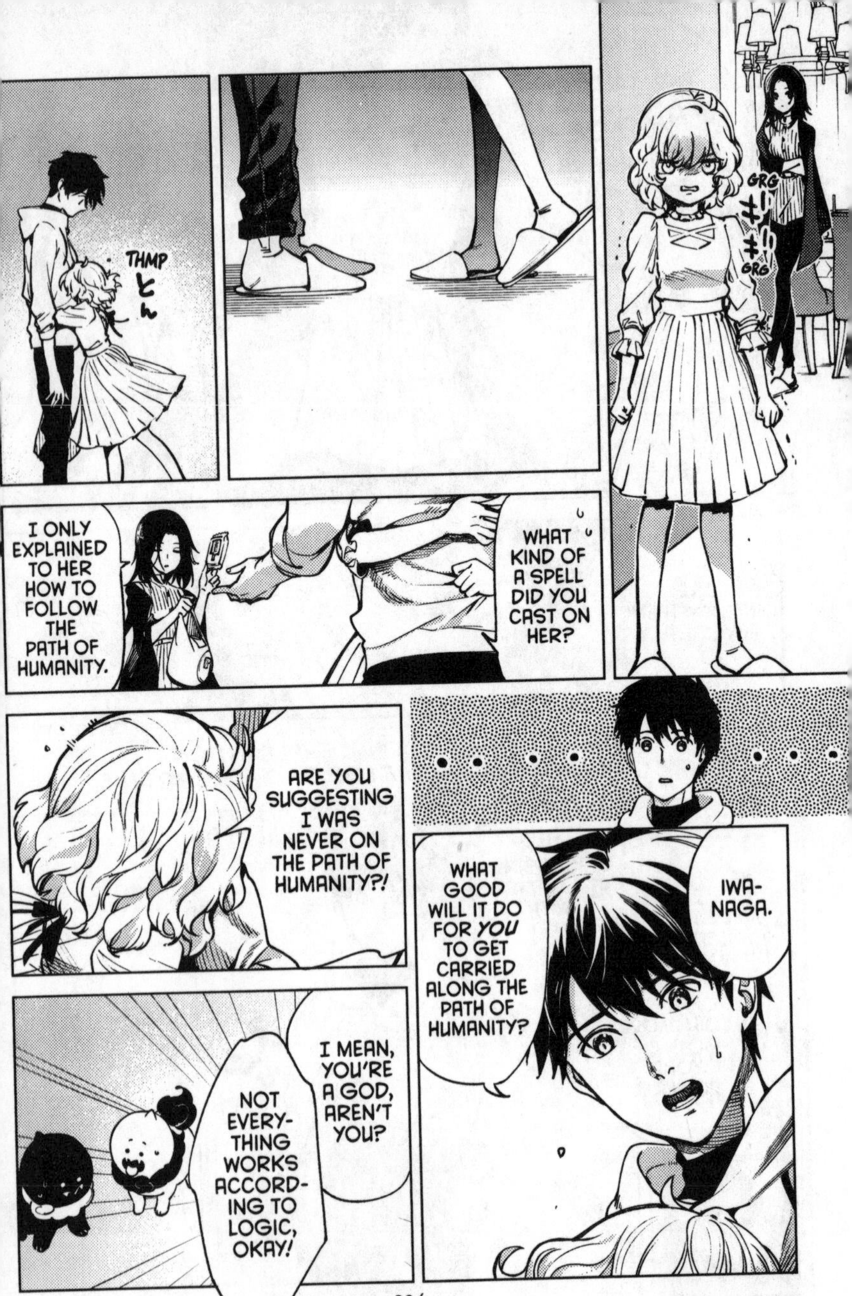
GRG ギリ
ギリ GRG
THMP とん
WHAT KIND OF A SPELL DID YOU CAST ON HER?
I ONLY EXPLAINED TO HER HOW TO FOLLOW THE PATH OF HUMANITY.
. . . . . .
IWA-NAGA.
WHAT GOOD WILL IT DO FOR *YOU* TO GET CARRIED ALONG THE PATH OF HUMANITY?
ARE YOU SUGGESTING I WAS NEVER ON THE PATH OF HUMANITY?!
I MEAN, YOU'RE A GOD, AREN'T YOU?
NOT EVERY-THING WORKS ACCORD-ING TO LOGIC, OKAY!

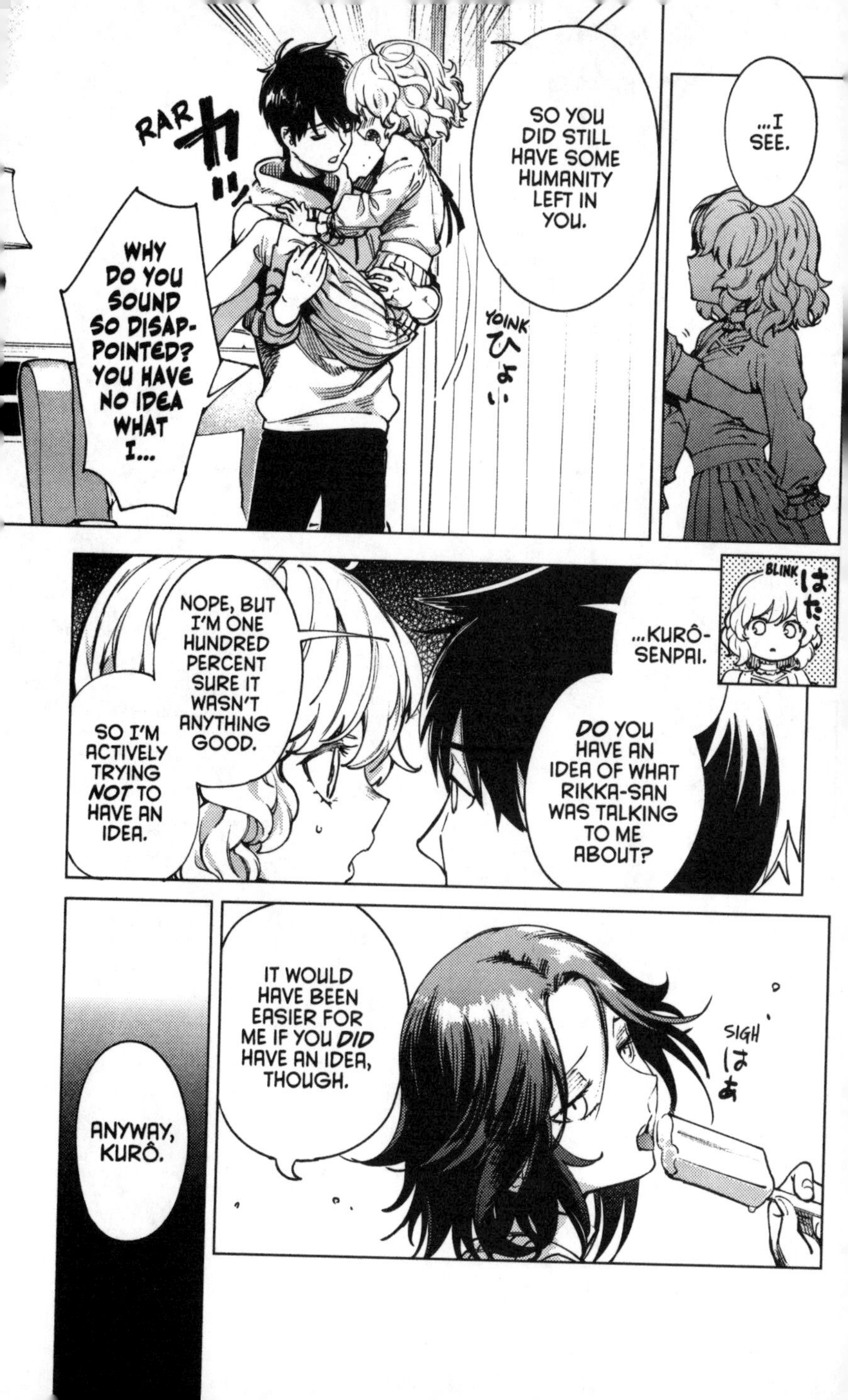
...I SEE.
SO YOU DID STILL HAVE SOME HUMANITY LEFT IN YOU.
YOINK
ひょい
RAR
ガッ
WHY DO YOU SOUND SO DISAPPOINTED? YOU HAVE NO IDEA WHAT I...
BLINK
はた
...KURÔ-SENPAI.
DO YOU HAVE AN IDEA OF WHAT RIKKA-SAN WAS TALKING TO ME ABOUT?
NOPE, BUT I'M ONE HUNDRED PERCENT SURE IT WASN'T ANYTHING GOOD.
SO I'M ACTIVELY TRYING *NOT* TO HAVE AN IDEA.
SIGH
はぁ
IT WOULD HAVE BEEN EASIER FOR ME IF YOU *DID* HAVE AN IDEA, THOUGH.
ANYWAY, KURÔ.

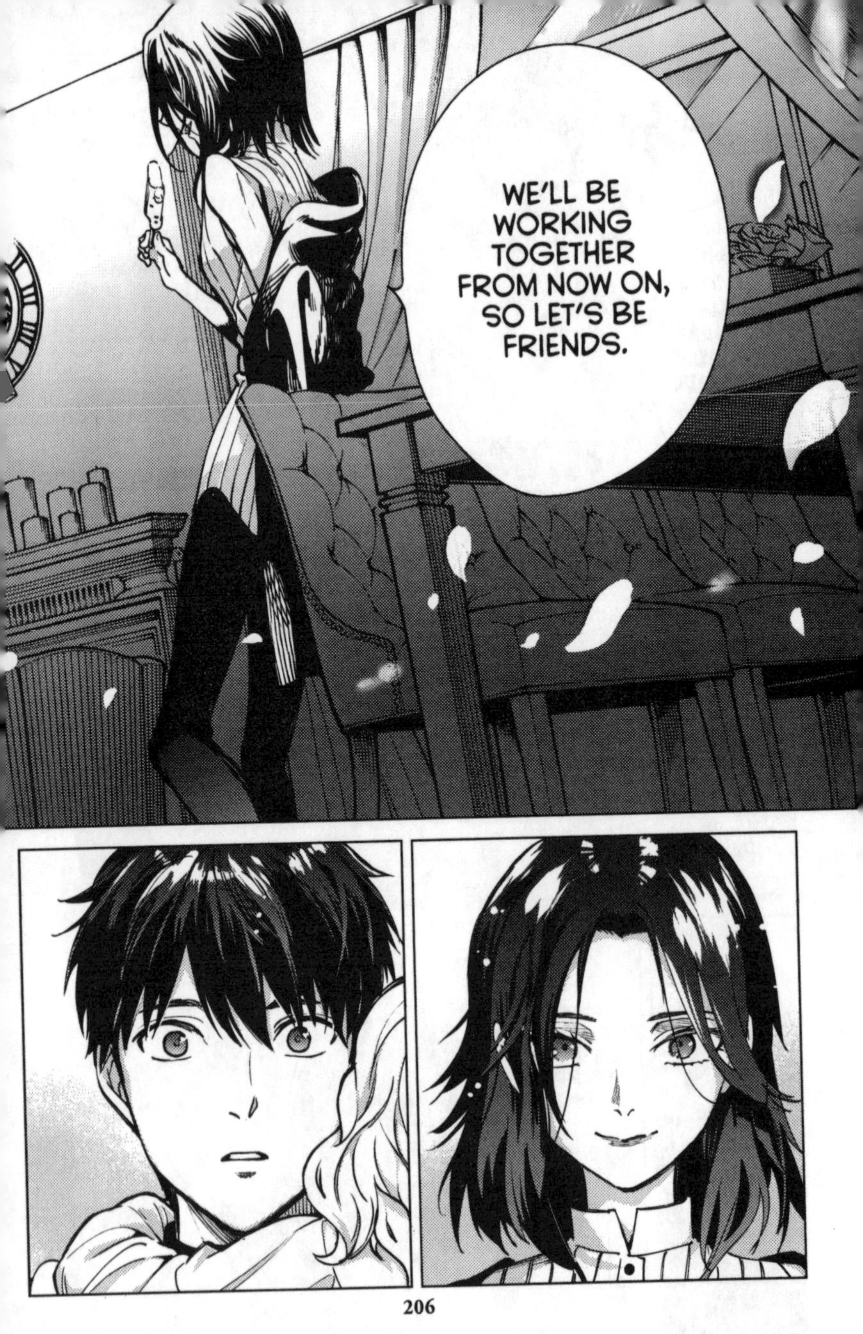
WE'LL BE WORKING TOGETHER FROM NOW ON, SO LET'S BE FRIENDS.

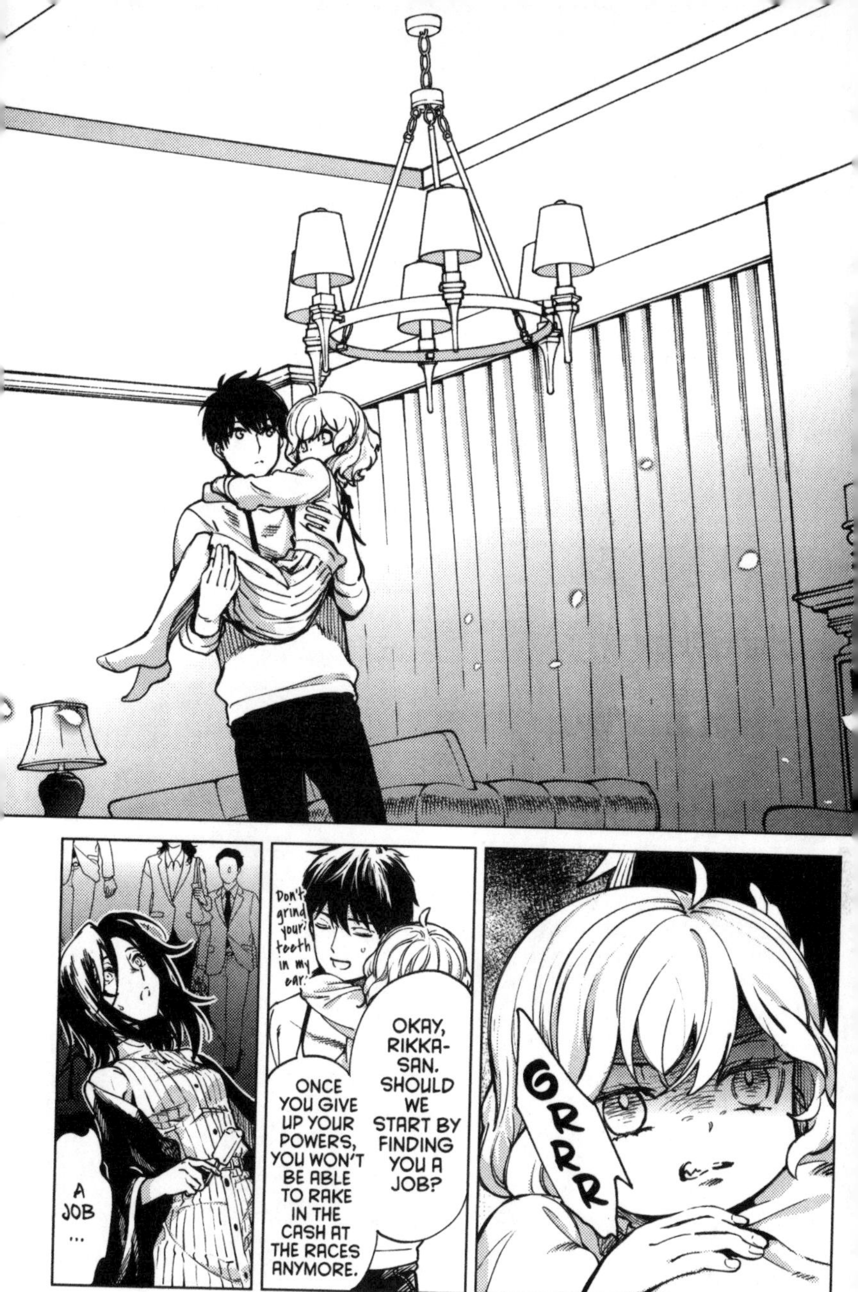
GRRR
Don't grind your teeth in my ear!
OKAY, RIKKA-SAN. SHOULD WE START BY FINDING YOU A JOB?
ONCE YOU GIVE UP YOUR POWERS, YOU WON'T BE ABLE TO RAKE IN THE CASH AT THE RACES ANYMORE.
A JOB ...

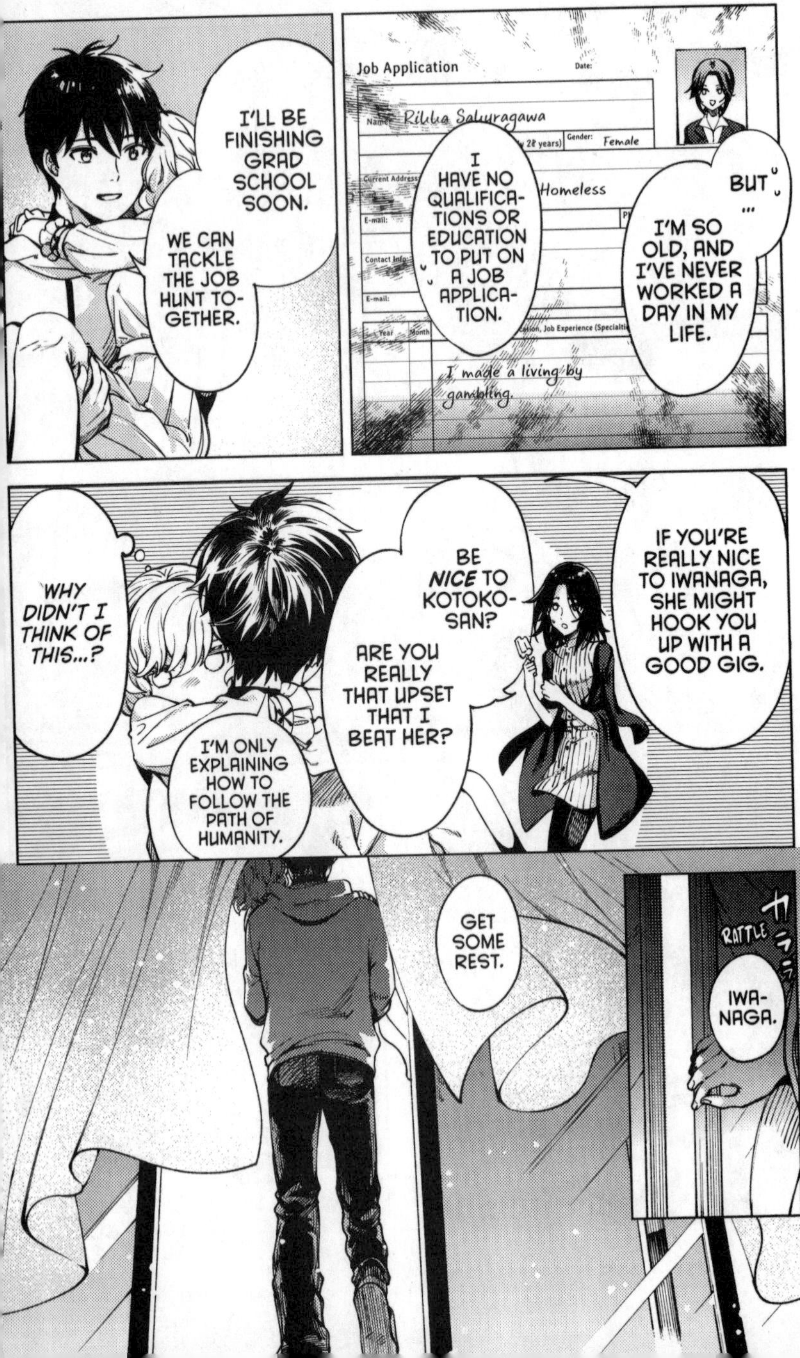
Job Application
Date:
Name: Rikka Sakuragawa
(y 28 years)
Gender: Female
Current Address: Homeless
E-mail:
Contact Info:
E-mail:
Year Month ation, Job Experience (Specialtie
I made a living by gambling.
BUT... I'M SO OLD, AND I'VE NEVER WORKED A DAY IN MY LIFE.
I HAVE NO QUALIFICATIONS OR EDUCATION TO PUT ON A JOB APPLICATION.
I'LL BE FINISHING GRAD SCHOOL SOON.
WE CAN TACKLE THE JOB HUNT TOGETHER.
IF YOU'RE REALLY NICE TO IWANAGA, SHE MIGHT HOOK YOU UP WITH A GOOD GIG.
BE *NICE* TO KOTOKO-SAN?
ARE YOU REALLY THAT UPSET THAT I BEAT HER?
I'M ONLY EXPLAINING HOW TO FOLLOW THE PATH OF HUMANITY.
WHY DIDN'T I THINK OF THIS...?
RATTLE
IWANAGA.
GET SOME REST.

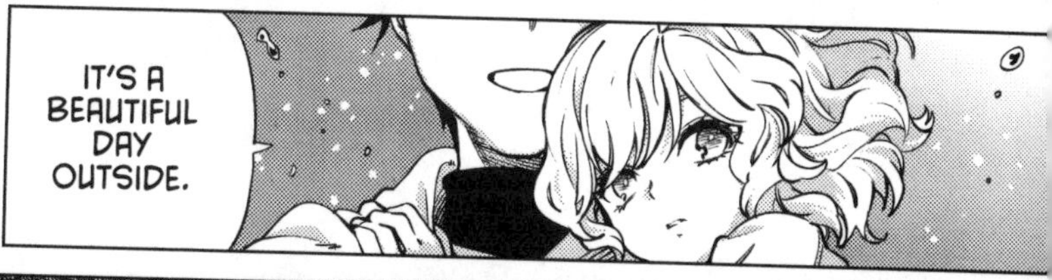
IT'S A BEAUTIFUL DAY OUTSIDE.
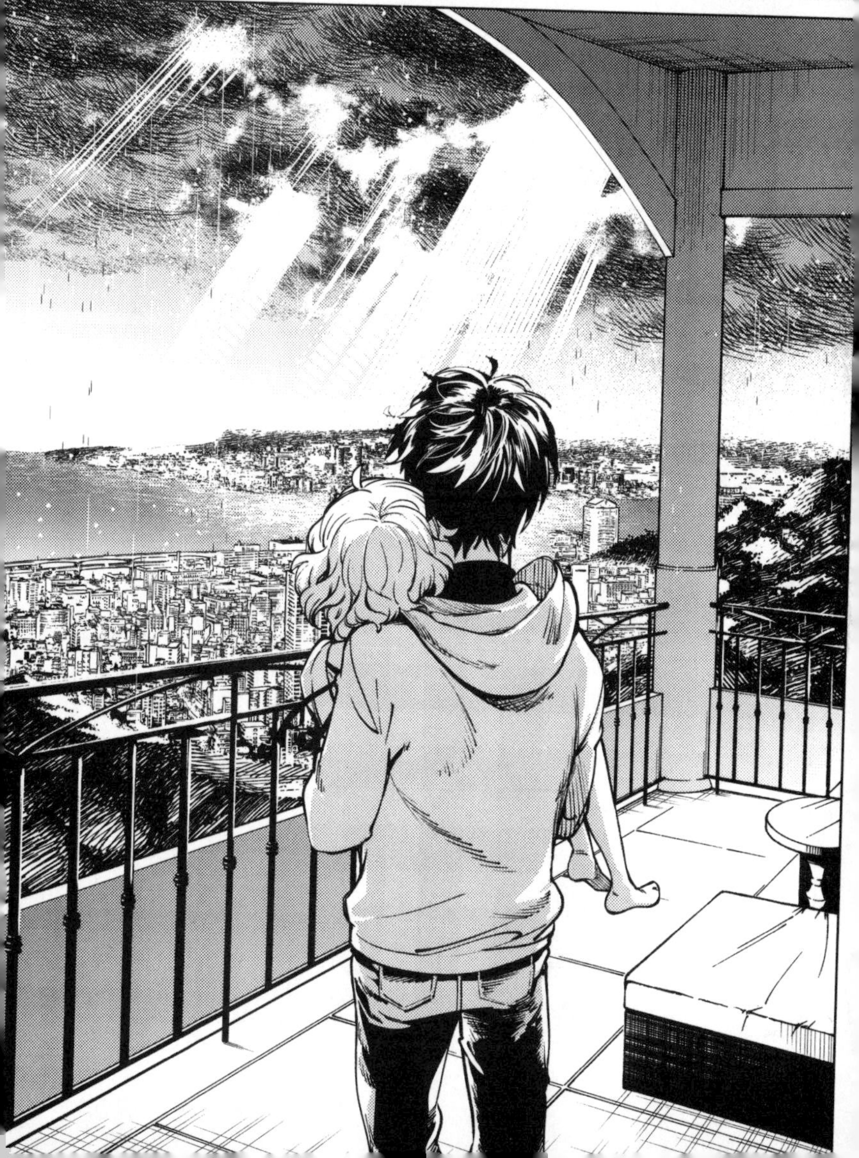

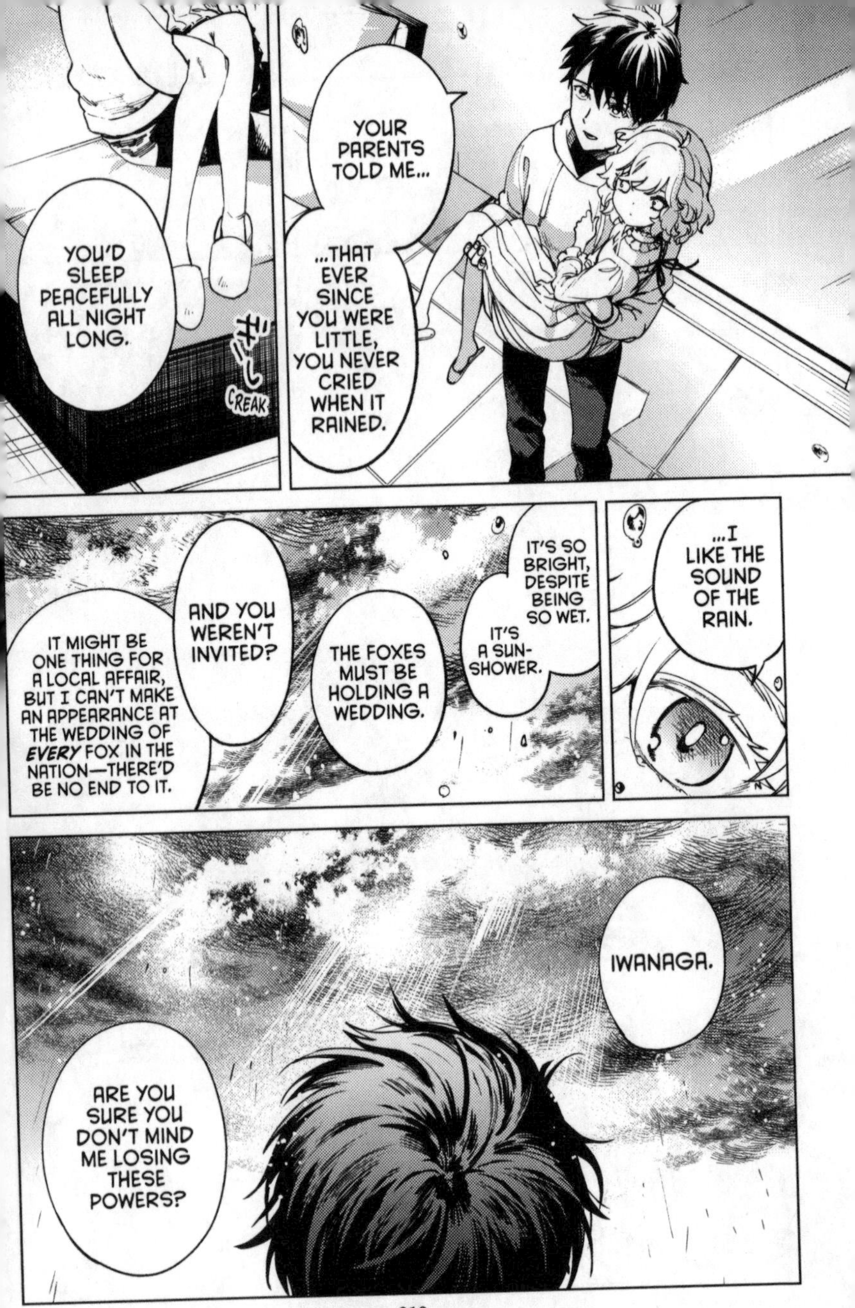
YOUR PARENTS TOLD ME...
...THAT EVER SINCE YOU WERE LITTLE, YOU NEVER CRIED WHEN IT RAINED.
YOU'D SLEEP PEACEFULLY ALL NIGHT LONG.
ぎし
CREAK
...I LIKE THE SOUND OF THE RAIN.
IT'S SO BRIGHT, DESPITE BEING SO WET.
IT'S A SUN-SHOWER.
THE FOXES MUST BE HOLDING A WEDDING.
AND YOU WEREN'T INVITED?
IT MIGHT BE ONE THING FOR A LOCAL AFFAIR, BUT I CAN'T MAKE AN APPEARANCE AT THE WEDDING OF *EVERY* FOX IN THE NATION—THERE'D BE NO END TO IT.
IWANAGA.
ARE YOU SURE YOU DON'T MIND ME LOSING THESE POWERS?

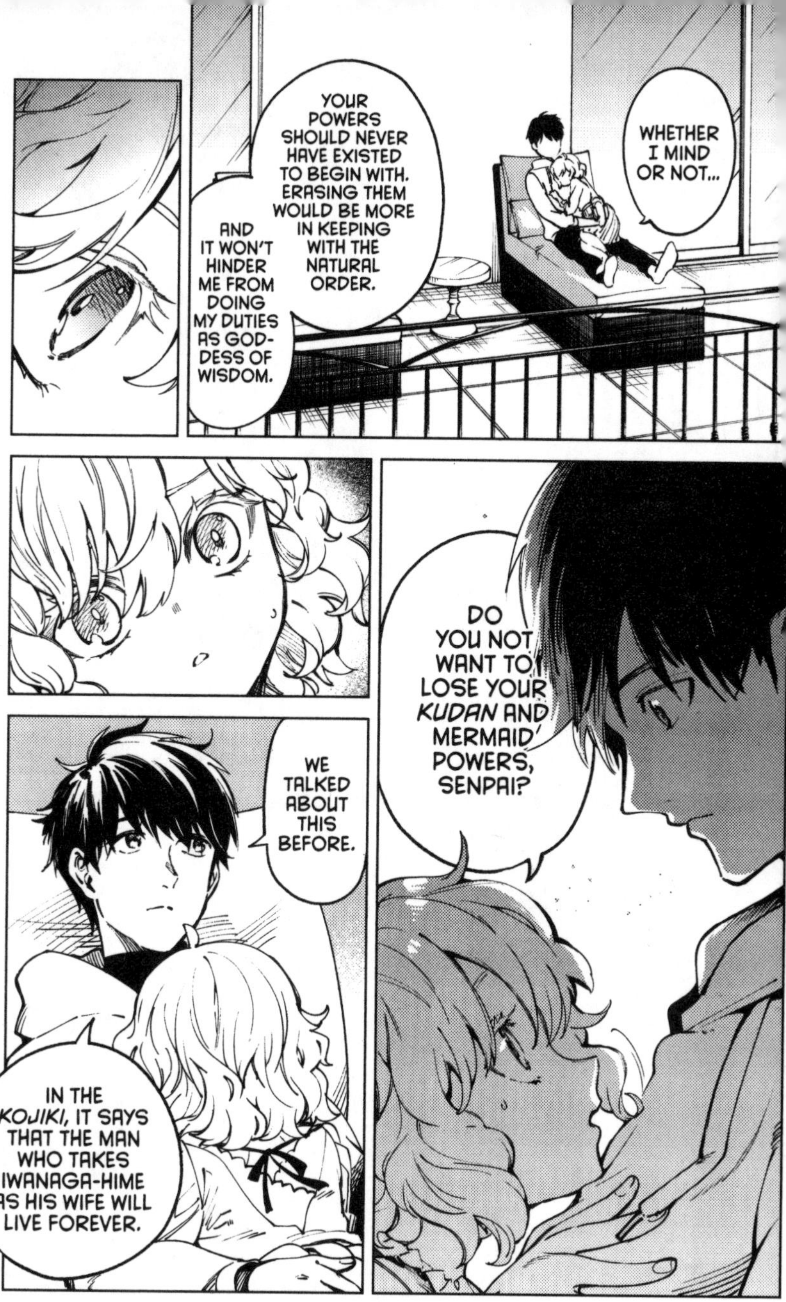
WHETHER I MIND OR NOT...
YOUR POWERS SHOULD NEVER HAVE EXISTED TO BEGIN WITH. ERASING THEM WOULD BE MORE IN KEEPING WITH THE NATURAL ORDER.
AND IT WON'T HINDER ME FROM DOING MY DUTIES AS GOD-DESS OF WISDOM.
DO YOU NOT WANT TO LOSE YOUR *KUDAN* AND MERMAID POWERS, SENPAI?
WE TALKED ABOUT THIS BEFORE.
IN THE *KOJIKI*, IT SAYS THAT THE MAN WHO TAKES IWANAGA-HIME AS HIS WIFE WILL LIVE FOREVER.

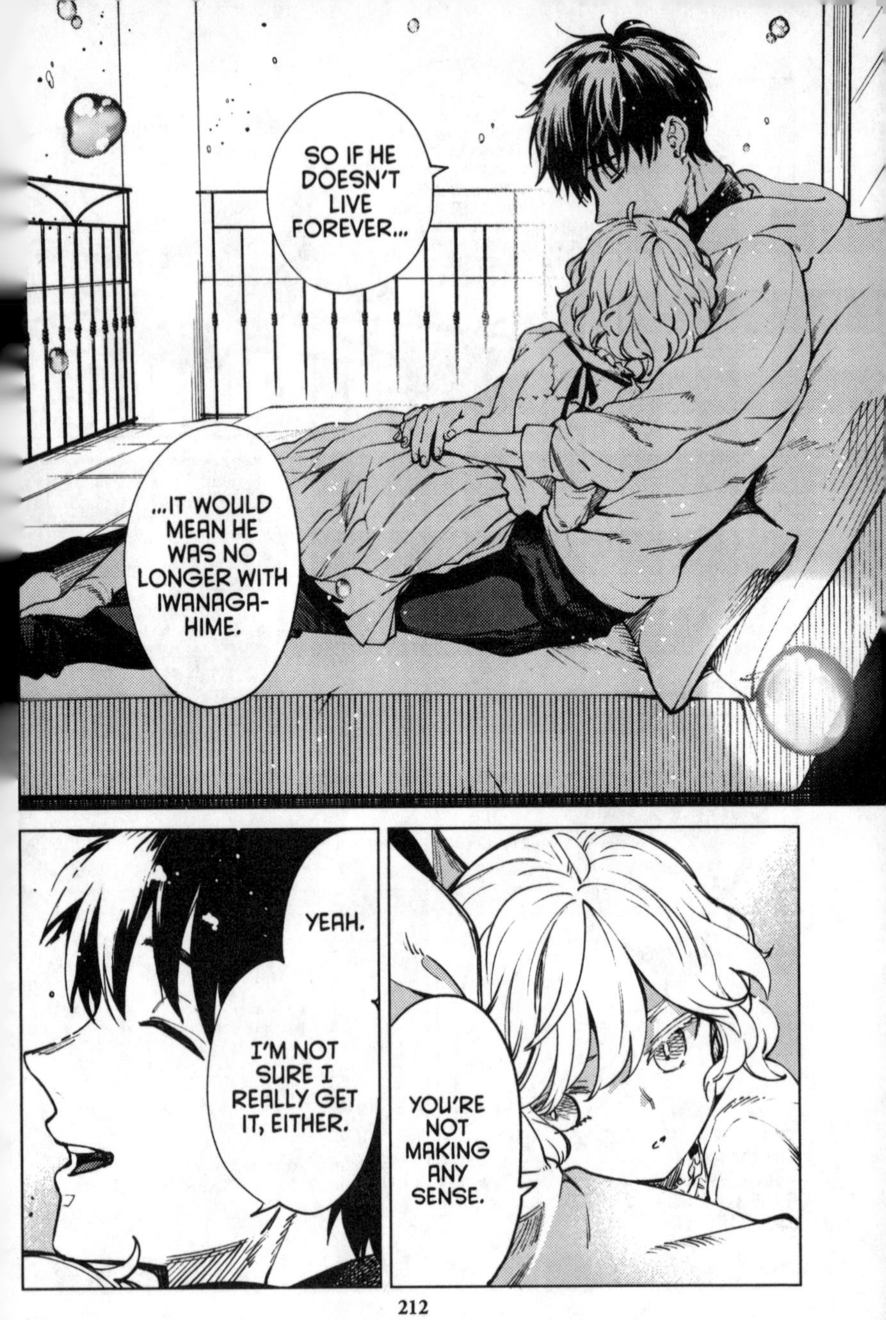
SO IF HE DOESN'T LIVE FOREVER...
...IT WOULD MEAN HE WAS NO LONGER WITH IWANAGA-HIME.
YOU'RE NOT MAKING ANY SENSE.
YEAH.
I'M NOT SURE I REALLY GET IT, EITHER.

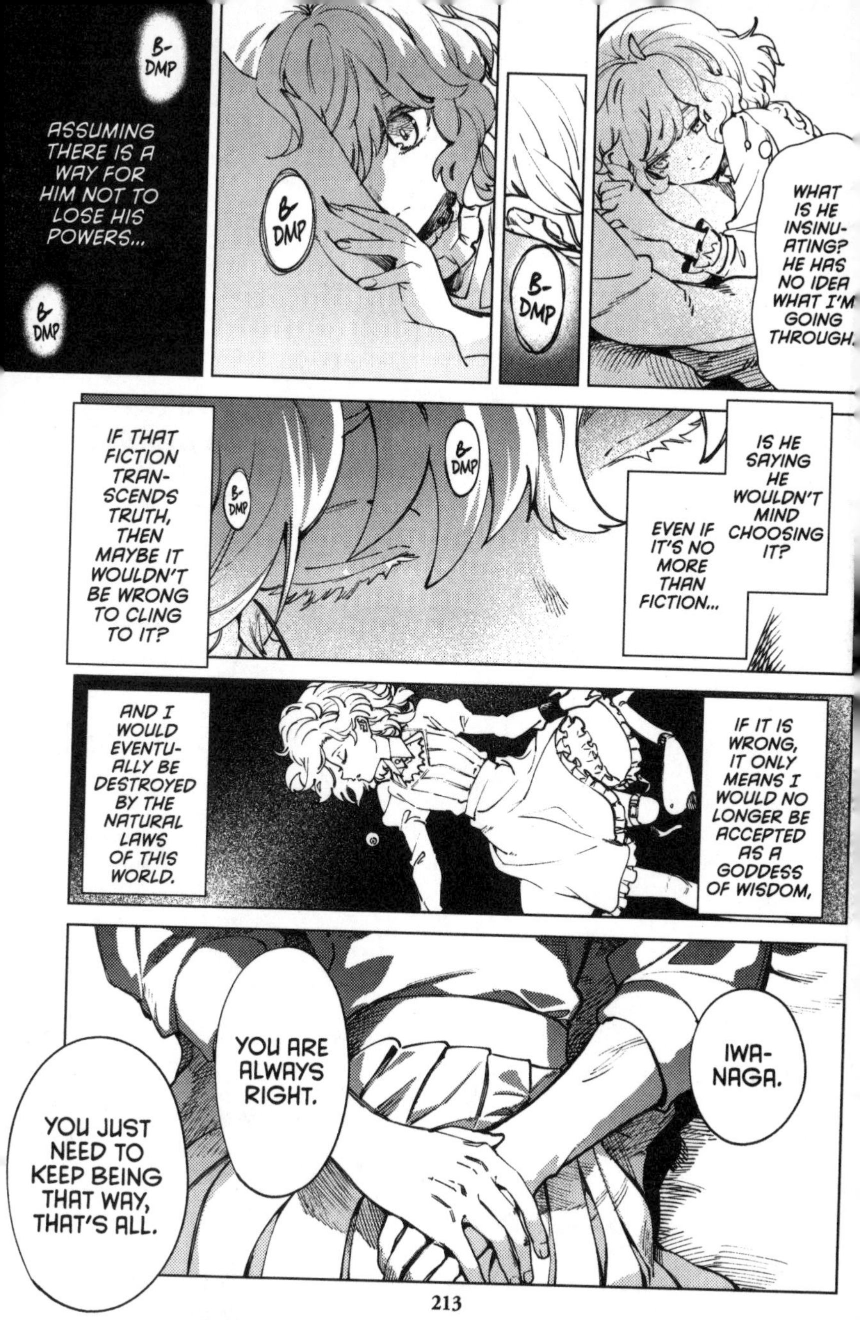
WHAT IS HE INSINUATING? HE HAS NO IDEA WHAT I'M GOING THROUGH.
B-DMP
B-DMP
B-DMP
ASSUMING THERE IS A WAY FOR HIM NOT TO LOSE HIS POWERS...
B-DMP
IS HE SAYING HE WOULDN'T MIND CHOOSING IT?
EVEN IF IT'S NO MORE THAN FICTION...
B-DMP
B-DMP
IF THAT FICTION TRANSCENDS TRUTH, THEN MAYBE IT WOULDN'T BE WRONG TO CLING TO IT?
IF IT IS WRONG, IT ONLY MEANS I WOULD NO LONGER BE ACCEPTED AS A GODDESS OF WISDOM,
AND I WOULD EVENTUALLY BE DESTROYED BY THE NATURAL LAWS OF THIS WORLD.
IWA-NAGA.
YOU ARE ALWAYS RIGHT.
YOU JUST NEED TO KEEP BEING THAT WAY, THAT'S ALL.

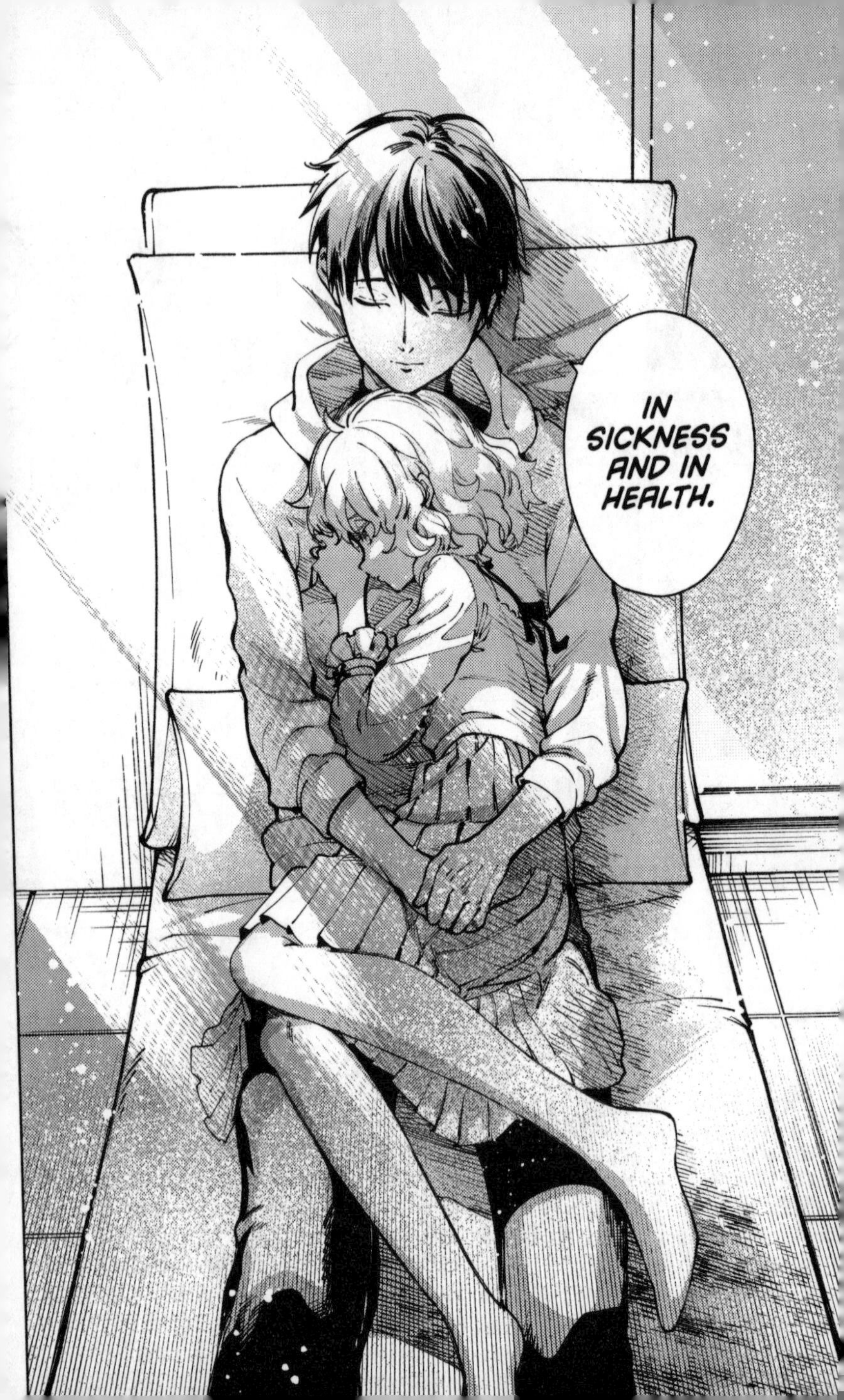
IN SICKNESS AND IN HEALTH.

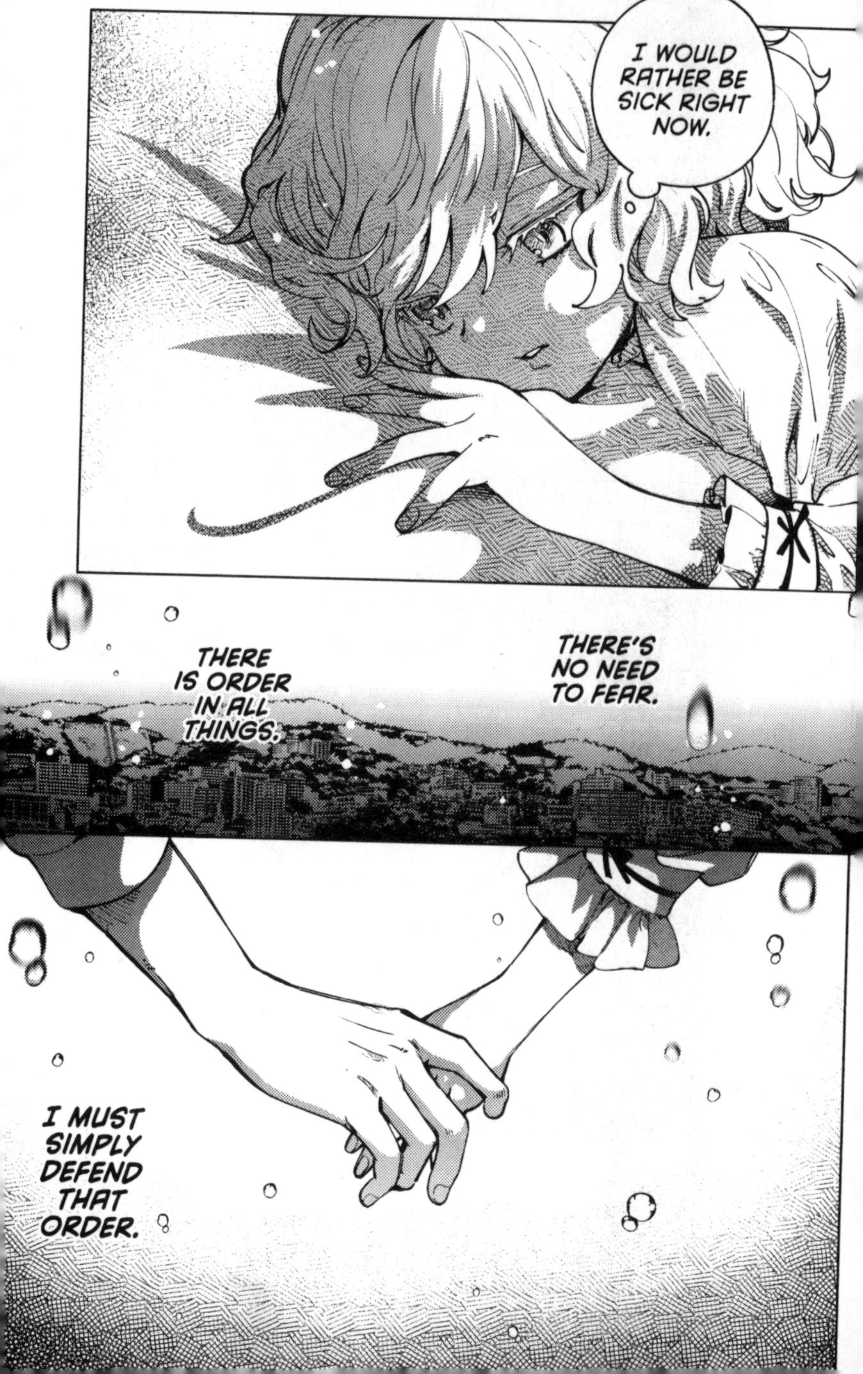
I WOULD RATHER BE SICK RIGHT NOW.
THERE'S NO NEED TO FEAR.
THERE IS ORDER IN ALL THINGS.
I MUST SIMPLY DEFEND THAT ORDER.

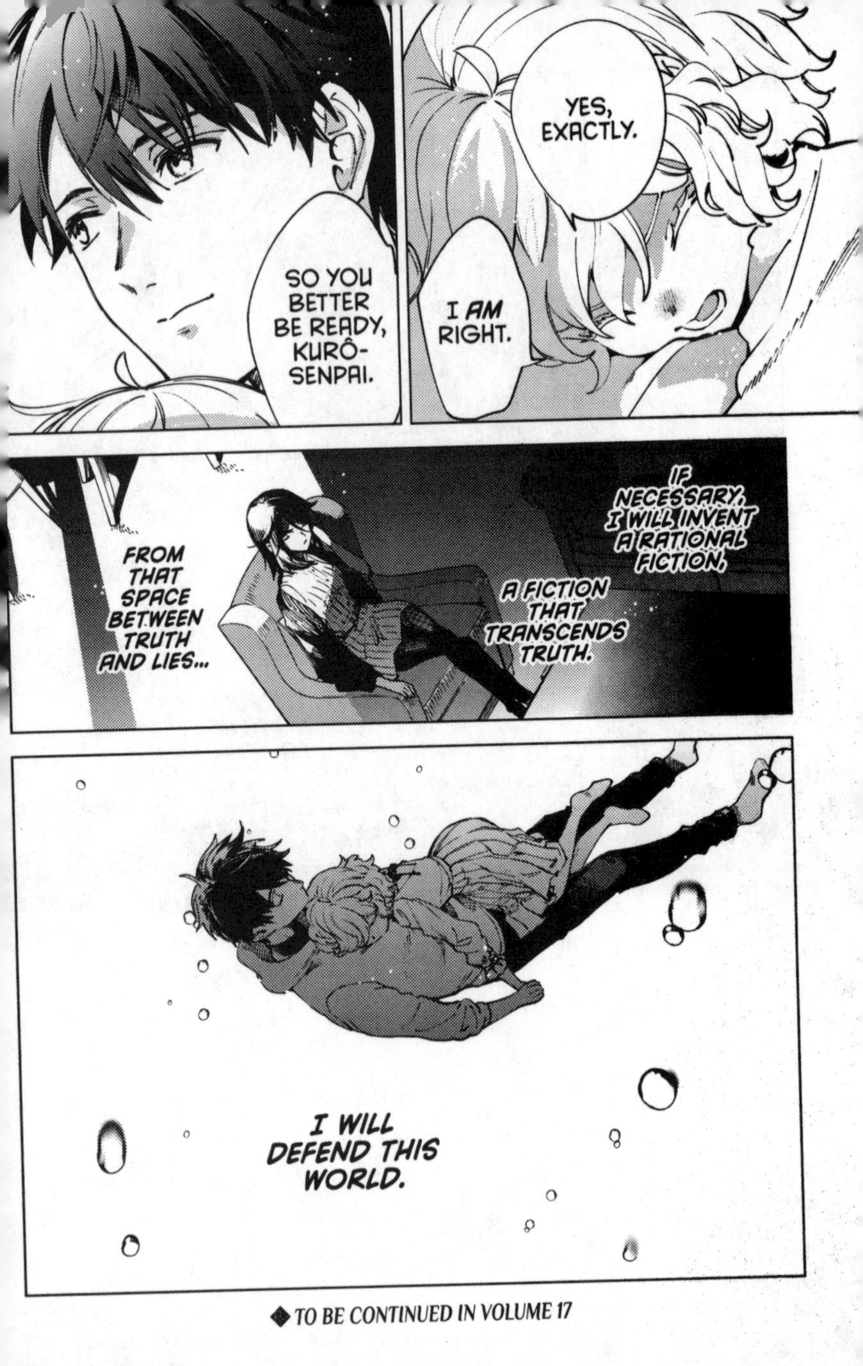
YES, EXACTLY.
I AM RIGHT.
SO YOU BETTER BE READY, KURÔ-SENPAI.
IF NECESSARY, I WILL INVENT A RATIONAL FICTION,
A FICTION THAT TRANSCENDS TRUTH.
FROM THAT SPACE BETWEEN TRUTH AND LIES...
I WILL DEFEND THIS WORLD.

◆ TO BE CONTINUED IN VOLUME 17

IN/SPECTRE

I am the author, Kyo Shirodaira. And this is volume 16. Here, the secret feud that has been going on with Rikka Sakuragawa since Steel Lady Nanase has reached a conclusion of sorts. It's not a complete resolution, but a temporary truce has been struck, and the story has reached the end of an arc. My goodness, but it was a long time coming.

However, this arc, "The Retaliation and Defeat of Kotoko Iwanaga," won't really be concluded until the end of one more chapter, its epilogue. That chapter will reveal something that has never been made clear before: Kurô's real feelings, and his opinion on the current outcome of the battle. In mystery writing terms, Kurô is sort of in a Watson-type position, but also not really; he seems like he's never thinking of anything, but also, like, maybe he is. So while we have reached a conclusion, it's also true that something will be lacking if we don't explain his inner workings.

Now, to remind you all, In/Spectre exists as a novel and as a manga. The novel is written first, then used for the basis of the manga version, although it can get complicated as some parts are published in the manga first. To illustrate that point, the final epilogue of this arc will be different in the manga than it is in the novel. Until now, any differences between the two were all left to Katase-sensei's interpretation and adaptation of the story, and I almost never did anything to participate in that, but this conclusion will be an exception.

Essentially, when it comes to Kurô's feelings, their revelation may or may not signify the close of the entire story, so I considered presenting them only in the novel, and then have the manga end the arc with the chapters in

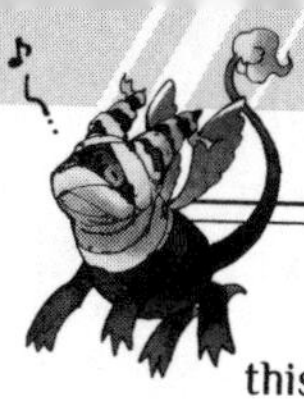

this volume, moving on to the next story without revealing too many details. You could say that, in a manga, it's better to leave a few mysteries. Nevertheless, if you're going to conclude an arc, it's best to put a clear ending on it—tying up all the loose ends can make it easier to move on to the next arc. So, in order to strike the right balance, I went ahead and wrote a separate epilogue for the manga. And I tried to make sure that reading the manga would leave you with a different impression than reading the novel.

There will be things that are only written about in the novel, and other things that are only expressed in the manga, so for those of you who have read the novel, I do hope you look forward to reading the next volume of the manga.

As for what happens after that, I hope to present a mystery that maintains the order through a different kind of fiction than what has been restricted by Rikka Sakuragawa and her subterfuge. I have just a little bit more freedom for what I can do with the story, and it may once again end up as something that's not quite what most people expect from the mystery genre.

Still, mystery fiction has been around for significantly more than 100 years, and there are not a lot of things that haven't already been done. It's not uncommon to come across something that seems new, but actually does have a precedent and is nothing more than an old trick used in a new story or a remake. I mean, there is a story published around 1951 where a history professor from the early 20th century makes a pact with the devil and goes back in time to the late 17th century, solves a mystery there, and changes history.

As for me, I am constantly praying that, as I learn from my forebears, I'm managing to create stories that include a certain amount of originality. Well, I hope you'll continue to read.

Kyo Shirodaira

The story so far
~Timeline of Kotoko Iwanaga~

			First Year in College		High School Student	
		(Iwanaga age 19, Kurô age 24, Rikka age 27)				
Mar.	**Nov.**	**Oct.**	**Sept.**		**Mar.**	
Electro-shock Pinocchio: Or, When You Wish Upon a Star	Lucky Day at the Unagi Restaurant	What the Guardian Serpent Heard	In/Spectre: Steel Lady Nanase		What Was Seen	Kotoko Iwanaga Was A High School Student
②	②	②	①		⑤	③	Novel
Vol. 8	Vol. 7		Vol. 1-6		Vol. 14	Vol. 9	Manga

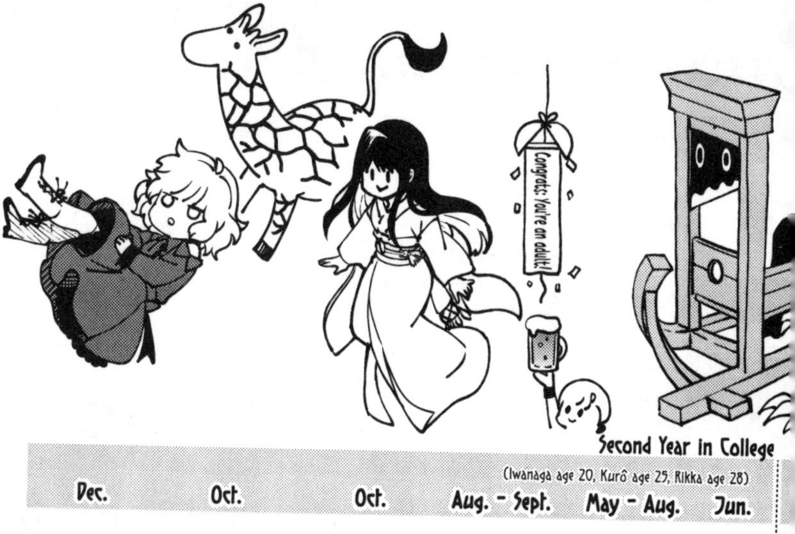
Congrats: You're an adult!

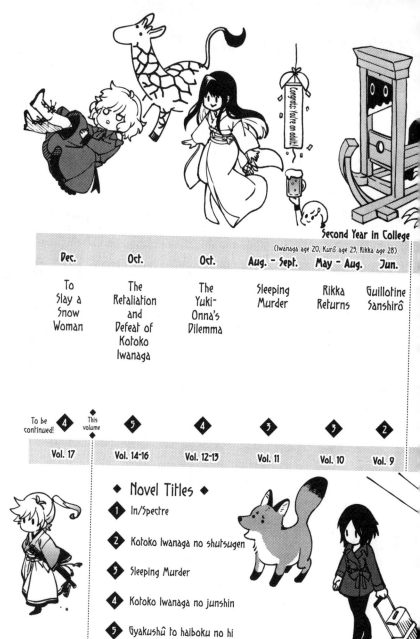

Second Year in College

(Iwanaga age 20, Kurô age 25, Rikka age 28)

Dec.	Oct.	Oct.	Aug. - Sept.	May - Aug.	Jun.
To Slay a Snow Woman	The Retaliation and Defeat of Kotoko Iwanaga	The Yuki-Onna's Dilemma	Sleeping Murder	Rikka Returns	Guillotine Sanshirô
To be continued! 4	This volume 5	4	3	3	2
Vol. 17	Vol. 14-16	Vol. 12-13	Vol. 11	Vol. 10	Vol. 9

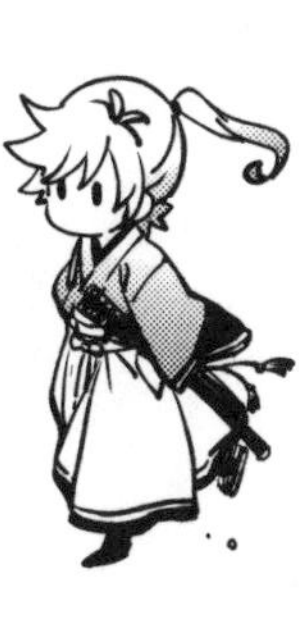

◆ Novel Titles ◆

1. In/Spectre
2. Kotoko Iwanaga no shutsugen
3. Sleeping Murder
4. Kotoko Iwanaga no junshin
5. Gyakushû to haiboku no hi

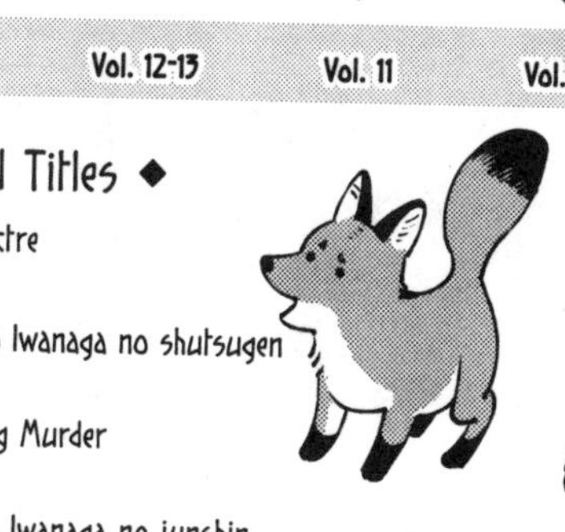

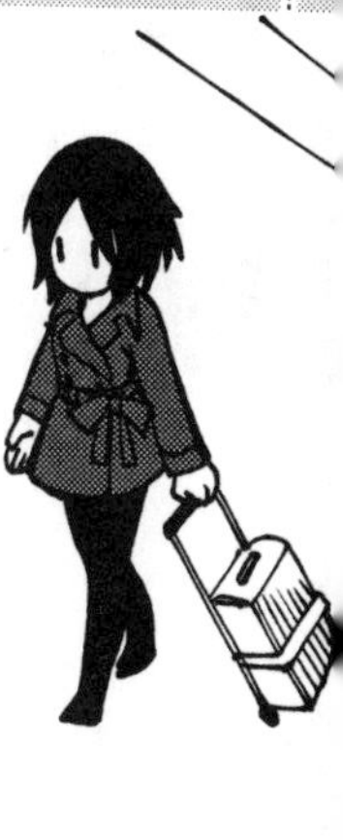

I hope you'll read the next volume!

TRANSLATION NOTES

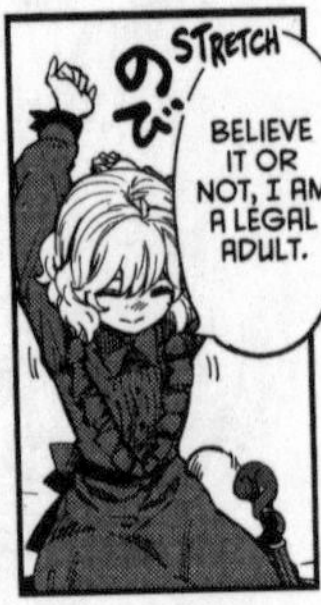
のび
STRETCH
BELIEVE IT OR NOT, I AM A LEGAL ADULT.

A legal adult, page 14
In Japan, one becomes an adult, and can therefore legally drink, at age 20.

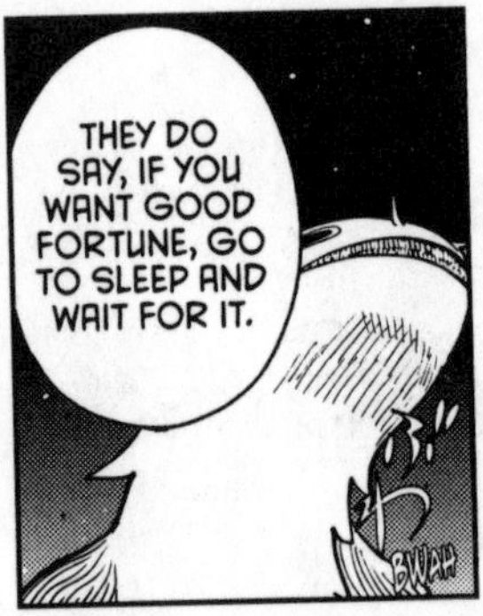
THEY DO SAY, IF YOU WANT GOOD FORTUNE, GO TO SLEEP AND WAIT FOR IT.
BWAH

If you want good fortune, page 78
This is a saying in Japan that indicates a resignation to the fact that mere mortals have very little control over good luck, so we may as well calm down, take a nap, and wait patiently. The English-speaking world's equivalent would be, "Good things come to those who wait."

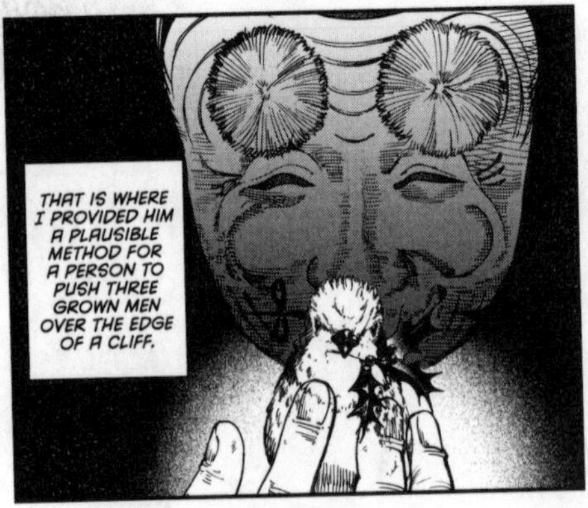
THAT IS WHERE I PROVIDED HIM A PLAUSIBLE METHOD FOR A PERSON TO PUSH THREE GROWN MEN OVER THE EDGE OF A CLIFF.

Holly sprig, page 137
Here we see Kotoko's ghost friend offering Okamachi-san a bird carrying a sprig of holly. In addition to representing the information he needs to get out of his dilemma, holly also represents his beloved Hiiragi, whose name means "holly."

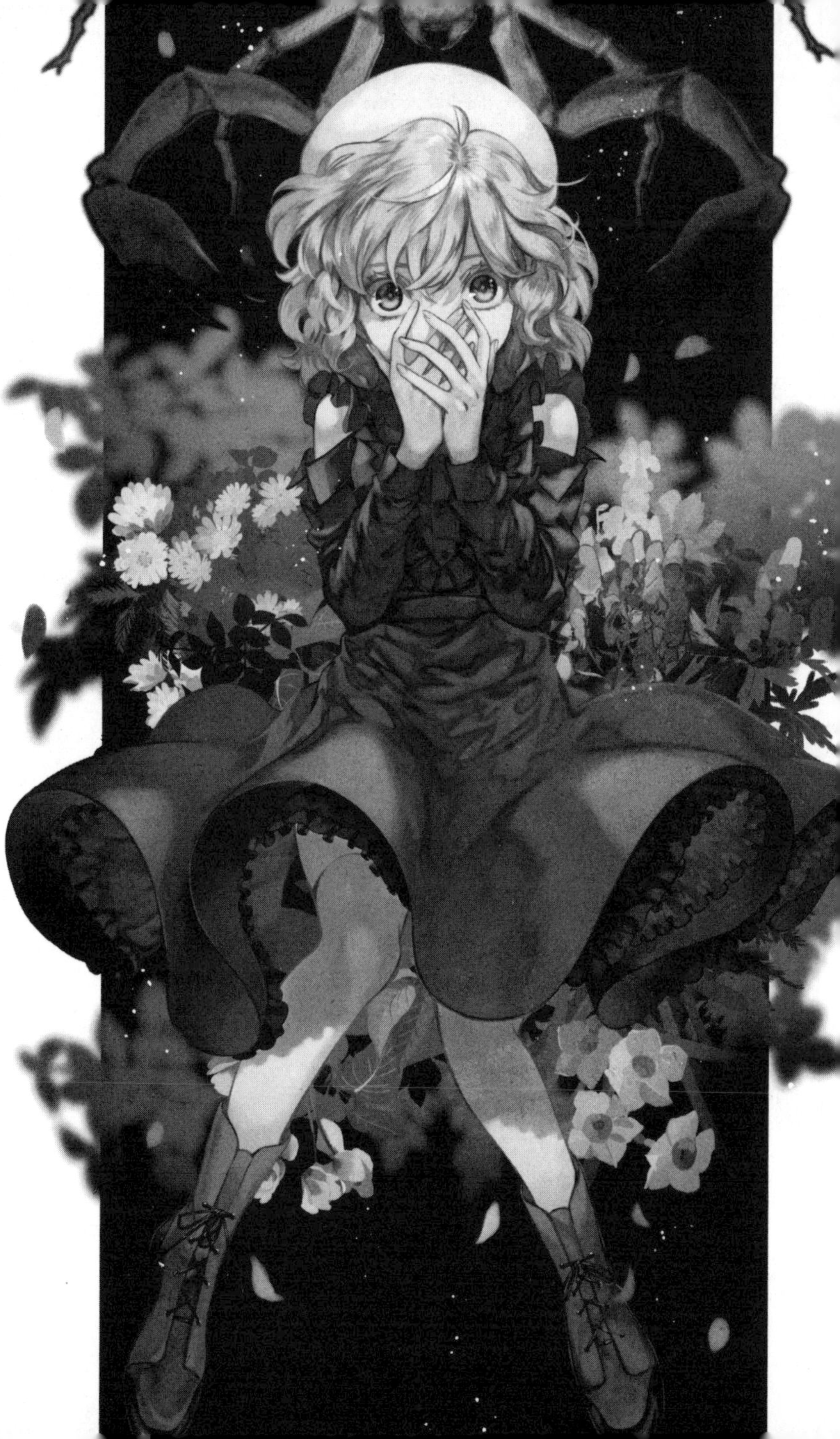

A Kodansha Comics Trade Paperback Original
In/Spectre 16 copyright © 2021 Kyo Shirodaira/Chashiba Katase
English translation copyright © 2022 Kyo Shirodaira/Chashiba Katase

Published in the United States by Kodansha Comics, an imprint of Kodansha USA Publishing, LLC, New York.

Publication rights for this English edition arranged through Kodansha Ltd., Tokyo.

First published in Japan in 2021 by Kodansha Ltd., Tokyo as *Kyokou Suiri*, volume 16.

ISBN 978-1-64651-578-3

Original cover design by Takashi Shimoyama and Mami Fukunaga (RedRooster)

Printed in the United States of America.

www.kodansha.us

1st Printing
Translation: Alethea Nibley and Athena Nibley
Lettering: Lys Blakeslee
Editing: Cayley Last
Kodansha Comics edition cover design by Phil Balsman

Publisher: Kiichiro Sugawara

Director of publishing services: Ben Applegate
Director of publishing operations: Dave Barrett
Associate director of publishing operations: Stephen Pakula
Publishing services managing editors: Alanna Ruse, Madison Salters
Production manager: Jocelyn O'Dowd